Unruly Americans
and the Origins of the Constitution

Unruly Americans and the Origins of the Constitution

Woody Holton

 Hill and Wang

A division of Farrar, Straus and Giroux

New York

Hill and Wang
A division of Farrar, Straus and Giroux
19 Union Square West, New York 10003

Library of Congress Cataloging-in-Publication Data
Holton, Woody.
    Unruly Americans and the origins of the Constitution / Woody Holton.
        p.   cm.
    Includes index.
    ISBN-13: 978-0-8090-8061-8 (hardcover : alk. paper)
    ISBN-10: 0-8090-8061-3 (hardcover : alk. paper)
    1. Constitutional history—United States.   I. Title.

KF4541.H58 2007
342.7302'9 — dc22

                                                      2007004931

Designed by Jay Colvin

www.fsgbooks.com

5 7 9 10 8 6 4

For Gretchen

Contents

V. Esau's Bargain

PREFACE

I WANT TO invite you to try your hand at a game I play with students in my American history classes. The game opens our discussion of the origins of the Constitution. Students shout out the specific clauses in the Constitution they most appreciate—the ones that make them feel safe and free. Having previously divided the blackboard into three sections, I place each clause that the students mention in one of the three categories. I number the columns but I do not label them. That is the students' challenge: to figure out, as the three columns fill up, what each one is.

Among the first things the students shout out are "freedom of religion" and "freedom of speech." Usually the right to bear arms also comes up early. All three of these go in the unlabeled Column 3. Sometimes students will offer me general concepts, such as "right to representation" or "no aristocracy." Both of those go in Column 1. Often a tattooed or pierced student in the back row will bring up freedom from illegal search and seizure. I write that in Column 3, along with "equal justice under law" and the right of all adults to vote.

It does not take the students long to notice that Column 2 is falling behind. After a while someone is likely to shout "checks and balances," and that becomes the first entry in Column 2—sometimes the only one—although on the rare occasion when a student mentions "right of habeas corpus" or "no religious test for officeholders," that goes in the middle column as well.

Using the clauses that I have placed in each of three columns, can you guess what labels to put on them?

Students are usually able to identify Column 3—it is the Bill of
Rights and the subsequent amendments. Often my classes figure out
that Column 2 is the basic Constitution before the Bill of Rights was
added to it. Usually I have to supply the label for Column 1. It consists
of provisions of the Constitution that were simply copied from its
predecessor, the Articles of Confederation—the United States's first
federal charter—which lasted from 1781 to 1789.

Once all three columns have been labeled, students are often struck
by the same thing that astonished me when I first began this study of
the origins of America's founding document: the vast majority of the
most popular constitutional clauses are not actually in the Constitution that the Framers signed on September 17, 1787. Nearly all of the
stirring phrases that Americans most cherish are actually in the Bill of
Rights or in later amendments, especially those adopted after the Civil
War. To be sure, the original seven articles do include some very important protections, but most of those were simply carryovers from the
Articles of Confederation.

There is irony in the fact that most of the best-loved portions of the
Constitution appear in the first ten amendments. The Philadelphia
Convention made a conscious decision not to give the new federal
charter a Bill of Rights. When the Constitution was sent out to the
states for ratification, however, thousands of Americans were aghast
that the delegates had codified the powers of government but not the
rights of citizens. They were even more appalled that as the ratification
battle wore on, the supporters of the Constitution, the Federalists,
continued to resist the idea of attaching a Bill of Rights. It was not that
the friends of the Constitution were uninterested in protecting personal liberty. What they feared was that the effort to amend the new
national charter to protect civil and states' rights would throw the
whole effort to strengthen the federal government off course.

Several state ratifying conventions ended up giving their approval to
the Constitution only on condition that it would later be amended to
include a Bill of Rights. Some supporters of the Constitution went
along with that stipulation, but they generally did so without conviction. They were simply making a strategic concession, accepting the
Bill of Rights in order to secure the adoption of the seven articles that
had been drawn up in Philadelphia.

Had there been no opposition to the Constitution, its supporters would not have felt the need to make concessions, and there would be no Bill of Rights. So if Americans are grateful for freedom of speech and religion, the right to assemble, the right to an attorney, the right to face their accusers, and other freedoms, it is not the Framers they should thank. It is the people who opposed the Constitution. They were the ones who extracted from the Federalists the strategic concession we call the Bill of Rights.[1]

Which raises a question: If the most compelling motive for the Constitution was not to safeguard civil liberties, what was it?

Unruly Americans
and the Origins of the Constitution

"Evils Which . . . Produced This Convention"

Introduction

THIRTEEN NORTH AMERICAN colonies left the British Empire in 1776, but that was not really the birth date of the American colossus. History's wealthiest and most powerful nation-state was not actually launched until the summer of 1787, at the Constitutional Convention in Philadelphia. Revolutionaries the world over have cribbed from the Declaration of Independence, but the successful ones, those who manage to overturn the social order and establish regimes of their own, find their inspiration not in the Declaration but in the Constitution. Anyone seeking the real origins of the United States must begin by asking why it was that, scarcely a decade after the free inhabitants of thirteen British colonies proclaimed each of them an autonomous state, they decided to meld those thirteen sovereignties together and launch an empire of their own.

Today politicians as well as judges profess an almost religious reverence for the Framers' original intent. And yet what do we really know about the motives that set fifty-five of the nation's most prominent citizens—men like George Washington, Ben Franklin, and Alexander Hamilton—on the road to Philadelphia? The Framers' motivations remain nearly as obscure today as they were that muggy summer of 1787, when the Constitutional Convention delegates voted to maintain the strictest secrecy—and thwarted eavesdroppers by keeping the fetid chamber's doors and windows closed and latched.

High school textbooks and popular histories of the Revolutionary War locate the origins of the Constitution in the nasty conflicts that kept threatening to tear the federal convention apart—and in the brilliant compromises that, again and again, brought the delegates back together. Should every state have the same number of representatives in Congress, or should representation be weighted in favor of the more populous ones? Solution: proportional representation in the House of Representatives and state equality in the Senate. Should the national government be allowed to abolish the African slave trade? Solution: yes, but not until 1808. In apportioning congressional representation among the states, should enslaved Americans be considered people, giving their owners bonus representatives? What about in allocating the tax burden among the states—should slaves be counted as people there? Solution to both controversies: count each slave as three-fifths of a person.

Whether the title is *Miracle at Philadelphia* or *The Grand Convention* or *The Great Rehearsal* or *The Summer of 1787*, it is almost as though the same book has been written over and over again, by different authors, every few years.[1]

The textbooks and the popular histories give surprisingly short shrift to the Framers' motivations. What almost all of them do say is that harsh experience had exposed the previous government, under the Articles of Confederation (1781–89), as too weak. What makes this emphasis strange is that the Framers' own statements reveal another, more pressing motive. Early in the Constitutional Convention, James Madison urged his colleagues to tackle "the evils . . . which prevail within the States individually as well as those which affect them collectively."[2] The "mutability" and "injustice" of "the laws of the States" had, Madison declared shortly after leaving Philadelphia, "contributed more to that uneasiness which produced the Convention, and prepared the public mind for a general reform, than those which accrued to our national character and interest from the inadequacy of the Confederation."[3]

Madison's preoccupation with what he later called the "the internal administration of the States" was by no means unique. On the eve of the convention, expressions of concern about the weakness of Congress, numerous as they were, were vastly outnumbered by complaints against the state governments. "What led to the appointment of this Convention?" Maryland delegate John Francis Mercer asked his colleagues. Was it not "the corruption & mutability of the Legislative Councils of the States"?[4]

Once the Constitution had been sent out to the thirteen states for ratification, its supporters affirmed that some of the most lethal diseases it was designed to cure were to be found within those same states. William Plumer of New Hampshire embraced the new national government out of a conviction that "our rights & property are now the sport of ignorant unprincipled State legislators."[5] In the last of the *Federalist Papers*—the series of eighty-five newspaper essays that are widely seen as America's premier contribution to political science—Alexander Hamilton praised the Constitution for placing salutary "restraints" on "the ambition of powerful individuals in single states."[6]

What was wrong with the state assemblies? Given the modern perception that the Founding Fathers had devoted their lives to the principle of government by the people, it is jarring to read their specific grievances. An essay appearing in a Connecticut newspaper in September 1786 complained that the state's representatives paid "too great an attention to popular notions."[7] At least one of those Connecticut assemblymen thoroughly agreed. In May 1787, just as the federal convention assembled, he observed that even the southern states, which under British rule had been aristocratic bastions, had "run into the extremes of democracy" since declaring independence.[8]

What these men were saying was that the American Revolution had gone too far. Their great hope was that the federal convention would find a way to put the democratic genie back in the bottle. Alexander Hamilton, the most ostentatiously conservative of the convention delegates, affirmed that many Americans—not just himself—were growing "tired of an excess of democracy."[9] Others identified the problem as "a headstrong democracy," a "prevailing rage of excessive democracy," a "republican frenzy," "democratical tyranny," and "democratic licentiousness."[10]

During the eighteenth century the primary means of land transportation—other than walking—was the horse. Writers and speakers often expressed their anxiety about the changes occurring in their fellow Americans by calling them "unruly steeds."[11] To Silas Deane it seemed that "the reins of Government" were held with too "feeble a hand."[12]

What had persuaded the Framers and many of the most prominent

Americans of the postwar era that the Revolution had gotten out of hand? Consider the case of James Madison, "the father of the Constitution."[13] Madison is widely credited with writing the "Virginia Plan," the Constitutional Convention's first draft. Having addressed the convention more often than all but one other delegate, he went on to become one of the two principal authors of the *Federalist Papers,* the best-known brief for ratification. When it became clear that roughly half the electorate would refuse to accept the Constitution until it contained a bill of rights, it was Madison who drew up those first ten amendments.

In seeking to explain the desperate urgency with which Madison championed the new national government, his biographers have made much of the fact that in 1784 he asked his friend Thomas Jefferson, the official American envoy to King Louis XVI of France, to rummage through the bookstalls on the left bank of the Seine and ship him a crateful of works on Renaissance and Enlightenment history and philosophy. We can easily imagine Madison's delight as one of his slaves pried open the chest, revealing everything from Plutarch's *Lives of the Noble Greeks and Romans* to Barthélemy de Felice's thirteen-volume *Code de l'humanité, ou La legislation universelle, naturelle, civile et politique.*

One reason historians have always found Madison such an appealing character is that he himself was something of a bookworm. Short and sickly, he more than once predicted that he would not live long. (As it turned out, he made it to the then-extraordinary age of eighty-five.)[14] It is difficult to imagine him mustering sufficient stamina for a modern political campaign and easy to conceive of him as something of a monk. Yet one subject seemed to fuel Madison with a limitless energy and to draw him from the tranquillity of his study. This was his disgust with the state governments that emerged from the Revolutionary War. Madison's desperate desire to rein in the thirteen state governments was not born in a contemplative philosophical vacuum; it reflected his own day-to-day experience as a political animal.[15]

Madison's political career began in earnest in 1776, when his Orange County, Virginia, neighbors sent him to the convention that wrote the state's first constitution. Elected to the founding session of the House of Delegates a short time later, he was defeated the very next year. No matter, for his real passion was for politics on a national scale. In 1780 his former colleagues in the assembly gave him his first year-long term in Congress, and he served until the three-term limit in the Articles of Confederation forced him out, whereupon he immediately got himself reelected to the Virginia legislature.

The Articles permitted former congressmen to reclaim their seats after a three-year hiatus, and as soon as Madison's three years were up, he was back in Congress. In the summer of 1787 this "feeble," "sickly" man would muster the energy not only to address the Constitutional Convention on scores of occasions but to take copious notes on nearly every speech given by every other delegate, a task to which he applied himself six days a week for nearly four months.[16]

By the spring of 1786, when Madison received Jefferson's "literary cargo," he no longer had any illusions about what he would find in those books. He did not need a crateful of ancient and modern philosophy and history to figure out why the young republic had lost its way, for he had already formed his opinions in the course of day-to-day political struggles.[17] What Madison was looking for as he performed his research was persuasive historical evidence for what his own practical experience had already taught him: that the state constitutions were fatally flawed. In his view, the Founders had rescued white Americans from kingly despotism only to subject them to something worse: the tyranny of "the major number of the constituents."[18]

What really alarmed Madison was the specific legislation the assemblies had adopted. More than anything else, it was the desire to overturn these state laws that set him on the road to Philadelphia. Nor was he alone. Another Constitutional Convention delegate, Pennsylvania's Gouverneur Morris, enumerated various kinds of iniquitous state laws he hoped his colleagues would guard against in the new national charter, concluding that "experience evinces the truth of this remark without having recourse to reading."[19]

What had the thirteen assemblies done wrong? The "evils which had more perhaps than any thing else, produced this convention," Madison told his colleagues in Philadelphia, were the states' countless "Interferences" with "the security of private rights, and the steady dispensation of Justice."[20]

All this talk about "rights" and "Justice" may seem today like glittering generalities. Actually, the transgressions that the Founding Fathers laid at the feet of the thirteen state legislatures were quite specific.

Most glaringly, representatives had shown excessive indulgence to debtors and taxpayers. They had refused to force farmers to pay what they owed.[21]

Insects, drought—even invading armies—fearsome as they all are, have rarely been what rural Americans dread most. That distinction belongs to the farmers' creditors—not only the men and women who have lent them cash but the merchants who have supplied them with tools and other merchandise on credit and the government officials who press them to pay their back taxes. In the wake of the Revolutionary War the thirteen legislatures had ridden to the farmers' rescue. They had allowed debtors to satisfy their creditors with property— even pine barrens and "old Horses"—instead of hard money (gold and silver).[22] In some cases public officials had temporarily shut down the legal system that was the neglected creditor's only recourse. Worst of all, Congress and every state assembly had funded the war effort partly by printing paper money. They emitted far more currency than the economy could bear, and the result was runaway inflation. In several states a person who owed £1,000 could get out of the debt with money that was actually worth only £1. Even after peace was declared in 1783, seven state legislatures printed additional currency.

The state governments also had debtors of their own to worry about. In most states thousands of citizens were behind on their taxes. Just like private debtors, delinquent taxpayers had received too much indulgence from state officials, the Framers believed. What may have seemed like a strictly state-level concern actually had national implications, since Congress relied upon the states for its own funding. The Articles of Confederation delegated the power of raising "Continental" funds to the thirteen state assemblies. To many Americans it seemed the states had botched this task. They knew why, too: representatives were reluctant to load their constituents down with burdensome federal taxes.

Tax relief crippled government operations. Even worse, it prevented public officials from meeting their single largest obligation, namely servicing the enormous debts they had amassed during the war. When Congress and the states failed to redeem the war bonds or even pay interest on them, Madison declared in *Federalist* Number 10, the owners of the securities were not the only ones who suffered. By begetting a "prevailing and increasing distrust of public engagements," this terrible "injustice" had doomed the state and federal governments themselves.[23]

For men like Madison, writing the Constitution was like appealing an unfavorable jury verdict to a higher court. If the thirteen state legislatures could not muster the fortitude to crack down on delinquent debtors and taxpayers, they reasoned, they would create a national government that could.

The Framers believed the only way to prevent state assemblymen from giving the taxpayer a free ride was to get them out of the business of collecting—or not collecting—"Continental" taxes. Article I, Section 8 gave the national government what it had never had before, its own power to tax. Article I, Section 10 imposed a similar crackdown on private debtors. It prohibited the states from rescuing farmers by issuing paper money or by "impairing the obligation of contracts" using any of the other devices they had discovered during the 1780s.

As a result of the protection that Section 10 afforded creditors, more people proclaimed that clause "the best in the Constitution" than any other in the document.[24] Section 10 was even touted as "the soul of the Constitution."[25] Virginia governor Edmund Randolph pronounced Section 10 "a great favourite of mine."[26] "Nothing, in the whole Federal Constitution, is more necessary than this very section," a New Jersey Federalist claimed.[27] Two prominent Pennsylvanians, attorney James Wilson and physician Benjamin Rush, independently reached the conclusion that even if the Constitution did nothing more than ban paper money, that alone would still, in Rush's words, be "eno' to recommend it to honest men."[28]

Rush was exaggerating, of course, but suppose for a moment that the Constitution had contained no other provisions besides those found in Sections 8 and 10 of Article I. The danger would have remained that the new national government would itself go easy on debtors and taxpayers—or at least look the other way when the states did so. It was largely in order to eliminate these possibilities that the Framers made the Constitution considerably less responsive to the popular will than any of the states. Only one element of the new government, the House of Representatives, would be elected directly by the people, and its initiatives could be derailed by the senators (who would not be chosen directly by the voters until 1913), the president, or the Supreme Court. Whereas most state legislators and even governors had to run for reelection every year, presidents would serve for four years and senators for six. As long as they committed no crimes, judges could remain in office for life.[29]

Even the one element of the national government that would be elected directly by the people, the House of Representatives, would be considerably less responsive to the voters than any of the state assemblies. The reason was that every congressman would represent many more voters than state legislators did. The best way to shield the government from popular pressure, Madison believed, was to "extend the sphere" of both individual election districts and the overall polity. Expanding legislative constituencies would enhance the likelihood that representatives would be wealthy men. Larger districts would also offer congressmen a measure of protection against grassroots pressure. Finally, as Madison famously pointed out in *Federalist* Number 10, the new national government would embrace much greater diversity than any of the states. With a wide variety of interests and proposals jockeying for popular support, none was likely to attract a majority. Thus members of Congress would be free to make their own decisions.[30]

A month before writing *Federalist* Number 10, Madison privately summarized it, employing an expression he did not dare use in that public essay: "Divide et impera, the reprobated axiom of tyranny, is under certain qualifications, the only policy, by which a republic can be administered on just principles."[31] "Divide et impera" is Latin for "divide and conquer."

It appears that by the mid-1780s the vast majority of free Americans shared James Madison's suspicion that the American Revolution had lost its way. And yet many, perhaps most, ordinary citizens disagreed with him about what had gone wrong. In fact, both their diagnosis of the nation's political ills and the cures they championed were essentially the reverse of his.

This alternative perspective on the new nation's growing pains was evident even in Madison's home state of Virginia. Indeed, in May 1787, just as the Framers were gathering in Philadelphia, a Virginia tax, designed to reduce the enormous debt that the state government had run up during the Revolutionary War, pushed a group of farmers in Greenbrier County (now part of West Virginia) into rebellion. The leader of the revolt was a local tavern-keeper named Adonijah Mathews.[32]

The war had brought tremendous hardship to men like Mathews, but the peace that followed was, in many ways, even worse. As late as the summer of 1787 the Greenbrier settlements still endured occasional attacks from Native American war parties.[33] Indians were not the settlers' most serious concern, however. The state government sided with the land speculation firms that claimed hundreds of thousands of acres in western counties like Greenbrier, mandating, according to one petition, that the farmers' money be "Extorted" from them by the land jobbers.[34] And yet even land speculation was not the greatest threat. In the 1780s Virginians believed they paid "greater Taxes than any people under the Sun."[35]

In the spring of 1787 Greenbrier farmers tried to redress their grievances. First "some Ilminded person or persons" burned down the county jail. Then at the May meeting of the county court, at least a hundred and fifty Greenbrier citizens signed an "Instrument of Writing" in which they pronounced themselves victims of "Great oppressions." The associators vowed "not to pay the certificate tax"—a special levy aimed at calling in war bonds. The certificate tax required each householder to turn in a certain number of war bonds for every worker under his or her roof. It also taxed property and several specific activities—including tavern-keeping, which may explain why Mathews rose to the forefront of the antitax movement.[36] After "binding themselves to stand by each other, in preventing the Sheriff from taking their property for debt or taxes," the Greenbrier associators "sent copies of the association paper to the other back counties."[37] It was also reported that they had made a still more radical agreement. When the county justices gathered for their August 1787 session, an opponent of the rebellion claimed, the rebels planned to "prevent the Court from Sitting."[38]

Inevitably the Greenbrier uprising put gentry Virginians in mind of the farmers' revolt that had broken out less than a year earlier in Massachusetts. Bay State leaders had made the mistake of blaming the 1786 insurgency on a single charismatic leader—they christened it "Shays's

Rebellion," and the name stuck—and officials in Virginia made a similar assumption, ascribing their own backcountry revolt to Mathews, who had recently been successfully sued for debt.[39] Betraying a long-standing prejudice against New England Puritans, one of Adonijah Mathews's fellow Virginians deduced from "the Length & sound of his christian name" that he "must have come from New-England."[40]

As the association document was being circulated, the sheriff made a bold attempt to nip the rebellion in the bud. He arrested Mathews for not paying the debt judgment that had been levied against him. Yet the sheriff's strategy only further radicalized at least four of the rebels, who overpowered him and rescued Mathews. "They Seemed the Strongest party," reported George Clendenin, the commanding officer of the county's militia.[41]

By the time Clendenin wrote, Adonijah Mathews—known in Greenbrier County as "Black Mathews"—had disappeared. No one would have been surprised if he had joined the tide of U.S. citizens who headed farther west in the 1780s, searching not only for opportunity but for respite from creditors and tax collectors. But Mathews did not escape to the West. He announced instead that he was headed to Richmond, the state capital, where he apparently expected to use the threat of an expanding insurrection to force legislators to repeal the certificate tax—which in fact they did.[42]

Adonijah Mathews probably never met James Madison. Yet these two Virginians' conflicting views neatly encapsulated the state-level controversies that led to the adoption of the U.S. Constitution. Both what Adonijah Mathews demanded from the House of Delegates (tax relief) and the mechanism by which he sought it (rebellion) indicate that his analysis of the economic and political plight of the United States during the Confederation period was diametrically opposed to the viewpoint that men like James Madison were just then expressing as they themselves rebelled against the state governments of the 1780s by writing the Constitution. Even as the Framers lamented that excessive democracy—an overreliance on the popular will—had turned the United States into a farmers' paradise, many of the farmers themselves complained that they could redress their many grievances only by taking up arms.

During the Revolutionary War, Madison's and Mathews's factions had both been aggressive advocates for home rule. Now, however, they disagreed about who should rule at home.[43] In numerous petitions and anonymous newspaper essays, Virginians like Mathews expressed grave doubt that the electoral process that had been established in the state constitution of 1776 actually allowed the majority to work its will. In other states, too, farmers and their supporters complained that the internal revolution had not gone far enough. Like the farmers of Greenbrier County, they often resorted to rebellion, expressing in the process a view of American politics that could scarcely have been more different from the Framers' belief that the major problem of the 1780s was an excess of democracy.

This great philosophical divide reflected a conflict over specific government policies. Even as men like Madison argued that the assemblies had been too lax about collecting taxes, others like Mathews declared their tax burden unendurable. During the same years when some Americans feared a return to the runaway inflation that had afflicted the United States during the war, others called attention to the extreme scarcity of hard currency and pleaded with their representatives to give them a mechanism—paper money—with which to pay their taxes and debts. These were not trivial differences, for no peacetime governmental policy has a greater impact on ordinary citizens than taxation and the money supply.

The schism was painfully clear at the time. Halfway through his last year at Harvard, John Quincy Adams reported to his mother, Abigail, that poor and wealthy citizens were equally disgusted with the Massachusetts constitution, but for opposite reasons. "While the idle, and extravagant, and consequently the poor, complain of its being oppressive," he wrote, "the men of property, and consideration, think the constitution, gives too much liberty to the unprincipled citizen, to the prejudice of the honest, and industrious."[44] Adams's analysis revealed his class bias, but it also demonstrated his acute awareness of just how deeply divided Americans were.

The state-level struggles that led to the Constitution spill forth from a cornucopia of documents that have come down to us from the eighteenth century. The number of American periodicals exploded in the years after the Revolutionary War—Charleston, South Carolina, had four newspapers by 1786, two of them dailies—and editors filled their columns with essays opposing and supporting a wide range of projects. Meanwhile freemen of all walks of life flooded the legislatures with petitions. After more than two centuries, many of their ideas retain the power to stir the imagination.

It would be a mistake to conflate the state-level struggles that preceded the summer 1787 federal convention with the better-known conflict that followed it—the debate over whether to ratify the Constitution. Many of the people who fought the Constitution in the ratifying conventions had stood shoulder to shoulder with the Framers against paper money, tax abatements, and other relief measures. On May 31, 1787, Elbridge Gerry, one of only three federal convention delegates who would later refuse to sign the Constitution, described the states' chief malady using exactly the same phrase Alexander Hamilton would employ more than two weeks later. The problem, he said, was an "excess of democracy." On the same day that Gerry uttered these words, both of the other two convention members who would ultimately withhold their signatures from the Constitution—George Mason and Edmund Randolph, both of Virginia—offered similar interpretations. Mason pronounced the thirteen state assemblies "too democratic." Randolph contended that "the evils under which the U.S. laboured" during the 1780s were rooted "in the turbulence and follies of democracy."[45]

All three of the delegates who refused to sign the Constitution also expressed (in Mason's words) "a mortal hatred to paper money."[46] Dozens of Anti-Federalists had tried as hard as Federalists like Hamilton and Madison to prevent the legislatures from granting relief to debtors and taxpayers. Men like Gerry and Mason fought the Constitution almost entirely because they feared it threatened states' rights and civil liberties. They did not object to the crackdowns on debtors and taxpayers envisioned in the new national charter, and most were easily reconciled to it once the Bill of Rights was adopted. In many ways the questions that the Anti-Federalists raised were less fundamental than those raised in the 1780s by Americans who believed the Revolution had not gone far enough.

It would be just as wrong to assume that the men who had battled

Madison on the question of tax and debt relief were bound to oppose
the Constitution he championed. In fact many Americans who spent
the 1780s decrying the plight of indebted and overtaxed farmers believed the Constitution would provide just the sort of relief they had
been demanding. Perhaps the most prominent of these was Abraham
Clark, a New Jersey signer of the Declaration of Independence. Clark
was the leading sponsor of paper money legislation in the New Jersey
assembly. Since the Constitution prohibited all state currency emissions, many New Jerseyans expected him to oppose ratification, and indeed a rumor to that effect spread through the state. Yet Clark could
see that the Constitution would allow the federal government to levy
duties on goods imported into the United States, greatly reducing its
revenue demands on the states and allowing them to cut taxes. The fiscal relief would be especially pronounced in states like New Jersey,
which, lacking major Atlantic ports at which to collect customs duties,
were forced to derive most of their tax revenue from farmers. Clark
could not bring himself to endorse the Constitution, but he did not
openly oppose it, either.[47]

Most Americans know at least a little about the men and women who
tried to keep the document signed in Philadelphia in September 1787
from being ratified. This book focuses instead on the citizens who had
done battle against men such as Madison and Hamilton in the years before they wrote the Constitution. Parts I and II investigate one of the
Framers' chief motivations by fleshing out their complaints against the
thirteen state legislatures that governed the land during the decade following the adoption of the Declaration of Independence. The authors
of the Constitution believed state assemblymen had performed far too
many favors for the debtors and taxpayers among their constituents,
not only defrauding public and private creditors but harming the entire nation. Parts I and II also consider the grievances that came to
the state legislatures from essentially the opposite direction—from
Americans who believed the assemblymen had damaged American
society by caving in to the demands of private creditors and speculators
in government bonds.

Eventually, as Part III shows, many Americans concluded that they would never obtain tax and debt relief using established political procedures. Some, like Mathews, felt compelled to play the trump card of rebellion. All the while they argued with men such as Madison about whether the assemblies were too responsive—or not responsive enough—to the popular will.

Part IV shows how Madison and most of the nation's other leading citizens, feeling just as outgunned in the struggles over relief and reform as their opponents did, played their own trump card. A distinguished collection of Americans gathered in Philadelphia to create a national government powerful enough to prevent the state legislatures from heeding grassroots demands for relief. Part V describes the campaign for the Constitution. For ordinary American farmers, the question of ratification represented a stark choice. The Federalists made a persuasive case that strengthening the federal union would revive the economy. Yet the new national government would be even less accountable to ordinary citizens than were the state assemblies.

From the complex struggles of the 1780s, the Founding Fathers extracted a simple lesson: that the uneducated farmers who seized the ship of state during the American Revolution had damn near driven it aground. From the Founders' perspective, the policies adopted by the state legislatures in the 1780s proved that ordinary Americans were not entirely capable of ruling themselves.

The Framers wove that message right into the fabric of the nation's founding document, and it remains there still. Indeed, the period between Philadelphia's two great signing ceremonies—for the Declaration of Independence in 1776 and for the Constitution in 1787—is often put on display, alongside such tragedies as slavery and the persecution of ethnic and religious minorities, to illustrate the dangers of democracy. For instance, Bernard Bailyn, the eminent Harvard historian, affirms that by 1787, James Madison "had observed the evil effects of legislative majorities within some of the states over the previous five years. Again and again minority property rights had been overwhelmed by populist majorities."[48]

In its own way, this traditional account of the events that led to the Constitutional Convention has become as powerful an institution as the Supreme Court or the Electoral College. It has instilled in many well-to-do and well-educated Americans a breezy sense of political entitlement. It has had just the opposite effect on ordinary citizens, chipping away at their self-confidence.

Maybe scholars such as Bailyn are right; perhaps popular government really did break down during the 1780s, just as the Framers claimed. But many Americans who lived through the postwar era—probably, in fact, the vast majority of them—saw things differently. They admitted that the state assemblies had badly damaged the American economy. In sharp contrast to the future Framers of the Constitution, however, they attributed the recession of the 1780s to elite, not popular, misrule.

Seeing as how the Founding Fathers' view of the origins of the Constitution has long been the dominant one, this book will focus on the alternative interpretations offered by Americans like Adonijah Mathews. A host of the Framers' contemporaries—men and women whose names have long since been forgotten—were firmly convinced that the recession that followed the Revolutionary War could have been ended without making the United States a less democratic country. Better than we do today, those ordinary farmers understood what was at stake in this great contest. Far from simply griping about particular policies, they were making the case that they possessed the ability to govern themselves.

PART I

THE GREAT DEBATE

CHAPTER 1

"BRICKS WITHOUT STRAW"

GRIEVANCES

NOAH WEBSTER was not known for his humility. Although born into a region (New England), a family background (pedigreed but poor), an era (the Enlightenment), and a gender that each produced more than its share of healthy egos, Webster far surpassed his peers in what one critic called "vanity and ostentation."[1]

And yet for all that, in the spring of 1787 Webster did something few people ever do: he printed a public confession of error. In an essay appearing in the *Pennsylvania Gazette*, the Philadelphia newspaper once owned by Benjamin Franklin, Webster affirmed that his initial response to the farmers' revolt that had erupted in Massachusetts during the summer of 1786 — history knows it as Shays's Rebellion — had been flawed. Webster had fallen "into the common opinion, that the opposition consisted of a rabble," and that "force should be used to check" it. "Subsequent events," he wrote, "proved that this was a mistake."[2]

Webster's repudiation of his previous view was all the more remarkable in light of his earlier attempts to cast himself as the ordinary farmer's mentor. Today, of course, Webster is best known for teaching his fellow Americans how to spell, but he also tried to tutor them in public policy.[3] When the Massachusetts insurgents refused to heed his advice that they throw down their weapons, Webster announced that Shays's Rebellion had annihilated his faith in ordinary Americans' capacity for self-government. "I was once as strong a republican as any man in America," Webster declared in November 1786. "*Now*, a republican is among the last kinds of governments I should choose. I should infinitely prefer a limited monarchy, for I would sooner be subject to the caprice of one man, than to the ignorance and passions of a multitude."[4]

Yet here was Webster, less than a year after publishing his first denunciation of Shays's Rebellion, telling *Pennsylvania Gazette* readers that after reexamining the tax policies that had provoked the uprising, "I frankly confess, that the result of my enquiries is, a decided opinion that the people are right."[5]

What caused Webster's extraordinary turnabout? Finding satisfactory answers to this question may illuminate another, much better-known mystery: Why was it that Webster and other illustrious Americans decided that the thirteen independent states that had declared independence from Britain must be fused into a single nation? The first step toward addressing both questions is to discover what turned Founding Fathers as well as obscure farmers against the thirteen state legislatures.

Why were so many Americans so eager to rescue bondholders and private creditors from the clutches of the farmers and their friends in the state legislatures? The answer was simple, Charles Beard argued in his enormously influential *Economic Interpretation of the Constitution of the United States*, which appeared in 1913. Beard pointed out that most of the Framers were themselves private creditors, investors in government securities, or both. He believed that they supported the Constitution because without it, they would never get their money.

Bondholders and private creditors were, in fact, among the Constitution's most avid supporters. But Beard's interpretation does not explain the enthusiasm that the proposed national government inspired in men such as Madison and Alexander Hamilton (the principal authors of the *Federalist Papers*), neither of whom was a major creditor and neither of whom owned government bonds.[6]

Today debt and tax relief are typically represented as worrisome less in themselves than as symptoms of a deeper malaise. The Framers are said to have held to a set of ideas that hearkened all the way back to the fall of the Roman Republic. This tradition, known as classical republicanism, insisted that no republic could survive unless its citizens remained virtuous—willing to sacrifice themselves for the community. By 1787 the men who had led the nation into the Revolutionary War were convinced that they had lost control of nearly every state assembly to demagogues who lacked this essential quality of manly virtue.[7] The only way to have a virtuous government, they decided, was to create a national one.

This ideological interpretation of the origins of the Constitution has its merits, and yet a thorough reexamination of the context in which the new national government was created reveals a still more pressing motive. By the mid-1780s the nation's leading citizens had come to believe that unless the federal government was thoroughly overhauled, the American economy would never be able to attract capital.

The dire postwar shortage of investment capital received emphasis from all three authors of the *Federalist Papers*. Under the Articles of Confederation, John Jay claimed, "scarcely any man can borrow of his neighbor." In the last *Federalist* paper, Alexander Hamilton praised Article I, Section 10, of the proposed Constitution for its "precautions against the repetition of those practices on the part of the state governments, which have undermined the foundations of property and credit."[8] And Madison, the man who is most often quoted in support of the hypothesis that the Framers' primary objective was to replace selfish demagogues with men of virtue, affirmed that his motives for pursuing this ideological goal were chiefly economic. Restoring virtue to government would revive the economy, because it would reopen the credit valve. Cracking down on debtors and taxpayers, Madison was convinced, would end the terrible recession that had followed the Revolutionary War. It would do more than that. It would fuel rapid economic growth—a matter that for him was intensely personal.

In the spring of 1787 the thirty-six-year-old Madison still lived at Montpelier, his father's estate in Orange County, Virginia. Eager to acquire the wealth that would allow him to live both comfortably and not with his parents, he had recently embarked upon a classically American get-rich-quick scheme: land speculation. The outcome of the venture fell far short of Madison's expectations, however—for reasons that had nothing to do with the quality of the soil.

In the fall of 1784 Madison accompanied the Marquis de Lafayette, the young French hero of the Revolutionary War, up the Hudson and Mohawk Rivers to Fort Stanwix, in present-day Rome, New York, to witness an Indian treaty. At the conference U.S. officials browbeat their Iroquois counterparts into ceding them a vast tract of land (most of which was ac-tually inhabited and hunted by other Indians).[9] By that time Madison and Lafayette had already gone back east, but at least for the Virginian, the excursion to Fort Stanwix had not been a waste of time.

As he sailed the Mohawk River, Madison could not help noticing the richness of the soil in what had once been the Iroquois heartland. A year after the Fort Stanwix treaty was signed, on a visit to Mount Ver-non, he asked George Washington about the advisability of buying land in the region.

Madison could not have come to a better place. "The greatest Estates we have in this Colony," Washington had discovered back when he was Madison's age, were made "by taking up and purchasing at very low rates the rich back Lands."[10] "If he had the money to spare and was dis-posed to deal in land," Washington now told Madison, the Mohawk Valley was "the very spot which his fancy had selected of all the U.S." Indeed, Washington and a partner had just purchased their own Mo-hawk River tract.[11]

In the spring of 1786 Madison entered into a partnership with Vir-ginia congressman James Monroe (who was destined, three decades later, to succeed him in the presidency) and "made a small purchase"— nine hundred acres—on the Mohawk River nine miles from the site of the Stanwix treaty.[12]

Madison and Monroe knew their plan contained a fatal flaw. Shortly after they made their initial purchase, in August 1786, Madison wrote his friend Thomas Jefferson saying "nothing but the difficulty of raising a sufficient sum restrained us from making a larger" one. The young en-trepreneurs had run up against the direst economic evil of the 1780s: well-to-do Americans' growing reluctance to lend money to their fellow citizens. Madison came from the wealthiest family in Orange County, Virginia, but it was becoming harder and harder even for men like him to convert their land and slaves into cash. In fact, Madison had had to rely on Monroe for the entire down payment, and repaying him took Madison much longer than anticipated.[13]

It occurred to Madison that Jefferson, who was then the American envoy to France, might have better luck "raising a sufficient sum" in Europe. Assuring Jefferson there was "prospect of advantage to your self as well as to us," Madison invited him to become a partner. This involved Jefferson "borrowing say, four or five thousand louis" d'or (French coins named for the king)—oh, and putting up a portion of his own considerable estate as collateral. Madison reminded Jefferson that "scarce an instance has happened in which purchases of new lands of good quality and in good situations have not well rewarded the adventurers."[14]

Jefferson had once demonstrated a voracious appetite for Indian land, but Madison's proposal left him cold, for he knew the "Monied men" of Europe would be no likelier than their American counterparts to invest in it. Jefferson had recently tried to interest wealthy Parisians in a similar loan request from George Washington's Potomac River canal company. But he soon found that no one would lend to the canal-builders when they could earn the same interest rate on French government bonds, upon which interest was paid "with a religious punctuality." Louis XVI's financial situation would soon grow considerably more precarious, but that was in the future. For the moment Jefferson could understand why French aristocrats would rather invest at home than in Virginia. If a Parisian lent a large sum to Madison and the two of them ever landed in a Virginia court, the judges' "habitual protection of the debtor would be against" the investor, Jefferson said.[15]

James Madison had a personal stake in government reform, but he was seeking to do much more than line his own pocket. His central insight was that he would never be able to borrow money until American legislators and judges enforced the collection of earlier loans. On May 3, 1787, when Madison left his seat in Congress and crossed the Hudson River—the first stage of his journey from New York to Philadelphia—what he was really seeking was the right to lose a lawsuit.

Like other Framers, Madison was convinced that cracking down on delinquent debtors would, ironically enough, solve many of the problems that farmers had complained about. Were the "lessons which the mercantile interest of Europe have received from late experience" starting to "check their propensity to credit us beyond our resources"? Well then, "the true mode" of "bringing in specie" (gold and silver) was "to enforce Justice"—to crack down on delinquent debtors.[16]

It seems likely that Madison's frustration was not only economic but psychological. Prevented by America's poor investment climate from borrowing the money that he needed to buy his way out from under his father's patriarchal care, the man who was about to become "the father of the Constitution" was, economically speaking, still a child. It must have been humiliating.[17] Madison would not really reach manhood until he became the head of his own household, and to do that he would first need to establish a gilt-edged credit rating, not only for himself but for the nation as a whole.

Madison recognized that thousands of Americans shared his frustrations. Under the Articles of Confederation, he declared in *Federalist* Number 62, "no great improvement or laudable enterprise, can go forward," because the "want [lack] of confidence in the public councils damps every useful undertaking."[18] If that confidence could be restored, if ambitious men like Madison could obtain the loans they needed to buy land, expand their trade networks, and develop manufacturing enterprises, they would set in motion a commercial revival that would shower its bounty on even the poorest tenant.

Not everyone agreed with James Madison's analysis of the infant nation's travails. Like Madison, Americans such as Adonijah Mathews based their economic analyses on their own experience. Today the Revolutionary War is seen as clearing the way for the unprecedented prosperity that has made the United States the envy of much of the world. But for the Americans who fought the war, the decade that followed it was disastrous—as bad, according to some modern analysts, as the Great Depression of the 1930s.

As always, the distress of multitudes spelled opportunity for some. In Boston a doctor who provided dental work to wealthy clients published an advertisement seeking "persons inclined to dispose of LIVE TEETH, for cash."[19] In Richmond, Virginia, an advertiser offered the extraordinary sum of "TWO GUINEAS"—about what a day laborer would earn in two weeks—for a living person's tooth. Virginia law defined nearly half the people of the state as property, so the Richmond notice included a clause "excepting slaves," since unfree African Americans' teeth were not their own.[20]

The economic slump of the 1780s had many sources. During the American Revolution, as in most wars, soldiers destroyed massive quantities of property. But what they did caused less harm to the economy than what they did not do: their normal jobs. During the war the nation's economic output plummeted. True, most farm families also drastically reduced expenditures—the virtual cessation of transatlantic trade left them little choice. But few households were able to scrimp enough to make up for what they lost when their young men exchanged wheat and tobacco fields for battlefields. Many plunged deep into debt.

Another kind of loss went hand in hand with one of the war's greatest instances of liberation. Throughout the rebelling colonies, enslaved men, women, and children took advantage of wartime chaos to declare their own independence. Some simply melted into forests or swamps, but many more responded to British emancipation proclamations that were not too different from the one Abraham Lincoln would publish nearly a century later. In a typical case, when an imperial fleet sailed up the Cape Fear River in the spring of 1776, the African-born slave Thomas Peters, a Wilmington, North Carolina, millwright, managed to get aboard one of the British warships. He signed on with the "Black Guides and Pioneers," served throughout the war, and received his freedom afterward, settling first in Nova Scotia and later in the new British colony of Sierra Leone on the West African coast.[21] During the war thousands of African Americans blazed a wide range of trails from slavery to freedom.[22]

Liberation for Americans like Thomas Peters meant tremendous financial loss for those who claimed to own them. For George Robertson of Chesterfield County, Virginia, the year 1781 was less memorable for the British surrender at Yorktown in October than for the white "people being so Distressed with the war and loseing their negroes." Owing to slave escapes and other wartime disruptions, Robertson said, "there was but a very few hogsheads [outsize barrels] of Tobacco made in the County."[23]

Some farm families believed that when the war ended, their tribulations would, too. Actually, the hardship had only begun. For one thing, reconciliation with Britain did not always mean peace. During the war citizens of the new nation had told themselves the only reason Native American war parties attacked their western settlements was that the

British had (in the words of the Declaration of Independence) "endeav-
oured to bring on the inhabitants of our frontiers, the merciless Indian
Savages." Actually the "Incursions of the Savages" continued long after
the Paris peace treaties of 1783.[24]

Back in 1776, when free Americans had announced their secession
from the British Empire, many had envisioned vast new economic opportunities opening to them once they escaped the mother country's
monopoly of their trade. Indeed, for many, the promise of free trade
was one of the primary attractions of independence.[25] After the war,
however, citizens reached the grim conclusion that being confined to
the British imperial trading bloc was not nearly as bad as being excluded from it. In 1783, the same year the Crown formally recognized
the independence of the United States, imperial officials also announced that they had no intention of allowing American merchants to
recover what had been one of their greatest sources of income before
the war: the trade with the British sugar islands in the Caribbean. No
longer would American vessels be allowed to carry fish, livestock, grain,
and forest products to the slave plantations in island colonies like Ja-
maica and Barbados.

All of these were real grievances. Within a few years of the victory at
Yorktown, however, free Americans seeking explanations for their distress increasingly focused on a single source. Their greatest tormen-
tors, they believed, were their own state governments.

The consensus that the thirteen state assemblies had let their constituents down was nearly universal. Where Americans differed was in
identifying what exactly the legislators had done wrong. Indeed, that
seemingly obscure question held the key to the creation of a national
government that was destined to become the most powerful institution in world history. Even more than that was at stake. Each of the
thirteen contests over arcane fiscal and monetary matters concealed a
more fundamental debate over whether ordinary Americans possessed
the capacity for self-government. If debtors and taxpayers could make
a convincing case that they were not the perpetrators of unjust legislation but the victims of it, they could vindicate their ability to govern
themselves.

Many Americans believed the assemblies' greatest crime had been to levy what one South Carolinian called "oppressive, grinding taxes."[26] There was no better way of "relieving the good people of this state, from their present distresses," the Virginia newspaper essayist "Plain Reason" asserted in September 1787, than by "speedily freeing them, from the pressure of their taxes."[27] Even before the Massachusetts legislature adopted the £311,000 tax that was widely seen as triggering Shays's Rebellion, a Bay State writer declared that "the people are taxed quite up to their bearing."[28] In neighboring New York the state government was able to obtain more than a third of its revenue from a nearly painless duty on European manufactured goods—predominantly textiles—arriving in the vast natural harbor at the mouth of the Hudson River. But even in New York, farmers were said to "labour under the most excessive weight of taxes, that ever country was burdened with."[29]

This was not mere rhetoric. To finance their war against British "taxation without representation," Americans had committed themselves to higher taxes than they had ever faced as British colonists. After the war, taxes in most states remained three or four times higher than colonial levels.[30] In the colony of Rhode Island annual revenue needs had seldom exceeded £2,000. Two years after the signing of the Paris peace treaty, however, the assembly imposed a tax with a face value of £20,000 and an actual value (in gold and silver) of about £11,000.[31] In 1786, the year of Shays's Rebellion, the portion of Massachusetts farmers' income consumed by taxation was four to five times higher than it had been under British rule.[32]

Americans were acutely conscious of the irony of having rebelled against British tax collectors only to face even more voracious ones at home. In the midst of Shays's Rebellion, the town meeting in Greenwich, Massachusetts, recalled that back during the struggle against Parliament "our Grievances Ware Less Real and more Ideal then [sic] they are Now."[33]

Even many citizens who initially favored the high taxes of the mid-1780s later came to see them as an "intolerable" form of "oppression."[34] Second thoughts about heavy taxation were especially common in Massachusetts. Rufus King, an early champion of the state legislature's harsh fiscal policies, later declared that assemblymen had "pressed the subject of Taxes, *of the direct Kind*, beyound what prudence would authorise."[35] In several states even the representatives who imposed the onerous taxes of the 1780s doubted the public's ability to bear up under the burden. After Shays's Rebellion broke out in Massachusetts, state legislators allowed that they might have "misjudged of the abilities of their constituents."[36] On the first day of 1788 Virginia representatives acknowledged that state taxes were "heavier than the circumstances of the people will admit of, without suffering great distress."[37]

Americans of the 1780s had to contend not only with new levies but with increasingly aggressive efforts to collect old ones. The men charged with extracting money from taxpayers could seize their belongings if they did not pay. If the collectors did not meet their quotas, their own property could be confiscated and sold. Sometimes they were even thrown in jail. These prospects were often sufficient to dissolve even the most kind-hearted tax-gatherer's qualms about carting off delinquent taxpayers' property.[38]

The taxes imposed in the 1780s were even heavier than they appeared on paper, for the citizens of the United States were suffering through an acute shortage of the hard money—gold and silver—that was often the only acceptable form of payment. During the 1780s, numerous writers complained that in imposing taxes while starving the economy of the currency that was needed to pay them, state assemblymen were making the same demand of taxpayers that Pharaoh had made of the children of Israel: "there shall no straw be given you, yet shall ye deliver the tale of bricks."[39] "A Friend to the Public," a Rhode Island writer, went further. "To call on the owners of little farms, the tradesmen, labourers and sailors to pay their proportion of a [£20,000] tax, when perhaps there is not half that sum in circulation is something harder than being forced to make bricks without straw," he wrote; "it is to make them without clay." He imagined a farmer who paid his state taxes every year by selling an ox. The shortage of circulating coin cut the price of livestock in half, meaning that the ox would discharge only half of the tax bill. "Pray honest farmer," this writer asked the character he had created, "where is the other half of your ox?"[40]

The shrinking money supply swelled private debts as well as taxes. Like the backcountry Virginian Adonijah Mathews, William Manning of Billerica, Massachusetts, was a tavern-keeper. He was also a farmer who had fought at the Battle of Concord. In a 1790 essay the forty-two-year-old Manning contended that every society consists of two great interests, the Few and the Many. "There is nothing," Manning wrote, "which excites jealousy between these Few and Many more than the alterations of money affairs."[41] Since "the interests and property of the Few consist chiefly in rents, money at interest, salaries, and fees," Manning wrote, the Few "are interested in having money scarce and the prices of things as low as possible. For instance, if they could reduce the prices by one half, it would in its operation be just the same to them as though their salaries were doubled." As the money supply tightened in the 1780s, livestock prices fell by roughly half, while land lost at least two-thirds of its value. Frequently a farmer who bought a horse on credit could raise sufficient funds to pay for it only by selling that animal and two others. "The debtors in general now pay as much as three pounds for every one pound they owe," Manning claimed.[42]

Sometimes the property that debtors found themselves selling off at a fraction of its face value consisted of human beings. In those cases the debtor was not the one who suffered most, for the sale of slaves often resulted in the permanent dissolution of enslaved families.

The shortage of circulating currency helps explain why Massachusetts farmers demanded that their governor, James Bowdoin, take a pay cut of more than 50 percent, from £1,100 to £500. The governor's defenders could not understand why farmers would "raise a mob to reduce the governor's salary, which does not amount to three pence per man per annum."[43] In response the town of Dracut explained that "five hundred pounds Represents as much Property at this time . . . as eleven hundred pounds did when the Governors salary was Established."[44] Everyone knows what inflation does to people on fixed incomes. For Bowdoin and everyone else who was lucky enough to earn a fixed salary during the 1780s, the process was reversed. As the money drained out of the economy, the governor received a continuing succession of automatic pay raises—even as the same process magnified farmers' tax burden.

For all their symbolic importance, government salaries accounted for only a fraction of the taxes that were levied in the 1780s. Between the Peace of Paris in 1783 and the ratification of the Constitution five years later, the single heaviest government expense, at both state and federal levels, was the war debt. Congress and all thirteen states printed paper money during the war, and loans and subsidies eventually came in from overseas. But one of the most crucial mechanisms of war finance had been the issuance of promissory notes. The IOUs went not only to people who lent cash to the government but to army contractors and soldiers. Eventually much of this paper was converted into bonds like today's savings bonds. In nearly every state two-thirds of direct tax revenue was earmarked for public creditors.[45] Sometimes the proportion was even higher. For instance, in 1786, the South Carolina legislature paid the annual interest on the state's war debt by imposing new poll and property taxes and decreeing that bondholders would receive every penny.[46]

Americans were acutely aware that most of the tribute that public officials exacted from them went to bondholders. In the wake of Shays's Rebellion a *Massachusetts Centinel* writer blamed the *"great possessors* of what is called publick securities," intent on "the carving of the *loaves and fishes,"* for the "abominable system of enormous taxation, which is crushing the poor to death."[47] In February 1786 Thomas Tudor Tucker reminded his colleagues in the South Carolina House of Representatives that if it were not for their obligations to bondholders, they could have gotten by with "a very light tax."[48] Indeed, many states could have stopped imposing property and poll (head) taxes altogether, obtaining all the revenue they needed from the nearly painless tariff they levied on imported merchandise. James Madison, who advocated aggressive collection of high taxes in order to service the war bonds, allowed that the states' other expenses amounted to a "pittance."[49]

Much of the debate over the Revolutionary War debt came down to who owned it. The bondholders' defenders said the securities mostly belonged to men like Thomas Mansfield of Abington, Massachusetts. Three years after the war the eighty-four-year-old Mansfield told the state assembly he had "no Estate Except what lies in State Secur[it]ies." Mansfield had tried to redeem his bonds, but he could "get no money from the tre[a]sury," despite having "made repeated application." "As Winter is now approaching," he told the representatives in September 1786, "your Pet[it]ioner must unavoidably suffer Except something be done for his Relief."[50]

It seems likely that Mansfield was the original owner of his bonds.

Perhaps he had received them in return for supplying the army. But thousands of other bondholders had acquired their securities on the open market. Every soldier in the Continental Army had received bonds to make up for the months when Congress—and after 1778 his home state—had fobbed him off with paper money that was worth only a fraction of the amount printed on its face. Most state militiamen also received part of their compensation in the form of securities.

Although Mansfield held on to his bonds, other Americans sold theirs. Joseph Plumb Martin was a Connecticut farmer's son who enlisted in the Continental Army in 1776 and served throughout the war. At the end of his life Martin was still bitter about the way he and his comrades had been discharged in 1783. The men in his unit who stuck around long enough to collect their bonds immediately sold them "to procure decent clothing and money sufficient to enable them to pass with decency through the country, and to appear something like themselves when they arrived among their friends." "I was among those," he recalled.[51]

Many of the bonds that had initially been issued to soldiers like Martin, as well as those given to the farmers and merchants who supplied the army, eventually ended up in the hands of speculators. Some wealthy Americans made enormous investments in depreciated government paper. Nicholas Brown of Providence, Rhode Island, acquired Rhode Island, Massachusetts, Connecticut, and United States notes with an aggregate face value in excess of £80,000. By November 1786 his federal bonds alone filled a "small Trunk."[52] Sometimes wealthy Americans formed partnerships whose sole purpose was to speculate in securities. On June 7, 1784, Nathanael Greene, the Rhode Island Quaker turned Continental Army general, signed an agreement with Philadelphia merchant Charles Pettit (who also speculated extensively on his own). The two agreed to invest as much as $4,000 in federal bonds—enough to buy securities with a face value of $32,000. But the venture was doomed from the start. To put up his share of the capital, Greene drew a bill of exchange—similar to a modern personal check—on Hartford, Connecticut, merchant Jeremiah Wadsworth, who refused to pay it.[53]

One securities trader approached the business with enough zeal and cunning to produce not only enormous profits but an extensive docu-

mentary record. One reason the documents survive is that the speculator was Abigail Adams.

John Adams spent most of the decade from 1774 to 1784 away from
his wife, Abigail Smith Adams, and his home in Braintree, Massachusetts. In 1778 he crossed the Atlantic as an American diplomat, and
with the exception of a brief sojourn the following year, he did not return from Europe for another decade. Until 1784, when she finally
joined her husband in Europe, Abigail Adams represented her husband
in his American business dealings. In modern popular culture early
American women are sometimes caricatured as drones without wills of
their own. But it was actually common for them to assume control of
the family's financial affairs when the man of the house was away. Benjamin Franklin's wife, Deborah, had done that before the Revolutionary War. During the Revolution thousands of soldiers, politicians, and
diplomats chose to turn their finances as well as their farms over to
their wives.[54]

Early in the war Abigail Adams proved herself an adept securities
speculator. One of the bonds she purchased had depreciated to 15 percent of its face value, and she held on to it until it reached 85 percent—
more than five times what she had paid for it. Even after her husband
helped negotiate peace with Britain in 1783, Adams wished to continue
dealing in depreciated government paper. First, however, she would
have to contend with a husband whose investment preferences ran
toward real estate.[55]

In the fall of 1783, shortly after the Paris peace conference, John
Adams instructed his wife to find out what price two of his neighbors
would take for their farms. Responding in January 1784, Abigail agreed
to sound the two men out. But then she added, "There is a method of
laying out money to more advantage than by the purchase of land's,"
namely "State Notes."[56]

The following summer Abigail finally joined her husband in Europe.
Before sailing she handed control of his affairs to her uncle, Cotton
Tufts, a physician in Weymouth, Massachusetts. In September 1784
John instructed his new agent to purchase a farm from a couple who
lived near the Adamses, William and Sarah Veasey.[57] Three days later, in
her own letter to Tufts, Abigail pleaded with him not to buy the farm.

"Veseys place is poverty," she wrote, "and I think we have enough of that already."⁵⁸

There is no way of knowing whether Abigail told John she had countermanded his instruction, but on April 24, 1785, John started a letter to Tufts by affirming his determination to buy the farm. To pay for it, Tufts was to "draw upon" Adams—hand the seller a bill of exchange that would eventually make its way to John, who would pay it. Later in the same letter, however, John wrote, "Shewing what I had written to Madam she has made me sick of purchasing Veseys Place. Instead of that therefore you may draw upon me, for two hundred Pounds at as good an Exchange [Rate] as you can obtain and lay it out in such Notes as you judge most for my Interest."⁵⁹

Abigail's conviction that bonds were a better investment than land even prompted her to take the extremely rare step of openly criticizing John to a third person. In an October 1790 letter she told her sister Mary Smith Cranch that if she and her uncle Tufts

*had been left to the sole management of our affairs, they would have been upon a more profitable footing. . . . The money paid for useless land I would have purchase[d] publick securities with. The interest of which, poorly as it is funded, would have been less troublesome to take charge of then [sic] Land and much more productive. But in these Ideas I have always been so unfortunate as to differ from my partner, who thinks he never saved any thing but what he vested in Land.*⁶⁰

Securities were not the only investment to open a rift within the Adams family. Abigail also speculated in western land, eliciting from John an October 1782 letter saying, "Dont meddle any more with Vermont."⁶¹ In general, however, John was only too happy to leave financial matters to his wife. After she joined him in Europe, John wanted to trust her uncle to choose among various speculative investments, but Abigail had precise notions about which bonds were likely to yield the highest return. "I should think it might not be amiss to invest one hundred pounds in the Army certificates which tho not so valuable at present, will become so in time," she wrote Tufts in April 1785.⁶² A year later Adams told her uncle she wanted to make an additional "purchase of notes," observing, "I think they must rise, and I have advised mr Adams to request you to lay out a hunderd pound in them if you are of the same mind."[63]

In May 1785 Abigail Adams began playing the bond market on her own. She wrote Tufts saying her son John Quincy, who was headed home to Massachusetts, was going to bring him £50 (Massachusetts currency). "With this money which I call mine I wish you to purchase the most advantageous Bills and keep them by themselves," she wrote.[64]

"Money which I call mine"—an extraordinary phrase. In a famous letter she sent her husband in June 1782, Adams complained that under the English common law, which continued to govern relations among Americans wherever their state assemblymen had not overridden it, married women's "property is subject to the controul and disposal of our partners, to whom the Laws have given a soverign Authority."[65] Wives could not make contracts unless they acted as their husbands' authorized agents. And yet three years later Abigail proclaimed that some of the family property was, at least in her eyes, hers.[66]

Adams's prolonged separation from her husband seems only to have intensified her affection for him (a phenomenon that would not have surprised his political rivals), but she did resent what she called her "widowhood," and she seems to have reasoned that if she was going to pay the price of independence, she might as well enjoy some of the privileges as well.[67]

The bondholders' advocates contended that most of them resembled Thomas Mansfield, the old man in Abington, Massachusetts, who did not know how he was going to buy enough firewood to get through the winter. They were the farmers who had fed the soldiers and the army's draft animals. They had lent their money to the state and federal governments. Above all, the bondholders were battle-scarred veterans and their widows and orphans.

Tax relief advocates painted a different picture. They claimed that the market in government paper had been cornered by speculators like Nicholas Brown and the Adamses (which is not to say Abigail Adams's bond speculation was widely reported at the time—in fact she took pains to conceal it).[68] "By far the greater part of your military debt, is no longer due to your well deserving soldiery," "Plain Reason" told

Virginians at the end of August 1787, "pressing necessity has caused these HEROES . . . to become the prey of usurers and speculators, who have got almost all their certificates into their hands, and that at an enormous discount."[69]

It seems likely that both of these seemingly contradictory claims — that many of the bonds remained with their original recipients and that speculators had bought up most of the government debt—were correct. Although a host of farmers and soldiers had held on to their bonds, the majority had not, and *by value* most of the debt had concentrated in the hands of a few. Reporting in the fall of 1786 on the largest category of Rhode Island state bonds, a legislative committee noted that nearly half of them were owned by just sixteen people. A Pennsylvania newspaper contended in March 1789 that of the £111,000 that the state government had extracted from taxpayers and handed over to bondholders every year, £70,000 had gone to just twelve investors.[70] By 1790 only about 2 percent of Americans owned bonds.[71]

The state and federal governments paid interest on the face value of bonds, not the price speculators paid for them—a policy with momentous implications. Virginia's "military certificates" paid annual interest of 6 percent. However, since these securities traded at one-fifth of their face value, the speculators who acquired them actually earned an annual return of 30 percent. Petitioners in the region around Jamestown spoke for many Virginians when they claimed this rate of profit violated a state ban on "Excessive Usury."[72] In Pennsylvania, too, men and women whose securities came directly from the government received only 6 percent interest, but those who purchased bonds on the open market earned much more. Benjamin Rush, the Philadelphia doctor and signer of the Declaration of Independence, acknowledged in an anonymous essay that bondholders like himself could count on annual returns "from 6 to 20 per cent."[73] In June 1785, when the Delaware legislature disbursed five years' worth of back interest to citizens who had invested in the state's depreciation certificates, the bondholders received lump sums that were two and a half times greater than what they had paid for their securities.[74]

Abigail Adams's profits were also impressive. In 1784 she persuaded her husband to invest in a Massachusetts government security called the Consolidated Note. These bonds paid an annual interest of 6 percent, but the interest was not based on what was paid for them. Instead investors received 6 percent of the bonds' face value, which was about three times higher. Thus purchasers like Adams earned an annual return of about 18 percent.[75]

Securities speculators reaped these windfalls without in any way diminishing the principal of their bonds. The plan, at least, was that the state and federal governments would eventually redeem each security at the price printed on its face. By 1785 the face value of federal bonds exceeded the market price by a factor of eight, so purchasers of these notes stood to make an eightfold profit (not counting interest). The defenders of the investing class reminded its critics that they had every right to share in the feast. But precious few farmers possessed what Abigail Adams's uncle, himself a speculator, identified as the one prerequisite for participation in this profitable venture: "Cash to spare."[76] "I have lamented that in the general scramble for property I had not a small capital to employ," Noah Webster wrote securities trader James Greenleaf in October 1791, after the federal government began paying punctual interest on its bonds, dramatically raising their value and enriching speculators who had bought low. "As the purchase of paper was attended with no risk and I wished to add a few thousand dollars to my means of living," Webster told Greenleaf, whose sister he had married three years earlier, "it would have made more cheerful hours in my little family."[77]

Taxpayers in every state resented the sacrifices their assemblymen exacted on behalf of bond speculators.[78] "Justitia," a Boston newspaper writer, believed that "the efficient cause of taxation" was the government's desire to satisfy the "desperate band of monopolizers" who had cornered the bond market.[79] In New Hampshire, Jeremy Belknap reported, taxpayers were convinced that "the public securities . . . were engrossed by rich speculators, and the poor were distressed for the means of paying their taxes and their private debts."[80]

No slur was too base for the stockjobbers. Several writers accused them of being Jews. In attacking his newspaper adversary, a New Hampshire essayist named "Observator" drew upon long-standing prejudices against both Jews and the merchants who congregated in London's "Exchange Alley." He claimed securities traders had "advanced this JEW in the alley, to the important trust of defending and supporting their destructive commerce." (Actually, it appears that Observator's opponent was a Puritan minister.)[81] Not even John Adams was immune to this attitude. In June 1786, as he and his wife were buying federal paper at about three shillings on the pound, Adams wrote Thomas Jefferson claiming that European "Jews and Judaizing Christians are now Scheeming to buy up all our Continental Notes at two or three shillings in a Pound, in order to oblige us to pay them at twenty shillings a Pound."[82]

Most Confederation-era levies, taxpayers pointed out, simply paid *interest* to bondholders "without any diminution of the publick debt."[83] Several writers compared this sort of taxation to "a canker worm that consumed their substance without lessening their burdens."[84] In striving to escape the treadmill of "endless Taxes" that left the principal of the government debt intact, taxpayer advocates kept faith with one of the most celebrated threads of Revolutionary thought: a deep suspicion, inherited from English "Country" politicians, of speculators in the public funds.[85]

During the 1780s Congress and most of the state governments employed an ingenious method by which money could be transferred directly from taxpayers to bondholders without ever passing through the hands of public officials. Assemblymen adopted what were sometimes called "certificate taxes." These levies could be discharged using gold and silver coin, but taxpayers hardly ever exercised that option, because they could also tender depreciated government paper. Sometimes legislators taxed in the war bonds themselves. More commonly they disbursed interest using special certificates that they then taxed back into the treasury. The idea was for bondholders, who received far more in interest certificates than they needed to pay their own taxes, to sell their surplus certificates to taxpayers who owned no bonds.

Certificate taxes were frequently defended as "small in substance," even if "*large in sound*." Since farmers could purchase certificates at a discount, a levy payable in certificates was less burdensome than a hard-money tax of the same nominal amount.[86] Taxpayers could even procure certificates without giving up an ounce of silver or gold—so long as they had something else to sell. Securities could "always be obtained at their circulating value, with some commodity or another," a New Hampshire writer pointed out in June 1785.[87]

Farmers nonetheless resented having to purchase certificates using livestock and crops that otherwise could have been converted into the gold and silver they needed for other obligations (including certain taxes that could not be discharged with certificates). In 1784 the New Hampshire legislature decided to pay down the state debt by issuing certificates to bondholders and then taxing them back into the treasury in six annual installments. "Observator," a Hillsborough County writer, said the only citizens who would benefit from this plan were those "who had engrossed those securities at seventy per cent. discount; in short the RICH men ONLY."[88]

American bondholders were acutely aware that the value of their investments hinged on the willingness of the state legislatures to impose taxes. In the summer of 1785, when Josiah Harmar, the ex-Quaker who became commander in chief of the United States Army after the war, learned that the Pennsylvania legislature had enacted a law "granting interest to original holders of certificates," he conjectured that his bonds "must certainly now become valuable."[89] A year later John Webb witnessed the opposite phenomenon in Connecticut. "Our State Notes have fallen to four shillings on the pound—oweing to the Assembly's not laying any Tax of any kind this Session," he told his brother in a June 1786 letter.[90]

Bond prices were even more responsive to the rigor with which taxes were collected. In the spring of 1786 the interest certificates that were disbursed each year to the holders of Connecticut soldiers' notes were trading at around half their face value, or ten shillings per pound. In March John Webb learned that "every [Tax] Collector in this State is now serv'd by the Treas[ur]y" with legal papers requiring the sale of his own property if he did not immediately fill his quota. "If you send on your certificate," he told his brother, the tax crackdown "may ennable me to turn them at 13s4d on the pound"—an increase of one-third.[91] The market price of federal securities likewise rose and fell with the state governments' readiness or reluctance to enact and enforce Continental taxes. A report by the federal treasury board asserted that investors who purchased U.S. bonds in April 1784 and sold them in

September 1787 actually lost money on the deal, since the states' failure to impose and collect Continental taxes had hammered down the value of both principal bonds and interest certificates.[92]

Many bondholders, recognizing that political events determined the value of their investments, made efforts to influence politics. In August 1787, for example, a group of Delaware bondholders petitioned the legislature to crack down on delinquent taxpayers.[93] State officials also heard from individual bondholders. The bond portfolio assembled by Nicholas Brown, a Providence, Rhode Island, merchant, included the "Army Notes" that had been distributed to Massachusetts soldiers starting in 1781. The holders of Army Notes were supposed to receive their annual interest payments out of the state's land and poll tax revenue. On a visit to Boston in August 1785, Brown persuaded state treasurer Thomas Ivers to instruct the sheriff of Bristol County (which bordered Brown's home state of Rhode Island) to pay Brown his interest out of the money coming in from tax collectors. Brown also elicited from Ivers a promise that Bristol County tax collectors who did not turn in their quotas within two weeks would be "executed," meaning that Ivers would order the sheriff to make up their shortfalls out of their own estates. That would leave the tax collectors no choice but to extract the deficient sums from delinquent taxpayers, sending their livestock and other belongings to the auction post. The proceeds from these forced sales could then be used to pay Brown and other bondholders their interest.

Despite the treasurer's assurances, Brown received no money when he met with the Bristol County sheriff on October 9, 1785, because Ivers had empowered the sheriff to execute only one delinquent tax collector. Brown implored Ivers to "Issue the Executions he promised me he wo'd" so the sheriff could begin seizing and selling other tax collectors' property.[94]

It is impossible to say how large a role bondholders like the Delaware petitioners and Nicholas Brown played in persuading the state legislatures to extract large sums of money from taxpayers, but certainly in the eyes of their countrymen, the speculators' influence was enormous. In Massachusetts, "Probus" charged public officials with using their positions to profit at the expense of "those who do not possess so *high a pile* of governmental obligations [bonds]."[95] "Plain Reason" knew better than to expect his tax relief proposal to receive a fair hearing from Virginia assemblymen, since "the figs have been too good, to be left for the mouths of those alone, more especially designed by the name of speculators."[96]

At election time bondholders were accused of advancing protax candidates. After John Hancock won the bitterly contested spring 1787 Massachusetts gubernatorial race, a supporter of the defeated incumbent, James Bowdoin, claimed the majority of the Bostonians who had voted for Hancock were "Labourers, servants, &c." Replying three days later, a Hancock man charged that most of Bowdoin's Boston supporters were "Speculators in Publick Securities."[97]

In time Americans would embrace a radical solution to the problem of excessive taxation. The adoption of the U.S. Constitution in 1788 and of a national debt-refinancing law two years later transferred responsibility for redeeming the bonds from the thirteen states to a federal government that was better equipped to handle it and less likely to cave in to taxpayers' demands for relief. Thus what historians say about the American and French Revolutions was also true of the Constitution: it might never have come about if the government had not previously run up an enormous war debt.

It was not always obvious that state action ranked high among farmers' grievances. One reason was that elite Americans tended to misrepresent smallholders' motives—a process that was never more in evidence than during Shays's Rebellion in Massachusetts. In his first report to George Washington on the revolt, Henry Lee, Jr.—known to history as "Light-Horse Harry," the Revolutionary cavalry commander who in his old age would sire Robert E. Lee—acknowledged that "some attribute it to the weight of taxes." Scarcely two weeks later, however, Lee claimed that what the insurgents really sought was "the abolition of debts, the division of property and re-union with G. Britain."[98]

Farmers were indeed worried about their private debts during the 1780s, but few wanted them abolished. Moreover, many ascribed their "inability to discharge our private debts" to the weight of their taxes, the tax man having carried away the money they needed to satisfy their private creditors.[99]

In the early days of the United States no less so than today, wealthy

Americans liked to attribute their good fortune to successful competition in a free market. Often enough that was the case. But when modern students of the conflicts that led to the U.S. Constitution focus exclusively on disputes between debtors and creditors, they forget that thousands of Americans established or expanded their fortunes not by selling goods or services in an open marketplace but by obtaining favorable policies from the government. That simple fact, so obscure today, was painfully obvious at the time. "Our misfortune," a western Massachusetts writer proclaimed early in 1786, "proceeds from the hand of government."[100]

Whether a family's distress was caused by taxation, private debt, or some combination of the two, the consequences could be dire. Often farmers were forced to sell livestock and sometimes even pots, pans, and family heirlooms. The shortage of circulating coin ensured that few buyers would attend the sale, with the result that the property fetched only a fraction of its face value. When these private sales failed to produce sufficient money to satisfy the merchant or tax man, he often sued, won, and directed the sheriff to sell off whatever remained of the debtor's or taxpayer's belongings.

If the property seized on behalf of creditors and tax collectors failed to make them whole, the next step was often the seizure of the delinquents themselves. Although conditions inside debtors' prison seldom rivaled what jailed criminals and recaptured slaves had to endure, they were often horrific. Former prisoners remembered the damp cold (jailors were notoriously stingy with firewood) as well as the "Suffocating . . . Stench."[101] To modern eyes, the idea of debtor's prison may seem absurd, since imprisonment precluded the debtor from earning the money he needed to satisfy his creditor.[102] Actually, the system contained a cruel logic, since it forced the delinquent debtor to reveal hidden assets, obtain loans from relatives or neighbors, or sell property that was legally exempt from seizure.[103]

The "hardship of being imprisoned for taxes" or debt could, like sheriffs' sales, reach even into the gentry class.[104] Before the Revolutionary War, Thomas Chandler had been a powerful judge in Albany County, New York. But by June 1785 he was in the Westminster, Vermont, debtors' prison, where he died. Chandler's troubles did not end with his death.

The townspeople feared that removing his corpse from the prison could be interpreted as assisting in a jailbreak, and anyone helping a debtor escape the prison bounds—which included the jail itself and several acres of land surrounding it—could be forced to pay the escapee's debt. As the people of Westminster argued over whose responsibility it was to give Chandler a decent burial, his corpse continued to rot. Finally the sheriff found that by "stretching the chain" that defined the prison bounds, he could almost reach the town cemetery. A crew was set to work digging a grave that began within the prison bounds but then slanted into the graveyard. The "jailor, in company with a few individuals, entered in the silence of midnight the cell where the putrescent mass was lying, placed it in a rough box-like coffin," and carried it to the end of the prison bounds, where it was lowered into the grave.[105]

Chandler appears to have died of natural causes, but other debtors became so despondent that they took their own lives. "Many have been the self-murders committed in this city, &c., within a few weeks past," a New York newspaper reported in June 1787.[106] During the colonial era most of the suicides reported in American newspapers had occurred in Europe. With independence, editors throughout the United States began taking a much larger proportion of their news from other periodicals published in the United States, with one result being that citizens mostly read about suicides that had occurred on their own soil. The impression given was that a European malady had crossed the Atlantic. A Hartford, Connecticut, newspaper called the 1785 suicide of John Cooper, an English immigrant, only "the latest instance that has come to our knowledge" of a disturbing trend: "The celebrated English method of getting rid of the troubles of life, by suicide, has lately been performed with wonderful success, in a variety of instances, in different parts of this country."[107]

In an era when both faith and reason argued powerfully against taking one's own life, the most common explanation for individual cases of suicide was insanity, which was often linked to religious fanaticism.[108] But many of the self-murders that occurred in the 1780s were attributed at least in part to financial problems. In one of the more dramatic cases, Philip Peeble of Frederick County, Maryland, who by 1785 had fallen on hard times, killed his entire family before turning his weapon, an axe, on himself.[109]

Even General Nathanael Greene, the man primarily credited with chasing the British Army out of the southern backcountry during the final years of the war, was reported to have killed himself. After the war Greene moved to Georgia to try to recoup his fortune, and just before his death, purportedly from sunstroke, he wrote a series of despairing letters to his former comrades in arms. "My family is in distress," he informed fellow general Henry Knox three months before his death, "I am overwhelmed with difficulties and God knows when or where they will end."[110] After Greene's death in June 1786 his friends were hard put to persuade one another that he had died of natural causes.[111]

Critics of the state legislatures' harsh fiscal and monetary policies sometimes claimed they not only oppressed families but threatened to tear them apart. A New Jerseyan asserted in a 1786 pamphlet that as more and more debtors' belongings were "sold far below the value," the inevitable result was "the breaking of families."[112] Even if a distressed family managed to stay together, the man of the house could not claim to head it if he was unable to keep it financially afloat. The farmers who closed the Worcester County, Massachusetts, court in September 1786 complained of the "sufferings which disenabled them to provide for their wives and children."[113] Unless the New Hampshire legislature relieved rural husbands' and fathers' distress, one writer claimed, they would be unable to "meet their families with conjugal and parental affection."[114]

The recession overthrew other patriarchs as well. When Connecticut residents Naomi and Benjamin Richards married, they "stipulated that neither of the contracting parties should . . . acquire any right belonging to either of them." A wise move on Naomi's part: by October 1786 Benjamin was under "confinement for debt." Although Connecticut did not officially recognize prenuptial agreements, the legislature agreed to make an exception, denying Benjamin's creditors access to the property Naomi had brought to the marriage.[115]

CHAPTER 2

"THE FAULT IS ALL YOUR OWN"

REBUTTALS

As MORE AND MORE AMERICANS insisted that the harsh fiscal and monetary policies of the 1780s had spread desolation through the countryside, most of the defenders of these policies acknowledged that farmers were in trouble but denied that official crackdowns on debtors and taxpayers were to blame. "The disorder under which you at present labour and complain," "Mentor" told his fellow Marylanders during the summer of 1786, "is only to be ascribed to your own misconduct."[1]

The opponents of relief legislation said their fellow citizens would find their debts much more manageable if they would simply repay them rather than waiting to be sued, tacking court costs and both sides' attorneys' fees onto the original balance.[2] The farmer's most grievous transgression, however, was his unwillingness to "live within his bounds."[3] "Unless you import less than you export," a Connecticut essayist told smallholders during the winter of 1786–87, "you will eternally be poor."[4]

Jeremiads against luxury were nothing new, either in America or Europe. For decades writers had contended that sumptuous clothing and other frivolities not only drove consumers into debt but ruined their morals. Today economists point out that Americans' debts, which really did start to grow around the middle of the eighteenth century, were often signs not of extravagance but of productive investment—like the debt carried by any expanding enterprise.[5] At the time, however, this benign view won little support.

Starting in 1764, the British colonists' misgivings about luxury began to acquire a distinctly American flavor. Most of the luxury goods the colonists consumed came from the mother country, and when Parliament tried to tax the colonies, Patriot leaders conceived the idea of turning British merchants' and manufacturers' dependence upon the American market into a weapon. What if colonists were to stop purchasing British goods? British subjects who depended on the American market would quickly perceive that the only way to stem the erosion of their fortunes was to persuade Parliament to repeal the American taxes. Moreover, as more and more British manufacturing hands—many of them already impoverished—were laid off, they would resort to persuasive tactics of their own.[6]

The three boycotts of British merchandise that Americans organized between 1765 and 1774 did in fact capture Parliament's attention. "Non-importation" also proved a valuable weapon against homegrown evils. George Washington, who successfully promoted a boycott to a rump session of the Virginia House of Burgesses in May 1769, privately called nonimportation "a pretext to live within bounds." It would give indebted Virginia gentlemen like himself an excuse to restrain their conspicuous consumption while avoiding the humiliation of individual abstention. Long before anyone in the thirteen colonies seriously contemplated political independence, agreements to forgo British merchandise inspired thousands of Americans with a vision of escaping the despotism of their creditors.[7]

Although the United Kingdom recognized the sovereignty of the United States in 1783, Americans' economic bonds to the former mother country remained as firm as ever. Indeed, the conclusion of the Revolutionary War led to a boom in orders for British manufactured goods as American shopkeepers rushed to replenish inventories depleted by the wartime disruption in transatlantic trade. By the mid-1780s nearly everyone agreed that a large segment of the free population was in deep trouble. Many of the burdens under which the country labored were beyond any American's control. Algerian pirates drove up insurance rates for U.S. merchants trading to the Mediterranean. Britain excluded American ship captains from the Caribbean trade. And so on. Most Americans agreed that the farmers' distress also had domestic roots. But what were they? Were Americans in trouble because the legislatures had failed to maintain a healthy flow of currency and then im-

posed excessively high taxes? Or was the real problem the Americans'
own tendency to spend more than they earned?

Recall that Noah Webster initially defended high taxes, then experi-
enced a conversion. Before his change of heart, Webster had distinguished
himself in the battle against plebeian indolence and extravagance. It was
not legislative policies that needed to be reformed, he insisted; it was
the farmers themselves. At the end of the Revolutionary War, just as he
was initiating his famous campaign to impose discipline upon Americans' use of language, Webster also began trying to rein in their spending. "Luxury rages among you," Webster told his countrymen, "and
luxury is *the devil*."[8]

In an effort to underscore their belief that unwise personal decisions
rather than draconian legislative policies were to blame for the nation's
economic straits, several groups of prominent Americans launched collective assaults on conspicuous consumption. Acting on the belief that
hardly anyone could bear the shame of single-handedly adopting frugal
habits, they formed anti-extravagance associations.[9] In the midst of
Shays's Rebellion the governor whose tax policies had helped stir Massachusetts farmers to revolt trumpeted his belief that the state's distress
was rooted in irresponsible consumer choices. James Bowdoin joined
with about seventy-five state senators and representatives in a "solemn
agreement and association" to reduce consumption of "articles of luxury and extravagance." At a time when farmers' advocates were blaming
heavy taxation for reducing to a trickle the amount of money that circulated in the Massachusetts countryside, the signers of the association affirmed that what was really "exhausting our circulating medium"
was "the excess use and consumption of articles of foreign manufac-
ture." The first state senator to sign the association was Samuel Phillips,
Jr., who owned one of the largest war-bond portfolios in the state.[10]

The antiluxury associations of the 1780s were founded on the belief
that since it was emulation—the tendency of the poor and middling to
mimic the spending habits of the wealthy—that had trapped Americans in debt, only emulation could save them. "Were the sons of affluence to deviate from the high-way of wide-wasting extravagance," a
Virginia essayist declared in the fall of 1786, "the plebians of our country would, probably, more generally embrace frugality and virtue." "Example," he affirmed, is "more powerful than precept."[11]

During the 1780s the long-standing assault on luxury not only intensified but took several unexpected turns. Two decades earlier, while boy-
cotting British merchandise, Patriots had resolved to dress simply, as
Indians did.[12] Yet by the 1780s authors were using Indians to illustrate the
consumer choices that Americans ought to avoid. One writer told Connecticut farmers they could easily discharge their tax bills if they would
simply drink less rum. "A stranger would think you to be a nation of Indians by your thirst for this paltry liquor," he wrote. This same essayist urged
men to "pull all the plumes from the heads of your wives and daughters.
Feathers and fripperies suit the Cherokees, or the wench in your kitchen;
but they little become the fair daughters of Independent America."[13]

In depicting his countrywomen adorning themselves with "feathers and
fripperies," the Connecticut essayist joined in a growing tendency to pin
the country's economic decline on women.[14] During the same period
when writers often claimed men could have discharged all their "rates"
(taxes) with just the money they spent on alcohol, one Connecticut essayist contended that farmwives "will annually spend as much money for
gauze, ribbons and other such trifling articles as would pay their rates."[15]

Another writer, a self-professed farmer, reported that before his first
daughter moved in with her husband, she spun her own trousseau.
When the second daughter married, her mother insisted upon tricking
her out in store-bought calico. The third bride wore silk, and now the
family was in danger of losing its farm.[16] According to male authors, the
woman who draped herself in luxury garments was not actually interested in increasing her comfort, just in keeping up with the neighbors
or even standing "at the head of her acquaintance."[17]

Sometimes men's attacks on female extravagance carried a sexual
charge. One author reminded American women that "feathers and
other frippery of the head, are badges of prostitutes in Europe." A New
Jersey writer urged women to forgo an article that had become fashionable on both sides of the Atlantic: "artificial rumps." In one presumably
fictitious newspaper item, a man reported that his wife had persuaded
him to buy her a coach—which she allegedly used "to indulge herself in
an impure, illicit way."[18]

Women not only demanded sexually charged articles for themselves
but also forced seductive clothing on men, male writers claimed.[19]
Ironically, these garments were often said to make men look like

women—and cross-dressing went both ways. A South Carolinian hated seeing "women accoutred like little infantry soldiers—and Men like dancing Misses."[20]

At the same time that women consumed too much, they also produced too little, a host of male writers complained. In postrevolutionary New Jersey, it was reported, "matrons and maids, instead of attending the duties of the distaff, as formerly, are employed in talking politics, and haranguing on the necessity of a free importation of gauzes and other vile trash."[21]

Writers frequently suggested that one reason women produced too little and consumed too much was that their husbands and fathers had abdicated their positions as family patriarchs. The farmer with the three increasingly expensive daughters affirmed that he was "determined to alter my way of living to what it was twenty years ago," since, after all, "I am still master in my own house."[22] Another author claimed his wife not only "grew proud of dress" but insisted upon the even greater indulgence of buying her daughter a classical education: "Our Elce shall PRACTICE Latin, aye and Greek; that she shall; and get wiser and more in her head than miss———." Having ruefully reported his wife's ambitions, this writer concluded by comparing her to an unruly horse. "Had I broke her at first," he wrote, "I might still have a good wife."[23]

Thus masculine anxiety about losing control of the family spanned the political spectrum. Some men believed the state legislatures' harsh fiscal and monetary policies had driven husbands and fathers from their rightful positions of authority. Others contended that family patriarchs had willingly abdicated their thrones.

While most women were castigated for exacerbating the economic downturn, others were celebrated as pointing the way to recovery. Female participation had ensured the success of Revolution-era boycotts of British merchandise, and during the 1780s male essayists cited numerous cases of women reprising that patriotic role.[24] In the fall of 1785 a South Carolina writer who claimed to be a backcountry farmer told white Charlestonians that "we country folks work up our *Homespun*, and our wives and girls are carding and spinning, whilst yours are *shopping*."[25] Even as these women drew praise for silently doing what virtuous wives and daughters were supposed to do, a small group of female citizens launched ostentatious assaults upon their own extravagance. In the fall of 1785 newspapers as far away as Charleston, South Carolina, published an extraordinary report from Boston: "many ladies of the *first character* and *fortune*, in this metropolis, have in contemplation, in consequence of the present melancholy state of their country, to desist, the approaching season, from all *public amusements*; and to discourage all in their power, every species of *luxury*, *extravagance* and *dissipation*."[26]

Acutely conscious that the reason individuals had trouble trimming their expenses was that they could not bear the humiliation of falling behind their neighbors, women in several towns agreed to "unite their influence" — to embark upon frugality together. On November 6, 1786, more than one hundred women in Hartford, Connecticut, did what several groups of men did at this time: they agreed to confront their conspicuous consumption together. They signed an "Oeconomical Association" pledging to "dress their persons in the plainest manner." The Hartford associators clearly did not agree with the numerous Connecticut essayists and assemblymen who attributed the state's economic problems to high taxes and a cramped money supply. "Our calamities," they said, "are in a great measure occasioned by the luxury and extravagance of individuals." Endorsing the widespread view that fashion was fueled by mimicry, the signers of the Hartford association tried to divert the force of emulation into a positive direction. Their hope was that the very "ladies that used to excel in dress" would now "endeavour to set the best examples" of frugality.[27]

The Oeconomical Association was modest in both its scope and its duration. During a period when male essayists were condemning women for underproducing as well as for overspending, the signatories narrowed their focus to the consumption side of the ledger and especially to fancy clothing. They committed to dress simply for only eight months, at which time they would be free catch up with their fashionable neighbors if the association idea failed to catch on.

Women in several other towns soon followed Hartford's example. Male reaction was mixed. One essayist praised the Hartford association but went on to say, "Should any married lady, at the request of her husband, refuse to join" in the effort, "I should esteem her guilty of the highest act of fornication," meriting "banishment from her husband."[28]

Many women, on the other hand, were taken with the idea that national redemption once again depended, as it had during the 1760s and 1770s, upon the actions of women. "Let no one say that the Ladies are of no importance in the affairs of the nation," Mary Cranch wrote her sister, Abigail Adams, in July 1786. "Perswaide them to renounce all their Luxirys and it would be found that they are."[29]

Men often called upon women to reform their husbands' and sons' habits along with their own. Since female influence had drawn men into the slough of luxury, who better to haul them out?[30] The Andover, Massachusetts, town meeting wished female citizens "would by their engaging examples, as well as in other proper ways, devote that power of influence, with which nature has endowed them, to the purpose of encouraging every species of economy in living."[31]

The Americans who defended the high taxes and restrictive monetary legislation of the 1780s by attributing farm families' distress to their "own laziness and extravagance" were naturally curious about the origins of these bad habits.[32] A striking number of essayists reached the ironic conclusion that when Americans severed their transatlantic political ties in 1776, they made themselves more dependent than ever on British merchandise. Although the colonists had separated themselves from the empire partly in order to preserve their virtue, the ensuing war had, according to New Haven, Connecticut, attorney David Daggett, "vitiated the morals of the people."[33] This process took a variety of forms. A group of Newcastle, Delaware, petitioners said that "the Relaxation of Civil Authority during the War" had led to "Idleness," which had in turn produced "Licentiousness."[34] According to this viewpoint, the Americans whose morals had been most damaged by the Revolutionary War were its heroes, the Continental soldiers. In his history of Shays's Rebellion, George Minot advanced the theory that "the discipline and manners of the army"—which commanded obedience from soldiers but never called upon them to take initiative—had "relaxed the industry of the yeomen."[35]

Even the arrival of peace did not restore the old colonial restraints, because the new state governments were much more beholden to the popular will than were their predecessors. Legislators dared not chastise their countrymen who lapsed into indolence and extravagance for fear of being punished in their turn at the polls. The sons of liberty had become libertines. Maryland gentleman Charles Carroll believed that as his fellow citizens grew "accustomed to a feeble govt. & familiarized with its defects," they inevitably sank into "idleness, & profligacy."[36] A third source of Americans' downfall was the pride that inevitably accompanied their triumph over the world's mightiest army and navy. In a parody of a New Hampshire farmers' convention, a delegate declares, "As conquerors we know / Whate'er we please we ought to do."[37]

Even as these writers sought to explain why Americans consumed so much more than they produced, thousands of their fellow citizens denied that any such slippage had occurred. In particular, women and farmers did not like being told they had provoked the economic crisis by spending beyond their means. "When we complain of our taxes," one self-described Massachusetts farmer stated, protax essayists "tell us of our fine feathers and dinners, and other extravagance." Actually, he declared, these were "the exclusive pleasures and privileges of men who draw from 20 to 60 per cent, from their country" in annual interest on their government securities.[38]

A few writers rebutting claims that farm families were responsible for their own predicament offered an extraordinary new defense. Bucking what had seemed like an ironclad American consensus against luxury, they asked whether it was really so terrible for farmers—and their wives—to indulge themselves once in a while.[39] Writing for the *New Hampshire Gazette* in July 1786, "Crisis" chided members of his own gender who presumed that every woman who donned "a gaudy ribbond, or a flimsy cap of gauze," was obsessed with the aristocratic lifestyle and bent on social "mimickry."[40] In neighboring Massachusetts "Modestus," a critic of Shays's Rebellion, urged young women to be "pleased with the product of their own loom and web" instead of "envying the foppery of the more wealthy." Replying a month later, "A Member of Convention" wondered that Modestus would "deny the maid her ornament, or the bride her attire, those innocent incitements to love, the source of virtuous and manly offspring."[41]

Even more remarkable than these male writers' vindication of female luxury were the women who mounted the same defense. In May 1780, after John Adams implored his wife to live frugally, Abigail penned an acid reply. "A little of what you call frippery is very necessary towards looking like the rest of the world," she declared. The couple's fourteen-year-old daughter, also named Abigail but generally called Nabby within the family, shared her mother's determination to keep up with fashion trends. Nabby told her mother she wanted "a few yard of Black or White Gauze, low priced black or white lace or a few yards of Ribbon," asking her to "write to Pappa at the same time that she has no passion for dress further than he would approve of or to appear when she goes from home a little like those of her own age."[42]

Although Abigail Adams condemned the extravagance she witnessed on the European diplomatic circuit, she came home determined to puncture American men's illusion that the United States was some new Sparta where no one had any need or desire for luxuries. Indeed, this determination provoked from Adams one of the few witty retorts George Washington ever had to endure. At a formal dinner he hosted shortly after assuming the presidency, Washington, who had never crossed the Atlantic, asked the vice president's wife if she was not relieved to have returned from the fleshpots of Europe to the American world of plain frugality. Adams replied that she thought Americans actually "approachd much nearer to the Luxury and manners of Europe according to our ability, than most persons were sensible of, and that we had our full share of taste and fondness for them."[43]

One self-professed female writer, "Eliza," even defended women who engaged in the widely condemned practice of compelling men to spend more on their clothing, affirming that nothing but "contempt" for others could prompt a man to "neglect his dress."[44]

CHAPTER 3

"TO RELIEVE THE DISTRESSED"

DEMANDS

FARMERS AND THEIR SUPPORTERS, blaming the hard times of the 1780s not on individual failings but on deliberate government policy, naturally looked to the government for redress. They petitioned the state assemblies to close the courts temporarily, to allow people to pay their debts and taxes using produce and property instead of hard money, and to reduce attorneys' and government officers' fees.[1] The primary cause of rural distress was overtaxation, they said, and assemblymen should shunt some of the farmer's fiscal burden over onto trade goods and luxuries.[2]

Since most tax money went to bondholders, they were the targets of numerous proposals. A few radicals, including a group of Harrison County, Virginia, petitioners, suggested "Striking off the Interest" the state government had been paying its creditors.[3] Taxpayer advocates in at least nine states proposed to treat the original recipients of bonds differently from those who had purchased them on the open market. If a security was still in the hands of the soldier, supplier, or investor who had originally received it from the government, they said, it should be redeemed in gold or silver. On the other hand, speculators should be paid not the face value of their notes but the much lower amount they themselves had paid for them.

Other tax relief advocates urged assemblymen to discriminate against speculators in the disbursement of interest.[4] Some assemblies reduced bond traders' interest income—and saved taxpayers tens of thousands of pounds—by multiplying the annual interest rate times the market value of their securities rather than the face value. Legislators in other states, recognizing that they would probably not be able to take in enough tax revenue to pay interest to all public creditors, showed speculators to the back of the line, decreeing that no secondary holder would receive a shilling until every original creditor had been paid.[5] Several states withheld interest from secondary holders altogether.[6]

The supporters of the various proposals to discriminate against securities speculators did not conform to the modern caricature of early American farmers as wary of the impersonal market forces that were encroaching upon their world of face-to-face contacts.[7] Indeed, many taxpayer advocates actually employed rhetoric that was aggressively pro-market. "When publick securities GENERALLY pass, among the citizens of a commonwealth, UNDER PAR," a western Massachusetts writer argued at the end of January 1786, "their sense is declared, and their consent given in the plainest manner, for a redemption at THE SAME RATE." Two months later a Connecticut essayist contended that the speculators "themselves being judges set the value" of the securities when they bought them. "That sum with interest is all they can justly demand," he declared. These writers were arguing that the market, like the ballot box, reflected a popular will that public officials had no right to thwart.[8] Occasionally the penetration of market forces into everyday life has prompted American farmers to seek government protection. In the 1780s, though, what farmers were pleading for was protection from the government.

In Massachusetts one strategy for easing the tax burden came to life on the front page of the *Hampshire Herald*, the hometown newspaper in the western Massachusetts village of Springfield. The publication of a pair of essays entitled "Publick Faith" and "Excise" in the winter of 1786 marked the emergence of the previously obscure *Herald* as the nation's leading host to unorthodox economic and political proposals.[9]

In time the decision to publish essays like these two would cost editors John Russell and Gad Stebbins their pride and joy, the newspaper Russell and a previous partner had established two years earlier with a battered old printing press and a short line of credit. They had launched the *Herald* not in one of the rising nation's commercial entrepots but in the little town of Springfield on the Connecticut River, nearly a hundred miles from Boston. Russell and Stebbins remained faithful to their region. At a time when most Americans were able to discern the existence of tax and debt relief schemes only by reading criticism of them—since that was all the local editor would publish— Russell and Stebbins opened the pages of their little weekly to the advocates for a wide variety of relief measures.

Newspaper editors in those days exchanged subscriptions with their counterparts in distant towns, and it was common for a particularly sensational item—a grisly murder, a suicide, an Indian speech—to reappear in dozens of papers throughout the nation. So it was with "Publick Credit" and "Excise," which ramified through the American journalistic network like a stone striking still water. Isaiah Thomas, the editor of the influential *Worcester Magazine*, pointedly refused to reprint either essay, but both soon appeared in two Boston papers, then spread to other New England states and beyond.[10] Often a cautious editor would introduce the essays with a note explaining that they had debuted at the *Hampshire Herald* and were being reprinted only at some reader's particular insistence.

"Excise" made essentially the same suggestion that had appeared in numerous other *Herald* essays: government securities that had been bought up by speculators ought to be scaled down to their market value. Although "Publick Faith" came from the same anonymous pen, it was considerably more original. Like most states, Massachusetts earmarked all the revenue from the tariff it levied on goods imported from overseas— at once its most lucrative and least painful tax—for the payment of interest on state bonds, specifically on the Consolidated Notes, which had been distributed to the possessors of an earlier series of state securities at sixteen times their market price.[11] The *Hampshire Herald* writer urged the assembly to take the tariff revenue away from the owners of the Consolidated Notes. Instead this money should be used to buy up the state's war bonds, as well as Massachusetts's share of the federal securities, at their greatly depreciated prevailing price. Once every bond in Massachusetts was in the state treasury, the General Court could repeal the onerous taxes it had levied on behalf of bondholders. Essentially the author of "Publick Faith" was proposing that the state government beat the paper speculators at their own game.[12]

Another relief proposal was endorsed by thousands of farmers in every state: paper money. The advocates and enemies of paper currency could not even agree on why it attracted so much support. One anticurrency petition claimed its champions were actuated by motives "more powerfull than pure."[13]

The impure motive that critics discerned in paper money advocates was debt repudiation. They predicted that if the legislature were to print fiat money (which creditors could not lawfully refuse), debtors would drive its market price far below the nominal value, then snap it up and use it to erase enormous hard-money debts.[14] Americans who opposed paper currency frequently compared its supporters to the enemies of private property who stalked the pages of history and the Bible. During New Hampshire's currency battle, "A Friend to the Rights of Mankind" accused one adversary, "Observator," of promoting "levelizm," the seventeenth-century English effort to level all distinctions in property ownership. What Observator was really seeking, he said, was a "jubilee" like the one Jehovah mandated in the book of Leviticus. In the year of the Jubilee, all debts were forgiven and everything that had been pawned was returned to its original owner.[15] Paper money advocates were also compared to Greek and Roman property-redistributors. "The Antients were surely men of more candor than We are," declared Dumfries, Virginia, attorney William Grayson. "They contended openly for an abolition of debts in so many words, while we strive as hard for the same thing under the decent & specious pretense of a circulating medium."[16]

The claim that paper money was a scheme to defraud creditors reached a crescendo during Shays's Rebellion in Massachusetts in 1786 and 1787. No one articulated this view more forcefully than Henry Knox. After the United States and Britain made peace in 1783, Congress had rewarded Knox for his success as Washington's chief of artillery by making him secretary of war. In October 1786 Knox told his old commander that the Shaysites were "determined to annihilate all debts public and private," a goal "easily effected by the means of unfunded paper money."[17]

This notion of paper money advocates as modern-day Robin Hoods was not quite as far-fetched as it might seem. If a government forces creditors to accept currency that is not worth the paper it is printed on, it might as well have decreed that the debt not be paid. Hyperinflated fiat money allows anyone who has bought an item on credit essentially to have it for free.[18]

In the 1780s the idea that property could be redistributed through currency manipulation was not simply a theoretical possibility, for something very close to that had just occurred during the Revolutionary War. A prominent victim of the wartime hyperinflation was Thomas Jefferson. Jefferson's father-in-law, John Wayles, died two years before the war, in June 1773, leaving Jefferson a three-part inheritance. The thirty-year-old Virginian acquired several tracts of land totaling more than 11,000 acres, 135 slaves (including an infant named Sally Hemings)—and a third of Wayles's debts. Jefferson decided to sell about half the land to raise the money he needed to pay off his share of the Wayles debt. The men who bought Jefferson's land agreed to pay him a combined total of £4,200, but not all at once. Before Jefferson could collect everything he was owed, the war came, and the Virginia House of Delegates printed paper money that soon depreciated. The assembly designated the money legal tender, meaning creditors had no right to refuse it. The purchasers of Jefferson's real estate discharged their debts to him using paper money that was, as he later wrote, "not worth oak leaves."[19]

George Washington's creditors also foisted depreciated paper money on him. While he was commanding the Continental Army, people to whom he had lent £10,000 (sterling) worth of cash and merchandise repaid their debts with paper money that was worth, on average, one-fourth of its face value.[20]

Another victim of the hyperinflation of the Virginia currency was Continental soldier Joseph Martin. As Lord Cornwallis's army moved through the south in 1781, hundreds of African Americans—including eight of the slaves Thomas Jefferson had inherited eight years earlier—managed to escape their owners and cast their lots with the redcoats. In October, as French and American troops laid siege to the British Army at Yorktown, Virginia, the general unceremoniously ordered his men to chase the hundreds of African Americans who had joined him out of the British camp. After Cornwallis surrendered, slaveholders offered rewards for the return of their human property, and Martin helped capture one of the fugitives. His share of the reward came to $1,200 in Virginia currency—nominally a princely sum but actually just enough, given hyperinflation, to buy Martin a celebratory quart of rum.[21]

Eventually all of the states complied with Congress's spring 1781 recommendation that they stop allowing debtors to foist paper money on their creditors. They returned to the gold-and-silver standard. But the memory of hyperinflation lingered on. In the mid-1780s, when numerous Americans suggested that their state governments once again resort to printing paper bills, many of the most prominent men and women in the nation shuddered. Americans, three essays published in Boston in 1785 independently declared, should avoid paper money just as a "burnt child dreads the fire."[22]

The friends of paper currency recognized that "the injurious consequences of the depreciation of the continental and state-monies" during the war had "left impressions extremely unfavourable to it."[23] They denied that fiat money would suffer the same fate during peacetime, and they repeatedly pointed to its widespread success during the colonial era.[24] Historians observe that the most fervent advocates for the U.S. Constitution tended to be "the young men of the Revolution," whose earliest adult memories were of Congress's frustrations maintaining the Continental Army, while many of the Anti-Federalists had formed their political convictions earlier, during the struggle against Parliament. Old men who had cut their teeth on British tyranny, the argument goes, approached the Constitution more cautiously than youngsters who had stared into the face of anarchy.[25] There may be another reason why the Constitution opened a generational divide. On the all-important topic of paper money, the older Americans were, the more deeply rooted were their memories of the successful currency emissions of the colonial era.

Some of the fiat money printed during the 1780s did depreciate, but that was rarely its supporters' intention. Indeed, the most severe currency inflation, in Rhode Island, was widely ascribed not to devious debtors but to the skittish creditors who refused to accept the new money. Widespread suspicion of the new currency guaranteed its depreciation—a self-fulfilling prophecy.[26]

Although constitutional scholars routinely describe the paper money emitted during the 1780s as debtor relief, the reality in several states was that the men who petitioned for currency were actually less eager to facilitate the payment of their debts—much less to defraud their creditors—than to ease the burden of taxation.[27] Since what made the era's tax levies so painful was the dire shortage of coin with which to pay them, allowing farmers to sell their crops and livestock for paper money that they could then hand the tax man would dramatically ease their distress.[28] New Hampshire legislators were not alone in recognizing that the principal reason "the cry for paper money has been great among the people at large within this state" was not to alleviate their debt burden but to "enable them to pay their outstanding taxes."[29] Since farmers recognized that most of the money they forked over to tax collectors eventually ended up in the hands of public creditors, their mounting cries for fiat currency were one more indication of their growing frustration with the bondholders.

Some petitioners and essayists suggested a more radical use of paper money. They urged assemblymen to force bondholders to exchange their war bonds, which paid interest, for paper money, which did not. The freemen of Swanzey, New Hampshire, spoke for thousands of Americans when they asked for an "Emission of paper Currency" and then urged that it "be applied Solely for the purpose of Redeeming the State Securities, which we conceive will be a great easment, by stopping the interest of those Securities."[30] Campbell County, Virginia, taxpayers petitioned the House of Delegates to print enough currency "for the redemption of the military claims, and all others, that do involve the state with Interest, and consequently accumulate endless Taxes thereon."[31]

Although many anticurrency writers claimed its supporters' goal was to repudiate their debts, others acknowledged that the demand for currency came at least as often from taxpayers. "The only plausible Argument held up by the Promoters of the *Paper-Money-Scheme*," observed a Rhode Islander who opposed it, "is, that many or most of the public Debts have been purchased by Sharpers and Monopolizers for trifling Considerations, and they think it hard to pay them the whole Value, according to the Letter of their several Securities; they therefore would make a Paper-Currency to pay them all off."[32]

Thus the movement for the Constitution, which prohibited state-issued paper, was rooted partly in state-level struggles over how much property the government should convey from taxpayers to bondholders. Modern claims that procurrency farmers were simply seeking to defraud their private creditors perpetuate the myth that the constitutional ban on paper money rescued Americans from a failed experiment in self-government.

• • •

Although most currency advocates renounced any desire to see its market value decline, a few actually embraced depreciation. But even these radicals were less interested in rescuing private debtors than in erasing the war debt. Under one proposal—so controversial it was never actually introduced in Congress or any state legislature—government creditors would have been forced to exchange their bonds for new notes that would have, by law, lost a certain percentage of their value every year until they became worthless.[33] The most well-developed version of this scheme appeared in a 1778 pamphlet called *A Proposal, or, A General Plan and Mode of Taxation, Throughout the American States*. The author was a western Pennsylvania religious seeker named Herman Husband, and this was neither his first bold suggestion nor his last.

Husband was born into the Anglican church in Maryland in 1724. Formal religion did not satisfy him. "It seem'd to me there was no true Worship in Spirit among them," he would say of his fellow parishioners many years later; "he seemed the best Fellow who first found the Place of the Book the Minister was in, and to answer him, and to know when to rise up and sit down."[34] As a teenager, Husband witnessed sermons by George Whitefield and Gilbert Tennent and then converted to evangelical Presbyterianism.

For many Americans, New Side religion was far too emotional. After attending a New York church service in 1790, the Old Light Congregationalist Abigail Adams would declare that "the oratory of a Clergyman here consists in foaming, loud speaking, working themselves up in such an enthusia[s]m as to cry."[35] For Husband the New Side was too tame. He joined the Society of Friends, better known as Quakers.[36]

As a young man Husband moved to North Carolina, and in a short time he became one of the largest landowners in backcountry Orange County. In 1764 he was expelled from his Quaker meeting for his obstinacy in standing by a woman minister who had incurred the majority's wrath. Although a pacifist, Husband took a leading role in the Regulator Rebellion of 1768–71, when North Carolina farmers challenged the oppressive exactions of land speculators, lawyers, and—most of all—predatory public officials: judges, clerks, and royal governor William Tryon.[37]

Husband published a brace of pamphlets publicizing the rebels' grievances, and he won election to the legislature on a relief platform.

His assembly colleagues twice expelled him, sheriffs threw him in jail three times, and government troops sent to suppress the rebellion destroyed his farm. But it was only after learning that Governor Tryon had put a price on his head that Husband fled the province. Briefly taking the alias "Tuscape Death," he resettled in Bedford County, Pennsylvania, and prospered there.[38]

It was common in the eighteenth century for political partisans to frame their complaints and proposals in biblical language. For Husband, though, the Bible was more than a thesaurus. "The Happiness of ourselves, and our Posterity, in this present World, and in the future Times of this World, depends on the right understanding of those Parts of the Scriptures which relate to the right Government of Mankind in this World," he declared in a 1782 pamphlet. That work, *Proposals to Amend and Perfect the Policy of the Government of the United States of America, or, The Fulfilling of the Prophecies in the Latter Days, Commenced by the Independence of America*, seamlessly combined Husband's paper money proposal, his suggestions for constitutional reform—and his biblical prophecies.[39]

Convinced that Jehovah hated injustice, Husband warned in 1789 that "the same men" who had refused to allow "British tyrants to oppress them" were "now willing to tyrannize over others." It would have been no different if an ex-slave had set himself up as "master and owner over hundreds of his fellow blacks."[40] For more than a decade, Husband argued that the only way to thwart these would-be tyrants was with a constantly depreciating paper currency. Devaluing the money a certain amount every year would essentially be a self-collecting tax—no different from taxing any other form of property at the same rate.[41]

Husband noted in 1782 that "in the *New Testament* . . . Publicans, and Tax-gatherers, are always ranked with Sinners." He was determined to "lessen those Swarms of Tax-gatherers, Excise-men, and Custom-house Officers, so much complained of by the Spirit and Feelings of a free People." Toward that end, he would hasten the redemption of the war bonds with taxes on luxuries, liquor, and land. Husband's real estate tax specifically targeted speculators and reflected his dismay at seeing the American wilderness, the very region where he envisioned the emergence of the New Jerusalem, "engrossed by Office Titles." Husband's tax reforms would allow the Pennsylvania assembly to dramatically reduce the tribute it exacted from farmers and artisans.[42] His most important proposal, however, was his paper money.

Studying the policy battles that raged through the American countryside during and after the Revolutionary War can help clarify the origins of the Constitution. Charles Beard argued that bond speculators wanted to give the national government its own taxing authority because they could see no other way to redeem their securities. Beard's critics accused him of exaggerating the speculators' influence. It now appears that the more important way in which bondholders influenced the adoption of the national charter was indirect. In order to pay interest to securities speculators like Nicholas Brown, Nathanael Greene, and Abigail and John Adams, state assemblymen made such heavy demands on taxpayers that they in turn demanded paper money and other forms of tax relief. Abolishing this relief legislation then became a primary motive for distinguished Americans like James Madison to insist on the adoption of the Constitution.

CHAPTER 4

"SAVE THE PEOPLE"

REQUISITION

MOST DESCRIPTIONS of the road to the Constitution draw attention to the same mileposts. The federal convention mustered a quorum on May 25, 1787, and completed its work four months later, on September 17. Delaware became the first state to ratify, on December 7, 1787. And so on. Inevitably these timelines omit one of the Constitution's most pivotal red-letter dates. On September 27, 1785, Congress sent the thirteen state legislatures a bill for $3 million. This "requisition" set off several initially distinct chains of events that, upon merging, immeasurably intensified the momentum for the Constitution.

There was nothing new about Congress's placing huge demands on the states. It had done that throughout the Revolutionary War. Back then, though, paymasters and purchasing agents working for the British and French armies had scattered gold and silver through the countryside, making taxes much easier to pay. Moreover, Americans could discharge many of their wartime taxes using paper money that had depreciated to a fraction of its face value.

Congress had no power to enforce its demands, so the state legislatures could simply have ignored the 1785 requisition. But most made good-faith efforts to fill their quotas—with dire consequences. In three states taxes levied in compliance with the requisition helped turn farmers' earlier requests for paper money into irresistible demands. The states' attempts to raise the revenue that Congress had requested also provoked some of the most wide-ranging farmers' revolts in American history. Witnessing what happened in the states that tried to comply with the 1785 requisition, two state assemblies explicitly announced that they would not even try to fill their quotas. No piece of legislation—at either the state or federal level—did more to advance the movement for the Constitution than the virtually unknown requisition of 1785.

One million dollars of the requisition had to be paid with hard money (gold or silver)—only half as much as the previous year. With the definitive conclusion of the Revolutionary War, Congress was gaining control of its budget, and only 30 percent of the real value of the money it sought was earmarked for operating expenses. Another 30 percent, also payable in hard money, would go to foreign lenders. Since gold and silver were in scarce supply, the dramatic reduction in the hard-money portion of the requisition undoubtedly came as a great relief to taxpayers.

Americans were considerably less happy about what Congress wanted them to do for its domestic creditors. The previous requisition, levied in April 1784, set aside $668,000 for the bondholders. In 1785 the amount more than quadrupled, reaching $2.8 million.[1] Two-thirds of the nominal value of the 1785 requisition—40 percent of its real value—would go to American bondholders. No other category of beneficiaries would receive as much. Taxpayers could discharge the domestic creditors' portion of the 1785 requisition using special certificates called "indents" (so named because government officials cut a unique indentation into the edge of each bill to frustrate counterfeiters). Like other government paper, the indents depreciated. Still, to purchase an indent, taxpayers in most states had to come up with about one-third of its face value in gold or silver. Americans did not need $3 million worth of hard money to comply with the 1785 requisition, but they would still have to lay hands on about $1.7 million. In a nation starved for currency, that was an immense sum.

One-time accounting anomalies explain part of the steep increase in what Congress requisitioned on behalf of the bondholders, but other factors were more enduring and more controversial.[2] The 1785 levy was the first in which congressmen asked the legislatures to levy new taxes in order to pay a year's interest—totaling about $300,000—on a controversial new bond. "Commutation certificates" were the offspring of a mutiny—to date the single most extensive and sustained effort by Americans in uniform to use their military might to extort legislation from civilian officials.[3]

What sort of attitude might a traveler expect to find in the Continental Army camp at Newburgh, New York (sixty miles up the Hudson River from New York City), in the fall of 1782, after major combat operations had concluded? Elation? Relief? The truth was that the officers, at least, were nursing a tremendous sense of injury. The Continental officers' numerous critics claimed they had taken advantage of wartime opportunities — ranging from sweetheart supply contracts to loose accounting practices — to enrich themselves at public expense. For their own part, the officers believed they had sacrificed the best years of their lives for the Revolutionary cause, and many were beginning to ask, "For what?" Even those who had managed to avoid injury and illness had suffered economically, they said, because Congress and the state legislatures had rarely managed to pay them their modest salaries. What made the officers' losses so galling was that scores of their countrymen had used the war to amass fortunes. Some had hit it big as privateers — government-sanctioned pirates. Although British navy ships patrolling the Caribbean and the North Atlantic seized hundreds of American trading vessels, merchants whose ships successfully ran the blockade reaped lush profits from wartime shortages and the accompanying price spikes. Other enterprising Americans had struck it rich without even taking risks, most commonly by winning contracts to supply the army.

Many of the officers were convinced that their families' disproportionate sacrifice had earned them only ingratitude. In the fall of 1780 officers had conspired to resign en masse unless Congress found some tangible way to recognize their contribution. Finally, on October 21, the delegates capitulated, promising officers the same retirement package their British counterparts enjoyed: half-pay for life. But by the fall of 1782 Congress still had not lifted a finger to implement this promise, so the officers sent a delegation to Philadelphia. The representatives carried a memorial declaring the officers' willingness to have Congress's original offer "commuted" into a bonus equal to five years' worth of salary at full pay. Since five years was longer than the median period the officers had served, if Congress approved the bonus, the typical officer would receive more after the war than he had during his entire period of service. The total cost of Commutation was put at $5 million.[4]

As the weeks passed and Congress failed to vote Commutation up or down, some officers began to contemplate more forceful action. In the unlikely event that the war dragged on, the officers could attract Congress's attention by marching the army west of the Appalachian Mountains, leaving the United States vulnerable to British attacks until their demands were met. This threat lost its sting as the peace negotiations advanced. So some officers begin advocating a new and more ominous strategy: the army should refuse to lay down its arms until Congress met its demands.[5]

Not all federal officials were appalled at the officers' threats, for some saw them as potentially useful. Indeed, Robert Morris, the federal financier, encouraged the officers to throw out dark hints of a military coup. He was hoping to scare congressmen into doing what he had so far failed to convince them to do: vote the officers their pensions and then ask the states to finance those and other obligations by empowering federal officials to collect a tariff on foreign merchandise as it entered American ports.[6] The officers' threat did indeed persuade many congressmen to support Commutation and the federal tariff.[7] By March 9, 1783, Commutation was only one state delegation short of adoption. Then, several days later, as rumors regarding the officers' intentions flooded into Philadelphia, the capital of the confederation, Eliphalet Dyer, a Connecticut congressman who had opposed Commutation, switched his vote. That moved Connecticut into the yes column, and the officers received their pensions.

George Washington is often—and rightly—praised for his role in persuading the would-be mutineers to abandon their plans.[8] But it is also clear that the Continental Army officers had succeeded in extorting Commutation from a reluctant Congress by floating the threat of a military coup. By contrast, enlisted men (other than invalids) would not receive pensions until 1818—and even then only if they could demonstrate poverty.[9]

The officers' pensions quickly became an object of speculation—and of protest.[10] "If Officers are allow'd five years," former enlisted men asked, "why should not soldiers be allow'd[?]"[11] In both Connecticut and New Hampshire delegates from dozens of towns gathered for protest conventions. The New Hampshire convention pleaded with Congress not "to Raise the Officers to a State of Opulence," especially

not "at the Expence of the happiness of those full[y] as Deserving"—
namely the common soldiers whose tax dollars would fund Commutation.[12] Noah Webster believed the vigorous stand he took in favor of
the officers' pensions explained much of the criticism that rained down
on his grammar textbook.[13] When, a month after Newburgh, Congress
asked the states for a federal tariff on merchandise imported into the
United States, taxpayers in several states demanded that their representatives either reject the tariff or at least provide assurances that
none of the revenue would go to the officers.

By the middle of 1786 even many of the men who had received Commutation bonuses had turned against the idea. "The Officers of the late
Army have most of them sold their Certificates," Massachusetts congressman Rufus King explained, and they were "now clamarous against
their Redemption except at a depreciated amount."[14] Six years after it
was adopted, Commutation provoked Herman Husband's one and
only criticism of George Washington. On June 8, 1783, Washington had
sent the state legislatures a circular letter supporting the officers'
bonuses. In a 1789 pamphlet Husband declared that the commander in
chief should have "shewn as much care and concern for the people
(who were all half ruined in their estates by the war) in his circular letter, as he did for the officers, who made their fortunes by the war."[15]

Opposition to Commutation persisted longest in New England. Although Benjamin Gale, a Killingworth, Connecticut, physician and
businessman, shared Herman Husband's interest in biblical prophecy,
he was no populist. In 1782 he had published a pamphlet urging the legislature to shift some of Connecticut merchants' tax burden onto farmers. But the bestowal of the Commutation bonuses the following year
drove Gale into the radical camp. Since his countryman Eliphalet
Dyer's indispensable vote in favor of the pensions had been "extorted
from him through fear," Gale told the Killingworth town meeting on
November 12, 1787, the bonus certificates did not represent a just
debt.[16] Massachusetts taxpayers also kept up the campaign against
Commutation. In January 1785 an anonymous writer claimed that Massachusetts had a *self-created nobility* that was "rioting with [co]mmuta-
tion money*, turning day into night [and ni]ght into day." "This is one
cause of your TAXES [being] heavy," he declared.[17]

The Commutation bonuses were not the only bittersweet fruit of the

Newburgh conspiracy. Two months after winning their pensions, the officers, recognizing that their army days were numbered, formed an alumni association, naming it for Roman general Lucius Quintus Cincinnatus. Having prevailed in his countrymen's battles, Cincinnatus won their hearts as well by not following the normal pattern of coming home to Rome and using his foreign conquests to snatch the reins of political power. Instead he returned to his plow. When Americans learned that the founders of the Society of the Cincinnati had decided to bequeath their memberships to their first-born sons (and so on forever), to award themselves ostentatious badges, and to use the new organization to put collective pressure on Congress and the state legislatures to come through with their pensions, many concluded that the members looked less like Cincinnatus than like Julius Caesar.[18] In a pamphlet published late in 1783 Aedanus Burke, a justice of the South Carolina supreme court, pronounced the society "a deep-laid contrivance to beget, and perpetuate family grandeur in an aristocratic Nobility, to terminate at last in monarchical tyranny."[19]

In 1782 Congress decreed that federal bondholders would henceforth receive their interest in the form of special certificates, which would then be taxed back into the state treasuries.[20] To the officers' chagrin, this decentralized system allowed individual states to discriminate against the holders of Commutation certificates. Nearly half did so.[21]

New Jersey lawmakers discovered a subtle way to snub the officers. On December 20, 1783, they agreed to levy an annual tax to pay interest to the state's federal bondholders. The tax act specified that no bond would earn interest unless it had been issued before May 2, 1783. Congress had approved the Commutation bonus only the previous March, and the first officers did not begin receiving their certificates until after the May 1 deadline. The New Jersey legislation enumerated certain federal bonds that would receive interest no matter when they were issued, but Commutation certificates were conspicuously absent from the list.[22]

Other middle-state assemblies also found ways to avoid paying interest on the Commutation certificates. In 1786 New York legislators agreed to "assume" a portion of the federal government's debt to their countrymen. The owners of several categories of federal securities were invited to trade them in for new interest-bearing state bonds. Excluded from this offer were "final settlements," a broad category of federal securities that included the Commutation certificates.[23] Pennsylvania discriminated against final settlements that had changed hands.[24] By 1787 it was clear that few officers would be able to collect the interest Congress owed them until the federal government obtained its own power to levy taxes. By this time more and more American leaders were saying that what the United States really needed was a national legislature that was powerful enough to withstand grassroots opposition to measures such as Commutation.

A host of Americans recoiled not only from the idea of paying interest on the Commutation certificates but from the whole September 1785 requisition. James Madison, who expected the requisition's price tag to "startle" taxpayers, predicted that complying with Congress's request, especially the hard-money portion, would "try the virtue of the States."[25]

He was right. One provision of the 1785 requisition was designed to return errant state legislatures to the federal fold. By the fall of 1785 nearly half the states had devised their own schemes, outside the congressional indent system, of paying interest on their citizens' federal bonds. Initially Congress tolerated this freelancing, but the September 1785 requisition in effect prohibited it. Early in 1786 Pennsylvania assemblymen yielded to congressional insistence that they stop disbursing interest to the state's federal bondholders. But the law they adopted was anything but a surrender. The legislators invited Pennsylvanians to bring their federal securities to Philadelphia, where they would be converted into new state bonds. By offering to incorporate its citizens' portion of the Continental debt into its own financial system, Pennsylvania outfoxed Congress. How could the federal government prevent a state, any state, from paying interest to its own bondholders?[26]

Pennsylvania was not the only state where the congressional crackdown backfired. Since 1783 New Jersey had been using paper money to pay the interest on its citizens' federal securities. The 1785 requisition was a frontal assault on this system, and it infuriated the state's taxpayers. So did Congress's demand for a year's interest on the officers' pensions. One writer, "A Fellow Citizen," claimed that paying interest on the Commutation certificates and other federal bonds would subject citizens to "heavy and insupportable taxes."[27] On February 20, 1786, the New Jersey legislature became the first in the nation explicitly to vote down a congressional requisition. Alarmed congressmen dispatched a delegation to Trenton to try to reason with the assembly. The representatives did back down, but they never made any effort to fill the state's quota—of this or any subsequent requisition.[28]

The 1785 requisition produced its most explosive results in New England. In Connecticut, it could hardly have come at a worse time. There state assemblymen had already imposed heavy poll and property taxes in order to keep up interest payments on the state bonds. These direct levies were especially high in Connecticut, since the government derived little revenue from trade. Few seagoing ships sailed directly into Connecticut harbors, so cloth from Europe, rum from the West Indies, and other merchandise entered the state indirectly, first passing through Rhode Island, New York, or Massachusetts. With borders too porous to prevent smuggling, Connecticut was unable to collect duties on these goods. As "X" explained in a June 1785 essay, no tariff would ever "be collected in this State till we come to import our goods directly from Europe."[29]

Connecticut taxpayers were not shy about blaming their heavy tax burden on securities speculators. One writer argued that it was only by dramatically reducing the "heavy state debt" that the legislature could "save the people from perpetual taxes."[30] These taxes provided the context in which Connecticut received word of the September 1785 requisition. Few citizens could imagine assuming an additional burden that would, on average, triple their direct taxes.[31]

Connecticut taxpayers' resistance to the requisition received support from an unexpected quarter. The owners of state securities worried that when the legislature came to grips with the average farmer's inability to satisfy the holders of both state and federal bonds, it might suspend interest payments on the state notes. Thus many of them joined the campaign against the congressional requisition. Under pressure from this unlikely coalition of government creditors (bondholders) and debtors (taxpayers), the Connecticut House of Representatives announced in October 1786 that it was not going to comply with the federal government's request. The assemblymen simply could not imagine subjecting their fellow citizens to an enormous new Continental tax at a time when they were still "labouring under Embarrasments by reason of Arrearages of former Taxes."[32] Connecticut became the first and only New England state to balk at the 1785 requisition. Unlike New Jersey, it never backed down.

When New Hampshire legislators confronted the same impossible challenge as Connecticut—servicing federal as well as state bonds—they chose the opposite path. The assembly adopted sufficient taxes to comply with the congressional requisition but scaled back earlier plans to redeem state securities.

In the spring of 1785 New Hampshire assemblymen levied a tax aimed at paying off one-sixth of the state debt. They planned to reenact the tax during each of the subsequent five years, ridding themselves of the entire state debt by 1790. As it turned out, the program lasted all of one year. The legislature, fearing taxpayers could not afford to gratify federal as well as state bondholders, did not call in any state securities in 1786. Indeed, no New Hampshire state bonds would be redeemed until after the adoption of the U.S. Constitution.[33]

Despite the assemblymen's prudence in reducing state levies at this time, the new tax they imposed on behalf of federal bondholders fell heavily upon the states' agrarian majority. Some town meetings argued that in light of the monetary famine, the legislature should "not grant the Requisition of Congress at present."[34] Dozens of towns, as well as several county conventions, pleaded with the representatives to give taxpayers a medium with which to discharge the new Continental tax. That meant paper money.

The assembly met in Exeter in September. The widespread demand for immediate recourse to the printing press was brushed aside. So on September 20 about two hundred men who had traveled to Kingston for a pro-currency convention marched six miles to Exeter and surrounded the building where the legislature was meeting. Militiamen armed with muskets and cannon were able to drive the rebels off, and cavalrymen soon arrested most of their leaders, but the New Hampshire establishment had received a shock. The assembly, which had earlier commanded the state treasurer to sue delinquent tax collectors, now rescinded that order.[35]

• • •

The 1785 requisition placed Massachusetts legislators in the same unten-able position as their counterparts in Connecticut and New Hampshire. Unlike its southern and northern neighbors, however, Massachusetts tried to have it both ways—to pay interest on federal as well as state bonds. It was a decision that many assemblymen would soon regret.

On March 23, 1786, the General Court approved a comprehensive tax package. Much about this legislation was new. It was the first law Mas-sachusetts had ever enacted on behalf of the holders of Commutation certificates. Moreover, owners of the state's Consolidated Notes, who had previously obtained all their annual interest from the state's tariff on merchandise arriving from overseas, would now receive money ex-tracted from farmers in the form of taxes on polls (people) and prop-erty as well. Earlier assemblies had infuriated taxpayers by giving the holders of the Consolidated Notes a monopoly of the tariff revenue, but by the end of 1785 even this lucrative funding source had proved in-adequate.[36] The deficiency in the tariff revenue was keenly felt by bond speculators such as the Providence, Rhode Island, merchant Nicholas Brown. In mid-March 1785, when Brown's partner George Benson tried to obtain the interest due on Brown's Consolidated Notes, Massachu-setts treasurer Thomas Ivers initially refused to give him anything. "Oblig'd to apply every soothing & Gentle address" and forced to pave "an easy avenue" to Ivers's "feelings" (this may have been a reference to a bribe), Benson later informed Brown that he had "Tarry'd" at the treasury office "so long that I am almost *initiated* in the service."[37]

Benson "was Determin'd not to give out & at length prevaild." The tariff collector for Boston Harbor happened to be a friend of his, and Benson prevailed upon him to say he would disburse a portion of the interest Brown was owed—£150—if Ivers would authorize the pay-ment. Benson's badgering, and the tariff collector's willingness to ap-pease him, finally overcame Ivers's objections. In the months that followed, though, the business of extracting money from state officials grew even harder. In the fall of 1785 Benson reported to Brown that the treasury "office is now nine months back in paying [interest on] Con-solidated notes."[38] By spring nothing Benson could say or do would per-suade Treasurer Ivers to pay Brown his interest. Other bondholders had trouble collecting their money, too, with the inevitable result that the market price of the securities continued to stagnate.[39]

Brown, Abigail Adams, and other owners of Consolidated Notes would never receive the money they felt they deserved until state assemblymen obtained additional revenue on their behalf. Accordingly, the spring 1786 session of the legislature imposed a new tax on property and people in the amount of £29,000. It promised all the income to the owners of Consolidated Notes, who would also continue to receive all the tariff revenue.

The assembly imposed other direct, hard-money taxes as well.[40] In doing so, it departed from its own recent practice. Legislators had not ordered citizens to pay their property and poll taxes with gold and silver since 1783. Back then much of the gold and silver pumped into the economy by British paymasters and purchasing agents in New York City reached New England, giving the region an adequate money supply.[41] The situation in 1786 was starkly different.

In addition to levying more than £114,000 worth of hard money, the assembly imposed nearly £200,000 in certificate taxes. It taxed in the last of the state's Army Notes, which had a face value of £100,000. Taxpayers would also have to obtain from federal bondholders nearly £100,000 worth of federal interest indents, issued in compliance with the congressional requisition of 1785. All together the March 1786 tax had an official value of £311,000 and an actual cost of about £165,000.[42] Roughly two-thirds of the 1786 tax would go to the state and federal governments' creditors. More than half was earmarked for domestic bondholders alone.[43]

The March 23, 1786, tax provoked one of the most significant agrarian uprisings in American history. Abigail Adams, who by this time was living in London with her diplomat husband, received regular reports on the tax revolt, one of them emphasizing that "the Requisitions of Congress" were among "the principle Bones of Contention."[44] Shays's Rebellion, usually described in textbooks as a western farmers' revolt that erupted in Hampshire County on August 29, 1786, actually began more than two months earlier, on June 13, in Bristol County in southeastern Massachusetts, with a failed effort to close the county court.[45] None of the participants in the Massachusetts insurgency ever referred to it as "Shays's Rebellion." They called themselves Regulators.[46]

By January 1787 government troops and the agrarian rebels were at war. The insurgents did not win a single battle, but their effort to force the assembly to ease up on taxpayers was notably successful. In the fall of 1786 the General Court postponed an earlier order seizing the property of sheriffs who refused to execute the estates of delinquent tax collectors.[47] Representatives also agreed to let citizens pay some levies with produce and to postpone tax deadlines. One immediate result of this massive tax relief was that Abigail Adams, Nicholas Brown, and everyone else who had purchased Massachusetts securities saw the value of their portfolios plummet.[48] The price of state securities was destined to fall even lower, because bondholders would henceforth be sharing the tariff revenue with a new set of public creditors: the wealthy citizens who lent the government the money it needed to suppress Shays's Rebellion. Benjamin Lincoln, who commanded the army that subdued the rebels, explained to George Washington that these investors had become "loaners of part of their property" in order "to secure the remainder."[49] More than half the contributors to the suppression fund were also holders of state bonds. The largest donation, £300 in scarce silver, came from William Phillips, a banker and state senator who owned at least £28,000 worth of Massachusetts state securities.[50]

The government's violent suppression of the revolt shifted it to the political realm. In the midst of the spring 1787 elections a Boston newspaper writer claimed that "the *great possessors* of what is called publick securities, appear very solicitous to get into the Legislature" in the hope of "continuing that abominable system of enormous taxation, which is crushing the poor to death."[51] If the bondholders really did make a concerted effort to obtain additional assembly seats in the elections held that spring, they were singularly unsuccessful. The government's treatment of the Regulators infuriated voters, who produced a 74 percent turnover in the House of Representatives. The new assembly surpassed its predecessor in granting tax relief.[52] Indeed, for the year 1787 the state government imposed no taxes at all.[53]

The Bay State's radical turn toward tax relief was painful not only for the owners of Consolidated Notes but for Congress, its creditors, and everyone who cared about the state and federal governments' credit ratings. Although the General Court had levied a hard-money Continental tax of more than £40,000 in March 1786, the amount of gold and silver that Treasurer Ivers and his successor were able to hand over to Congress between October 1786 and March 1787 was only £93.[54]

Massachusetts was not even able to pay its share of an October 1786 congressional requisition that would have fielded a federal army to help suppress Shays's Rebellion.

Northern New England's retreat from compliance with the 1785 requisition provided additional ammunition to Americans who believed Congress needed its own authority to levy taxes.

The most controversial response to the September 1785 congressional requisition came from Massachusetts's tiny southern neighbor, Rhode Island. In the process Rhode Islanders, quite inadvertently, did more to boost the momentum for the Constitution than their counterparts in any other state.

Earlier Rhode Island had single-handedly blocked Congress's proposal for a national tariff, making the state, in the eyes of all federally minded Americans, a pariah. The faction that dominated the assembly in September 1785 greeted the congressional requisition as a godsend— an opportunity to redeem Rhode Island's reputation. Determined to make their state the first in the country to meet its quota, assembly leaders did not even wait for Congress to act. A month before the adoption of the requisition, in August 1785, legislators estimated Rhode Island's proportion of the forthcoming levy and laid a Continental tax of £20,000 to pay it. By deciding to "provide for, beforehand, the constitutional demands of Congress," exulted Rhode Island congressman David Howell, the state "could not fail to make a good impression on our sister states." Howell also pointed out that "a large balance of the sum called for to pay domestic interest must ultimately come into the pockets of our citizens," which undoubtedly contributed to the legislators' zeal.[55]

Eight months after the assembly levied its £20,000 tax to comply with the 1785 requisition, Rhode Island was the site of an electoral revolution. Voters swept the governor, half the council, and two-thirds of the assembly out of office, replacing them with mavericks committed to printing paper money that taxpayers could use to discharge their Continental taxes.[56] As the only New England state to resort to paper currency during the Confederation era, Rhode Island resumed its pariah status. What produced this turnabout? What was so irksome about Congress's September 1785 requisition? An anonymous Rhode

Islander who took the name "A Friend to the Public" declared that he and other taxpayers resented the idea of "fetching from the mines of Peru gold and silver, sufficient to realize those numerous obligations given by government to pacify a tumultuous soldiery"—a reference to the Newburgh conspirators who had extracted the Commutation certificates from Congress—"and which have been nearly all transfered to other hands for one quarter of its nominal sum."[57]

In Rhode Island the federal securities clustered in even fewer hands than elsewhere. By 1790 more than 38 percent of the value of the U.S. bonds in Rhode Island was owned by just nine individuals.[58] Another reason for Rhode Islanders' heightened contempt for securities speculators was that an unusually high proportion of the federal bonds in the state—more than two-thirds—were Loan Office certificates, which were second only to Commutation certificates in arousing taxpayers' indignation.

Congress had started selling Loan Office certificates in 1776, accepting Continental paper money—at face value—as payment. Some Americans lodged money in the Loan Office out of a sense of patriotic duty, but the Loan Office certificates owed most of their popularity to the declining fortunes of Continental paper money. As the market value of the currency printed during the war steadily eroded, more and more debtors sought to fob it off on their creditors. Until 1781 no one could legally refuse paper money, which left creditors no choice but to try to evade their debtors—exactly as the debtors had dodged them before the war. Creditors who got stuck with paper money increasingly sought refuge in Loan Office certificates. They used their currency, which did not pay interest, to purchase certificates, which did.[59] Nathaniel Peabody of Atkinson, New Hampshire, spoke for other investors when he said his "securities were obtained for paper money that was forced upon me."[60] For Americans like Peabody, loan certificates were the lesser of two evils. They depreciated, but at nothing like the rate of Continental or state paper money.[61]

One category of Loan Office certificates, those issued before March 1, 1778, received special treatment. Congress decided to pay the owners of these bonds their interest using the subsidy it received—secretly at first—from the French government. That made the certificates astonishingly profitable. In June 1777 Abigail Adams bought a Loan Office certificate using £100 worth of Massachusetts currency that had been foisted upon her by her husband's creditors.[62] This paper was worth about £25 in gold and silver. Three months later Congress decided to pay bondholders like Adams their 6 percent annual interest out of the French subsidy, ensuring her a 24 percent annual return on her investment.[63] By March 1782, when Congress finally halted these special payments, Adams had collected £27 in interest—slightly more than the £25 she had invested four years earlier—all while retaining her £100 Loan Office certificate.

Like modern savings bonds, the Loan Office certificates were initially designed simply to raise cash. But as the conflict wore on and government finances deteriorated, army commissaries and quartermasters increasingly resorted to handing out Loan Office certificates to the army's suppliers, who otherwise would have received nothing at all. Recognizing that the recipients of the certificates would be unable to sell them at their face value, the public officials who used them to buy livestock, grain, firewood, and other supplies deliberately paid highly inflated prices.[64]

Eventually Congress, recognizing that most of the Loan Office certificates had either been disbursed to suppliers at high prices or purchased with greatly depreciated paper money, resolved to liquidate them, which meant they would not be redeemed at their face value. Instead, federal officials would determine the actual value, in gold and silver, of the depreciated paper money or high-priced commodities the government had received for each of the securities, then pay the owner that figure. This was a fraction of the amount printed on the bond.[65]

On its face, this was a major defeat for the holders of the Loan Office certificates. Actually it was nothing of the kind. Congress resolved to scale the bonds down to a value that was much greater than what the paper money tendered for them had fetched in the open market. Recognizing that a person wishing to purchase a Loan Office certificate with a face value of £1,000 would have first needed to come up with paper money of the same nominal value, Congress assumed that on March 1, 1778, $1,000 worth of paper money must have cost $570 in gold or silver. Actually it had cost $160. In 1790 Congress redeemed all federal bonds with a package of new securities that soon traded at 90 percent of their face value. Thus an investor who laid out $160 worth of gold or silver in February 1778 in order to buy a $1,000 Loan Office certificate could, by September 1791, convert the bond back into hard money in the amount of $513—more than three times what he or she had invested.[66]

Rhode Island had the nation's highest per capita ownership of Loan Office certificates. Federal officials issued more than ten dollars' worth for every man, woman, and child in the state—which is not to say the bonds were distributed evenly across the population. By the end of June 1777 Nicholas Brown had already purchased more than $40,000 worth of them. His brother John ended up with even more—more, in fact, than anyone else in the state.[67]

The enormous profit that the Browns and other speculators stood to make from the September 1785 requisition helps explain the vehement opposition it generated. Rhode Islanders were particularly angry at the privileged treatment Congress accorded to people who had purchased their Loan Office certificates before March 1, 1778. These were the investors who had initially received their interest out of the French subsidy—but that was not the perquisite that most angered Rhode Islanders. Congress, in calculating how much annual interest to pay on certificates issued before March 1, 1778, did not liquidate them. Federal officials were instructed to multiply the 6 percent annual interest rate not by the actual market value of the depreciated paper money with which the securities had been purchased, nor even by the inflated value Congress ascribed to the other Loan Office certificates, but by the bonds' vastly higher face value.[68] The Smithfield town meeting expressed "Great Surprize and Astonishment" at the legislature's decision to levy taxes in compliance with a "Requisition of Congress, Wherein was contained the paying the Interest of the Loaned Money on the Principle Sum Loaned Though they acknowledge It is Subject to a Liquidation."[69]

Numerous Rhode Island town meetings and newspaper writers called on the legislature to print paper money, emphasizing that it would both "ease taxation, on account of the national debt," and also enable taxpayers to "pay the principal and interest of our State debt."[70] In May 1786 newly elected Rhode Island legislators granted the citizenry's wish, printing £100,000 worth of paper money and requiring tax collectors as well as private creditors to accept it at face value. For many Americans, Rhode Island's emission, which quickly depreciated, became one of the most persuasive arguments in favor of the Constitution, which prohibited the states from printing currency. At the federal convention, where Rhode Island had chosen not to be represented, hardly anyone remembered that the currency emission had primarily been not a life-ring thrown to debtors but a direct response to the congressional requisition of September 1785.

Modern Americans who study the genesis of the U.S. Constitution frequently draw attention to the failure of the Articles of Confederation to grant Congress sufficient authority. While it is true that before 1789 congressmen wielded little formal power, their influence on state assemblymen was considerable. Indeed, the legislation that the state governments adopted in response to the £3 million congressional requisition of September 27, 1785, played a critical role in bringing on the crisis that looms so large in nearly every account of the origins of the Constitution. If none of the states had tried to comply with the requisition, many of the dramatic events of 1786—from the rebellions that shook New Hampshire and Massachusetts to the emission of paper money in Rhode Island, New York, and New Jersey—might never have occurred. And without those events, the case for strengthening the national government would have been considerably weaker.

When the Connecticut and New Jersey assemblies explicitly refused to comply with the requisition, they contributed their own ammunition to the nationalists' arsenal.

Most accounts of the genesis of the Constitution endorse, implicitly or explicitly, the Framers' view that in the immediate aftermath of the Revolutionary War, ordinary Americans had persuaded the thirteen state assemblies to adopt irresponsible legislation. For instance, debtors had demanded the right to force worthless paper money on their creditors. Meanwhile taxpayers, conveniently forgetting that loans from the French, the Dutch, and thousands of individual Americans had financed the Revolution, sought to enjoy the benefits of independence without bearing their share of the cost.

To investigate the impact of Congress's September 1785 requisition is to invite a different characterization of the era's farmers. Ordinary Americans denied wishing to obtain paper money simply in order to depreciate it and foist it on their creditors. On the contrary, they said, they were simply seeking some means of alleviating their enormous tax burden. Most tax money, they repeatedly stressed, was used to service the state and federal governments' war debts—obligations that might have been bearable if public officials had not inflated them, first by caving in to the demands of mutinous army officers and later by overvaluing the war bonds. Determining which group's arguments were more valid is a matter for the moralist, not the historian. What can be said with certainty, however, is that the long-standing assumption that the farmers acted irresponsibly is overdue for reassessment.

PART II

VIRTUE AND VICE

CHAPTER 5

"WHO WILL CALL THIS JUSTICE?"

QUARRELS

WHY DID SO MANY AMERICANS object to the legislation that the state assemblies adopted on behalf of debtors and taxpayers?

For a host of citizens, the case against relief legislation was intensely personal. Richard Cranch was a Braintree, Massachusetts, watchmaker whose financial fortunes sank even as his brother-in-law John Adams grew rich. Like Adams, Cranch went into public service. During the 1780s Cranch's neighbors elected him to the state senate. The salary was modest, but for Cranch it was indispensable. And yet in the fall of 1786 his wife, Mary, reported to Abigail Adams that "Mr Cranch has been labouring for the Publick for three or four years without receiving Scarcly any pay." She knew why, too: "The People will not pay their Tax."[1]

Abigail Adams hated seeing her sister suffer as a result of tax relief, and in fact by the mid-1780s Adams had begun to see herself as a victim, too. Two types of government securities in her family's portfolio, federal Loan Office certificates and Massachusetts Consolidated Notes, had initially paid punctual interest in gold and silver. But by 1787 the owners of these and most other government notes received their interest in greatly depreciated certificates. In a September 1789 letter to her sister, Adams expressed regret at "being cheated by our Friends"—the taxpayers who demanded relief and the legislators who gave it to them. Five months later Adams told Cranch the owners of government securities were "sufferers by the instability of Government."[2]

In portraying herself as a hapless victim of low bond prices, Adams forgot that it was this very depreciation that had allowed her to purchase her securities at bargain-basement prices and then, interest being paid on the face value, to reap an astronomical rate of return. In March 1787, when Adams asserted that people like her who dealt in "the paper of America" had to "run risks," she went on to acknowledge that "at all events it will fetch what is given for it."[3] Few investments offered that guarantee.

At least one of Adams's kinsmen also cried foul when their speculative investments yielded less than fabulous returns. In the fall of 1787 Abigail's uncle, Isaac Smith, died owing more than £6,000 to Champion & Dickason, a major British mercantile firm. Smith left behind "public Securities" that were roughly equal in value to his debt—at least on paper. Another of Abigail Adams's uncles, Cotton Tufts, told his niece "there would still remain on hand some Estate to be divided among the Children" if only Champion & Dickason would accept these government certificates at their "nominal Value."[4] Actually, no creditor in his right mind would agree to such an arrangement, given that the market price of the bonds was vastly below what Champion & Dickason was owed.

Tufts described the sorry state of Uncle Smith's affairs as a "Consequence of the Depreciation of our public Securities." In order to satisfy Champion & Dickason, the executors would be forced to sell Smith's property, leaving nothing for his heirs. What Tufts failed to mention— and what may in fact have slipped his mind—was that Smith had purchased his bonds with paper money that had depreciated even more than the bonds had. Had the government mistreated him, as Tufts implied? Only by not giving him the windfall he had anticipated.[5]

Bondholding families like the Adamses do not fit either of the two most popular explanations of the origins of the Constitution. In 1913 Charles Beard suggested that the Framers and Federalists were cynically trying to advance their own economic interests. In particular, he noted, many of the Constitution's strongest supporters were bondholders who received tremendous windfalls when the federal government finally obtained the revenue it needed to pay their claims. Beard's analysis attracted a host of followers, but today most historians are more charitable to the Founding Fathers, crediting them with an ardent desire to serve the common good. Neither of these models allows for the possibility that the friends of the Constitution (and of earlier, state-level, policies favoring bondholders) were motivated by a sense of grievance that was genuine and questionable at the same time. Abigail Adams's feeling that the government had "cheated" her was undoubtedly sincere, but that does not mean it was accurate.

Private creditors also expressed a genuine sense of persecution. "We are in a wretched condition at present, no money to be got for any practice or old debts," one Virginian lamented in September 1787. "Unless a new Government forms some permanent System we shall all be ruined by rascals and faithless debtors."[6] Another group that suffered when public officials indulged common farmers was landlords. James Duncanson complained early in 1788 that judicial debt collection was so lax that "my Rents are fallen to nothing."[7] George Washington's rental agent, Battaile Muse, informed him in November 1787 that the lax "Execution of our Laws" hampered his efforts to "Collect the full amount" that Washington's tenants owed him.[8] As the largest landowner in Orange County, Virginia, James Madison's father undoubtedly shared in his fellow landlords' frustration.

Debtor relief also injured local officials who derived their income from fees. Isaac Huger, the sheriff of the Charleston, South Carolina, district court, told the legislature its Pine Barrens Act of 1785, which essentially closed the state's courts, had "in general deprived him of [the] Emoluments of office."[9] Eleazar Burr, a deputy sheriff in Bristol County, Massachusetts, was deprived of his fees after an angry crowd forced the justices of the county court to halt judicial proceedings. Burr's reaction was more dramatic than Huger's; he cut his own throat.[10]

Disruptions in judicial proceedings could prove costly to lawyers as well as court officers. All through the spring of 1783 Virginia attorney Edmund Randolph worried that the next session of the House of Delegates was going to "limit, if not wholly abolish, executions" against debtors, which would "cut off the means of supporting my family."[11]

Thus countless Americans were painfully aware of how tax and debt relief legislation had harmed them personally. At the same time a host of writers and speakers affirmed that relief was also bad for society as a whole. Philadelphia merchant Charles Pettit reportedly owned $267,000 worth of bonds, but he was not worrying only for himself when he lamented that, as Americans succumbed to the "intoxicating Draughts of Liberty run mad," Congress's requisitions and other "Recommenda[tions]" were "as little regarded as the Cries of an Oysterman."[12] As a bondholder, Abigail Adams would benefit immensely if her fellow Massachusetts citizens promptly discharged the entire £311,000 levied by the legislature in March 1786, but she also saw compliance as a sacred duty. If Massachusetts taxpayers were "harder-prest by publick burdens than formerly," she wrote, "they should consider it as the price of their freedom."[13] In 1790, as Congress contemplated legislation that amounted to an enormous gift to bond speculators, Adams did not hesitate to identify the measure with "the General Good."[14]

How, exactly, did tax cuts, paper money, and debtor-protection legislation undermine the social order? In many ways. Relief was described as unjust and unbiblical. Tax abatements threatened the federal and state governments' credit ratings, and delinquency on foreign loans also posed a threat to national security. At the same time debtor relief exacerbated the very economic difficulties it was designed to combat. The opponents of relief legislation believed it even posed a threat to republican government. It was a daunting bill of indictment, but every item in it was vigorously contested by Americans who favored light taxation and an ample money supply.

The first specific goal enunciated in the preamble to the U.S. Constitution is "to establish justice." That seemingly vague phrase had a very specific meaning. The Framers believed the state legislatures had meted out injustice both to private creditors and to owners of government bonds. One of their principal goals in drafting the Constitution was to do justice to these two groups. George Washington was speaking for a large segment of American society when he affirmed, a year before the federal convention assembled, that "the origin of the evils we now feel" was "the want of disposition to do justice."[15]

Americans who favored tax and debt relief recognized that the charge of legislative injustice was among the sharpest arrows in their adversaries' quiver, and they mounted a spirited defense on multiple fronts. One of the tax-cutters' claims was that their fellow citizens who demanded justice for the bondholders were not really interested in that abstract principle. A western Massachusetts writer who wanted to redeem the war bonds at their depreciated current value said the enemies of his proposal were not lovers of justice but "a class of men called publick creditors."[16] The targets of this particular criticism sometimes surprised their critics by cheerfully pleading guilty. Only by confessing that their vision of justice was distorted by self-interest, they apparently reasoned, could they hope to extract similar confessions from their opponents. In March 1786 the low-tax faction in the Massachusetts House of Representatives painted its antagonists as greedy bondholders. "Some members had accused that side of the House with holding the notes," one protax assemblyman observed in reply. "If this observation was made to infer that interest dictated their votes, gentlemen should recollect, that those who made the observation, acknowledged themselves not to be holders of notes, and of course, were interested in not paying them."[17] Scolded during a fall 1785 floor debate for being influenced by his speculative investments, South Carolina assemblyman Alexander Gillon replied that "if speculation were the matter to be investigated, he believed we should appear to be all speculators."[18] Apparently Gillon and the unnamed Massachusetts representative had both concluded that their opponents' inflated pretensions to objectivity could be punctured only with a double-edged sword.

Several relief advocates also attempted to highlight their opponents' partiality by admitting their own. In his 1790 pamphlet opposing Alexander Hamilton's plan to fully fund government bonds that had been bought up by speculators, William Manning compared self-interest to a veil. He was apparently referring to himself as well as to the stockjobbers when he wrote, "Self in the best of men is too much like an object that is placed before the eye, which hinders the sight of anything beyond; and that touch a man's interest (or his ideas thereof)."[19]

Another Massachusetts relief advocate, signing himself simply "O," ridiculed his opponents' pretensions to objectivity but did not stop there. "It is not to be expected of human nature," he declared, "that the rich should be always attentive to the interests of the commons." On the other hand, O could understand why "the rich" were "continually fearful of Agrarian laws, and the division of property." This acknowledgment that the rich are justified in fearing the poor paved the way for O's main point, which was that "the poor have equal reason to dread the influence of the rich to produce monopolies, and to lay restraints on personal liberty." Everyone feels "an involuntary bias towards those of their own rank."[20]

For many Americans on all sides of the dispute over whether tax relief created an injustice or remedied one, the whole question came down to how much money soldiers who had sold their securities should, in their new role as taxpayers, hand over to the speculators who had bought them. Although some of the bondholders' advocates acknowledged that this transfer of wealth might sometimes be distasteful, they usually went on to insist that it simply could not be avoided. In an essay published in Virginia on July 4, 1787, "Amicus" contended that whether a particular security "be now in the hands of the veteran, or rapacious speculator, to us, ought to be a matter of indifference."[21]

Other Americans questioned whether the soldiers' decision to part with their bonds had actually been voluntary.[22] William Manning contended that "by compelling [soldiers] to pay their private debts and taxes in hard money" instead of with the certificates it had foisted on them, the Massachusetts legislature had in effect "obliged them to sell their public securities for what they would fetch."[23] Antitax writers pointed out that if the state and federal governments were to redeem the speculators' war bonds at the market price rather than the far-higher face value, they would only be following their own precedent.[24] The policy of partial repudiation had already been applied to federal and state paper money and even to several series of interest-bearing bonds. Why should the securities that remained in circulation in the 1780s be any different?[25]

The bondholders' advocates recognized that precedent was a powerful weapon in their opponents' hands. One of their replies was simply that two wrongs never make a right.[26] Americans who wished to redeem the securities at face value called the congressional decision essentially to repudiate the Continental paper money a war measure that could never be justified during times of peace.[27] Their opponents replied that the economic emergency of the mid-1780s was nearly as dire as the earlier military crisis. In their view, the more significant difference between 1780 (when Congress had voted to scale down the Continental paper money and the Loan Office certificates) and the mid-1780s was that now a much larger proportion of government paper was owned by wealthy and well-connected speculators. In Connecticut a relief advocate asserted in March 1786 that if the "worthy soldiers" to whom the bonds had been issued "had held their notes, I dare say we should not have heard so much about public faith."[28] Numerous Americans shared this writer's belief that public officials were less attentive to the cry for justice when it came from the poor. Decades after the war Continental Army veteran Joseph Martin recalled that the government had been "rigorous in exacting my compliance to *my* engagements to a punctilio" and yet "careless in performing her contracts with me."[29]

Today it is an article of faith that American farmers used the new powers bestowed upon them in the early state constitutions to treat government bondholders and private creditors unjustly. At the time, however, few Americans could see the justice in cracking down on debtors and taxpayers when doing so would force them to sell property at a fraction of what they had paid for it. It pained "Americanus," a South Carolina writer, to watch debtors "give up £50" worth of property "to pay £10." "Who will call this *Justice*?" he asked.[30]

Nearly every American who championed harsh fiscal and monetary policies saw justice as a straightforward matter of principle, and so did most of their opponents. On the other hand, some relief advocates struggled toward a more nuanced view. A Georgia writer named "Tullius" acknowledged that his proposal to let citizens pay their debts in installments would deviate from "rigid justice," but he went on to affirm that that was precisely what "justice" required.[31] Herman Husband and other writers located justice at the golden mean. "It is just and right to drink—yet drinking to excess becomes a vice," Husband wrote. "Just so it is with justice."[32] He warned public officials who wished to keep "holding the reins of government" to avoid an "excess in justice."[33]

Once liberated from the belief that justice was an abstract imperative admitting of no deviation, some relief advocates began to treat it as a commodity, one that was not only tangible but divisible. In the spring of 1786 a group of Delaware citizens sought permission to settle their debts with property. By ensuring that all creditors got their fair share, they declared, a property-tender law would "distribute Justice more equally."[34]

• • •

Americans also disagreed about whether increasing or reducing pressure on taxpayers and debtors was more consistent with biblical principles.

Advocates for austere fiscal and monetary policies never doubted that God was on their side.[35] Poems and essays satirizing the pro-relief position routinely associated it with the devil.[36] Judging from the substantial body of printed sermons that survive from the era, preachers' opposition to relief was nearly unanimous. Sometimes an entire congregation would take a stand against relief. The Little Compton, Rhode Island, church "suspended a deacon from his office and fellowship with them, for tendering the present depreciated paper money at par in discharge of real specie debts."[37]

Americans who strayed from economic orthodoxy were often accused of holding deviant religious views as well. Nathaniel Peabody, allegedly a leader in the New Hampshire paper money movement, was said to have called Jesus Christ "*Mary's bastard*."[38] Citizens who favored a hard line against debtors and bondholders were particularly fond of associating their opponents with the "New Light" evangelical revival. "I have often heard *mighty religious saints*, with holy grunts and uplifted sighs, say, 'they should think it extremely hard to tax these poor people to pay our *Great Men* these notes which they had bought for much less than their nominal value'" from "the *poor soldiers*," a Connecticut essayist complained in October 1786. Grunts and sighs were just the sort of "enthusiastic" self-expression the defenders of the Standing Order had long imputed to the excessively passionate New Lights.[39]

Other opponents of agrarian relief claimed that its champions possessed no religious principles at all. Denouncing a proposal to scale speculators' securities down to their face value, a Massachusetts writer created a fictional character who favored the idea. "An Old Rogue" acknowledged there were "some passages in the BIBLE which timid, conscientious people may think a little opposed to what I have advanced." His solution? "Burn the *Bible*."[40]

Americans who asked the state assemblies to ease up on debtors and taxpayers denied that doing so would violate biblical principles. A South Carolinian claimed his proposed emission of £200,000 worth of paper money would appeal to "every one whose God is the Lord Jehovah."[41] Like their opponents, prorelief writers often turned biblical in-

junctions into political barbs.[42] The ubiquitous allegation that harsh
fiscal and monetary legislation had the effect of "grind[ing] the faces of
the poor" was drawn straight from Isaiah 3:15.[43]

Relief advocates compared creditors and bondholders to the Bible's
basest villains and ordinary American farmers to its most wretched victims. Drawing a parallel between bond traders and Judas Iscariot, Hunterdon County, New Jersey, petitioners grieved at seeing "the Door left
wide open for the speculator" to "sell his country for a few Pieces of Silver."[44] Plympton, Massachusetts, taxpayers equated themselves with
"the Jews in the Days of Nehemiah," who had bemoaned the taxation,
famine, and debt that compelled them to "bring into bondage our sons
and our daughters."[45]

In what was possibly the most audacious attempt to use the Bible
to justify relief legislation, an essay appearing in Massachusetts in
September 1786 compared paper money to Jesus Christ. The author
permitted paper currency to speak in its own defense, reminding
Americans that it had sacrificed its life for them. Even as its own value
melted away, the currency recalled, it had funded the war that secured
American independence. Paper money then prophesied that, like Jesus
Christ, it would soon return. "I died for their deliverance from foreign
foes," it declared, "and will rise again to deliver them from their domestick ones."[46]

Americans who found biblical justification for relief were annoyed
at the nearly universal opposition it elicited from ministers. One Connecticut writer compared the seizure of debtors' and taxpayers' property to Pharaoh's mass confiscations, noting, however, that the Egyptian
had allowed one segment of society to keep their belongings: the
priests. It seems Pharaoh, like Connecticut's nearly as oppressive ruling elite, "had received great advantages from them in the government
of his kingdom, for which he was not ungrateful."[47]

Although the relief cause attracted adherents from every religious
faith, there was a grain of truth in its critics' effort to link political and
religious nonconformity. Two of the most articulate critics of heavy taxation and tight money, Herman Husband in the mountains of Pennsylvania and William Manning near the Massachusetts coast, were also
enemies of religious liberalism. But the two criticized the Old Lights
from different directions. Whereas Manning was a Calvinist, Husband

went through an evangelical phase but was most heavily influenced by his sojourn with the Quakers.[48]

Few of the attempts to use religion to shape Americans' attitudes toward tax and debt relief bore much fruit. Consider the New Jerseyans whose resistance to tax collectors earned them "a seasonable reproof from the pulpit," as Joseph Lewis reported in his diary early in 1785. Reminded by their minister of "the command of rendering to Caesar the things that are Caesars," the congregation did not change its ways. Indeed, Lewis wrote, "some of the people were offended."[49]

In the eyes of many Americans, relief legislation was not only unjust to creditors and bondholders and sinful in the eyes of God but a threat to national security. If lax tax collection prevented the government from servicing its foreign loans, "A Freeholder" warned, "France, Spain, [and the Netherlands], to whom we are so much indebted," might not "wait any longer without making reprisals."[50] Back in the spring of 1776 Patriots had warned British Americans to declare independence soon, lest the mother country divide the colonies among the great powers of Europe. Now Freeholder revived the specter of partition. "May not these nations, provoked by our unworthy treatment of them [attempt] to divide the states amongst them, making such a partition as they are well acquainted with in Europe?" he asked.[51]

Relief advocates scoffed at the specter of reprisal and partition. Benjamin Gale attributed the warnings about "our Foreign Creditors, Making *reprisals* upon us" to a campaign by the Society of the Cincinnati to secure the officers' Commutation bonuses by "*Terrifying Weak Minds*."[52]

An even more pressing motive for the United States to satisfy its creditors, both abroad and at home, was to ensure access to future loans. Repudiating the war bonds would "discourage all people from ever helping us any more," "Phydelius" declared in 1786.[53] Writers frequently contended that a government's credit rating required the same vigilance as a woman's chastity. Back in 1779 the Continental Congress had called on the state legislatures to collect taxes more aggressively, warning that "a bankrupt faithless republic would . . . appear among reputable nations like a common prostitute among chaste and respectable matrons."[54] In 1784 Philadelphia bondholders petitioning against plans to withhold their annual interest declared that "credit may be considered as the chastity of the state." For the government to pick and choose among its creditors—to allow original holders' claims while denying "an interest of 40 or 50 per cent [to] a few speculators"—would be "as indelicate, as it would be to measure female honor by calculations in arithmetic."[55]

Americans demanding tax relief ridiculed their opponents' pose as guardians of public faith. "To hear a speculator, in this country, declaim on [the] importance" of the government's credit rating, "Plain Reason" declared in an essay appearing in Virginia just as the Constitutional Convention completed its work, "is really a great act of barefacedness." After all, it was the bond broker who had not deigned to purchase securities until they had "already depreciated 500 *per cent* and who by his cheapening; and higgling, would, were it then in his power; have reduced [them] still lower!"[56] Some antitax writers went so far as to contend that if the government granted the bond speculators' wishes, its credit rating would actually suffer. The author of the boldly titled *Hampshire Herald* essay "Publick Faith" distinguished between the money the government legitimately owed foreigners and its bloated domestic debt. "Reducing our domestick debt within the bounds of justice, reason and common sense," he pointed out, "would enable us to do justice to our foreign creditors, and so to keep our faith, and maintain our reputation abroad."[57]

CHAPTER 6

"IDLE DRONES"

ECONOMICS

ONE ARGUMENT against tax and debt relief eclipsed every other. Even today it remains the single most powerful justification for the adoption of the Constitution. This is the claim that the plebeian politicians who came to power during the American Revolution attempted to alleviate their constituents' economic distress with hamfisted schemes that actually made matters worse.

Take the shortage of gold and silver. A New York editor argued that what had "lock[ed] up the coin of the country in the chest of the possessor" was would-be creditors' "fear of unrighteous laws and practices, to avoid the payment of honest debts."[1] Abolishing relief would even eliminate one of the great anomalies of the 1780s: cautious American investors, reversing the natural flow of capital from the Old World to the New, had sent their money to Europe for safekeeping.[2]

The currency shortage was aggravated not only by debtor relief legislation but also by public officials' excessive indulgence toward delinquent taxpayers. According to James Madison, "the relaxation in collecting the taxes" in his home state had had the unintended consequence of "diverting the money from the public Treasury to the shops of merchandize." Virginians took the gold and silver they would otherwise have handed the tax collector and instead used it to buy European frippery. Shopkeepers then sent these coins "out of the Country to balance the increased consumption," leaving the state bereft of circulating cash.[3]

If sheriffs were to extract every shilling delinquent taxpayers withheld, Madison and others affirmed, they would expand the money supply in another way as well. Financially flush state governments would be able to make regular interest payments—in hard money—to bondholders. That in turn would raise the market value of the securities. Once every war bond traded at par with a coin of the same nominal value, the notes would become a useful addition to the circulating currency.[4]

Undoubtedly the most urgent complaint about debtor relief was that it had stalled economic growth by chasing away would-be investors. "What men will lend money," "Aristides" asked, "when the law does not enforce payment at the time agreed?"[5] Even more important than cash loans were the clothing, tools, and slaves that European merchants were becoming increasingly reluctant to supply free Americans on credit. In a 1786 broadside urging the Virginia assembly to crack down on delinquent debtors, George Mason, the patriarch of Gunston Hall on the Potomac River, contended that what had "deterred foreigners from trading with us" was the "interference of our laws with private property and contracts," specifically "regulations calculated to defraud creditors."[6]

Another Virginian took the name "A True Friend" and offered his fellow citizens some friendly advice. The Old Dominion abounded in "immense and fruitful lands." To "grub them up," free Virginians needed a constant infusion of capital for the purchase of tools and slaves. Thus the state was "of necessity a borrower." As British subjects, Virginians "could pass no act tending to hurt, or annihilate the rights and interests of British creditors." English and Scottish merchants, confident in their ability to recover whatever money they invested in the province, "did not fear to advance considerable sums." Now, however, Virginians were "deprived of the assistance, advances and credit, which the metropolis, used to sell us," and A True Friend knew why. "As long as it will be by the tediousness of the courts of justice almost impossible to force the debtor" to pay what he owed, he wrote, "we shall not find money lenders."[7]

If European merchants could only "find in America, the punctuality and security, which alone gain credit and support confidence," True Friend declared, they would be "eager" not only to lend Americans money but to sell them merchandise on credit. These loans, and nothing else, would "revive our agriculture," he wrote.[8] A South Carolinian argued that the only way Americans could persuade British merchants once again to provide them with goods on credit would be for every state to adopt a battery of debt enforcement legislation and then require all of its citizens "to swear or affirm that they would aid and contribute all in their power (and by force of arms if necessary) to enforce the execution of said laws."[9]

The widespread claim that relief legislation had discouraged foreign investment was more than mere rhetoric. One of the many causes of the economic distress that "depresse[d] the mind" of Nathanael Greene was his inability to borrow money in Europe, which Greene and all his friends attributed to anticreditor American legislation.[10] Louis Guillaume Otto, comte de Mosloy, the French chargé d'affaires in the United States, observed in May 1786 that American credit had "considerably suffered by the jolt given to it by several laws prejudicial to foreign creditors."[11] As European credit dried up, American wholesalers in turn demanded that their own customers, the crossroads retailers, pay cash on delivery. How could they do otherwise, wondered Philadelphia merchant Stephen Collins in April 1786, at a time when there was "so little Dependance in Public measures"?[12]

The enemies of relief legislation believed it cast suspicion even upon entrepreneurs whose personal credit ratings were impeccable. Peter Colt, a wholesale merchant in Hartford, Connecticut, allowed in June 1787 that "there may [be] punctual dealers in those parts" of northern New England beset by relief legislation and agrarian revolt, but he was "not sufficiently acquainted with them to risque the property in their hands." Even a New Jersey paper money advocate acknowledged in December 1785 that earlier, ill-advised, relief legislation had made it "next to an impossibility for an honest man . . . to procure money on interest."[13]

It was not only legislation that made moneyed men and women both at home and abroad reluctant to give Americans credit. As the Maryland senate pointed out early in 1787, it was also the infamous "delays and difficulties, which the lenders experience when compelled to have recourse to law, to enforce the payment."[14]

Another argument in favor of more aggressive tax and debt collection resembled the modern "supply-side" economic theory. A dollar in the hands of a farmer benefited only him and his family, many leading Americans argued, but a moneyed man or merchant would use that same dollar to grow the larger economy. In a July 1782 report to Congress, federal financier Robert Morris affirmed that if legislators were to transfer wealth from taxpayers to the men who had purchased government bonds "at a considerable discount," they would furnish the bondholders with "those funds which are necessary to the full exercise of their skill and industry." Morris proposed a package of federal taxes aimed at "distributing property into those hands which could render it most productive." He was confident that the benefits of his plan would eventually—the anachronistic term seems unavoidable—trickle back down to ordinary free Americans. Similarly "Amicus" contended in an essay appearing in Virginia on July 4, 1787, that cracking down on delinquent debtors would "put the property into the hands of those who would manage it better."[15] It was only by summoning the courage to crack down on delinquent debtors and taxpayers that legislators could revive the economy, Americans like Morris and Amicus contended, because there was no other way for entrepreneurs to acquire capital.

Advocates for harsh fiscal and monetary policies expected them to produce beneficial effects not only on potential investors but also on ordinary farmers and their families. For the segment of society that blamed Americans' misery on their own failure to produce more than they consumed, one of the harmful effects of relief legislation was that it aggravated farmers' worst tendencies. Early in 1787 a Marylander contended that the "lax principle in our laws, and the administration of justice, ha[d] greatly tended . . . to relax the natural springs of industry." "A Native of Virginia" was blunter, declaring that "the relaxation of our laws" had led to "inactivity and torpor."[16] It followed that "accelerating the Adm[inistrati]on of Justice" would actually relieve "the present distresses of the Countrey," as another Virginian, Edmund Pendleton, contended in a December 1786 letter to James Madison. How? By "producing Industry & Oeconomy" among debtors.[17]

Taxpayers would also someday thank legislators for making them produce more and consume less, several writers contended. "When it is considered how much men are disposed to indolence and profusion," Robert Morris told Congress in 1782, "it will appear that . . . it would be wise to carry taxation to a certain amount," for taxes "stimulate industry to provide the means of payment." "To neglect taxation," a Bostonian declared, "would produce a *famine*," since it "would relax the spirit of industry and oeconomy, and thereby bring poverty and want."[18]

In the eyes of many of America's most prominent citizens, the thirteen states' frequent recourse to tax and debt relief legislation revealed that they were fundamentally flawed. Again and again state representatives had yielded to their constituents' most reckless demands, adopting policies that ended up harming even their intended beneficiaries. The lesson was clear: in their first flush of revolutionary enthusiasm, the Patriots had created governments that were far too sensitive to public pressure.

Numerous citizens rejected the Founders' explanations for the economic ills of the 1780s—and their proposed remedies as well. What may have appeared to be merely a policy dispute had larger implications. The Americans who refused to blame the recession on tax and debt relief were equally dubious about the Framers' claim that the legislation emerging from the state assemblies revealed them to be excessively democratic.

Early in the twentieth century Charles Beard and other "Progressive" historians launched a challenge to the long-standing view that the Revolutionary War had been followed by a protracted recession. The Progressives lauded the first state assemblymen as highly competent stewards of the economy. For the Progressives, the Constitution fixed a system that had not been broken.[19] But this rosy interpretation of the postwar economy attracted very few adherents at the time. Most ordinary citizens shared the Framers' belief that the economy was in trouble during the 1780s, and they agreed that the state assemblies deserved much of the blame. There was also broad consensus that the state legislatures had reduced farmers' output and driven away currency and investment capital.

Elite and ordinary Americans were equally critical of the thirteen state legislatures, but their criticisms were not identical. Whereas the Founding Fathers believed the legislatures had stunted the nation's growth by granting too much relief to debtors and taxpayers, thousands of other Americans contended that the remedy for the recession was not to press harder on taxpayers and debtors but to ease up on them.

The opponents of the record-high taxes of the 1780s denied that punctual interest payments would make the war bonds a useful addition to the currency. William Manning, the Billerica, Massachusetts, farmer and tavern-keeper, said inflating the market price of government securities to equivalence with their face value would meet the monetary needs of only the wealthiest Americans, since the bonds only came in large denominations and were "chiefly owned in the seaports."[20]

Not only did heavy taxation fail to replenish the money supply, anti-tax writers charged, it was actually one of the chief culprits in draining the countryside of its gold and silver. Taxpayers were forced to scour their neighborhoods for gold and silver that ultimately passed into the hands of bondholders, who shipped it to Britain in exchange for manufactured goods. Even James Swan, himself a Boston merchant and bond speculator, believed, "Every public contribution [tax] in money, forms the means of a greater exportation of it, which the government facilitates by inforcing the collection."[21] The Virginia writer "Plain Reason" blamed the "decay of specie in this country" on "the consumption of the greater part" of it "by the non-productive speculators, in European articles."[22]

Americans who opposed heavy taxation and procreditor legislation also had another, still more fundamental, objection to them. Bearing down on taxpayers and debtors drained the American economy of its real lifeblood, which in their view was not capital but labor. When their opponents contended that stepping up enforcement of farmers' obligations would have the salutary effect of keeping them from becoming "indolent," relief advocates turned this argument on its head, contending that rigorous tax and debt collection had prevented Americans from realizing their full potential as laborers.

Fiscal and monetary austerity had, for instance, deprived debtors and taxpayers of their tools and livestock—what a later generation would call their means of production. The town of Bernardston in western Massachusetts warned that "for want of Cattle our lands must be untild."[23] To "distress the labouring Part, and take their Implements of Labour, their Horses, Oxen, &c. is to stab ourselves to the very Heart," Herman Husband declared in 1782. On the other hand, a New Jerseyan who took the name "Willing to Learn" declared at the end of 1785, if the government were to relieve farmers by printing paper money, they would be able to "save their estates" and remain "useful members of the community."[24]

As important as tools and draft animals were to the labor process, the most crucial element was of course the farmer himself, and many Americans contended that aggressive tax and debt collection prevented them from working to their full potential. For instance, when producers who were accustomed to payment in cash confronted the monetary famine, they sometimes curtailed their output. Noah Webster's 1785–86 lecture tour included a stop at Princeton University. Only sixteen paying customers showed up for his first grammar lecture, the others explaining that they had "no cash." Webster canceled his Princeton appearances, informing a friend, "I shall not read Lectures on such prospects but to day move on to N York."[25]

The shortage of circulating currency reduced Americans' output in other ways as well. William Manning reported that debtors were forced "to spend a vast deal of time and money in settling their affairs and quieting their creditors." So scarce was money in the New Jersey countryside, "Willing to Learn" claimed in 1786, that artisans spent nearly as much time dunning their customers as they did at their benches. A Rhode Islander reported that the currency shortage often compelled artisans to receive their wages in commodities such as tea and salt. The result was that "a labourer after his day's work is done, must spend another in bartering away his tea or salt, into three or four articles more suitable."[26]

Still more work hours were squandered when the debt or tax collection process ended up in court. "The waste of time attending law suits . . . oppress[es] industry," "A Husbandman" told readers of the *Maryland Journal* on June 6, 1786. Even if an American faithfully paid his debts and taxes and managed to collect from his own debtors, he could still be dragged into a time-consuming legal process as a witness or juror. "If we should value the time" of everyone involved in the typical debt suit, "Willing to Learn" mused, "perhaps it would amount to a larger sum than what is due."[27]

The most dramatic way to stop a debtor or taxpayer from working was to throw him in jail. Petitioners in Sanbornton, New Hampshire, claimed that "People of all Ranks, & Conditions, are Sued & meney Put into Prison all of which tends to Impoverish Individuals, & Consequently the State in General." William Whiting, the chief justice of the Berkshire County, Massachusetts, court, wished imprisoned debtors could be "at home Employed about their ordinary business," in which case they "would be benneficial to the Community at Large."[28]

Thus fiscal and monetary austerity wore away at farmers' output by depriving them of both tools and time. These corrosives, lethal enough in themselves, also wrought secondary damage to the nation's economic output that was potentially even more destructive. If farmers' distress was not alleviated, a host of essayists and assemblymen contended, word would get back to Europe, discouraging would-be immigrants from crossing the Atlantic. A Maryland paper money supporter asserted in the spring of 1785 that "foreigners will not be encouraged to emigrate and settle among us, should they once be informed and persuaded that we are very deficient [i]n our quantum of circulating cash."[29] On the other hand, if assemblymen were to grant tax relief, a Massachusetts writer declared, "the inhabitants of other countries" would come "rushing hither as air to a *vacuum*."[30] Sometimes Americans' anxieties about the threat to immigration were accompanied by an even darker concern: that more and more of their neighbors were escaping to other parts of the country. The most dire warnings about emigration were sounded in New England. If the sale of taxpayers' property at a fraction of its real worth continued, a Connecticut writer warned, thousands of farmers would "bid farewell to a country, which holds out nothing but poverty and prisons."[31]

One of the relief advocates' most extraordinary claims was that the transfer of wealth from debtors and taxpayers to creditors and bondholders had stymied farmers' productive capacity by breaking their spirits. When the friends of fiscal and monetary austerity asserted that farmers and artisans needed to be prodded to work harder, their opponents replied that Americans' "dissipation" was actually "a natural and unfailing consequence of despair"—what one western Massachusetts writer called a "dead weight which lies on their spirits."[32]

A remarkable number of petitioners and essayists described themselves or other Americans using variants of the word "discouraged." "A Citizen of Connecticut" was typical in asserting that the currency shortage "discourage[d]" farmers "from making any attempts towards extricating themselves; who otherwise would act with spirit and vigour."[33]

Several prorelief writers claimed that despondency had had an actual physical effect on farmers' bodies, disabling them from performing the labor upon which the entire American economy depended. The anonymous author of the widely reprinted "Publick Faith" declared that heavy taxation had driven farmers into "torpid despair, which congeals their blood and stiffens every nerve." The following August "Plain Reason" told his fellow Virginians he knew they were "bowed down and dispirited by the weight of your taxes." In Maryland "A Husbandman" claimed, "The labour necessary to increase our crops, greatly depends upon peace of mind, and pleasant prospects of the effects of our labour; for who has not been sensible of more strength, when cheerful, th[a]n when sad? Whatever therefore promises cheerfulness, increases industry."[34]

Writers who worried about the psychological impact of rigorous debt and tax collection often asserted that when farmers became too dispirited to work at their full capacity, it was not only their families but the whole economy that suffered. A group of Delaware petitioners described themselves as "disabled, dispiritted and cast down, bereft of our Peace and Tranquility . . . incapable of doing any farther good, for Ourselves, Families, or Country."[35] The town meeting in Lancaster, Massachusetts, warned that the "present mode of taxation" would "discourage the industrious husbandman (on whom this commonwealth will probably ever depend for its greatest strength)."[36] Even some Americans who wanted to extract more money from debtors and taxpayers acknowledged that taking too much could so dismay them as to diminish their productivity. The Massachusetts legislature imposed an unprecedented tax in March 1786 but rejected proposals to demand even more money from farmers out of fear that "increasing the demands might rather tend to dishearten them, and to lessen those exertions, which were, in fact, within their power."[37]

Since aggressive debt and tax collection had "dispirited" farmers and "rendered [them] in some measure useless to Society," it followed that relieving their distress would revive their spirits, expanding both individual and national output. In April 1787 a Marylander proposed that the state government replace its £200,000 worth of interest-bearing bonds with paper money, which did not pay interest. He noted that "lessening the public debt" in this way would allow the assembly to slash the state property tax, "thus animating the hopes of a desponding

people." Similarly, a western Massachusetts writer claimed his tax reduction plan would prompt farmers "to manly and generous exertions
for the common good, by calling hope to their aid."[38]

Today few Americans question the Founding Fathers' claim that
Confederation-era state representatives, acutely aware of their political vulnerability, overindulged their rural constituents, adopting relief
legislation that chased away investment capital and crippled the economy. At the time, most free Americans shared their leaders' conviction
that the nation was on the road to economic ruin, but many rejected
their explanation of how it had gotten there. In their view, state representatives had ignored the popular voice and embraced harsh fiscal and
monetary regimes that depleted farmers' ability to produce. It was,
they said, the government's excessive demands, not the shortage of investment capital, that had depressed the economy. Accordingly the
remedy for the recession was to make state representatives more, not
less, sensitive to pressure from below.

The most insistent claims that heavy taxation and tight money weakened the economy all reflected a belief that the key ingredient in a successful economy was not land, capital, or managerial expertise. It was
labor. Many Americans had already articulated this labor theory of
value before the Revolutionary War, and during the 1780s it ripened
into a systematic ideology.[39] The "Midling and Lower Orders of the
people" were the "most useful and Laborous Part of the Community,"
William Whiting asserted in a fall 1786 essay that was never published.
"Some other orders" were "of much Less Importance to the Community." The critics of the high taxes and stringent monetary policies of
the 1780s often insisted that it was possible to describe the United
States as comprising just two classes. On the one hand, there were the
"industrious members of the community." High taxes and tight money
transmitted their "Property, the Production of Laborious Industry," to
"the non-productive class," the "useless and idle drones, who [were] living on the common stock." Herman Husband declared that the nation's rulers "can indeed handle a knife and fork at table; but are as
ignorant and awkward how to supply the table with provisions, as if
their hands were cut off."[40]

Many opponents of tax and debt relief were alarmed by its supporters' advanced level of class consciousness. The town of Newton, Massachusetts, which opposed Shays's Rebellion, said the revolt was animated by "a principle of opposition, between debtor and creditor—the rich and the poor."[41] While most advocates for strict tax and debt enforcement disputed the relief advocates' depiction of the Many carrying the Few on their backs, one implicitly accepted it, observing with concern the growing prejudice against "those, whose subsistence is derived from the labours of others."[42]

One diagnosis of the nation's economic ills attracted the support of nearly all free Americans, no matter where they stood on fiscal and monetary questions. This was the belief that the stagnation of the 1780s was caused in part by bond speculation.

Stockjobbing starved the economy of both labor and capital. It caused citizens to work less, as they wasted countless hours buying and selling bonds. Even worse, as the Virginian "Plain Reason" explained to the state's freeholders, "the pernicious traffick of Military Certificates" tempted Americans with the prospect of "acquiring great profits, with little trouble; thus relaxing the honest industry of your citizens."[43] It was not only the stockjobbers' critics who made this claim. Even Virginia congressman Henry Lee, no stranger to bond speculation, professed disgust that "all orders" of Americans had chosen "to relinquish every profession and place their attention to jobbing in paper securitys."[44]

An even broader consensus formed around the notion that securities speculation diverted capital away from projects—from livestock-raising to shipbuilding—that created wealth instead of simply redistributing it. "Plain Reason" regretted seeing bond trading swallow up funds that otherwise "would have gone to improve a farm, and increase the wealth of the state."[45] A Massachusetts writer wished "the great, instead of dabbling in publick securities," would "apply their wealth to the cultivation of the land."[46] John Adams observed the harmful effects of speculation from his diplomatic post in London. "While a Bit of Paper can be bought for five shillings that is worth twenty," he told Jefferson during the summer of 1786, "all Capitals will be employed in that Trade, for it is certain there is no other that will yeild four hundred Per Cent Profit, clear of Charges and Risques." It was only by putting a stop to stockjobbing that Americans could re-direct capital to the export trade, Adams declared.[47]

By the time he wrote those words, Adams had for nine years tacitly consented to his wife Abigail's decision to invest his money in depreciated government securities. But he went even further than bond trading's other critics, contending that by soaking up capital that would otherwise have gone to private borrowers, it increased interest rates. If the state and federal governments could stop investors from speculating in their securities, he contended, "the interest of money would instantly be lowered."[48]

Alexander Hamilton attacked the speculators in his own way. Shortly after becoming secretary of the treasury on September 11, 1789, he urged Congress to make punctual interest payments on the securities, raising their market value to equivalence with the price printed on their face. Even as it enriched those who had bought bonds in the 1780s, Hamilton's proposal would prevent future speculation by taking the profit out of it.[49] Despite their diametrically opposed solutions, Americans who wished to fully fund the securities and those who wished to partially or completely repudiate them agreed that bond speculation eroded the nation's scarce supply of capital.

CHAPTER 7

"THE FATE OF REPUBLICAN GOVT"

REDEMPTION

BY THE MID-1780S most of the men who would later contribute to the design of the Constitution had come to the conclusion that measures such as tax abatements and currency emissions threatened not only the American economy but the republic itself. Among foreigners and Americans alike, relief legislation sullied the reputation not only of the United States but of the very idea of popular government. It might even convince the friends of order that the only way to restore it was to establish an aristocratic or monarchical government. At the Constitutional Convention, James Madison told his fellow delegates that they "were now digesting a plan which in its operation w[oul]d decide forever the fate of Republican Govt."[1]

Other Americans, much less well known than the Framers, shared their apprehension that republican government was imperiled in the postwar era. But they had their own ideas about why. For them the real threat lay not in relief legislation but in the same oppressive fiscal and monetary policies that harbored such grave dangers for individuals and the economy. High taxes and tight money eroded one of the foundation stones of American popular government: the roughly equal distribution of property.

William Whiting, the Berkshire County, Massachusetts, justice who sympathized with his state's beleaguered taxpayers, wondered "what more ready method can be devised to enrich and aggrandize a number of individuals at the expence of the community at large and thereby put it in their power to introduce that odious state of Aristocracy, to the utter subversion of our present republican constitution, than by permitting them to draw from the people near fifty p[er] Cent interest" on their war bonds every year.[2] "We may as well think to repeal the great laws of attraction and gravitation," a Connecticut assemblyman pleading for tax relief told his colleagues on May 30, 1787, as to think of "continuing a popular government without a good degree of equality among the people as to their property." He even recommended the example of the biblical Jubilee, which mandated that "lands were to revert to their former owners at the end of every fifty years."[3]

Few Americans located their commitment to widespread landownership in the passion for social justice that had motivated the Levellers, the religious radicals who had sought to level out the gaping inequities that characterized seventeenth-century England. Citizens of the new nation considered equitable property distribution important not for its own sake but as a precondition for republican government. Farmers who became "tenants," Pennsylvania state representative William Findley warned, would "be dependent upon their landlords and vote as they direct."[4] As Pennsylvanians debated how to distribute the land the state had acquired from the Iroquois Indians in the 1780s, Herman Husband declared that everyone who moved west was "entitled to a preemption right," since "the granting of larger quantities to private persons, is creating of a nobility and lords to be over tenants—not freemen."[5] Albemarle County, Virginia, petitioners worried that if they were forced to sell their belongings, "power will natur[al]ly follow property, then god help the poor."[6]

Tenants and other citizens who lacked personal autonomy posed the greatest threat to popular government, but relief advocates were also wary of what could happen at the opposite rim of the economic chasm. "An enormous Proportion of Property vested in a few Individuals is dangerous to the Rights, and destructive of the Common Happiness of Mankind," a rejected clause of Pennsylvania's 1776 constitution declared, "therefore every free State hath a Right by its Laws to discourage the Possession of such Property."[7] William Whiting reminded his western Massachusetts neighbors that whenever a citizen of ancient Greece acquired a certain level of wealth, he was banished.[8] Numerous advocates for tax and relief contended that the state governments were not simply failing to prevent wealth disparity but actually encouraging it. The town meeting in Farmington, Connecticut, worried that the Continental Army officers' Commutation bonus would put "an excessive Power, the constant attendant of property . . . into the Hands of a Few."[9]

Of all the tax and debt relief proposals that circulated through the country during the 1780s, none excited more alarm than paper money. Opposition to state-issued currency generated tremendous support for the Constitution, which prohibited it. The critics of currency emissions charged that depreciation amounted to an unjust assault not only on private creditors but on Americans who held war bonds. An essay published in New Jersey in May 1786 warned that dumping still more currency into an economy already awash in various forms of government paper would "reduce public-securities to one half their present value."[10] Nor were creditors and bondholders paper money's only victims. The fear of getting stuck with depreciated currency allegedly prompted creditors to charge "exorbitant interest" and to sue debtors whom they might otherwise have been willing to indulge.[11] Most crucially, paper emissions sapped Americans' willingness to make loans. "What Man of Sense would risque his Money, and have his Gold metamorp[h]osed into old Rags?" a citizen of Foster, Rhode Island, asked in early 1786 as his state pondered an emission.[12] It is true that James Madison feared that fiat money would "disgrace Republican Govts. in the eyes of mankind," but he also voiced the more practical concern that legislators who resorted to the printing press inevitably ended up "destroying that confidence between man & man, by which [the] resources of one may be commanded by another."[13]

When the friends of paper money tried to disarm its critics by distinguishing the admittedly volatile emissions that funded wars from the land banks that had proven so successful during the colonial era, opponents countered that what really determined whether a paper emission held its value was the type of government that issued it. In this analysis, credit for the success of the colonial currency actually belonged to the British government. Imperial officials on both sides of the Atlantic, determined to protect English and Scottish merchant-creditors, had prevented the colonial assemblies from printing too much paper. Eventually Parliament seized control of the colonial money supply, prohibiting the North American provinces from forcing creditors to accept paper currency at its face value.[14] A New Jersey writer, "Eugenio," conceded in a January 1786 essay that the market value of the paper money emitted during the colonial era had often exceeded its face value, owing to its "convenience of carriage." He nonetheless opposed a new emission, for the simple reason that democratically elected legislators would fall short of their colonial forerunners' capacity for self-restraint. "If by elections and petitions this castle of paper can be erected," Eugenio wrote, "by the very same means it can be demolished."[15]

Writers like Eugenio identified several distinct factors that could cause republican paper currency to depreciate. State representatives who were too beholden to their constituents could fuel inflation by printing too much money. Or, as the Maryland senate warned, the "debility of our government" might lead to a "remissness in the collection or payment of taxes," which would leave too much money in circulation, causing it to "depreciate very considerably."[16] Americans who opposed currency feared that in a popular "Government like ours," legislative policy was "so liable to alteration" that the public's confidence in a particular emission of paper money could even be destroyed by the prospect that some future assembly might possibly fall behind in taxing it back into treasury.[17]

In an effort to allay these fears, some currency advocates suggested that it not be simply foisted upon bondholders, as others had proposed. The money would stand a much better chance of maintaining its value if it passed into the economy through willing hands. For this reason, the government should distribute the new bills through a loan office. Most of the seven state assemblies that issued paper money during the 1780s chose to establish loan offices rather than simply force the money on unwilling bondholders. (In doing so they gave modern observers the false impression that their sole motivation was to relieve desperate debtors.)

The state loan offices invariably failed to allay the fears of paper money's most inveterate enemies. When a popularly elected assembly lends out currency, it may resemble other creditors, they said, but it is actually not the same. Private-sector moneylenders can take care of themselves. That is what courts are for. But men who borrow money from a republican government are also voters, and they can use their electoral influence to prevent state officials from requiring timely re-payment of their loans.

The danger that the state's debt collection procedure would grow too lax seemed especially great in Pennsylvania, which had the most democratic of the state constitutions. In March 1785 Pennsylvania assemblymen voted to lend £50,000 to private citizens—by colonial standards a very modest sum. More than a year later a critic of the scheme—and of the state's "feeble constitution"—doubted the ability of public officials to "compel the *early* and *punctual* payment of the interest or principal" owed to the loan office.[18] Even in Maryland, with arguably the least democratic constitution in the United States, senators warned that voters might prevail upon the assembly to "procrastinate the term of payment."[19]

Thus opponents of paper currency made the ironic argument that in declaring independence from Britain and inaugurating a more democratic regime, Americans had obligated themselves to revert to a less progressive monetary policy. Paper money had worked well enough in many of the thirteen colonies; in the newly independent republics it was doomed.[20]

Americans seeking currency emissions struggled to allay their opponents' concerns. One of their strategies was to remind skeptics of the restraints on grassroots influence that were built into the state constitutions. This argument was especially appealing in Maryland, the state that granted the longest terms to members of the upper house of the legislature (Maryland senators served five years) and, more important, the only state where senators were selected by special electors rather than by the voters. "The manner in which our Senate is chosen," a procurrency Marylander affirmed in June 1786, "affords an admirable check to the *momentary* ebullitions of popular caprice."[21]

Some Americans who called for currency emissions predicted that the thirteen new republics would actually outshine their colonial predecessors at maintaining its value. The United States was "possessed of independence, a vast property, and numberless resources," a Maryland essayist declared in a spring 1785 article. "There can be no doubt of her being adequate to the business of emitting and supporting a paper credit."[22]

Not every American who questioned the ability of republics to maintain the stability of their paper emissions was a wealthy merchant-creditor. Thomas Paine made his name championing the rights of artisans and common soldiers, and during the Revolutionary War he witnessed firsthand what hyperinflation could do to these two groups and to everyone else on a fixed income. By the mid-1780s it was too late to do anything for the soldiers, but Paine was determined to protect Pennsylvania's artisans—who generally endured long intervals between settling on a price for their wares and receiving payment for them—from another ruinous wave of currency inflation. That brought Paine into conflict with backcountry agrarians like Herman Husband who wanted the legislature to print paper money. True, Paine had to admit, the currency printed by the Pennsylvania provincial assembly had held its value, but that was only because Britain had been "a restraining power over the conduct of the house; as to the quantity to be struck, which prevented depreciation."[23]

Paine's opposition to paper money helped turn him against the Constitutionalist party, the defenders of Pennsylvania's highly democratic state constitution. In a 1786 essay Paine declared that his earlier arguments in favor of the state's unicameral legislature—where there was no upper house to restrain the assembly—had been mistaken.[24]

By May 1787, when the federal convention gathered in Philadelphia, partisans on both sides of the depreciation question had accumulated hard evidence in support of their positions. The enemies of paper money could point to inflation in North Carolina, Georgia, and (especially) Rhode Island. But in New York, New Jersey, and South Carolina—and even in Paine's adopted home state of Pennsylvania—the currency printed in the 1780s by and large held its value.[25] Alexander Hamilton was certain the money printed by the New York legislature in 1786 would depreciate. By February 1787 he was ready to acknowledge—in a speech on the floor of the assembly—that "the event has, however, turned out otherwise."[26] If inflation in Georgia, Carolina, and Rhode Island threatened wealthy citizens economically, the stability of the currency printed in the other four states was in some ways even more disconcerting, since it undercut a belief in the incompatibility of paper money and republican government that was fundamental to their worldview.

Even in the three states where the currency did depreciate, the critics' depictions of creditors and bondholders as helpless victims was considerably exaggerated. The savviest and most powerful public and private creditors were able to mitigate the harmful effects of depreciation. This was true even of Rhode Island, the state that suffered by far the worst inflation. Shortly after the 1786 emission was approved, its opponents obtained special protection for the state's charitable institutions, most notably Rhode Island College (the future Brown University). The legislature prohibited people who owed money to charities from paying them back ahead of schedule. It may seem strange that creditors would consider early repayment an act of aggression, but the reality was that the college and other charities had done what nonprofit organizations generally do today. Having built up financial reserves, they had lent them out at interest. The charities worried that the people who had purchased their bonds would redeem them using depreciated paper currency. That was the tactic the 1786 law prohibited.[27]

Private creditors and bondholders also found ways to protect themselves. The two Columbia University professors who charged students higher tuition when they paid with the paper money emitted in 1786 were by no means unique in granting customers a discount when they paid with gold or silver.[28] Some people resorted to elaborate ruses to avoid having to accept paper currency. Creditors to whom debtors had mortgaged land or other property pretended to sell the mortgages to friends or relatives who lived outside the state. If your debtors could not find you, they could not force you to accept paper money.[29]

Nicholas Brown used a similar strategy to protect his investment in government securities. In March 1788 he sent his Rhode Island bonds to Philadelphia "to be Negotiated [sold]." So, at least, he wrote at the top of his "List of State Notes . . . Del[ivere]d [to] Mr. John Francis." Actually, as Brown noted elsewhere on the same document three years later—after the U.S. Constitution had been adopted and Congress had assumed responsibility for redeeming the state notes with new federal bonds that were nearly as good as gold—he had only sent the securities to Francis "To be Secured." Francis returned them in February 1791. Pretending to sell his bonds in Philadelphia, Brown had actually just hidden them there.[30]

These were desperate schemes, fraught with danger, and they did nothing to dilute the mounting opposition to paper money. Since anti-currency writers worried that even the possibility of hyperinflation might discourage the wealthy from putting their gold and silver in circulation, many believed the only way to reassure would-be investors was to place the printing press beyond the legislature's reach. They would eventually hit upon a dramatic national solution to the problem, but they made numerous efforts at the state level first. "Plain Reason" recommended to his fellow Virginians "the calling of a Convention, with the avowed purpose of doing away all future dread of Paper-Money, by putting it out of the power of your Assembly, to terrify people every year with the expectation of it."[31] New Jerseyans and Rhode Islanders proposed similar currency bans for their own state constitutions.[32]

Even the most impassioned adversaries of paper money apparently recognized that there was very little chance of any state's adopting a constitutional prohibition. Thus some writers suggested a different approach: the legislature should simply construe existing clauses in the state constitution as banning currency emissions. Since New Hampshire's founding document did not allow the legislature "to alter the nature of private contracts," Jeremy Belknap asserted in his history of the state, it did not matter whether "the majority of the people petition the government" for paper money. The assemblymen must still "reject the petition as unconstitutional."[33]

In several states citizens who believed that fiat money violated the constitution talked of obtaining a judicial ruling to that effect. In no state, however, were the courts able to overturn a currency emission, and the opponents of paper money increasingly sought protection by the federal government.[34] "Congress should have the power of preventing the States from cheating one another as well as their own citizens by means of paper money," the Virginia congressman William Grayson suggested to a receptive James Madison in May 1786.[35] In 1786, when delegates were sent to Annapolis to consider amendments to the Articles of Confederation, several writers urged them to propose a ban on state-issued paper money.[36] The demand for a federal assault on state currency intensified the following year, as delegates gathered in Philadelphia for the federal convention.[37]

Many of the Americans who debated proposals such as paper money during the 1780s discerned fatal flaws not only in their opponents' policy positions but also in their mind-sets. Legislators, essayists, and orators frequently contended that their own beliefs were based on reason, while their opponents were slaves to their passions. Supporters of high taxes and hard money found this line of attack especially appealing. David Daggett, the young New Haven, Connecticut, attorney, gave voice to a widespread suspicion when, in his Fourth of July oration for 1787, he said Americans who wanted to scale down the speculators' bonds "never will be reasoned out of this idea, for they never reasoned themselves into it."[38] A Massachusetts newspaper writer attributed relief legislation to the "sentimental times."[39]

Even as citizens disputing the direction of the American Revolution accused each other of thralldom to feeling, the population as a whole had reached the conclusion that sentiment not only packed tremendous punch but deserved to. Long before the Revolutionary War a new literary form, the novel, had conquered western Europe and the American colonies. Books like Henry MacKenzie's 1771 *Man of Feeling* and Jane Austen's 1811 *Sense and Sensibility* celebrated characters who surpassed the common run of mankind in the richness and refinement of their emotional lives. One unmistakable index of the rising popularity of "sensibility" (as it was most commonly called) was that numerous participants in the debates of the 1780s contended that their position deserved the support of every person of feeling.

Sensibility had an artistic dimension: only a person with a high level of refinement could truly appreciate a Gainsborough portrait or a Mozart sonata. However, another sort of sensibility proved much more useful to the political partisans of the 1780s. "Fellow feeling" was roughly equivalent to the modern term "empathy" (which would not be invented until late in the nineteenth century). It was the ability not just to pity a person in distress but actually to feel his or her pain. Fellow feeling could come from suffering the same fate as the distressed person (or having done so in the past), but it could also be generated by the imagination.

The most influential eighteenth-century student of fellow feeling was, surprisingly enough, a man who is generally known today as the champion of self-interest. In 1759, seventeen years before writing *The Wealth of Nations*, Adam Smith published the lectures he had been reading to his students at the University of Glasgow. He called the book *The Theory of Moral Sentiments*. The only reason we hate seeing someone suffer, Smith argued, is that "by the imagination we place ourselves in his situation, we conceive ourselves enduring all the same torments, we enter as it were into his body, and become in some measure the same person with him, and thence form some idea of his sensations."[40] Americans who waded into the great fiscal and monetary contests of the 1780s understood that their listeners' or readers' ability to sympathize with the taxpayer's plight—or with the bondholder's, for that matter—depended upon their ability to imagine it. Smith had cautioned that humans feel "little for another, with whom they have no particular connexion."[41] Drawing upon this insight, the political partisans of the 1780s labored to forge a bond between the observer and the sufferer.

It was a daunting task, for the public speaker and even more so for the essayist. The playwright—and to some extent, the orator—can offer his audience a physical demonstration of his subjects' suffering. But as Thomas Sheridan pointed out, the writer's only resource is "the dead letter."[42] Since "the eye is the best avenue to the heart," Henry Home (Lord Kames) declared, it was incumbent upon authors to show "every thing as passing before our sight; and from readers and hearers transform us . . . into spectators."[43] Americans who debated relief legislation during the 1780s painted verbal tableaux where their audiences could see, for example, the pain a farm family suffered as the sheriff confiscated its livestock.

Often these word-pictures focused on the human body. European and North American thinkers of the eighteenth century were endlessly intrigued by the tendency of the emotions to leave a physical trace. These effects, which included blushing, crying, sexual responses, and salivation, can sometimes be explained by physical contact. Often, however, they cannot. The hungry person sometimes salivates at the mere thought of food, without any stimulation from the sense of smell, sight, or taste. Blushes, tears, and laughter can be provoked by physical contact but more often by the imagination.[44]

Fellow feeling could likewise produce an instinctive response. "The plaintive voice of misery," Adam Smith had explained, "forces us almost involuntarily" to aid the person who is suffering.[45] Participants in the great fiscal and monetary debates of the 1780s believed they could make converts if they could show that their opponents' policies had caused anguish so severe as to trigger the sort of automatic response Smith had described. Toward that end they often used their own bodies as canvases on which to demonstrate how a humane person should react to the tragic tales they told. The New Braintree, Massachusetts, town meeting pleaded with state leaders not to take up arms against the men who had closed several backcountry courts. "Our blood recoils in our veins with a chilling horror," the townsmen declared, "& our big swolen hearts palpitate at an idea so shocking."[46]

These unabashed appeals to sympathy and fellow feeling were all the more remarkable in light of Enlightenment thinkers' tendency to associate sentiment with women. By the mid-1780s it was a commonplace in the United States as well as in Europe that women were "the sentimental part of our species." Judith Sargent Murray, the Massachusetts writer and champion of women's rights, claimed that the "heart-rending emotions, which fill us at once with wonder, compassion and terror, always have belonged, and always will belong, only to Women."[47]

Authors and orators also wielded sensibility as a cudgel. Since the process by which suffering elicited sympathy was supposed to be automatic, to be unmoved was to be unnatural, and in an Enlightened age, no one wanted to be told he had fallen out of harmony with nature.[48] Americans who beseeched the legislatures to ease up on farmers used the same word over and over again in their characterizations of litigious creditors, wealthy Americans who bought up their insolvent neighbors' property, and bondholders who demanded action on delinquent taxpayers. All were described as "unfeeling."[49] Relief advocates lamented that some people's bodies seemed immune to the involuntary responses that a neighbor's distress was supposed to trigger. They drew special attention to their adversaries' hearts, which were said to be as hard and inflexible as the metal coins they demanded as the nation's sole units of exchange. In May 1785 "Observator" claimed that the men at the helm of New Hampshire's government could not "feel for others, through a callosity of heart, which makes them insensible to any one's interest but their own."[50]

Some prorelief writers warned that wealth tended to prevent a man from experiencing the proper degree of fellow feeling. Right before the May 1787 Massachusetts elections, a newspaper essayist urged voters to replace their bondholding representatives with others "more likely to *sympathize with*, and relieve the distresses of their brethren."[51] Americans who favored rigorous debt and tax collection often replied in kind, contending that it was not the few but the many who lacked fellow feeling. An essay appearing in the *Pennsylvania Journal* in 1783 warned bondholders not to expect sympathy from "the callous multitude."[52]

Few audiences could have missed the message these accusations were meant to convey: if they disagreed with the speaker or author addressing them, they, too, must lack feeling. A group of Delaware petitioners who sought a temporary closure of the state's courts allowed that the idea would hold little appeal for people with "unfeeling hearts." But "those who Enjoy those soft and virtu[o]us feelings of the Human Heart, which Simpathizes with the Distressed," could hardly "turn a Deaf Ear to the Voice of Lamentation which pervades their Country."[53]

When advocates for stringent fiscal and monetary policies claimed their opponents were actuated by emotion rather than reason, pro-relief writers sometimes replied with vigorous defenses of sensibility. Occasionally they used a candid acknowledgment that not everyone possesses the same capacity for reason as a springboard for an aggressive challenge to the notion that political judgments must be founded on reason. "Few can reason," one Massachusetts tax relief advocate wrote, "but all can feel."[54]

The problem with this argument, of course, was that if listeners and readers could be convinced that political questions were best decided by reason, not by emotion, then ordinary citizens would have to defer to the nation's best minds. At least one advocate for harsh fiscal and monetary legislation, apparently a Philadelphian, spotted this opening. He began his contribution to the debate with a concession of his own. Many people understand "the principles of liberty," which are "matters of feeling," but not "the principles of government . . . which are objects of reflection and reason," he declared.[55]

The complex fiscal and monetary debates of the 1780s did not simply split the nation into two factions. Actually there were many more, and every broad grouping was split into numerous subcamps. The difficult questions of the 1780s even divided the minds of many individuals.

Neither of the principal parties to the relief debate was monolithic. Some Americans who sympathized with distressed farmers opposed paper money while supporting other forms of relief. Some currency supporters wanted it to be legal tender, but not all did.[56] Sometimes advocates for tax or debt relief chose to link arms with one probondholder faction against another. In Connecticut taxpayers who did not want the legislature to comply with Congress's September 1785 requisition, which would require it to add burdensome "Continental" taxes to the heavy state levies they were already paying, found an unlikely ally: holders of state bonds. It was widely feared that there was not enough money in Connecticut to pay both state and "Continental" taxes, and the state government's creditors were reluctant to share the state's limited tax revenue with Congress and its creditors.[57]

In Pennsylvania the dispute involved rival groups of federal bondholders. The legislature announced in the fall of 1784 that it was going to pay interest to Pennsylvanians who owned federal securities. Every federal creditor was to receive his or her interest in paper money. The assembly's proposal encountered opposition not only from beleagured taxpayers but from some of the bondholders themselves. Pennsylvanians who had obtained federal securities directly from the government did not want the assembly to pay secondary holders anything, since cutting them off would enable it to pay the original holders their interest in silver.[58]

The harshest punishment ever suggested for a group of bond traders—namely, that the state utterly repudiate its debt to them—came in a petition that the Delaware assembly received from a rival group of speculators.[59]

To add to the complications surrounding the struggle between the friends and enemies of tax and debt relief, many Americans did not fall neatly into either camp. Some were simply ambivalent. On the one hand, the American envoys in London (John Adams) and Paris (Thomas Jefferson) both fretted that tax and debt relief endangered their country's reputation among European investors. On the other hand, both contended that earlier European loans had caused Americans nothing but trouble.[60] Jefferson's ambivalence was especially acute. On the one hand, he was highly critical of the relief laws that numerous states, including his native Virginia, adopted in the 1780s. On the other hand, he defended a proposal to allow Virginians like himself to pay their prewar British debts in seven annual installments, and in doing so he used the same arguments that had been advanced on behalf of the relief schemes he denounced.[61]

John Adams's ambivalence about bond speculation manifested itself as a long-running dispute with his wife, Abigail. John initially balked at investing in depreciated government paper, contending that real estate was safer—both for the investor and for his country. The ideal he constantly held before himself was the virtuous Roman senator whose vote was not for sale because his landed estate ensured his financial independence. Securities traders, by contrast, were what every republic had to avoid at all costs: a narrow faction with both the motivation and the clout to manipulate the government in its favor. Although born and raised on the Massachusetts coast near Boston, Adams partook of some of the same pastoralism we associate with Jefferson, who considered "those who labour in the earth . . . the chosen people of God."[62]

Abigail Adams's situation was different. As long as her husband lived (and as it turned out, he outlived her), she could never experience the pleasure of owning property. On the other hand, she played an even bigger role than John did in deciding how his money was spent. Entitled to use what she could not own, Abigail naturally cared less about what form the family's assets took than about the rate of return.

In any event, it may be less accurate to describe John Adams as ambivalent about bond speculation than to note that his actions did not always match his ideals. The simple fact is that he did allow his wife to make him a speculator. It was one more useful role she played in the relationship—the devil who made him do it.

The tidy image of a set-piece battle between supporters and opponents of aggressive debt and tax collection is further complicated by the fact that loyal members of one of the two main camps sometimes raided the other's armory of rhetoric and ideas. The archetypical rhetorical pirate was Philadelphia merchant Pelatiah Webster, who called upon the Pennsylvania legislature to use gold and silver to pay interest to Pennsylvanians like himself who had used depreciated paper money to purchase federal bonds back during the war.[63] Webster's proposal was an attack upon Pennsylvanians who had obtained their bonds on the open market. In 1784 the secondary holders, recognizing that the Pennsylvania government could not afford to pay both categories of bond owners their interest in gold and silver, proposed that all interest be paid in paper money instead.

The currency proposal infuriated Webster and other original holders, who balked at the idea of receiving their interest in the form of "another deluge of *public promises*" destined to depreciate. They pointed out that the government could afford to pay them their interest in gold and silver—so long as the secondary holders received nothing at all. Webster's war against the secondary holders generated some of the decade's most eloquent denunciations of bond speculation, which, he declared, "takes an immense property from those who had *earned* it, and would, of course, probably make the *best use* of it, and places it in the hands of people who have *not earned* it, and who would, of course, probably make the *worst use* of it."[64]

Echoing a claim made by many tax relief advocates, Webster contended that the reason Pennsylvania legislators wanted to pay interest on secondary holders' securities was that they themselves had purchased government paper. It was common, he said, for bondholding state assemblymen to "vote the money of their constituents by thousands into their *own pockets*." Whenever the assembly took up legislation related to the public debt, he said, each representative should have to reveal the extent of his own investment in government paper, and speculators should not be allowed to vote.[65]

Webster's indictment of securities speculation drew extensively upon the relief advocates' economic vision. The speculators were wrong to say easing up on taxpayers would reduce Americans' output, he claimed. Quite the contrary. "There are, it is said, 5000 people in Pennsylvania, who live by broking and speculating, who would otherwise be employed in lawful trades, or in agriculture," he wrote. "They are infinitely more hurtful to our country than the Hessian fly."[66] "When the speculators are paid," he predicted in 1785, "they will all at once become so *amazingly rich*, that they will probably set up their carriages, and run into other courses of *idleness and pleasures, luxury and dissipation*, which are ever hurtful to the public." Like tax relief advocates, Webster cautioned that excessive public demands "cast a damp and deadening languor on the very *first springs*, the *original principle* and *source* of our national wealth," namely the work performed by ordinary farmers and artisans. He also repeated the popular warning that state assemblymen, in their zeal to satisfy bondholders, might scare off would-be immigrants. "Heavy taxes on the country," he wrote, "will discourage people from coming to settle on our lands." Webster even joined the fiscal reformers in rejecting the "stupid and cruel argument . . . that taxing labor has this advantage, that it promotes industry, because it increases necessity. . . . that it is best to make every body poor, because it will make them work the harder." Instead of being "*goaded on* by dire necessity and the dreadful spurs of pinching want," he said, farmers and artisans should be "*animated* by an increase of happiness and hope of reward."[67]

Webster appears to have been expressing a genuine sympathy for distressed taxpayers at the same time that he cynically appropriated relief advocates' arguments for use against a rival group of securities speculators. Webster's embrace of prorelief rhetoric is one indication of just how popular those ideas were.

PART III
UNRULY AMERICANS

CHAPTER 8

"A REVOLUTION WHICH OUGHT TO BE GLORIOUS"

DISENCHANTMENT

URING THE HALF-DECADE that preceded the adoption of the Constitution, every state legislature granted at least some tax and debt relief, inevitably prompting charges that assemblymen were "desperate men" who had secured election in order "to screen themselves from their creditors."[1] Local officials who eased up on debtors and taxpayers faced similar accusations. When New Hanover County, North Carolina, judges postponed all but a few of the lawsuits that creditors had filed against debtors, Archibald Maclaine was sure he knew why. "The truth is," he told James Iredell in July 1787, "they and their friends were all sued."[2] These charges were not entirely unfounded. Numerous officeholders shared their constituents' distress. Throughout the 1780s the Virginia House of Delegates kept the state's courts closed to British merchants seeking to recover prewar debts. Many of the assemblymen owed their old colonial creditors much more than they could pay. Sometimes citizens received legislative indulgence in response to their petitions or representative instructions.[3] Not very often, though. And so even as some Americans complained that the political establishment had been too kind to debtors and taxpayers, others described it as insufficiently responsive to pressure from below.

The difficulty that ordinary Americans faced in trying to sway their elected officials was never more in evidence than in the fall of 1785, when farmers in the South Carolina backcountry asked the state assembly to do something about the African slave trade. Thousands of black Carolinians had escaped to the British lines during the Revolutionary War, and when peace came, slaveholders, especially in the backcountry, imported thousands of replacement workers from Africa. But many of their less wealthy neighbors, themselves unable or unwilling to purchase Africans, feared that the boom in slave purchases had increased the danger of slave revolt. It had also drained the region of cash. According to one contemporary estimate, South Carolinians buying Africans had sent £300,000 worth of hard money out of the state. Citizens in several western counties entreated the assembly to suspend the transatlantic slave trade. So many men signed one petition that it stretched to seven feet long.[4]

Unfortunately for these backcountry petitioners, many of their region's assembly representatives had purchased Africans and wished to continue doing so. Ralph Izard, a lowcountry assemblyman who favored the upstate petitions against the slave trade, told the state House of Representatives he "hoped, that when [assemblymen] belonging to that part of the country from whence a petition had been transmitted, signed by 600 names, one section of which complained of the importing negroes, returned home, they would carry a list of those members that had voted against the proposition, for the information of their constituents." The backcountry representatives did not follow Izard's suggestion, for such a list would have contained their own names.[5]

Where petitions and instructions failed to produce the desired effect, tax and debt relief advocates sometimes urged their fellow citizens to defeat recalcitrant politicians at the polls. A New Jerseyan hoped that state legislators would grasp the need for paper money. "If not," he wrote, "our only remedy is the next election of representatives."[6] In June 1787 the Delaware legislature agreed to pay two years of interest to holders of state bonds. During the ensuing election season "the public prints resounded with exhortations not to chuse any man as a representative, who had purchased certificates, or advocated the payment of them." The voters of New Castle County replaced their representatives, and in November the assembly adopted legislation effectively denying interest to everyone who had acquired their securities through speculation.[7]

But farmers' efforts to influence elections encountered numerous

obstacles. In most states the tallest challenge was defeating obstruc-
tionist members of the upper house of assembly (called the senate in
some states and the council in others). One reason senators and councilors were less vulnerable to grassroots pressure than assemblymen
was that they were chosen by many more voters. The sheer size of their
districts often made it almost impossible to drive them from office.

Massachusetts voters learned how difficult it was to replace senators
in the wake of the legislature's March 23, 1786, vote to levy a £300,000
tax. Opponents blamed the new tax on the state's senators, and a year
later they launched efforts to turn them out of office. Appropriating a
tactic that had long been used by more established political interests,
they published the names of prorelief senate candidates. Meanwhile
town meetings in Suffolk and Worcester Counties proposed countywide conventions to nominate relief advocates for the senate.[8] An antitax newspaper essayist proposed in October 1786 that conventions
assemble in each county twice a year: "once to instruct their Senators,
and once, at the close of the General Court, to examine their conduct,
that they might be able to judge whether they are safe persons to be
trusted in [the] future."[9] Little came of the effort, however.

Farmers in southern New England faced an even taller challenge. In
both Connecticut and Rhode Island the members of the council (the
upper house of the legislature) were elected statewide.[10] In 1783 the
Connecticut Council of Assistants blocked a lower house proposal
to condemn the Continental Army officers' Commutation bonus. In
September angry citizens held a convention and agreed on a slate of
council candidates, but the campaign fizzled.[11] In neighboring Rhode
Island, however, relief advocates did manage to overcome the political
liabilities that came with large election districts. How did they succeed
where other New Englanders failed?

Rhode Islanders seeking an emission of paper money knew they
would face their greatest test in the council of assistants, which was
elected statewide. Voters seldom knew any of the candidates personally, and they usually just ratified the "proxe"—the slate—proposed to
them by the state's political establishment.[12] In the spring of 1786,
though, a group of currency advocates held a pair of conventions in
East Greenwich and proposed a proxe of their own. Under the slogan

"To Relieve the Distressed," they circulated a list of candidates for council and other statewide offices. If the so-called country-proxe came to power, its first order of business would be to print currency.

Rhode Islanders who opposed paper money rallied against the country-proxe. Providence merchant Nicholas Brown knew that few of his numerous creditors would foist paper currency on him the moment it was printed, since doing so would disable them from obtaining future loans. Still, an emission would shift the balance of power in the debtor-creditor relationship. With paper money in circulation, if Brown threatened to sue one of his customers, the debtor could retaliate with a threat of his own. Brown was also loath to receive either the interest or the principal of his Rhode Island bonds in paper.[13] And he was convinced that an emission would devastate the state's economy.

Brown drew on his network of contacts throughout Rhode Island for information on the progress of the country slate. He even managed to get his hands on a "List of Persons Present 3d Apl. E Greenwich."[14] To no avail. Voters turned out in record numbers, and most of the men appearing on the country-proxe were elected, as were the majority of the pro-currency candidates for the lower house. The new assembly wasted no time in ordering the emission of £100,000 worth of paper money that could be used to pay not only personal debts but state and federal taxes. It also delayed the due date for the tax that its predecessor had levied in compliance with Congress's September 1785 requisition.

By organizing on a statewide basis, paper money advocates showed they understood the point that James Madison would make in the early 1790s: "a general intercommunication of sentiments & ideas among the body of the people, as a free press, compact situation, good roads, interior commerce &c. is equivalent to a contraction of the orbit within wch. the Govt. is to act."[15] But this effort succeeded only in Rhode Island, the Confederation's smallest state. Elsewhere relief advocates' campaigns did not fare so well. Indeed, farmers who got involved in politics sometimes ended up making matters worse for themselves. In 1783 a group of Bedford County, Pennsylvania, citizens who tried to turn out their representative not only came up short on election day but were successfully sued for libel.[16]

Even in states where the legislature did ease up on debtors and taxpayers, many believed the relief did "not go far enough."[17] Several assemblies adopted legislation allowing debtors to satisfy their creditors with property instead of hard money, but these measures were inevitably denounced as inadequate.[18] Seven states printed paper money in the mid-1780s, but even in the majority of those, currency advocates complained that the assembly had done too little.[19] Often the quantity of currency was considered too low. Moreover, four of the legislatures that printed currency chose not to make it "legal tender," which would have required creditors to accept it at its face value.[20] Barely a year after the Pennsylvania legislature issued £150,000 worth of paper money, Philadelphia newspapers reported that "petitions to the Legislature are now circulating in Bucks county in this state, praying them to increase the quantity of paper money, and to make it a legal tender." Only one-third of the currency was put out on loan (the rest being disbursed as interest to the state's federal bondholders), prompting Bucks and Lancaster County citizens to call the loan office "too small . . . to give adequate relief."[21]

The Americans' remarkable triumph over the British Empire—the most powerful nation the world had ever known—had filled them with hope for the future. But by the mid-1780s that optimism was giving way to despair. Brunswick County, Virginia, petitioners spoke for farmers everywhere when they claimed in 1786 that "the honest labourour who tills the ground by the sweat of his brow Seams hithertoo to be the only sufferors by a revolution which ought to be glorious but which the undeserving only reap the benifit off."[22] Growing numbers of Americans were beginning to wonder whether they had been better off under British rule. "Has not many been oppressed a Hundred to one more then ever they had been by Brittan Before[?]," John Reed of Massachusetts asked in the fall of 1785.[23] Two years later Connecticut attorney David Daggett noted that the state's "heavy taxes" had prompted many citizens to ask, "Is this liberty—is this independence[?] . . . How preferable the years of 1772 or 73!"[24] Relief advocates in both Massachusetts and Virginia suggested the formation of committees of correspondence—a tactic Patriots had used against the British.[25]

Farmers in northern New England found a remarkable way to express their disappointment with the course that the revolution had taken. Dozens of New Hampshire and Massachusetts town meetings resolved that the next time the state assembly met, they would go unrepresented.

In both of the two northernmost states, members of the General Court were paid by taxpayers in their hometowns, not out of the state treasury, and town meetings often reduced expenses during hard times by forgoing representation. By the spring of 1786, however, the withholding of legislators had become something else: a political statement.[26] "If our Representative goes to Court," the Massachusetts General Court could hear many country people saying, "he will do us no service: For the measures he is in favour of, will not be adopted."[27] In April 1787 the editors of the *New Hampshire Spy* noted that several town meetings had "resolved not to send any representatives to the ensuing General Court." The newspaper attributed this extraordinary decision to the widespread belief among farmers that assemblymen did nothing but "sit on their bottoms and eat up the provisions," thus adding to "the expenses of the state without contriving any means to lessen them."[28]

The New England towns' occasional failure to elect legislators during the immediate postwar era has sometimes been chalked up to indifference. But the residents of a town like Loudon, New Hampshire, which voted to forgo representation in the spring of 1787, could hardly be called apathetic. Loudon *had* sent delegates to Concord for a Rockingham County protest convention less than a year earlier, instructing them to seek "a Bank of [paper] money." Other New Hampshire towns also chose to be represented in protest conventions but not in the legislature.[29]

The question of whether to elect assemblymen often proved divisive. It even led Cambridge, Massachusetts, to take the rare step of criticizing the towns that had chosen "to forebear sending constitutional Representatives."[30] Elsewhere the tactic opened fissures within towns. The selectmen (town council) of Marlborough, New Hampshire, were so eager to dispatch a representative to the 1786 legislative session that they hired Phenious Farrer to ride around the village for two days seeking signatures on a petition in favor of being represented. The town meeting nonetheless "Voted Not to Send a Representative." In 1785 and 1786 the freeholders of Deerfield, New Hampshire, took the extraordinary step of petitioning the legislature for paper money. The request was denied, and in the spring of 1787 a group of Deerfield residents proposed that the town withhold its assemblyman. The selectmen initially refused to call a town meeting to discuss the issue, relenting only after receiving a petition signed by several townsmen. At the meeting Deerfield voted not to be represented—but then changed its mind a week later.[31]

Similar divisions afflicted towns in Massachusetts. On May 15, 1786, Paxton voted by "a large majority" not to send its incumbent state representative, Hezekiah Ward, back to the assembly. To the disgust of his townsmen, Ward "by some means or other, obtained a seat in the House of Representatives" anyway. In the spring of 1787 Abigail Adams, who had traveled to London to join her diplomat husband, learned from her sister Mary Smith Cranch that some of their Braintree neighbors were so angry at the state government's handling of Shays's Rebellion that they wanted to recall Ebenezer Thayer, the town's state representative. "Shays has not a small party in Braintree," Cranch reported. "They call'd a Town meeting about a week since to forbid colln. Thayers attending the general court but they could not get a vote."[32]

The militant fatalism of some Massachusetts towns helps explain one of the great mysteries of the so-called Critical Period, the half-decade preceding the adoption of the Constitution. In March 1786 the Massachusetts legislature hit the state's taxpayers with a bill for £300,000. Farmers not only refused to pay the new tax but protested this and other burdens by closing many of the state's courts. Which raises a question: why, if voters were so angry about the March 1786 tax, did they not use the spring 1786 elections to turn out the protax governor, representatives, and senators? Why did they take up arms when they could simply have taken to the polls?

Actually, many towns *did* replace their assemblymen that spring, and George Richards Minot, the clerk of the state house of representatives, reported seeing "a great number of new faces" in the session of the assembly that convened in late May 1786. Massachusetts politicians who admired the previous assembly for taking a hard line on taxation and private debt feared its decisions would be reversed by its successor. "Great alterations I hear, have taken place in the Country Representation," Samuel Henshaw told Nathan Dane. "Paper Money & Tender Acts I expect will be great & popular questions in the new [General] Court." Similarly, a New Hampshire essayist reported that in the state's

May 1786 elections voters "made a great change in the Representative body for the approaching session, in hopes" the legislature would emit a "paper medium."[33]

The opponents of tax and debt relief need not have worried. Even though numerous New Hampshire and Massachusetts towns defeated their antirelief assemblymen in the spring 1786 elections, their action was canceled out by other towns that expressed their anger at the legislature's harsh fiscal and monetary policies by withdrawing their representatives altogether. Fifty-two fewer assemblymen showed up for the summer 1786 session of the Massachusetts House of Representatives than had participated in the previous session. Absenteeism was especially high among western members, whose attendance fell to a three-year low. In New Hampshire, too, the towns that decided to send new representatives might have had an impact—except that other towns chose to send none. The legislature elected in May 1786, far from easing the tax burden imposed by its predecessor, added to it.[34]

More and more citizens were coming to the conclusion that the fundamental challenge of American politics was to find a way to relieve the distress of the Many (debtors and taxpayers) without injuring the interests of the Few (creditors and bondholders). There were, in fact, three possible ways to do so.

Both the debtor-creditor conflict and the one pitting taxpayers against bondholders had been aggravated by the shortage of circulating coin. Both disputes would become much less divisive issues if the American economy could somehow stop hemorrhaging gold and silver. As long as Americans imported more than they exported, they would have to make up the difference by shipping hard money to their overseas trading partners. Campaigns to eliminate the trade deficit by promoting "industry and frugality" yielded little in the way of tangible results.[35] Citizens could not even agree on whether it was taxpayers and debtors or bondholders and creditors who had undermined the economy by producing too little and buying too much. On the other hand, no one would be subjected to undue sacrifice if the trade gap could be filled using what economists would later call "invisible earnings." Revenue from the international carrying trade could turn a trade deficit into a surplus. During these years Caribbean and transatlantic shipping were dominated by the Americans' former colonial masters, the British. If some of that trade could be transferred from British to American ships, Americans would have the satisfaction of resolving their internal differences at their recent enemies' expense.

It was not necessary for the United States to dominate every shipping route. American merchants simply needed to claim a larger share of the trade between their own ports and the Caribbean sugar plantations. As British colonists, North Americans had played a major role in supplying the slaveholders in the West Indies with grain, livestock, fish, and forest products in return for their molasses and rum. The resulting profits had enriched the merchants as well as their home colonies. In July 1783, however, the British Privy Council prohibited the newly independent Americans from sending their ships to their former mother country's Caribbean possessions.

A host of wily American captains managed to evade the 1783 orders in council. A popular tactic was to invoke the ancient custom permitting any ship in distress to put into the nearest port, even if it would not normally be welcome there. A naïve person reading a Caribbean newspaper in the 1780s might have concluded that Americans were sloppy shipbuilders indeed, for their vessels were constantly seeking refuge in British ports in the sugar islands. But these ships never seemed to be too distressed to unload their cargoes and take on new ones. Still, the island trade never approached prewar levels. British navy captains and customs agents occasionally enforced the 1783 orders, leading to the confiscation and sale of an American ship's entire cargo and even of the ship itself (the arresting officer receiving a portion of the proceeds). John Adams, the American minister in London, pleaded with the British government to open the empire's ports to American ships, knowing full well his words would fall on deaf ears until they were backed by power. The only way the United States could break Britain's monopoly of the Caribbean trade was to retaliate, excluding British ships from American harbors until Parliament and the Privy Council backed down. Under the Articles of Confederation, though, Congress had no authority to regulate trade. Desperately needing the power to force British ports open to American ships, Congress asked the states to approve an amendment granting that power. Most of the legislatures agreed, but the movement to revise the Articles, which required unanimous approval, stalled. The trade between the British Caribbean and the American mainland would remain a virtual British monopoly.[36]

There were two other ways to resolve the conflict between the Few and the Many. Both were solutions to one of the fundamental problems of the 1780s: the federal government's need for nearly a million dollars a year to service its foreign and domestic debts. Each offered the prospect of satisfying the bondholders without placing an undue burden on taxpayers.

The Articles of Confederation gave the federal government no power to tax. In 1781 Congress proposed an amendment allowing it to levy a 5 percent tariff on all merchandise imported into the country. The plan was ratified by every state except Rhode Island. In the midst of a congressional effort to break the Rhode Islanders' resistance, Virginia rescinded its approval, and the amendment died. In 1783 Congress tried again, this time seeking direct taxes (on property and people) as well as a tariff. The direct tax amendment fell far short of the required unanimous approval. By 1786, on the other hand, every state had approved the federal tariff. But New York, the last state to consent, attached conditions to its adoption that Congress found unacceptable. The Confederation government never was able to levy a tariff.

Why did Rhode Island and then New York block the campaign for a federal tariff? It was universally understood that acceding to federal customs duties would have forced those and other states to stop levying their own tariffs on merchandise arriving in their ports. The New York tariff had proved especially lucrative, since New York harbor was the landing place for most of the merchandise that ultimately ended up in Connecticut and New Jersey.

The supporters of the federal tariff were especially cynical about New York's rejection of it, blaming the legislature's recalcitrance on New Yorkers who had invested in Continental securities. Why would federal bondholders oppose a federal tariff? For a very good reason. In February 1786 New York assemblymen, fearing that Congress would never redeem its war bonds or even pay punctual interest on them, offered citizens of the state the option of exchanging their federal securities for new state bonds.[37] If New York was going to service these new notes without oppressing taxpayers, it would have to hold on to its own lucrative tariff. Supporters of the federal tariff alleged that the assemblymen themselves were, in James Monroe's words, "possess'd to great amount (I mean the leaders of the party) of publick securities."[38]

There remained one more way to resolve the conflict between taxpayers and the largest group of bondholders—those whose securities had been issued by the federal government. Suppose Congress were to liquidate its domestic debt by selling western land? Instead of demanding gold and silver from its customers, the federal land office would allow them to pay with war bonds. The territory Britain had ceded to its former colonies in the Treaty of Paris in 1783, which stretched all the way out to the Mississippi River, contained vastly more land than was needed to wipe out the government's entire domestic debt.

Free Americans of all ranks clutched at this painless (to them) method of redeeming the bonds like a life-ring. "The sale of Lands, may Collect our Domestic Securities," New Hampshire congressman Jonathan Blanchard affirmed in a typical statement.[39] In September 1785, when Congress imposed a $3 million requisition on the states, it tried to soften the blow by promising that future requisitions would be smaller. Why? Because Congress had just "passed an Ordinance for the survey and sale of the Western Territory of the United States" and "the proceeds thereof will be applied as a sinking fund, to extinguish the domestic debt."[40]

The plan to use the land office rather than taxation to liquidate the federal debt might have worked if the region to the west of the United States had been empty. It was not, of course. Native American diplomats managed to complicate Congress's plans to use their land to solve its problems—as amply illustrated by a crisis that erupted shortly after Congress adopted its land ordinance.

In the fall of 1785, U.S. newspapers reported some alarming news about Joseph Brant (also known as Thayendanegea), a warrior and diplomat of the Mohawk nation (one of the Six Nations of the Iroquois). Brant, readers learned, had just gotten back from London. It was not his first trip. During the Revolutionary War the Mohawks and most of the other Indians who lived anywhere near the rebel colonies, acutely aware that the rebels had designs on their land, had sided with the British. During a visit to London in the winter of 1775–76 Brant had helped forge the Anglo-Indian alliance.[41] For the imperial government the Native Americans proved to be very useful allies, taking terrible losses but holding their own in most of the western theater even as British generals surrendered their armies at Saratoga and Yorktown.[42] Then in the Paris peace conference of 1782 and 1783, Britain abandoned the Indians, ceding their land to the United States.

Even before news of the treaty arrived in America, some of the Indians who had allied with the British during the war had launched their own effort to halt the United States's westward advance. They announced that no matter what European diplomats decided, they would not permit American citizens to settle west of the Ohio River.

None of the native nations was naïve enough to think it could thwart American expansion singlehandedly. The Indians' only hope was to combine forces. Yet unity was easier to talk about than to achieve, given the long-standing animosity among—and within—the various Native American nations, phratries, and villages. Still, a series of diplomatic overtures in the last years of the Revolutionary War culminated in a large-scale gathering at the Wyandot town of Sandusky on Lake Erie in September 1783. The meeting attracted delegations from the Iroquois, Shawnees, Delawares, Wyandots, and the "Lake Indians" who lived along the Detroit River. Ominously for the United States, small groups of Creeks and Cherokees—southern nations with long histories of conflict against their northern hosts—also attended.[43] The diplomats' ability to build a pan-Indian confederacy capable of resisting U.S. encroachment would hinge upon the support they received from the British officers who had just deserted them. Like other Americans, the natives were unable to make war without European weapons and ammunition. Even more important, the promoters of the Native American coalition knew it was the rare Indian nation that would willingly submit to the leadership of any other. Yet the coalition needed a leader, and the only candidate that was both suitably well connected and sufficiently unthreatening was Great Britain.

Would London help the Indians? United States officials received a partial, and frightening, answer to that question on July 8, 1785, when two native headmen who had previously shown themselves willing to accommodate American demands, Guyasuta and his nephew Cornplanter, arrived in Pittsburgh and demanded a meeting with Colonel Josiah Harmar.[44] Born and raised a Quaker, Harmar had fought with distinction in the Revolutionary War and then succeeded George Washington at the head of the much-reduced U.S. army. At the July 1785 meeting, Harmar learned from Guyasuta and Cornplanter, whose Seneca nation was part of the Iroquois confederation, that Joseph Brant had spent the winter of 1784–85 in London. There he had made a remarkable discovery, one that undermined the very basis on which a small group of Iroquois leaders, including Cornplanter, had signed the October 1784 Fort Stanwix treaty—the agreement in which they ceded the area west of the Iroquois homeland in upstate New York to the United States. At the Stanwix conference (the same one where James Madison scouted out Iroquois land for future real estate speculation) the new nation's Indian commissioners had assured the Iroquois that British diplomats attending the Paris peace conference the previous year had consented to their former colonists' occupation of the Indians' land. But during his trip to London, Brant had learned that the American agents' assertion was false.

Brant's voyage to London was the reason for Guyasuta and Cornplanter's fall 1785 trip to Pittsburgh. They had come to renounce the Fort Stanwix land cession, and they ostentatiously handed over their copy of the treaty.[45]

Actually, British diplomats attending the 1783 Paris peace conference really had ceded the Indians' land to the United States. But the revelation that they had denied doing so in their meetings with Joseph Brant alarmed Harmar and other U.S. officers. They knew that even if Britain never came through with the backing that Brant had sailed home expecting, the native coalition builders' confident anticipation of British support would help them draw the more cautious Indian villages into their league. The news that "the celebrated and noted *Brant* had arrived from England" with British endorsement for the Indians' territorial claims appeared in newspapers from South Carolina to New Hampshire.[46] Small wonder, because almost every U.S. citizen, from the land speculator to the potential pioneer, wanted Indian land. Not to mention the widespread hope that land office revenue would permit a drastic reduction in taxes.

There was just one problem with the whole story of Joseph Brant's voyage to London in the winter of 1784–85. It was not true. He had made no such trip.[47]

Why did Guyasuta and Cornplanter say Brant had just returned from England? Maybe they were simply mistaken. Another possibility, however, is that someone in Iroquois country—perhaps Guyasuta and Cornplanter themselves—had deliberately invented the story of Brant's successful diplomatic mission in order to make British support for the Indians' anti–United States coalition seem stronger than it really was.[48]

If so, the Brant story was only one piece of a larger strategy on the part of the anti-American Indian confederates to create the illusion of British support. Another of their tactics was to communicate with each other using British government employees as messengers. Often the Indians could have gotten the messages to their destinations sooner using their own runners. In one case, for instance, a message from the Ohio Valley to the Niagara River seems to have been routed through Detroit—not exactly the most direct path. Apparently the reason Indian diplomats sometimes insisted upon using British messengers was to stamp their league with British fingerprints.[49]

The confederacy's effort to clothe itself in the appearance of British backing was aimed both at impressing Indians who had remained noncommittal, assessing the alliance's strength, and at intimidating the United States. It is not known whether any Indians fell for these ploys, but plenty of people in the United States did.[50] One reason the Native American diplomats' deception worked was that nearly everyone in the United States considered Indians incapable of constructing a powerful alliance without help. Ironically, however, the image of the Indians as British puppets was manufactured in part by the Indians themselves.

The same native diplomats also exaggerated the number of Indians who had joined their coalition.[51] Over the objections of cautious British Canadian officials, Joseph Brant once tried to arrange for deputies from the Seven Nations of Canada to attend an upcoming congress with the United States. British Indian agent John Johnson understood that Brant's purpose was to "give their Confederacy a greater Consequence at the intended Meeting."[52]

The U.S. Congress was acutely aware of the threat that Indian unity posed to American interests. In March 1784 a congressional committee chaired by Thomas Jefferson suggested that U.S. commissioners "treat with the several nations at different times and places" in order to "discourage every coalition and consultation which might tend to involve any one nation in the wars of the others." American Indian agents did their best to hew to that policy, holding one meeting with the Iroquois in 1784 and then additional sessions with two separate groups of westerners in 1785 and 1786.[53] "We are aware of your design to divide our Councils," Piteasewa, a Shawnee speaker, told American messengers in the fall of 1785. He insisted, however, that "we are unanimous."[54]

Actually, Piteasewa exaggerated the Indians' unity—as he well knew. But he and other native diplomats did a remarkably effective job of persuading the United States that they had unified. In mid-February 1787, on the eve of the Constitutional Convention, Levi Todd informed Virginia governor Edmund Randolph that he and other white westerners expected "as soon as the season permits, to experience the united efforts of all the neighbouring Indian Tribes."[55]

Of course in the end the Indians were unable to prevent white Americans, who massively outnumbered them, from seizing their land. But the native diplomats did manage to exert a significant impact on American politics. On May 20, 1785, Congress ordered Thomas Hutchins, the "Geographer of the United States," to begin surveying the region west of the Ohio River. Hutchins was instructed to mark off a neat array of ranges that he would then divide into townships and then plots. The resulting grid appears in nearly every American history textbook. It symbolizes the expansion of the new nation into the Old Northwest.[56] The reason for the neat lines is that Congress, in its determination to maximize its profits from the Indians' land, abandoned the old colonial system whereby well-connected people who wanted government land picked out their own tracts and paid little or nothing for them. Under the May 1785 ordinance, Indian land would be auctioned off to the highest bidder.

Almost all the textbooks that reprint the grid omit one essential fact. The famous 1785 land-grid ordinance did not actually result in the sale of a single acre of land. The reason was that Congress decreed that no land would be sold until seven ranges had been marked off and divided into townships, and Indians prevented the surveying team from completing those seven ranges.

This failure was not for lack of effort on the part of Hutchins and his crew of surveyors (one from each of the thirteen states). Hutchins even persuaded Captain Pipe, a Delaware headman who had previously collaborated with U.S. officials, to serve as an escort. The mere presence of Pipe and his band was expected to prevent the team from being attacked by the Indian "banditti"—a group of nativist renegades from the Six Nations (known as the Mingoes) and the Cherokees.[57]

No one attacked the surveying party. But soon after it began its work, in mid-October 1785, Pipe decided that the U.S. effort to survey the Indians' land was premature. Indeed, at the very moment Hutchins and his men were surveying the territory west of the Ohio River, another group of American officials was at Fort Finney on the Ohio trying to persuade headmen to come in to a treaty council and cede that very land. Pipe told Hutchins that "treating with them at one place and surveying their Lands in another lookd misterious and gave great cause for suspicion, and that he cou'd be no longer answerable for his safety, on which Capt. Hutchins very prudently retired to a place of greater security"—specifically, the east bank of the Ohio River.[58] Captain Pipe had brought the surveying process to a grinding halt.[59]

Hutchins's team made another attempt a year later, in the fall of 1786. By the end of September the men had started surveying the seventh range—the last one they needed to start selling land under the 1785 ordinance. But on October 1 they learned that they were in imminent danger. Indian warriors representing several nations had gathered at the Shawnee towns on the Mad River in present-day Ohio with the evident intention of attacking them.[60] News of the impending attack was conveyed to Hutchins by three men who dwelt on the cultural "middle ground," passing easily between U.S. settlements and various Native American societies. One was an American settler who had been captured by the Indians six years earlier and stayed on with them after the war; another was a European-American who had become a Wyandot sachem by marrying a woman of the tribe; and the third was a multiethnic fur trader.[61] It seems likely that native leaders had actually asked the three men to warn the surveyors off. For the vastly outnumbered

Indians, violence was most powerful when it was threatened but not used.

Although the immediate threat to the surveyors came from Chero-kee and Mingo banditti, the Indian diplomats who were trying to build a broad anti–United States coalition made it clear that they, too, ob-jected to the marking out of the seven ranges.[62] Like Joseph Brant's fab-ricated trip to London in the winter of 1784–85, the Indians' success at preventing the survey of their land in 1785 and 1786 alarmed both land speculators and would-be pioneers.[63] But the worst victim of the Indi-ans' success at hanging on to their land may have been the U.S. govern-ment itself. Congress faced a conundrum: the government hoped to relieve its poverty partly by selling Indian land, but it could not initiate land sales until it had conquered the Indians, and that required an army bigger than it could afford.

Congress was growing desperate. In April 1787 it repealed its two-year-old "Inhibition of any Sale 'till seven Ranges are compleatly Sur-veyed."[64] Even then federal officials were able to find customers for only a small portion of the land that Hutchins's team had surveyed: 108,000 acres, which brought in only $176,000 worth of war bonds.[65] The only major land sales of 1787 were to speculators—the very people the May 1785 ordinance had been designed to avoid. The land broker-age firms, the best known of which was the Ohio Company, paid one dollar per acre in government bonds—the minimum price the land had been expected to fetch at auction. Since the bonds had depreciated to one-eighth of their face value, and since the speculators were allowed to reduce the purchase price by up to one-third to allow for "bad land" and the cost of dividing their tracts into townships and lots, they ac-tually paid less than sixteen cents per acre.[66] The land sales scarcely dented the government's enormous war debt.

Congress opened the door to the land speculators in July 1787. That same month it also made two important concessions to the Indians. In the Northwest Ordinance it gave up its claim to have conquered the Indians' land and decreed that henceforth "their lands and prop-erty shall never be taken from them without their consent."[67] That was not all. Throughout the 1780s Congress had made a point of hold-ing as many separate Indian councils as it could afford—in order, as Thomas Jefferson said, to "discourage every coalition" of Indians. But in December 1786 a well-attended meeting of the Indian confederacy, held at Brownstown on the Detroit River, had demanded that the United States meet the entire coalition at once. On July 21, 1787, Secretary of War Knox informed Congress that its only options were capitulation and war—and that the country was "utterly unable to maintain an Indian war." Congress had no choice but to agree to a single meeting.[68]

The Indians' success at preventing the U.S. government from selling their land aggravated the financial crisis that had been gathering force ever since the Revolutionary War. Massachusetts congressman Nathan Dane was typical in placing the blame for the heavy Continental taxation of the postwar period squarely at the feet of the natives. "Had it not been for the hostile appearances in the Indians," he told the state assembly, "7,000,000 acres of the land belonging to the United States would now have been surveyed, and ready for sale."[69] If the Indians in the Old Northwest had been passive and insignificant, Congress might well have done what thousands of Americans had expected it to do: liquidate its domestic debts by selling western land. That would have resolved one of the fundamental internal conflicts that beset the United States during the 1780s: the controversy over how much money the state governments should extract from taxpayers for the benefit of bondholders. As it was, the battle over taxation raged on, and it threatened to tear the infant nation apart.

CHAPTER 9

"A MURMURING UNDERNEATH"

REBELLION

IN SEPTEMBER 1784 a deputy sheriff tried to hand Hezekiah Maham of South Carolina a writ ordering him to appear in court to answer his creditor's charges. Maham did not simply refuse the writ: he made the deputy eat it, graciously supplying him a beverage to wash it down.[1] Maham was by no means the only American who resisted the confiscation of his property during the 1780s. Like Maham, some of the debtors and taxpayers who defended themselves and their property during the 1780s acted alone. Others joined forces with fellow sufferers.

In what was probably the most common form of resistance, debtors often took sanctuary in their own homes; deputies were not allowed to force their way into houses to serve writs.[2] Others resisted violently. Today many Americans are familiar with Shays's Rebellion, the 1786 uprising of western Massachusetts farmers. But there were actually multiple revolts up and down the seaboard. For instance, a study of incomplete records in just three counties in the Virginia backcountry turned up 155 cases in which sheriffs and deputies who tried to seize property from delinquent debtors were "kept off by force of arms" during the mid-1780s.[3] The scuffles sometimes took a deadly turn. On September 14, 1785, a York County, Virginia, deputy sheriff impounded a horse belonging to a taxpayer named Roane. Roane "abused the sheriff, and swore he would have his horse again." As newspapers throughout the country reported, the sheriff turned and "shot him through the body, so that he died in about an hour afterwards."[4]

In about half the states groups of debtors and taxpayers assaulted the very symbol of government power in their community, the county court. Immediately after the New Jersey legislature refused to print paper money, "people in some parts of the state . . . began to nail up the Court-Houses" to prevent creditors' suits from going forward.[5] In Elizabethtown farmers planted a stake outside the local courthouse and impaled an effigy of Governor William Livingston, who had led the opposition to paper money.[6]

No one could say for sure who set fire to several Virginia courthouses in the 1780s—that was what made arson so attractive.[7] But when Lunenburg County records were burned in a fire that also destroyed the courthouse one night early in 1783, attorney general Edmund Randolph speculated that taxpayers were trying "to prevent the obtaining of those documents, which are necessary to execute the tax."[8] On the night of July 12, 1787, the financially troubled John Price Posey escaped the New Kent County prison and then rounded up three associates (two of them slaves named Sawney and Hercules), and the group burned down the jail and the county clerk's office. Posey was captured and hanged.[9]

It is remarkable that several white Virginians apparently burned public buildings in the mid-1780s, while hardly anyone in other states did. Why the difference? The fact that Posey enlisted Sawney and Hercules in his scheme may provide a clue. Slaves sometimes set fire to their owners' buildings, and even many natural fires were mistakenly attributed to them. Perhaps in Virginia, where nearly half of the population was African American—making Virginia the least free state in the union by 1800—debtors had been reminded of an effective tactic (one with deep roots in British soil, to be sure) by their enslaved neighbors.

Deputies who tried to confiscate delinquent debtors' and taxpayers' cattle, furniture, and other belongings frequently encountered collective resistance. In Berks County, Pennsylvania, in 1780, more than seventy-five men signed an association agreeing to defend one another's property from the sheriff.[10] Two Delaware tax collectors noted "a disposition in too many to throw every difficulty" upon them.[11] On April 6, 1786, a crowd in Washington County, Pennsylvania, seized a tax collector and "cut off one half of his hair, cued the other half on one side of his Head, cut off the Cock of his Hat, and made him wear it in a form to render his Cue the most Conspicuous."[12]

Even when debtors or taxpayers were unable to prevent their property from being seized, they could sometimes thwart government officials' efforts to sell it. In January 1785 William Grayson, a lawyer in Prince William County, Virginia, told Governor Patrick Henry that the local sheriff had made "fifty distresses"—attempts to auction off taxpayers' property—"at one time without effect, as no person would attend to purchase, least in the next instance it might be his fate."[13] Often the people of an area agreed not to bid on confiscated property, and anyone who refused to sign the pledge risked retaliation. A York County, Pennsylvania, crowd of at least two hundred stopped a sheriff's auction, prompting the sheriff to deputize ten men, whom the crowd "pretty severely handled." The members of the defeated government posse went home and armed themselves with pistols and swords.[14]

Farmers in Mendham Township, New Jersey, were angry at the state government for aggressively collecting from taxpayers while withholding the money it owed them. So they decided to "rise in opposition to authority by refusing to pay their taxes."[15] On New Year's Day 1785, outside a tavern called the Black Horse, "an attempt was made by a constable to sell some property at vendue [auction] which he had distrained [seized] for taxes," Joseph Lewis wrote in his diary. "But a party (who had previously prepared clubs &c.) would not suffer anyone to make a bid for the articles set up or exposed to sale."[16] New Jersey tax resistance did not end there. In 1787, when the assembly voted to comply with congressional requisitions by levying an excise tax, protest meetings were held throughout the state. In several counties taxpayers formed groups that pitched in to purchase the office of excise collector—all with the express purpose of not making anyone pay.[17]

Anxious witnesses often emphasized that agrarian insurrections were not isolated but widespread. Reporting to George Washington on the disturbances in New England, Henry Lee, Jr., warned that "the temper of the eastern people . . . is not confined to one state or to one part of a state, but pervades the whole."[18] North Hampton, New Hampshire, pastor Benjamin Thurston likewise fretted in 1786 that there had been "clamours and insurrections by so large a number of people in some of the states."[19] Connecticut lawyer David Daggett went further, asserting that heavy taxation had fueled "contentions and civil discord in almost every state in the union."[20] Dispatches from southern states confirmed this assessment. Benjamin Hawkins, a former North Carolina congressman who passed through South Carolina in the summer of 1785, reported that "in many parts of the State," the "Collection of Taxes . . . have been impeded . . . by the disorderly behaviour of some of the Citizens."[21] Hugh Williamson, another North Carolinian, noted that debtors had created "riots and combinations" not just here and there but "in many places."[22]

Even in Virginia, which had once had a reputation for social peace, "a tendency to Insurrection" manifested itself in several "quarters of the state," observed James McClurg, a Virginia delegate to the federal convention.[23] Another of Virginia's deputies, Governor Edmund Randolph, wrote his lieutenant governor from Philadelphia asking not only about Adonijah Mathews's rebellion in Greenbrier County but about rumors of "commotions . . . rising in some other important counties." Scarcely two months later a group of Henrico County petitioners claimed that "Riots" had "prevailed in many parts of the State."[24]

The spirit of rebellion was described as not only pervasive but growing. A Pennsylvania official reported on delinquent taxpayers' well-organized resistance to property confiscation and added, "This disorder I am nearly warranted to say is become epidemic."[25] The notion of rebellion as an "epidemical" contagion was especially common in reports on Shays's Rebellion.[26] When a group in Preston, Connecticut, was accused of trying to abet the Massachusetts insurgency, a *Middlesex Gazette* writer declared, " 'Tis by no means to be wondered at, that such an infection should take effect in this state, when many designing men stand ready to innoculate all who do not catch the distemper the natural way."[27] Virginia congressman Edward Carrington wondered "how far the contagion of the Eastern disorders will spread."[28] Others agreed with Alexander Hamilton that Shays's Rebellion seemed to "spread like wild fire."[29]

In two states farmers who blamed their problems on the state government pressed their demands by surrounding the legislature. On June 21, 1783, Pennsylvania troops, angry at being discharged without receiving their long-overdue pay, laid siege to the statehouse—the future Constitution Hall—in hopes of forcing the executive council to redress their grievances. Not only did the council refuse to consider the soldiers' demands, but Washington—who had used kind words to defuse the Newburgh officers' conspiracy just two months earlier—sent troops. Congress, which had held its sessions in the Pennsylvania statehouse ever since 1775, was so alarmed at the siege that it left town, not to return until 1790.[30]

Three years later, on September 20, 1786, about two hundred New Hampshire farmers who had been attending a protest convention demanding paper money marched to Exeter, where the legislature was meeting, to try to force assemblymen to comply with their demand. They surrounded the assembly building for several hours. The crowd, viewing itself as the continuation of the convention, had decided "to demand an answer in 1/2 an hour to a petition which they had before sent for an emission of paper money," as the preacher and historian Jeremy Belknap reported.[31]

Although these were the only cases where farmers marched to the state capital, more than one rebellion that seemed on the surface like a strictly local affair actually had a larger dimension. In the late summer and fall of 1786 Massachusetts farmers managed to close four of the state's county courts. Since Massachusetts courts seized property on behalf of creditors, not tax collectors (who could go straight to the sheriff), the assaults on the courts are typically ascribed to debtors, not taxpayers. Actually, the men who shut down the courts sought much more than a suspension of creditors' suits. George Richards Minot, the clerk of the state house of representatives and an opponent of the rebellion, recognized that the farmers had attacked the courts in order to "force the General Court into measures repugnant to every idea of justice."[32] William Whiting expected the farmers to "continue the present measures no longer then untill Such alterations Shall be made in the administration of Government as Shall Render the Same Tolerable."[33] The rebels themselves ratified this assessment, the Greenwich town meeting describing the closing of the courts as "the only means to Convence [the legislature] that We Need Redress."[34] In other states, too, farmers who attacked courts made it clear that they were seeking not only immediate relief from their creditors but changes in legislative policy.

The most organized rebellions of the 1780s were attempts to threaten violence without actually using it. When a "few old Continental officers" aimed a cannon at the New Hampshire farmers who had surrounded the state legislature to demand paper money, they went "scampering over the fences" without firing a shot, Jeremy Belknap reported.[35] Belknap and other critics of the rebellion delighted in re-counting this apparent act of cowardice, but the protesters appear to have been nearly as averse to shooting at government forces as they were to being shot at.[36]

The New Hampshire authorities were somewhat rare in calling the farmers' bluff, and Americans seeking tax and debt relief often found that threats of rebellion could be tremendously effective. "Lett the gentellmen of Boston [know] that we Countray men will not pay taxes, as the[y] think," a group of western Massachusetts farmers warned Governor Bowdoin during Shays's Rebellion. "Lett them send the Con-stubel to here and well Nock him Down for ofering to Come Near us."[37] Meanwhile, "in some of the low counties" of Virginia, John Dawson, a member of the House of Delegates, reported in April 1787, people were talking "boldly of following the example of the insurgents in Massachu-setts and preventing the courts proceeding to business."[38] Pittsylvania County, Virginia, petitioners cautioned state assemblymen that if heavy taxes drove them into the "Gulf" of tenancy, their "giting out again" might involve "a great Deal of [blood] Shed."[39] In September 1783 the man bringing the sheriff of Hampshire County, Virginia, official notice that he was about to be sued for overdue taxes turned back after being told "that if he went into that hilly County of Hampshire on that Er-rand he surely would be scalped."[40]

On occasion Americans who used threats of violence to obtain tax and debt relief encountered public officials who were willing to employ threats of their own. The result was often an intricate dance of mutual intimidation. One noteworthy example was the April 27, 1785, court riot in Camden County, South Carolina. Neither the farmers who tried to close the district court that Wednesday nor Judge John F. Grimké, who was determined to keep it open, placed much faith in persuasion. On the other hand, neither wanted to resort to force. Thus the judge was armed only with the threat of arrest, and the crowd could only threaten violence. April 27 unfolded as an exchange not of bullets or blows but of feints and bluffs, expressed not only verbally but through body language.

It all began when more than a thousand farmers surrounded the courthouse, and many went inside. As Judge Grimké worked his way through the criminal docket, which came before the debt cases, a man named Hill stood up and began reading off the names of the men who had been called to jury duty. His "Intention" was obvious, Grimké said: "intimidating the Jury from appearing" to hear debt suits. Hill had found a worthy adversary in Judge Grimké, himself no stranger to the art of intimidation. One difference, however, was that Grimké was more subtle about it. He knew how to transmit volumes of information simply by adjusting his position or the tone of his voice. When Hill refused to desist from calling out the jurors' names, the judge, intentionally speaking loud enough for Hill to overhear him, instructed the sheriff to arrest him. But (as Grimké later reported) Hill "was so far from being intimidated that he proceeded leisurely in calling over the list of names as before."[41]

Grimké's voice not having had the desired effect, he tried speaking a still more dramatic body language. He arose from the bench in order to, as he said, "prevent others from supporting [Hill] as they would be more immediately under my own Eye." Also, for the first time, Grimké spoke to Hill directly, "hoping that it would daunt" him. Instead, the judge later reported, Hill "replied to me tauntingly that it was [']not many words that would fill a bushell.'" Like Hill, his associates, who by this time were "surrounding him" to guard him, showed no sign of "relinquishing their stand as I reasonably expected," Grimké observed. So the judge asked the grand jury to help him arrest Hill. Once again his words were designed to be overheard. He made a point of addressing the grand jurors in "so sudden and decisive a manner" as to "have operated on Hill and his party so strongly as to have caused them to have abandoned so impudent an attempt."[42]

"I was again mistaken," the judge later reported. So in an effort to show that his threat to lead the grand jurors against Hill's party was serious, Grimké again resorted to body language. He "suddenly descended from the Bench and invited [the jurors] to assist me." Finally Hill and his associates withdrew, but not without accomplishing their goal. Grimké learned the next day that "the Persons who had assembled for the purpose of serving in the Capacity of Jurors . . . had quitted the Town with precipitancy and apprehension." The judge finished his criminal docket and went home without trying a single debtor.[43]

Grandiose, explicit threats like those made by the Camden rioters— and by the officers at Newburgh—were not common, for Americans recognized that they could often influence public officials with avowedly friendly warnings. In cautioning legislators to abandon their harsh fiscal and monetary policies, two writers, one in Connecticut and the other in Virginia, used the same words. Farmers, both warned, were "ripe for a revolt."[44] Not long after Adonijah Mathews and his neighbors plotted to close the Greenbrier County, Virginia, court, Patrick Henry predicted that other Virginia farmers would also resort to "rebellion if they are driven to despair."[45] Throughout the country writers predicting dire consequences of the state legislatures' harsh fiscal and monetary measures chose variants of the same word, warning of "a popular murmur," "murmurs and dissensions," "encreasing murmurs," and "universal Murmurings among the People."[46]

When Shays's Rebellion broke out in Massachusetts, relief advocates in other states quickly recognized it as a godsend. "Look to the northward," Colonel Thomas Seymour told his colleagues in the Connecticut legislature shortly after the Massachusetts Regulators were suppressed, "see the tumults; see the horrors of civil war. What occasioned these tumults?" The obvious answer was heavy taxation.[47] Months earlier, Alexander Gillon had reviewed recent events in Massachusetts for the South Carolina House of Representatives and then declared, "Behold the effects . . . of not timely listening to the complaints of their citizens! With arms in their hands now perhaps fighting for what our citizens now peaceably ask; that is, time to pay their debts."[48]

Insurrectionary threats and warnings were such powerful political tools that they were sometimes appropriated by people who were not desperate farmers. Legislators even received warnings from the opponents of relief. "A Friend to Justice" told New Jersey assemblymen that if they chose to redeem the state's depreciated wartime paper currency (much of which had been bought up by speculators) below its face value, "they must expect the people will become clamorous."[49]

Of course Americans with grievances had rebelled and warned of rebellions by others on numerous occasions before the 1780s. But things were supposed to be different now. Government was supposedly in the hands of the people. When Americans seeking debt and tax relief employed the tried-and-true strategies of rebelling and issuing threats and warnings, they revealed their conviction that the Revolution had failed to bring about the fundamental changes they had anticipated and desperately desired. Far from agreeing with the Framers that the thirteen state governments suffered from an excess of democracy, a large segment of American society considered the states insufficiently attentive to the will of the majority.

The rebellions, threats, and warnings of the Confederation era were remarkably successful at bringing about debt and tax relief. Faced with massive grassroots resistance, tax collectors, sheriffs charged with repossessing property, judges, jurors, and other government officials throughout the thirteen states deliberately neglected their duties.

The public servants who put the greatest effort into not doing their jobs were those with the heaviest burden to impose: tax collectors. The squeamishness of the southeastern Massachusetts officials who cracked down on taxpayers only after feeling the heat from bondholder Nicholas Brown was by no means unique. After farmers in York County, Pennsylvania, thwarted collectors' efforts to sell property confiscated from delinquent taxpayers—twice crowds reclaimed the delinquents' cows even as they were being auctioned off—a tax commissioner in neighboring Dauphin County stated that he and his colleagues had suspended rigorous tax collection out of fear that it "might possibly occasion Commotions similar to those which lately happened in York County."[50]

Debtors and taxpayers also won the sympathy of judges. John Nicholson, Pennsylvania's chief financial officer, complained that the state's justices had managed to "impede and protract the payment of the taxes."[51] Pennsylvania was one of the few states where judges had a hand in the tax collection process, but courts in every state were able to screen delinquent debtors. In Maryland a newspaper essayist observed on June 6, 1786, that "our courts, the sacred dispensers of justice," had been "under the dreadful necessity of delaying it" in order to avoid violence.[52]

Often state legislators proved no more immune than local officials to pressure for tax and debt relief.[53] Shortly after farmers in Greenbrier County, Virginia, rebelled against the certificate tax, the House of Delegates repealed it. The certificates would still be called in, but through a tariff on foreign merchandise imported into the state.[54] In

New Jersey the statewide campaign against the 1787 excise act forced the legislature to repeal it.[55] While serving in the Virginia House of Delegates in the fall of 1786, James Madison proposed an "Assize" bill that would have replaced the state's amateur county judges with full-time professionals who could be counted on to process creditors' claims against debtors quickly. Worried that "the bill for accelerating Justice would . . . endanger the public repose," the delegates defeated it.[56] The threat of rebellion also played a crucial role in Connecticut's decision to snub Congress by officially announcing its inability to pay its quota of the September 1785 requisition. It was, Alexander Hamilton observed at the Constitutional Convention, "in order to prevent those turbulent scenes which had appeared elsewhere"—most notably in Massachusetts—that Connecticut assemblymen did not "dare impose & collect a [Continental] tax on the people."[57] William Grayson, a member of Congress from Virginia, also believed that "Connecticut would have been in the situation of Massachusetts if she had passed the requisition."[58]

One state where the connection between fear and relief was especially clear was South Carolina, where the April 1785 Camden Riot was only the beginning of a wave of activism. During the subsequent spring and summer debtors and taxpayers throughout the state protected their property with a massive campaign of "knocking down of sheriffs."[59] "Americanus" emphasized that the reason backcountry property seizures had ceased was "not by the neglect of duty, or favour in the sheriff's officers, but from a dread they stand in of their lives in attempting to serve a writ beyond such a distance from the city" of Charleston.[60] One reason officials backed down was that they feared that conflict among whites might provide an opening to the enslaved half of the population. Even the Camden rebels shared this concern. In the midst of their effort to shut down the civil court, they "professed an anxious Desire of supporting the Criminal Department."[61]

A remarkable number of South Carolinians described what they were hearing from ordinary farmers using the same word that was applied to restless citizens in other states: "murmuring." Aedanus Burke warned of "hidden combustibles, like fires in a volcano, which . . . produce a murmuring underneath, like the affair at Camden, and end in a convulsion."[62]

In September Governor William Moultrie called the legislature into special session to confront the crisis. In his opening speech the governor pointed out that "civil Process" had been "confined to a small part of the State" (Charleston).[63] Everyone agreed on what *not* to do. There was no thought of trying to carry out court orders in the backcountry. Not even "5000 troops . . . could enforce obedience to the [Court of] Common Pleas," Burke said.[64] On the contrary, James Madison expected the legislature to "legalize a suspension of Judicial proceedings which has been already effected by popular combinations."[65] He was right. The assembly voted to print paper money and to close the courts until the new notes could be put into circulation. Three months later, when some legislators, harboring second thoughts about the paper currency, asked the assembly to reconsider the emission, Charleston attorney and planter Edward Rutledge, a signer of the Declaration of Independence, urged his colleagues not "to trifle with the people." Rutledge's warning was heeded, and the money was printed.[66]

The link between rebellion and relief was also clear in Massachusetts. In the fall of 1786, after western and southeastern farmers began closing county courts, Governor Bowdoin did what the governor of South Carolina had done a year earlier: he called the assembly into special session. The same legislators who had adopted the punishing taxes that provoked the rebellion—and who had voted down several relief measures during the spring and summer—now granted farmers a broad range of tax and debt relief. They postponed their earlier order seizing the property of sheriffs who refused to "execute" the estates of delinquent tax collectors. "From a consideration of the present burthens of the people," the legislature also decided to delay consideration of Congress's most recent requisition and acceded to farmers' demands that they be permitted to pay some levies with produce and that tax deadlines be postponed.[67]

On the other hand, the fall 1786 assembly session also endorsed Bowdoin's violent suppression of the rebellion. In January Bowdoin decided to create a special 4,400-man army to crush the revolt. Even Harvard students got into the act, forming their own company of Independent Cadets.[68] The easterners' decision to crack down on the Regulators ended up producing still more relief for debtors and taxpayers. By suspending habeas corpus, dispatching an army to suppress the revolt, and ultimately executing two rebels, the government of Massachusetts infuriated numerous citizens who had opposed the insurrection.[69]

One indication of the altered climate was the rapid circulation of a pair of ghost stories. On January 25, 1787, state troops under Colonel William Shepard repelled a rebel assault on the federal arsenal at Springfield using cannon and musket fire. Two eerie anecdotes about the battle made it into the diary of Joseph Lee, a Concord doctor. "It is afarmed to me by Joseph Baggon that Mr Edward Weber of South Brimfield Informed him the blood was fresh and without Clots that Ran from the wounds of those men that was slain by Coll Shepard at Springfield a weeke after [they] were killed," Lee wrote.[70] Nor was this all. The night after the attack "a compain[y] of men were seen by the guard and other[s] for some time March[ing] on the snow." The witnesses did not merely see the ghost soldiers, for Jones noted that their "Drums and fifes were he[a]rd." The frightened "Guards fired on them severall times," Lee reported, but without effect.[71]

In the May 1787 elections the Massachusetts town meetings replaced two-thirds of the assemblymen and soundly defeated Governor Bowdoin. The farmers had not suddenly turned against the government during the winter of 1787. The legislature had already provoked their ire the previous spring by levying unprecedented taxes. What made the April–May 1787 elections different from those held a year earlier was that by that time, anger at the government was such a common topic of conversation that farmers became convinced that like-minded individuals throughout the state were going to show up at their town meetings determined to replace the assembly majority. This conviction became circular, as the belief that voter turnout was going to be unusually high persuaded Massachusetts citizens to vote in record numbers.[72]

Although the members of the Constitutional Convention complained over and over again about the indulgence that debtors and taxpayers had received from assemblymen and local officials, they very rarely blamed these relief measures on farmers' insurrections and threats. Why? One reason was that the targets of insurgency tended to downplay its influence on their actions. This process was especially evident during Shays's Rebellion. A widely circulated account of the closing of the Bristol County court of common pleas on September 12, 1786, asserted that when the justices elected not to try any cases, they "were not influenced in their adjournment, by any threats of the insurgents" outside the courthouse—although there were approximately four hundred of them.[73] Two weeks later, when the superior court justices who were supposed to try cases in Springfield chose not to do so, witnesses insisted that it was not "fear of the rioters" that had forced the adjournment but simply "the noise and tumult that pervaded every part of the town."[74]

The same pattern of denial also prevailed in other states. On December 12, 1786, when Windham County, Connecticut, justice William Williams decided not to hear any cases, one reason he gave was that in Massachusetts excessive pressure on farmers had produced "a scene of *blood* and *carnage*" that he did not wish to see repeated in his own state. But in later accounts of his decision Williams omitted this concern, mentioning only a recent blizzard and his sympathy for the farmers' distress.[75]

Why did officials deny being influenced by fear? Some worried that admitting to caving in to violence and intimidation would encourage further rebellion. Thus one of the government officers' primary motives for concealing their fear was fear itself.[76] Another reason to deny being afraid was simple masculine pride. The targets of the insurgents may have been motivated by another sort of pride as well. Most public officials—even those who thought the Revolution had gone too far—were proud of having turned the thirteen colonies into republics. They did not want to believe they had simply replaced British imperial officials in the saddle.

The rebellions, threats, and warnings of the postwar years cast light on the origins of the Constitution. It seems natural to ascribe the drafting of such founding documents to "great men." Granted, very few of the delegates who deliberated in the Pennsylvania statehouse from May through September 1787 were common farmers. But ordinary Americans did influence the Constitution indirectly. During the 1780s relief advocates, the great majority of them farmers, frequently launched uprisings or warned that other people were about to revolt. The gentry class was frightened and infuriated, and one reason the Founding Fathers favored the Constitution was that it would, for the first time, give the federal government the funds it needed to field an army capable of suppressing farmers' rebellions. That is what the Framers were talking about when they stated in the preamble to the Constitution that one of their goals was "to ensure domestic tranquility."

But the agrarian insurrections of the 1780s actually influenced the adoption of the Constitution even more powerfully in an indirect way. Insurgents extorted substantial tax and debt relief from reluctant state legislatures, and overturning this legislation became one of the principal reasons the Constitution was written. What set men like Madison and Hamilton on the road to Philadelphia was not so much the farmers' revolts in themselves but the legislative indulgence that rebels managed to extract from public officials. Yes, the new national government would ensure domestic tranquillity. But it would also accomplish another goal announced in the preamble; it would, by abolishing relief, "establish justice" for government bondholders as well as private creditors.

Several Americans who witnessed the insurrections of the 1780s dedicated considerable thought to how they had influenced the nation's political life. For Edmund Randolph, who served as governor of Virginia during the mid-1780s, tax and debt relief resulted from a complex interaction between democracy and rebellion. In his opening speech at the federal convention, the one in which he presented the plan that served as the basis for the Constitution, Randolph drew the delegates' attention to Maryland, which had the nation's least democratic upper house. Maryland senators had the longest terms in the country—five years— and they received their appointments not from the people themselves but from special electors who had been chosen by the voters. Yes, Maryland had a "powerful senate," Randolph said, "but the late distractions in that State, have discovered that it is not powerful enough."[77] Randolph was referring to Maryland debtors' and taxpayers' numerous successes at preventing the confiscation of their property and especially to the violent closure of the Charles County court. Randolph did not say how a less democratic senate would have prevented these rebellions, but we may follow his logic to its natural conclusion. Suppose instead of a senate, Maryland had had a hereditary House of Lords. Liberated from the fear of being turned out of office, members of the upper house would have been able to stand firm in the face of agrarian revolt, thwarting the House of Delegates' proposals to redress the rebels' grievances and possibly even forcing the lower house (say, by holding up legislative salary appropriations) to send in the militia. Farmers, knowing all this, would have seen no purpose in launching rebellions. Of course, Randolph was not arguing for a Maryland House of Lords. He was simply saying that the democratic constraints under which Maryland senators operated, feeble though they were, had encouraged the state's farmers to rebel.

Another federal convention delegate, Elbridge Gerry, made a similar point later in the summer. He reminded his colleagues that in the spring 1787 elections both John Sullivan, the president of New Hampshire, and James Bowdoin, the governor of Massachusetts, had forfeited the voters' support by sending troops to put down farmers' rebellions. (Bowdoin was defeated; Sullivan placed second and managed to retain his position only because no candidate received a majority and the election was thrown into the legislature.) Gerry warned that at the national level, too, a popularly elected president who suppressed a rebellion would risk being "turned out for it like Govr Bowdoin in Massts & President Sullivan in N. Hamshire."[78] And if farmers nationwide obtained what citizens in Massachusetts and New Hampshire already had—the ability to turn out any chief executive who inflicted harsh punishment on rioters—they, too, would feel little compunction about rebelling.

Thus the opponents of the rebellions thought they had been caused in part by the excessive democracy in the thirteen states. What did the rebels themselves think? Many seem to have been interested less in whether the existence of formally democratic elections increased the likelihood of insurrection than in the possibility that the current of influence could run in the other direction. They believed that sometimes a rebellion could lead to a truly democratic election.

In the fall of 1786, after crowds in western and southeastern Massachusetts began shutting down county courts, numerous town meetings and county conventions resolved that the courts should remain closed only until the next session of the legislature. The plan was to hold the courts hostage in hopes the assembly would ransom them by granting debt and tax relief. Other Massachusetts insurgents, however, made a different demand. They wanted the courts to stay closed until after the April–May 1787 elections.[79] What made them think the 1787 canvass would come out any better than the one the previous spring?

The only possible answer was the rebellion itself. Farmers in western and southeastern Massachusetts recognized that closing their courts was going to attract an enormous amount of attention to their cause. This publicity might convince citizens throughout the state that a serious movement to redress grievances was afoot. If that happened, farmers would turn out to vote in record numbers. Thus closing the courts in the fall of 1786 would turn the formally democratic election process scheduled for the following spring into a genuine expression of the public will. The result would be a new governor and a new legislature.

Many of the people targeted by the agrarian insurrections of the 1780s believed they would not have occurred if the rebels' passions had not been excited by essayists and politicians who denounced oppression and demanded relief. Thus revolts sometimes led to crackdowns on relief advocates.

Such was the case in Massachusetts in 1786 and 1787. Both William Whiting, the Berkshire County judge who sympathized with the Regulators, and Moses Harvey, a state representative from Montague who endorsed their allegations, were convicted of seditious libel. And both were fined.[80] Another important voice in the Massachusetts backcountry was also silenced in the wake of Shays's Rebellion. Although John Russell and Gad Stebbins, the editors of the Springfield *Hampshire Herald*, criticized their fellow westerners for closing county courts, they had previously demonstrated profound sympathy for the farmers' grievances. It was in the pages of the *Hampshire Herald* that the essay urging the legislature to divert the tariff revenue away from the state bondholders—a scheme that would have allowed the state to reduce the direct taxes it levied on farmers—first appeared. Sometimes prorelief essays occupied the entire front page of the paper and were introduced by editors' notes urging the reader's favorable consideration.

Russell and Stebbins sometimes printed antirelief essays as well, but these were often preceded by disclaimers saying they had been printed only at the insistence of some gentleman from Boston. It was the opposite of what happened when prorelief essays from the *Hampshire Herald* were reprinted elsewhere.

On September 6, 1786, a new publication appeared in western Massachusetts. The *Hampshire Gazette* was printed each week in Northampton. "Its mission," the town's historian would note more than a century later, "was to oppose the malcontents."[81] Apparently the backers of the *Gazette* believed that the *Hampshire Herald* had helped foment Shays's Rebellion by legitimating farmers' grievances and publishing their proposals. It is possible that the enemies of the *Hampshire Herald* intended only to offer western farmers an alternative. What is certain is that they achieved more than that. Western Massachusetts was not big enough for two newspapers. Although the *Hampshire Herald* was two years older than the upstart *Hampshire Gazette*, somehow it was not able to compete. On September 26, 1786, its last issue appeared. In a note to readers Russell and Stebbins expressed regret at having to terminate the venture "at a time, when our country calls for every exertion from her real friends." Defiant to the last, the two asserted that it was "the laws of the government"—economic mismanagement by Bowdoin and the General Court—that had, "in a great measure, driven us to this disagreeable alternative."[82]

After the disappearance of the *Hampshire Herald*, items reprinted from the other Massachusetts newspapers, nearly all of them hostile to the Regulators, became most Americans' only sources of information on the revolt. These accounts often contained distortions. Initial reports of the suicide of Bristol County deputy sheriff Eleazar Burr attributed it to his despair at losing the fees he had collected for seizing property from delinquent taxpayers and debtors—a source of income that had dried up as Shays's Rebellion got under way. Apparently some newspaper editors thought this version of the story played into the Regulators' claim that local officials were living off the fees they extorted from debtors caught up in the legal system. Thus some accounts of Burr's suicide omitted the fact that he had been a deputy sheriff, leaving the impression that the source of his distress was the same economic downturn that weighed so heavily on everyone else.[83]

CHAPTER 10

"EXCESS OF DEMOCRACY"?

REFORM

AMERICANS WHO BELIEVED the state legislatures were asking too much from the public had something in common with those who found them too lenient. Each group judged the tree by its fruit, concluding that state assemblymen rejected its program because they had fallen under the influence of its antagonists. Thus each side's dissatisfaction with the state government's economic policies evolved into a critique of the government itself.

During the 1780s citizens who favored heavy taxation and strict monetary policies grew increasingly frustrated with lawmakers and local officers. Many continued to ascribe relief to public officials' fear of rebellion, but over the course of the decade a new orthodoxy began to emerge. With growing conviction, elite Americans contended that the real reason the states so often caved in to taxpayers' and debtors' demands was that they were too responsive to the whims of the voter. New Jersey governor William Livingston was speaking for an entire segment of American society when he decried the tendency of popularly elected legislators to yield to popular demands for relief, betraying a "passion" for getting themselves reelected "per fas & nefas"—by fair means or foul.[1] In his diary Timothy Ford expressed little surprise that South Carolina representatives had allowed debtors to foist worthless pineland on their creditors; "such is the nature of a republican government!"[2] When a group of Connecticut assemblymen proposed that citizens be allowed to pay their debts with property instead of gold and silver, one of their colleagues, Charles Phelps, contended that "the people in this state are not so much crouded with suits and executions now as they were in the year 1774," on the eve of the Revolution. But back then no one had demanded a property tender law. Why the difference? Was it not "the inconstancy of republican governments"? he asked.[3] One signal advantage of ascribing relief to public officials' fear of the voters rather than to their anxiety about agrarian rebellion was that while insurrections seemed nearly impossible to prevent, it would be relatively easy to make government institutions less responsive to popular whimsy. With increasing vehemence, the opponents of relief demanded precisely that transformation.

Meanwhile other Americans were imagining a very different sort of change. They insisted that public officials must protect the powerless. "Surely, it is the highest duty of the Legislature to attend to the distresses of the middling and lower rank of the people, as the most numerous part of the individuals, forming the community at large, more than to the superfluous wants of the rich," a South Carolina essayist declared in September 1785.[4] A New Jersey writer told state assemblymen it was their "business to help the feeble against the mighty, and deliver the oppressed out of the hands of the oppress[or]."[5]

Americans also had other reasons to believe their state governments suffered from either a glut or a shortage of democracy. Even as some citizens blamed the state representatives' excessive accountability for the wave of revolts that swept over the new nation in the 1780s, others put forward precisely the opposite claim, contending that the real reason so many farmers had rebelled was that they were unable to obtain redress at the polls. Herman Husband, the Bedford County, Pennsylvania, millennialist, predicted that insurgency would vanish once the government was fully democratized. If "regular Channels [were] opened to convey all Grievances and Complaints from their first Rise and Fountains," he wrote, "then they would scarcely if ever overflow or rise up into Inundations of Mobs and Insurrections."[6]

For many prominent Americans, what was most troubling about the rising tide of democratic aspiration was that it had spread beyond white men. Enslaved Americans did not need to learn the value of freedom from their Patriot owners—if anything, that lesson traveled in the other direction—but the Revolution did advance the antislavery cause.[7] Once slaveholding colonists started describing British taxation-without-representation as "slavery," slaves and their supporters were able to add hypocrisy to their bill of complaint. By the early nineteenth century every state north of the Mason-Dixon line had either abolished slavery or put it on the road to extinction. Many of the newly emancipated African Americans joined propertyless white men in demanding the right to vote. In 1780 the Cuffee brothers of Dartmouth, Massachusetts, protested their disenfranchisement by withholding their taxes.[8]

Revolutionary ideology also led many women to question their subjugation. Even under British rule female colonists had occasionally ridiculed their husbands' pose as "the Lords of Creation." When male Patriots asserted themselves against the mother country, these complaints multiplied.[9] Abigail Adams was not alone in wishing male lawmakers would "Remember the Ladies."[10] A tiny but growing number of brides even objected to having to vow obedience to their husbands.[11] Most remarkably, several men as well as women pointed out that in not allowing female citizens who owned property and paid taxes to vote, men violated the principle of no taxation without representation.[12]

Thus some Americans sought greater democratization for a host of practical reasons, while others had just as many motives for wishing to propel the country in the other direction. This clash reflected a fundamental philosophical difference. In the years following the Declaration of Independence a growing number of citizens embraced the slogan "VOX POPULI VOX DEI"—"the voice of the people is the voice of God."[13] State representatives, they claimed, were not trustees (who should be left alone between elections) but mere "substitutes and agents."[14] One reason ordinary freeholders increasingly claimed the right to govern the nation was that more and more of them became convinced that they were capable of doing it well. "Let us have a set of Farmers to serve us," a group in Bedford County, Pennsylvania, insisted in an election notice posted throughout the county in 1783, "and no doubt but we shall be honestly represented."[15] One Bedfordman, Herman Husband, found a typically outlandish way to express this new faith in the capacities of ordinary Americans. If Jesus of Nazareth's fate had been determined by majority vote, he claimed, he would not have been crucified. Instead his countrymen "would have elected our Saviour" to some "high Office."[16]

The segment of American society that seems to have gained the most self-confidence during the Revolutionary War was free women. Thousands of females became heads of households when their husbands' military, political, and diplomatic duties kept them away from home for long periods. Although most found the experience frustrating, many became convinced that they could succeed in what had been a man's world. Both Mary Bartlett, the wife of a signer of the Declaration of Independence, and Abigail Adams initially referred, in letters to their husbands, to "your" farm but ended up calling it "ours."[17]

As American farmers' "self-confident assurance" grew, they showed less and less deference toward the upper ranks of American society, and both trends troubled the gentry.[18] "Our states cannot be well governed," Noah Webster warned, "till our old influential characters acquire confidence and authority."[19] In a skeptic's imaginary description of a farmers' protest convention, one delegate offers a motion, another seconds it, and a third man jumps up and says, "I third the motion."[20] In the spring of 1787, when a Connecticut writer suggested that Daniel Shays, like George Washington, might have been sent by God, "Brutus" replied that ordinary Americans should "be content with the station God has assigned them, and not turn politicians when their maker intended them for farmers."[21] "I dread more from the licentiousness of the people, than from the bad government of rulers," Virginia congressman Henry Lee, Jr., told the state ratifying convention. (It was not revealed until much later that Congressman Lee had sold his vote to the Spanish government for $5,000.)[22]

What was it that had bolstered the ordinary freeman's self-esteem and sharpened his suspicion of his leaders? For the nation's most prominent citizens, the obvious answer was the Revolutionary War. "Men of sense and property have lost much of their influence by the popular spirit of the war," one New Englander declared in the fall of 1786.[23] "On the acknowledgment of our independence," a southern newspaper complained at about the same time, "we became intoxicated with Utopian ideas."[24] Edward Rutledge of South Carolina observed that Americans' "spirit of subordination" seemed to have "evaporated" during the Revolutionary War.[25] Gentry writers struggled to persuade their neighbors that the time for insubordination had passed. "Let us not adopt the ridiculous idea, that true whiggism consists in perpetual resistance!" a New Yorker pleaded.[26] "People once respected their governors, their senators, their judges and their clergy," another essayist declared in the fall of 1786. "Since the war, blustering ignorant men . . . have turned the clamours against British tyranny, against their own governments."[27]

Elite Americans were not the only ones who attributed their social inferiors' newfound self-confidence to the Revolutionary War. In the pamphlets he wrote—but failed to publish—in the 1790s, William Manning freely admitted that he was "no great reader," had never traveled "fifty miles from where I was born," and had not even "had the advantage of six months schooling in my life." But Manning did not hesitate to comment on public affairs, and one reason was that he had been "in the Concord fight"—the first battle of the Revolutionary War. Men like Manning believed their military service imparted the same significance to their opinions that a Harvard or Yale degree gave their wealthier contemporaries.[28] Manning also cited another reason he deserved to be heard: he had become "a constant reader of public newspapers."[29] Herman Husband located his own faith in ordinary men's political abilities elsewhere, in their status as minor patriarchs. Public office required few talents beyond those that free adult men had already honed in daily interaction with their servants, children, and wives. A "Man who will make a good Mechanick, or good Farmer, who can rule his own Family well, is also capable, with a few Years Practice . . . to make a good Assembly-man to rule the State," Husband declared.[30]

The conflict over whether patricians or plebeians were more capable of governing hinged on what sort of ability mattered. Most writers and speakers who favored heavy taxation and stringent monetary policies also held to the belief that one of the hard facts of American politics was that ordinary citizens simply did not share in their wealthier neighbors' abundant opportunities to sharpen their political skills. "The main body of a people cannot be politicians," an essay appearing in the *Hampshire Herald* early in 1785 declared. "They have not leasure to attend to, opportunity to be informed of, nor ability to understand all that variety of matters, which concern the community."[31] The wealthy man's superior education and his economic independence permitted him to act virtuously—that is, in the public interest—advocates for fis-

cal and monetary austerity believed. "I contend that the spirit of patri-
otism . . . is favored, in a popular government, by extent of private
property," William Beers declared in a pamphlet published in Connecticut in 1791.[32] Men like Beers saw a correlation between a man's
wealth and his ability to subject his emotions to the dominion of his
reason. The effect of electing ordinary farmers to the state legislatures,
Beers claimed, had been to "carry into the government the irregular
passions, caprices and fanciful wishes of the people."[33]

Some populist writers allowed that ordinary citizens were less familiar
with the details of public policy than their leaders, but they inevitably
went on to defend the common man's grasp of the basic issues. "The
body of the people do not understand politicks," a western Massachusetts writer conceded in the midst of Shays's Rebellion, "but they know
that money is grown very scarce, and that greater sums are demanded of
them in taxes than many of them can pay."[34] "Honesty is not engrossed
by the fortunate," a New Hampshire paper money advocate declared at
about the same time; "neither is wealth the test of wisdom; else whence
those lucky rogues, those wealthy fools, who roll in chariots?"[35]

According to most Americans who favored tax and debt relief, the
greatest threat to proper representation came not from uneducated or
overly emotional representatives but from those who could not sympathize with the plight of their constituents. In the fall of 1786 a convention in Worcester County, Massachusetts, lamented that "the rulers of
Massachusetts, being many of them born to affluence, and perhaps the
whole in easy circumstances, had not been under advantages of feeling
for the less wealthy."[36] George Mason, the author of the Virginia constitution and Declaration of Rights, was a fierce enemy of relief measures
such as paper money. Yet in the Constitutional Convention he pointed
out that delegates who wanted legislators to be superior to their constituents rather than similar to them were, in essence, advocating virtual representation—a concept the British had once used to justify the
lack of American representation in Parliament. In a republic, Mason
said, representation must be actual, not virtual, and "the requisites in
actual representation are that the Reps. should sympathize with their
constituents; shd. think as they think, & feel as they feel."[37]

The debate over political reform paralleled the dispute over whether the saviors of the economy were going to be moneyed men (who would invest in America as soon as they could do so safely) or ordinary farmers (who would become prodigiously productive once the government removed their fiscal and monetary shackles). Some Americans were convinced that the nation would be strengthened through the concentration, and others through the dispersion, of both wealth and political power. In politics as in economics, the question was whether redemption was going to come from above or below.

With all of these practical as well as philosophical reasons for wishing to make the state governments less—or more—accountable to the people, citizens of the new republic proposed a host of specific reforms.

Back during the colonial era, only Pennsylvanians and New Englanders had had the opportunity to elect—or reject—their assemblymen every year.[38] After the adoption of the new state constitutions, annual elections spread throughout the country. By 1777 the lower house of the legislature was elected annually everywhere but South Carolina and Connecticut. (Representatives served for two years in South Carolina—and six months in Connecticut.) It required only a few of these annual elections to persuade some Americans that officeholders should have longer terms. Even in New England and Pennsylvania the advocates for stringent fiscal and monetary policies soon pronounced them incompatible with annual elections.[39] Noting how frequently control of the Pennsylvania legislature passed from one party to the other, one writer warned that "annual elections, the choicest gem in the cap of liberty, are subject to very imminent danger of becoming a Pandora's box, replete with evils perhaps as pernicious as those annexed to despotism."[40] Thomas Jefferson and James Madison both wanted to lengthen assemblymen's terms from one year to three.[41]

In six of the eleven states where the legislature had an upper house, the members were elected annually, and many Americans thought they should have longer terms.[42] In Virginia, where the convention writing the 1776 constitution decreed that senators would serve for four years, Thomas Jefferson favored nine.[43] In several of the states where senators served for more than one year, their terms were not staggered, and Madison considered this a fatal flaw. He noted in August 1786 that in Maryland, "the clamor" for paper money had become "universal." Senate elections were coming up, and Madison feared that because "the whole body is unluckily by their constitution to be chosen at once . . . a paper emission will be the result."[44] This dire prophecy was not fulfilled, but Madison remained a strong advocate for staggering elections.

Other Americans wanted to move the state governments in precisely the opposite direction. They insisted that the legislatures open their sessions to the public, publish their votes on major legislation, accord more representation to growing western districts, and increase the number of polling places.[45] Nowhere was the populist critique of the new state constitutions more vehement than in Massachusetts. In fact, the town meetings rejected the draft constitution proposed to them in 1778 and narrowly approved a 1780 revision only after lodging a host of objections to it. Numerous towns denounced the 1778 convention's decision to disenfranchise propertied African American men. That provision was dropped in 1780, but other objectionable clauses survived. Judges, several town meetings said, should be elected, not appointed. Other towns declared that allowing the governor to veto legislation was "dangerous to the liberties of the People."[46]

One of the most often repeated Massachusetts demands—that the capital be moved west from Boston—was aimed at much more than equalizing legislators' travel time. Since deputies from the area around Boston could live at home, their expenses were minimal, and their constituents could afford to keep them in the assembly throughout even long sessions. Eastern representatives were also able to keep an eye on their private affairs. Backcountry legislators were not so lucky. Few of them could afford to neglect their farms for long stretches, and besides, their hometowns were able to pay their room and board for only short periods. During Shays's Rebellion a Hampshire County writer charged that a recent tax relief proposal had been "spun out and put off till July just at the close of the session, when many of the country members [were] under a necessity of returning to their farms."[47]

If legislators were determined to keep the capital in Boston, the Greenwich town meeting pointed out a short time later, another way for representation to be equalized would be for assemblymen to "receive their Wagers for their services out of the common stock" rather than from their hometowns. That would make the town meetings more diligent about sending representatives. Then—"and Never before then"—the assembly would ease up on debtors and taxpayers, the Greenwich freeholders insisted.[48] A motion to relieve the individual town meetings of responsibility for paying representatives' salaries had come up late in the spring 1780 convention that wrote the state's new constitution, when many backcountry members had already gone home. To no one's surprise, it failed.[49]

The 1780 Massachusetts constitution contained a clause saying it could not be amended for fifteen years, but during Shays's Rebellion several county conventions proposed to hold a constitutional convention ahead of schedule.[50] Voters in other states also demanded constitutional amendments. A Rhode Island writer wanted to overhaul the process by which statewide officers were nominated so "as to take the Voice of the Freeman at large."[51] Two groups of South Carolinians sent the House of Representatives petitions in favor of "revising the Constitution of this State, and accommodating it more perfectly to the principles of equal Freedom," specifically by giving the backcountry proportional representation in the legislature.[52]

Most of the Revolution-era state constitutions preserved the colonial policy of denying citizens the right to run for office unless they owned a certain amount of property, and the property qualification was invariably higher for officeholders than for voters.[53] Not everyone was happy with the carryover. A South Carolinian rejected the notion that "men who are indigent and low in circumstances, are more liable to yield to temptations and bribes, and therefore more likely to betray the public trust." Actually, he wrote, "experience proves, that none are more insatiable than the rich." If officeholding were to be restricted at all, he suggested, it should be to "those of moderate estates," who seemed least likely "to be corrupted."[54]

A small band of populist reformers proposed to reduce the size of election districts. In sharp contrast to James Madison, who wanted to "extend the sphere" of government in order to insulate lawmakers against pressure from below, they wished to make state legislators more responsive to the voters by giving them fewer constituents. In the same 1782 pamphlet where he urged the Pennsylvania assembly to print paper money, Herman Husband asserted that the ideal election district would be small enough to give every voter "an Opportunity to converse with the Representative." Such was not the case with Pennsylvania's districts, which spanned entire counties and were thus among the most populous in the nation. Knowing little of their assemblymen, ordinary voters were unable to "call them to any Account." It was even more difficult for farmers and artisans to run successful legislative campaigns of their own. A "County is too large a Bound," Husband declared, and there are only "a few Men in a County who are generally known throughout the whole of it." These prominent men who had the best chance of getting elected were "generally the most unsuitable, they being chiefly Tavern-keepers, Merchants, &c. in the County Towns, with the Officers, Lawyers, &c."[55]

Husband wanted to set up new county legislatures—each comprising representatives from every town in the county—that would, in turn, choose the state assemblymen. Farmers and artisans would easily win election to the county legislatures, and once there they could send one of their own to the statehouse. These new legislative bodies would not only increase the percentage of plebeian assembly candidates who won their races but also give more farmers and artisans the confidence they needed to seek higher office in the first place. As long as lawmakers were chosen countywide, Husband argued, ordinary men would be "apt to conceive of ourselves" as "too insignificant to represent the County." The county legislature would "prove as a School to train up and learn Men of the best Sense and Principles the Nature of all publick Business, and give them Utterance to speak to the same."[56]

Like Madison, Husband believed the size of the districts that sent men to the statehouse helped determine what sort of policies came out of it. If Pennsylvania assemblymen were chosen by fewer voters, he believed, they would permit debtors to satisfy their creditors with paper money. The 1776 Pennsylvania constitution, with no upper house of the legislature and no governor, was probably, for its time, the most democratic government charter on earth.[57] And yet in Husband's view, until the size of the election districts was reduced, it would not be democratic enough.

A principal source of Husband's political vision was the prophet Ezekiel, whose narrative blueprint for the temple to be built in Jerusalem was founded on the principle of gradation. After all, the dimensions of the parts of the human body build gradually, and indeed at a constant rate, from the smallest measurement—the distance between two knuckles—all the way to the largest, the person's height. By the same token, the United States should not consist simply of the rulers and the ruled but of a series of layers ascending gradually, pyramid style, from the citizenry through the county legislatures to the state assemblies and Congress. The key element the United States lacked was the county legislature. "Our Want [lack] of the proper Use of those lesser Joints in the Body-politick," Husband wrote, "is as though we wanted our Finger-joints in our Bodies natural; without which we could not carry on the finer Parts of mechanick Work."[58]

In 1782, the same year that Husband published his thoughts on the proper size of election districts, Benjamin Gale, the Killingworth, Connecticut, physician who would later become an outspoken critic of Commutation, addressed the same topic. Like Husband, he believed that putting more constituents in a representative's district tended to liberate him from grassroots pressure. Unlike Husband, Gale was an advocate for large districts. Connecticut voters elected the members of the council of assistants (the upper house of the legislature) statewide. Anticipating several of the arguments Madison would make in *Federalist* Number 10 five years later, Gale asserted that because each member of the council represented many more constituents than his counterparts in the lower house, who were chosen by the towns, the councilors had legislated more wisely and justly. Members of the house of representatives frequently fell victim to some "popular whim." Incumbent councilors, by contrast, were almost never defeated, because it was "not so easy to *electerize* the whole State with the spirit of party, faction and intrigue, as the narrow compass of a town."[59]

Gale's objections to small legislative districts were not only philosophical but practical. He believed the agrarian majority in the house of representatives had oppressed the state's mercantile minority by saddling commercial men with a disproportionate share of the tax burden. Had it not been for the wise restraining influence of the council, he contended, the lower house would have yielded even more often to "popular freaks and commotions."[60]

• • •

The advocates and opponents of aggressive tax and debt collection were so far apart that they tried to reform several elements of the state governments in opposite directions. In the few states where the governor or a council of revision could veto legislation, many citizens wanted to abolish the veto.[61] On the other hand, in Virginia, where there was no veto, Madison and others favored the creation of a council of revision similar to New York's.[62] In Massachusetts, where some people favored taking away the legislature's right to override gubernatorial vetoes, others wanted to get rid of the veto power altogether.[63]

The two groups also expressed contrary complaints about restrictions on the electoral franchise. Often the same people who opposed high taxes and tight monetary policies also objected to the colonial-era requirement that only property holders could vote, which persisted in most states.[64] At the same time other Americans—frequently the advocates for heavy taxation and tight money—thought the Revolution-era constitutions had made the electorate too large. Several states allowed Revolutionary War veterans to vote even if they owned nothing—a policy that "Americanus" denounced. "Legislation is an evil," he declared, "when the laws of property are fabricated by those who may probably shew a scar, but not an acre of land."[65]

Americans who opposed expanding the franchise offered several distinct arguments. Some worried that propertyless voters would sell their votes, others that they might choose "a Representative to go to court, to vote away the Money of those that have Estates."[66] Opponents of universal manhood suffrage wondered where the democratizing trend would end. One mockingly advised reformers to push for the enfranchisement of women, who would elect their own leaders, including "Her Excellency, Granny General."[67] Some advocates for fiscal and monetary stringency actually wanted to make the electorate smaller than it had been under British rule. A Virginia writer denounced the widespread practice, dating back to colonial times, of allowing long-term tenants to vote. "Men who have no property of their own," "Aristides" declared, ought not "to regulate the property of others."[68] Although the 1780 Massachusetts constitution slightly raised the colonial-era property qualification, Elbridge Gerry told his fellow Constitutional Convention delegates that "the proportion having a right of suffrage" was so high in his home state that "the worst men get into the Legislature."[69]

• • •

The fiscal and monetary debates of the 1780s often centered on the upper houses of the legislatures. In most states members of the senate or
council not only represented more constituents than their counterparts in the lower chamber but had to meet higher property qualifications—a distinction that was often reflected in the policies they
adopted.[70] In half of the six states that printed no paper currency in the
mid-1780s, the lower house actually gave initial approval to an emission, only to see the senate or council kill it.[71] When, by a two-to-one
margin, the Delaware House of Assembly sent the council a paper
money proposal, it came back covered with the labels "rejected,"
"R.E.J.E.C.T.E.D.," and even "rejected tetotally."[72] A currency emission
also made it through the lower house in neighboring Maryland. But the
senate unanimously defeated it, sending it back down to the other
chamber marked *"will not pass."*[73] Even in three of the states that did
emit paper currency in the years between the Yorktown victory and the
ratification of the Constitution, the upper house exercised a restraining influence on the lower chamber, delaying the emission, reducing
the amount printed, or both.[74]

The friends of paper money were certain they knew why it invariably
received a cold reception in the upper house of the legislature. In October 1785, nearly a year before the New Hampshire Senate blocked the
emission of currency, "Sentinel" correctly predicted that it would do so,
explaining that the senators were "very rich, and have a large number of
distressed persons indebted to them." If the legislature printed money
and it depreciated, he pointed out, the senators would "suffer great
losses in their private fortunes."[75] These charges were not entirely
without foundation. For instance, the family of Maryland senator
Charles Carroll had £30,000 out on loan.[76]

Populists in at least three bicameral states—New Hampshire, Massachusetts, and South Carolina—proposed to "abolish the order of the
Senate."[77] John Adams, who served as the United States minister in
London during the mid-1780s, recalled years later that "every western
wind brought us news of town and county meetings in Massachusetts . . . reprobating the office of governor and the assembly of the
Senate as expensive, useless, and pernicious." It was primarily in order

to defend the senate (as well as the governor's veto) that Adams wrote his three-volume *Defence of the American Constitutions*.[78]

Even as some Americans tried to deprive their state legislature of its upper house, others sought to establish one in the two states—Pennsylvania and Georgia—where none existed. Advocates for high taxes and hard money also searched for ways to stiffen the existing senates' and councils' resistance against popular pressure. In addition to proposing long, staggered terms for state senators, James Madison favored a high property qualification. He could "see no reason why the rights of property which chiefly bears the burden of Government & is so much an object of Legislation should not be respected as well as personal rights in the choice of Rulers."[79] Jefferson would have liked to take the power of choosing senators away from the voters, handing it over to special electors like those in Maryland.[80] A newspaper writer championed the same reform for Massachusetts, where, under the existing system, "a majority of the people . . . possessing a minority of the property, could controul the residue of it."[81]

Representative instructions also incited competing bands of reformers. Many of the British colonies in North America had recognized voters' right to instruct their assemblymen, but three of the four Anne Arundel County, Maryland, delegates to the 1776 convention that wrote that state's constitution were so dead-set against the idea that when their constituents instructed them, they resigned.[82] Some South Carolinians likewise denied that voters could instruct their members of the state house of representatives, whereupon one lawmaker, Thomas Tudor Tucker, proposed to enshrine that right in the state constitution, as four states had already done.[83] Other Americans asserted that members of the lower house were already obligated to follow their constituents' instructions, and a few New Englanders even sought a mechanism for instructing senators.[84]

The chasm in Americans' attitudes toward the state governments that emerged from the Revolutionary War was visible in miniature in one state, Pennsylvania. So dissatisfied were some Pennsylvanians with the 1776 state constitution that they formed an organization, the Republican party, with the express purpose of abolishing it. Throughout the 1780s the Republicans struggled to create a senate, shrink the electorate, lengthen officeholders' one-year terms, and replace the Supreme Executive Council with a governor who could veto legislation.[85] And yet even the Pennsylvania constitution was not democratic enough for Herman Husband. In addition to proposing to shrink election districts, Husband thought every major piece of legislation should be submitted to a plebiscite. Toward the end of each session of the legislature, the freemen of every township would assemble and vote "on each Law, and hand the same up, through the Counties, to the General Assembly; who shall confirm, or repeal the same, by the Majority of Votes of the Townships."[86]

Thus two distinct segments of American society championed vastly different visions of the Revolution they had just fought. For one group, the Revolutionary War had "only disconnected us from Great Britain."[87] Few internal changes were required. Other citizens felt differently. They believed the American Revolution had only begun.

PART IV
REINING IN THE REVOLUTION

CHAPTER 11

"THE HOUSE ON FIRE"

CREDIT

THE WAVE OF INSURRECTIONS and threats that swept over the United States during the 1780s—and more important, the relief legislation that the rebels managed to extract from lawmakers and local officials—convinced many of the nation's most prominent citizens that the time had come to launch a rebellion of their own. "If the people at large have not virtue enough to govern themselves, as republicans," a Rhode Island writer warned, "they must submit to a different form of government."[1] "A *military government* is better than *no government*," another New Englander declared.[2] According to a much later report, Nathaniel Gorham, the president of the Continental Congress, even sounded out Prince Henry of Prussia on becoming king of America.[3]

Few Americans wanted to go that far, but by the mid-1780s a growing number of them had turned against the state governments. Charles Lee bitterly protested the Virginia House of Delegates' penchant for tax relief in an April 1788 letter to George Washington, who was, like himself, a large-scale public creditor. Lee predicted that "the public debts and even private debts will in my opinion be extinguished by acts of the several Legislatures . . . unless there be a quiet and peaceable transition from the present American government, into another more powerful and independent of the people." Actually almost no one, not even the most radical insurgents, wished to abolish private debts or annihilate government bonds. But the fear Lee expressed was genuine.[4] More and more of the nation's most prominent citizens, convinced that the thirteen legislatures had yielded to agrarian demands for relief because they were too weak, paradoxically decided that the solution was to weaken them further. "The vile State governments are sources of pollution, which will contaminate the American name; perhaps for ages," declared Henry Knox in July 1787. The only way to end their career of injustice was to "Smite them in the name of God and the people."[5]

Knox was writing to Rufus King, a Massachusetts delegate to the Constitutional Convention. To the extent they could, King and his colleagues heeded the general's advice.

In 1781, when the thirteen state legislatures had ratified the "Articles of Confederation and Perpetual Union," they agreed never to alter them without unanimous consent. Six years later, during the winter of 1786–87, every state but Rhode Island elected delegates to a federal convention, to be held in Philadelphia the following summer. The meeting had been called, as Congress observed, "for the sole and express purpose of revising the Articles of Confederation." Delegates were to propose amendments that would take effect only after clearing Congress and every state legislature.[6] The members of the Philadelphia convention decided to ignore these instructions, proposing not to alter the Articles of Confederation but to abolish them. The regime they created would begin exercising sovereignty not when it was endorsed by Congress and all thirteen state assemblies, as the Articles required, but as soon as it received the approval of nine state ratifying conventions. Whatever else it was, the process that resulted in the U.S. Constitution was indisputably, according to the rules in place at the time, unconstitutional.

In defense of their unorthodox methods, the Framers of the Constitution boldly avowed that they had decided to ask their fellow citizens to assert the same prerogative they had insisted upon in 1776—their right of revolution.[7] The difference, of course, was that the Federalists, like the Shaysites, were rebelling against their own republic. Like the Massachusetts insurgents, some of the Framers claimed they simply had no choice. "The House on fire must be extinguished," Pennsylvania attorney James Wilson declared, "without a scrupulous regard to ordinary rights."[8]

The members of the federal convention did not suddenly come up with the idea of junking the Articles of Confederation after they all arrived in Philadelphia. Many, in fact, had decided years earlier to try to establish a new national government.[9] In plotting to ignore the instructions they had received from the state assemblies, the delegates displayed an extreme version of the belief that the elected representative is not simply an instrument of his constituents' will. He is instead an independent thinker who ought to execute justice as he himself defines it.

James Madison, Alexander Hamilton, Charles Pinckney of South Carolina, and other delegates brought proposals for overthrowing the Articles of Confederation with them to Philadelphia. But they did not discuss their intentions publicly. If they had, assemblymen in their home states probably would not have chosen them. It is an unsettling but inescapable fact that several of the principal authors of the U.S. Constitution, which has served as a model for representative governments all over the world, would never have made it to Philadelphia if their constituents had known their real intentions. There is more. If the various proposals to create a new national government drafted in the spring of 1787 had been made public, several state legislatures might have joined Rhode Island in steering clear of the convention altogether. The Constitution that the delegates were writing would consolidate the thirteen previously sovereign states into a single nation, John Lansing of New York declared three weeks into the deliberations, and his state "would never have concurred in sending deputies to the convention, if she had supposed the deliberations were to turn on a consolidation of the States."[10]

It has frequently been noted that hardly any of the federal convention delegates tilled the soil for a living. Since nine in ten free Americans were farmers, the Framers were, demographically speaking, unrepresentative in the extreme. And yet for all that, the nation's agricultural majority did exert a significant influence on the convention. In fact, farmers had begun to influence it even before it opened. As the delegates traveled to Philadelphia late in the spring, they were looking over their shoulders. Had they been confident that their constituents would meekly acquiesce in whatever plan they produced, the delegates who wished to overthrow the Articles of Confederation would not have felt the need to conceal their intentions.

• • •

Early in the federal convention it became clear that one of the delegates' most pressing goals was to revive the economy. Part of their plan was to give the national government the right to regulate American trade. Until American diplomats could credibly threaten other countries, especially Britain, with the loss of American markets and produce, they would never be able to open foreign ports (especially in the West Indies) to U.S. ships. An even more powerful way to promote economic development would be to make the United States more attractive to investors.

The delegates set their sights on recruiting capital because they believed the state assemblies had actively repelled it. The need to rein in the states weighed far more heavily upon the convention than the motive that has received the most attention from later generations of Americans, strengthening the Confederation. On the eve of the convention James Madison drew up a list of eleven "Vices of the Political System of the U. States." Only two of these were weaknesses of the federal government, for the list was dominated by Madison's indictment of the thirteen assemblies.[11] Addressing his fellow delegates in Philadelphia, Madison emphasized "the necessity" not only of "enlarging the bounds of the general government" but "of circumscribing more effectually the state governments."[12]

The Framers wrote into the Constitution a multipronged assault on the states' debtor- and taxpayer-protection schemes. First, the thirteen state assemblies would be prohibited from adopting debtor relief legislation. Second, to reduce the likelihood that national officials would themselves feel pressure to do something for debtors, they would be surrounded by a political stockade: a series of what Edmund Randolph called "checks agst. the popular intemperance."[13] And finally, as Chapter 13 will show, the responsibility for collecting the national government's revenue would no longer be delegated to the state legislatures. Under the Constitution, Congress would, for the first time ever, have the power to tax individual Americans directly.

The members of the federal convention were appalled by the state governments' failure to collect private debts. The most vocal champion of the most potent weapon for stopping the legislatures from screening debtors was Madison, who proposed to give the U.S. Senate the power to veto state laws.[14] Senators, he declared, should be able to overturn state legislation *"in all cases whatsoever."*[15]

The phrase Madison underlined was a deliberate provocation, a quotation from Parliament's 1766 assertion of absolute sovereignty over the thirteen colonies. As a congressman, Madison had tried to revise the Articles of Confederation to allow Congress to use soldiers to force the states to comply with its mandates—a proposal that had proven less than popular.[16] Now he was suggesting a new way for the federal government to rein in the assemblies. He would create a federal senate and then graft it into all thirteen state constitutions as an additional "branch of the State Legislatures."[17]

Madison's plan would allow the Senate to veto any state law it deemed unjust, but his principal target was debtor protection legislation. In promoting the federal veto to Virginia governor Edmund Randolph on the eve of the convention, Madison contended that there had "been no moment since the peace at which the federal assent w[oul]d have been given to paper money."[18] If it had had the power to do so, Congress would also have punished the states that violated the 1783 Paris peace treaty by blocking British creditors' access to their courts. Once the federal veto was in place, the Virginian observed, the assemblies would never again "violate national Treaties."[19]

To Madison's delight, the veto won praise from every corner of the convention. Several delegates had been meditating similar proposals of their own.[20] And yet the convention whittled Madison's veto down to nothing. Elbridge Gerry did not favor a blanket congressional veto, but he "had no objection to authoriz[ing] a negative to paper money and similar measures."[21] Some members, perhaps anticipating the constitutional ban on state-level relief legislation that the convention would adopt near the end of its deliberations, thought the federal government should be allowed to reject only those state laws that violated the Constitution. The delegates endorsed this limited version of the federal veto on May 31. Then, on July 17, they rejected the veto proposal altogether.

The reason for Madison's defeat was clear. As Charles Pinckney noted, the delegates feared the states would "reluctantly grant" the veto.[22] As much as George Mason liked the idea—indeed, he and several other delegates believed the national government should also be empowered to tell the states who their governors were going to be—he told the convention "the public mind would not now bear" such aggressive federal interference in state affairs.[23] As an alternative to these excessively blunt instruments, the delegates hit upon a solution that more precisely targeted the specific evils Madison had identified. They resolved to write creditor-protection language directly into the Constitution.[24] This decision followed a pattern that was evident throughout the convention's deliberations. The Framers never approved an inflammatory proposal if they could accomplish the same objective using a mechanism their fellow citizens would find easier to swallow.

The members of the convention indicated the significance they attached to the most important of their creditor-protection provisions by where they put it. As admirers of order and symmetry, the Framers purged most of the Constitution's seven articles of extraneous material. But near the end of the very first article, which defines the powers of the new national legislature, they inserted language prohibiting the states from rescuing debtors. Article I, Section 10, reads in part: "No State shall . . . emit Bills of Credit; make any Thing but gold and silver Coin a Tender in Payment of Debts [nor] pass any . . . Law impairing the Obligation of Contracts."[25] At first glance the famous "Contracts" clause at the end of Section 10 may seem like a blanket protection against all sorts of legislative meddling in commercial relations. Indeed, courts have applied it to a wide variety of circumstances.[26] Actually, however, the contracts clause had the specific purpose of abolishing debtor-relief legislation.[27]

Other provisions of Section 10 also grew out of the debtor-creditor conflicts of the 1780s. In both New Jersey and Virginia the enemies of paper money had tried to amend the state constitution to ban it. They had failed, but now the national charter would eliminate the currency option in every state.[28] The convention initially voted to bar the states from emitting currency without congressional approval. But the members were so "*smitten* with the *paper money dread*," observed Maryland delegate Luther Martin, who ended up opposing the Constitution, "that they insisted the prohibition should be *absolute*." The convention was "willing to risk any political evil, rather than admit the idea of a paper emission, in any *possible* event," Martin wrote.[29] William Davie told the North Carolina ratifying convention that the currency ban "became in some measure a preliminary"—a nonnegotiable demand—on the part of delegates from the six states that had not printed any currency since the Revolutionary War. They had told their colleagues from the paper money states, "By your iniquitous laws and paper emissions [you] shamefully defrauded our citizens. The Confederation prevented our compelling you to do them justice; but before we confederate with you again, you must not only agree to be honest, but put it out of your power to be otherwise."[30] The delegates also decided against explicitly allowing the federal government to print currency of its own. George Read of Delaware warned that a clause giving Congress access to the printing press "would be as alarming as the mark of the Beast in Revelations."[31]

By refusing to grant either Congress or the state legislatures the power to print any sort of paper money, the Constitutional Convention struck a more violent blow against currency emissions than even Parliament had. The Currency Act, adopted in 1764, had permitted the North American colonies to print money so long as it was not "legal tender," which obligated creditors to accept it. But the Framers decided to prohibit the states from issuing any kind of paper money. Why?

One reason was that private creditors were not the only Americans who needed protection from paper money. The Framers did not want to see currency foisted upon the possessors of government bonds, either. During the 1780s several states had used currency to pay bondholders their interest, and taxpayers in other states had pleaded for similar policies. Some tax relief advocates—from Virginia petitioners to the Allegheny prophet Herman Husband to numerous New Hampshire town meetings—had even suggested forcing securities traders to accept paper currency, which did not pay interest, in exchange for the bonds themselves. There would be no danger of any legislature complying with these demands once Section 10 became the law of the land.

It was fitting that Section 10 extended its protection against paper money to securities speculators and other public creditors. After all, the currency ban was, to a large extent, a product of the debate that had raged throughout the 1780s over how much money state officials should convey from taxpayers to bondholders. If the assemblies had not levied heavy taxes on behalf of public creditors, many fewer taxpayers would have demanded that they ease the fiscal burden by emitting paper money. Indeed, if there had been no bondholders, very few of the states would have printed currency, and there would have been no reason to prohibit it in the Constitution. In fact, without paper money as a focus for prominent Americans' ire, the Constitutional Convention might never have assembled. It is in this indirect sense that the holders of government bonds played their most crucial role in the genesis of the Constitution.[32]

It was all well and good for the convention to prohibit the states from rescuing debtors. Would the prohibition have teeth, though? Would the federal courts have the nerve to overturn state-level relief legislation? Throughout most of the country state laws had proven impervious to judicial review.

Things were going to be different in the new national government. The Constitution did not explicitly grant the Supreme Court the right of judicial review. Like Madison's proposal for a federal veto of state legislation, a clause allowing national courts to overturn state laws would have jeopardized ratification. But the Constitution declared itself (and all federal laws and treaties) "the supreme Law of the Land"— superior to all state legislation.[33] This provision was adopted the day after the delegates defeated Madison's federal veto of state laws and was obviously intended as a more palatable substitute.

Several Framers affirmed as individuals what they did not dare inscribe into the Constitution: when an unconstitutional law made it through a state assembly, federal judges would prevent it from ever taking effect. In *Federalist* Number 80, Hamilton pointed out that the proposed national charter prohibited the states from resorting to such expedients as "the imposition of duties on imported articles, and the emission of paper money." He noted that these "restrictions" would be pointless "without some constitutional mode of enforcing the observance of them." The mode the Framers had chosen was judicial review.[34] Federal judges' authority to overturn unconstitutional state legislation was confirmed in the Judiciary Act of 1789.[35]

The Constitution offered special protection to one class of litigants. Plaintiffs, including foreigners, who did not live in the same state as their debtors would be able to sue them in federal court. Furthermore the federal Constitution, unlike most of its state counterparts, gave civil defendants no right to a jury trial, so a debtor who was sued by, say, a British merchant would no longer be able to count on the protection of his friends and neighbors. Moreover, since federal treaties would be superior to ordinary legislation, the federal courts could overturn state laws that screened debtors in violation of the 1783 treaty with Britain. While the federal convention was meeting, Thomas Jefferson wrote Madison rejecting the idea of a federal veto over state legislation and endorsing the alternative that the Framers ultimately devised, namely allowing unsuccessful litigants who believed state judges had violated the Constitution to appeal their cases in federal court. In the 1790s hundreds of Virginians lost federal suits to British creditors, and Jefferson was one of them.[36]

Madison recognized that "the Judicial authority under our new system will keep the States within their proper limits, and supply the place of a negative on their laws." Unlike their state counterparts, who were often popularly elected for short terms, federal judges would be appointed by the president (and confirmed by the Senate) for life. Madison nonetheless continued to worry that judicial enforcement of Section 10 would be less effective than the federal veto he had proposed.[37]

The members of the federal convention recognized that no matter how explicitly the Constitution protected bondholders and private creditors from interventionist state legislatures, these provisions, on their own, would be inadequate. The danger remained that the constitutional clauses protecting creditors and bondholders would not be enforced. Or Congress could decide to cut taxes, print paper money, or grant debtors and taxpayers any of the other protections the Constitution had taken away from the state assemblies.[38] The Framers' awareness of these dangers led to one of the great turning points of American history. The convention decided to make the new national government considerably less responsive to the popular will than any of its state-level counterparts. Like other prominent citizens, the authors of the Constitution believed the American Revolution had turned ordinary farmers into "unruly steeds." There was but one solution, a Massachusetts newspaper essayist declared in March 1787: "the reins should be

resumed and held with a firmer hand."[39] This was a widespread sentiment. "The reins of Government," Elizabeth Smith Shaw of Haverhill,
Massachusettts, told her sister, Abigail Adams, less than a week before
the federal convention assembled, "must e'er long be drawn closer."[40]

One way the delegates promoted the independence of federal officeholders was by giving them the opportunity to entrench themselves in
office. Under the Articles of Confederation, members of Congress
could serve only three one-year terms in any six. Six state constitutions
mandated rotation in office for the governor as well, and three imposed
similar restrictions on state senators.[41] But no national legislator would
ever face any such term limits. Indeed, until the adoption in 1951 of an
amendment confining presidents to two terms, the Constitution did
not limit the service of any national officer.[42]

The president of the United States would be more powerful and
more independent of his legislative branch than any of the governors.
Although most state constitutions established executive councils — not
only to advise the governor but to keep an eye on him — there would be
none at the national level. Whereas the Articles of Confederation and
almost all of the state constitutions lodged the power of appointing top
officials in the legislature, most major appointments in the new national government would be made by the president (with the advice
and consent of the Senate). State governors were elected by the assembly or by the voters at large, but the president would be chosen by
special electors. A principal reason the Framers created the Electoral
College was to make it harder for a popular majority to elect a president whom leading Americans considered irresponsible.[43]

The Constitution awarded bonus presidential electors — as well as
extra seats in the House of Representatives — to states where a significant percentage of the population was enslaved.[44] It was in fact the desire to give the slave states additional weight in presidential elections
that led James Madison to oppose the direct election of the chief executive. Madison believed that in apportioning the power to choose the
president among the states, the Constitution should count slaves as
people. Although slaves were of course denied the vote, they did contribute to a state's taxable wealth, and Madison thought a state's weight
in presidential elections should be based upon its contribution to the
national treasury. The problem was that if the convention had allowed

voters to choose the president directly, there would have been no way to accord slave states extra weight. So instead Madison endorsed a system of president electors who would be apportioned among the states according to the number of their inhabitants. Then the legislature of each state would decide how its electors would be chosen. Madison and other southern delegates also wanted to count slaves in the apportionment of congressmen.

Gouverneur Morris of Philadelphia was appalled at the idea that "the inhabitant of Georgia and [South Carolina] who goes to the Coast of Africa, and in defiance of the most sacred laws of humanity tears away his fellow creatures from their dearest connections & dam[n]s them to the most cruel bondages, shall have more votes in a Govt. instituted for protection of the rights of mankind, than the Citizen of [Pennsylvania] or N[ew] Jersey who views with a laudable horror, so nefarious a practice."[45] Eventually the Convention decided that in apportioning congressmen and presidential electors among the states, slaves and freemen would not be counted equally, as Madison had suggested. Instead each slave would be considered three-fifths of a person. Even that was sufficient to give the freemen in slave states about one-third more congressmen and presidential electors, relative to their free inhabitants, than their counterparts in states with few or no slaves.[46]

The convention's decision to award bonus congressmen and presidential electors to states with large slave populations—a privilege not accorded to slaveholding regions in any state constitution—powerfully influenced politics in the new nation. Without the three-fifths clause, Jefferson would not have defeated Adams for the presidency in 1800, southerners would not have dominated the party caucuses that chose congressional leaders and nominated presidential candidates during the antebellum period, and Congress would not have voted in 1820 to permit slavery in Missouri.[47] During the nineteenth century, abolitionists denounced the Constitution for considering the enslaved American only three-fifths of a person. But they also understood that in apportioning the power to choose the president and Congress among the free and slave states, the Framers would actually have strengthened the slaveholders if they had counted slaves as equal to whites. In this one instance, the slaves' interests would have been better served if they had not been considered persons at all.

The powerful new president would find a potent ally in the U.S. Senate.[48] The "origin" of "the evils under which the U.S. laboured" was "the turbulence and follies of democracy," Edmund Randolph told the convention. "Some check therefore was to be sought for agst. this tendency of our Governments," he said, and "a good Senate seemed most likely to answer the purpose," since it would "restrain, if possible, the fury of democracy."[49] Gouverneur Morris believed the Senate should "check" the natural propensity in the House of Representatives "to run into projects of paper money & similar expedients."[50]

In several states during the postwar years, when the lower house of the legislature approved a plan to print paper money, the senate or council chose not to stand in its way, and the money was printed. On the other hand, the upper houses of New Hampshire, Delaware, and Maryland were instrumental in preventing paper emissions. The Maryland Senate withstood especially intense pressure from pro-currency forces both in the lower house and in the free population at large. Throughout the country the opponents of paper money hailed the Maryland senators as heroes. But everyone understood that what really distinguished Maryland from every other state was that its senate was not chosen directly by the voters. The state constitution established special electors whose sole responsibility was to choose the senators.

The Constitutional Convention patterned the federal Senate on Maryland's. Until 1913, when a constitutional amendment mandated direct election, senators were appointed by the state legislatures.[51] Under the Articles of Confederation, it made sense for congressmen to be chosen by the assemblies, since each of the thirteen member states retained its sovereignty. (In Connecticut and Rhode Island, congressmen had nonetheless been chosen by the voters.) Why did the Framers insist upon carrying the principle of indirect election into the new national government? One reason was that delegates from small states believed that election by the legislatures would bolster their claim that the United States was still partly a confederation. That would in turn strengthen the case for according every state equal representation in at least one branch of the national legislature.[52]

But indirect election also appealed to several delegates from large states. Elbridge Gerry of Massachusetts contended that "the commercial & monied interest wd. be more secure in the hands of the State

Legislatures, than of the people at large."[53] Even small-state delegates understood that their best chance of preventing the direct election of senators lay in appealing to their colleagues' anxiety about the perils of popular rule. John Dickinson of Delaware affirmed that senators should be "distinguished for their rank in life and their weight of property," and he thought "such characters more likely to be selected by the State Legislatures, than in any other mode."[54]

Another of the convention's strategies for preventing popular clamors from turning into Senate majorities was to stagger senators' terms. Dividing the senators into three classes, the Framers arranged for one class to finish its six-year term every two years. Madison, who had once worried that the failure of the Maryland constitution to stagger senators' terms would lead the upper house to acquiesce in the popular "clamor" for paper money, affirmed his determination to see federal senators "go out in such a rotation as always to leave in office a large majority of old members."[55] Decades after helping write the Constitution, he was pleased to find that the Senate had in fact proved itself "capable of stemming popular currents taking a wrong direction, till reason & justice could regain their ascendancy."[56]

Even as the Philadelphia convention took all these steps to keep federal officeholders from being too beholden to their constituents, it rejected others. Still others were adopted only after being heavily modified. In several crucial areas the delegates rejected blatantly undemocratic proposals in favor of other mechanisms that accomplished the same goals more subtly. Why did the Framers reject or moderate so many provisions they admired in theory? One reason was that nearly every delegate took pride in being a republican statesman, and none wanted to tarnish his self-image by endorsing every single effort to reduce ordinary citizens' political influence. There was also a more practical reason for the Framers to reject or at least tone down antidemocratic proposals. As Elbridge Gerry told his colleagues, "it was necessary to consider what the people would approve."[57]

Ordinary citizens were, as one historian has put it, ghosts at the Constitutional Convention, influencing it without being there in the flesh.[58] That was never more apparent than on June 18 — the only occasion during the long summer of 1787 when the delegates yielded the floor to a single colleague for an entire day. What is especially remarkable is that the recipient of this unique compliment was a man of low—indeed, illegitimate—birth. And yet Alexander Hamilton had earned his colleagues' respect, and he held them rapt as he talked on and on all through the morning of June 18 and well into the afternoon.

Like many of his contemporaries, Hamilton discerned a fundamental divide between "the mass of the people" and "the rich and well born." Government needed to strike a balance between the two primary classes. Since "the people . . . seldom judge or determine right," it was especially important to keep them in check. "To the want of this check," he said, "we owe our paper money[,] instalment laws[,] &c."[59] Under Hamilton's plan of government, the president and the Senate would initially be elected, but they would then serve life terms. Thus the one popularly elected branch, the House of Representatives, would be balanced by what would essentially be an elective monarch and House of Lords.

Even Hamilton knew there was no chance the architects of the Constitution would adopt his design. But historians err when they assume that the reason Hamilton's colleagues rejected his plan was that they did not like it. Actually, the transcripts of the convention debates reveal that Hamilton's philosophy was greatly admired—at least in theory. It was obvious to everyone present that the government Hamilton envisioned would rarely if ever cave in to debtors' or taxpayers' demands. That alone was sufficient to render it attractive, since abolishing debt and tax relief stood high on the convention's agenda. Even when a delegate favored amending some clause of the draft Constitution for reasons of his own, he often played these down in floor debate, knowing he could attract many more votes by showing how his amendment would stifle relief.

And yet the Framers were realists, too. Three days after Hamilton's speech William Samuel Johnson of Connecticut said it had been "praised by every gentleman, but supported by no gentleman."[60] The delegates never mistook themselves for philosophers ruminating about Utopia. They were realists, and they knew that the most radical mechanisms for freeing the new government from grassroots control would doom the Constitution. Even if the supporters of Hamilton's elective monarchy somehow managed to finagle its ratification, Americans would never accept it, and the members of the convention would have succeeded only in undermining the stability they had come to Philadelphia to try to restore.

The delegates' task, most of them soon realized, was to determine just how far they could go in limiting popular influence on the new regime without sacrificing popular support. The remarkable stability of American government in the years since 1789 has blinded us to what its architects understood all too well: if they had loaded it down with too many of their favorite projects, the whole edifice would have toppled. To avoid that outcome, the delegates rejected some of the most antidemocratic proposals altogether and moderated others. Still other restraints on popular influence were jettisoned in favor of alternative measures that accomplished the same goal less conspicuously. Much of the energy that pulsed through the Philadelphia convention was generated by the ongoing tension—not only among the members but within the minds of individuals—between two competing imperatives: ensuring ratification and liberating officeholders from the influence of debtors and taxpayers. Many of the Framers' battles concluded in the adoption of federal institutions that were considerably less responsive to the public will than their state-level counterparts—and yet more democratic than what some delegates had had in mind.[61]

Nowhere did the contrary winds that blew through the convention leave a more visible trace than in the design of the Senate. As independent of popular influence as senators would be, theirs was not to be the aristocratic bastion some delegates had envisioned.

Early in the convention's discussion of the upper house, George Mason told his colleagues he favored restricting Senate candidacy to the well-to-do, explaining that "one important object in constituting the Senate was to secure the rights of property."[62] Charles Cotesworth Pinckney, the South Carolina attorney who had risen to the rank of brigadier general in the Continental Army, believed "no Salary should be allowed" to senators. Since the Senate "was meant to represent the wealth of the Country," he argued, "it ought to be composed of persons of wealth," which it would be "if no allowance was to be made." Benjamin Franklin, who had volunteered for countless civic projects since his retirement from the printing business decades earlier, went further, proposing to make all government service voluntary. That would guarantee the election of independently wealthy men to every office.[63]

Members also suggested a variety of additional mechanisms to strengthen senators. Some wanted to allow them to originate appropriations bills. This was a power that even the House of Lords, Britain's avowedly aristocratic upper house, lacked, and the proposal to give it to federal senators provoked an outburst from Edmund Randolph. Reminding his colleagues that the ratification campaign already had "numerous & monstrous difficulties to combat," Randolph demanded, "When the people behold in the Senate, the countenance of an aristocracy; and in the president, the form at least of a little monarch, will not their alarms be sufficiently raised without taking from their immediate representatives"—the members of the House of Representatives—"a right which has been so long appropriated to them[?]"[64] Randolph's anxiety was widely shared. "The acceptance of the plan will inevitably fail, if the Senate be not restrained from originating Money bills," Elbridge Gerry warned.[65] The Framers' fear that an overly aristocratic Senate would prevent the ratification of the Constitution ensured the defeat not only of the bid to let senators initiate appropriations bills but also of the property qualification for Senate service and the proposal that senators not be paid.

One of the more extreme proposals for reducing the national government's susceptibility to popular influence came from Pennsylvania delegate Gouverneur Morris. No surprise there, for Morris had been, quite literally, to the manor born. Growing up at Morrisania, his family's feudal estate ten miles north of New York City, had influenced Morris powerfully, and he had been one of the first participants in the colonial struggle for home rule to see that it had the potential to trigger a struggle over who would rule at home.[66] In May 1774 New Yorkers gathered outside Fraunces Tavern to protest Parliament's harsh punishment of Boston for its famous Tea Party. Morris stood on the balcony of the tavern, literally looking down on the crowd below. "On my right hand were ranged all the people of property, with some few poor dependants," he later recalled. To Morris's left were "all the tradesmen," and it was to them that he turned his attention. "The mob begin to think and to reason," he later wrote. "Poor reptiles! It is with them a vernal morning, they are struggling to cast off their winter's slough, they bask in the sunshine, and ere noon they will bite, depend upon it. The gentry begin to fear this."[67]

Frequently during the Revolution and the 1780s, ordinary Americans proved Morris a discerning prophet, and he entered the federal convention determined to speak plainly about class conflict. This was partly a matter of personality, for Morris was the type who delighted in outraging his audiences by blurting out the one thought everyone else was trying to suppress. The tendency toward extroversion that Morris had demonstrated early in his youth had actually been exacerbated by the two incidents that disfigured him—the boiling water that tipped onto his right arm and side during his childhood, scarring him for life, and the carriage accident that tore off his left leg. The two calamities had, in an odd sense, liberated him. Since Morris was never going to be known for his poise, he learned instead to charm men and (especially) women with his wit. He was, as he once put it, "constitutionally one of the happiest of men." One biographer, noting that the federal convention chose Morris to give its handiwork a final polish, christened him "the rake who wrote the Constitution."[68]

Morris had something in common with the convention's better-known conservative, Alexander Hamilton. Both prided themselves on presenting the conflict between the Few and the Many in the starkest terms. Although Morris supported the presidential veto, he feared it would not be sufficient to prevent the adoption of irresponsible measures. As evidence, "he recited the history of paper emissions, and the perseverance of the legislative assemblies in repeating them, with all the distressing effects of such measures before their eyes." If "a war was now to break out," Morris claimed, Congress—even the reformed version the convention was busy creating—would not be able to resist popular pressure to emit paper currency. Suppose, on the other hand, the convention required a three-fourths vote to repeal any law. Representatives would think twice before adopting legislation if they knew it would be virtually impervious to repeal. Thus the three-fourths requirement would "prevent the hasty passage of laws."[69]

Morris's proposal was not adopted. In fact, none of the other delegates even mentioned it. It was as though the idea had never come up.

• • •

The list of antidemocratic devices that the Framers discarded altogether was not long. But frequently when the members adopted some proposal to curb popular influence, they first modified it to make it more palatable to the ratifying conventions.

Many delegates would have liked to restrict the franchise in national elections to "the freeholders of the Country"—property owners.[70] Others shared Oliver Ellsworth's concern that "the people will not readily subscribe to the Natl. Constitution, if it should subject them to be disfranchised."[71] The controversy created divisions not only within the convention but in the mind of its most active delegate. "Viewing the subject [on] its merits alone," James Madison told his colleagues on August 7, "the freeholders of the Country would be the safest depositories of Republican liberty." But Madison was too realistic to believe the issue should be decided on "its merits alone." Whether to allow men without property to vote in federal elections "would with him depend much on the probable reception such a change would meet with in States where the right was now exercised by every description of people," he said.[72]

In the end the Framers decided to tie the federal franchise to each state's rules governing assembly elections. Wherever the propertyless had gained the right to vote, they would be allowed to participate in congressional elections. But in states that had refused to enfranchise men without property, they would not receive congressional ballots, either. The delegates had found a way to exclude thousands of unpropertied Americans from federal elections without jeopardizing the popularity of the Constitution in states with universal manhood suffrage.

One of the most contentious questions at the federal convention was how long federal officeholders should serve. One-year terms were the norm in the old Congress, in the lower house of nearly every state legislature, and even in most of the councils and senates.[73] Most Americans still clung to the old adage "Where annual elections end, there slavery begins."[74] On the other hand, the Framers initially voted to give members of the House of Representatives three-year terms, and they hoped U.S. senators would serve even longer. Nine years sounded about right to James Madison. The federal government ought "to protect the minority of the opulent against the majority," he declared. "The senate, therefore, ought to be this body; and to answer these purposes, they ought to have permanency and stability."[75] Other delegates thought the president as well as the senators should remain in office for life (provided they engaged in no personal misconduct). Gouverneur Morris contended that senators needed unlimited terms if the United States was ever going to attract investment. "Ask any man . . . if he will lend his money or enter into contract? He will tell you no," Morris declared. "If we change our measures no body will trust us: and how avoid a change of measures, but by avoiding a change of men[?]"[76]

The delegates ended up scaling back these ambitious proposals. Elbridge Gerry warned that if congressmen were allowed to serve three times longer than their counterparts in twelve states, "the people will be alarmed, as savoring of despotism."[77] When the convention debated senators' terms, Georgia delegate William Pierce cautioned that "7 years would raise an alarm."[78] In the end the convention decided that senators would face the electorate every six years, the president every four, and members of the House of Representatives every two.

The delegates' wish to create a less-than-democratic government that could nonetheless pass muster with the ratifying conventions also forced a compromise on the president's role in lawmaking. Only in one state, Massachusetts, could the governor veto legislation.[79] But James Madison was speaking for other Framers when he said he considered a presidential veto essential "for the safety of a minority"—whether "the Rich," creditors, or members of dissenting religions—"in Danger of oppression from an unjust and interested majority."[80] Since unjust measures such as "emissions of paper money, largesses to the people [and] a remission of debts" would sometimes cruise through Congress on the irresistible wave of popular fervor, Gouverneur Morris declared, the president needed the power to scuttle them.[81]

James Wilson of Pennsylvania, whose biographers often portray him as a herald of democracy, proposed to give the chief executive "a complete and full negative," meaning that it could not be overridden.[82] Other delegates worried that an absolute presidential veto would not, in George Mason's words, "accord with the genius of the people." Mason "asked if Gentlemen had ever reflected on that awful period of time between the passing and final adoption of this constitution;—what alarm might possibly take place in the public mind."[83] In the end the convention allowed the president to veto legislation but also permitted two-thirds of both houses to override him.[84] Since only one governor possessed the veto power, the Framers' solution can hardly be described as middle-of-the-road. But it was more moderate than what many of them had envisioned, and for that reason it was not expected to jeopardize ratification.

As the convention delegates went their separate ways early in the autumn of 1787, it was clear that their republican idealism and their desperate desire to get the Constitution through the ratifying conventions had forced them to drop or moderate some of their favorite restraints on grassroots influence. But they still managed to make the new national government far less responsive to the popular will than any of its state-level counterparts. No law that passed the one elected branch, the House of Representatives, would take effect without the approval of the indirectly chosen Senate. The president, who would also not be elected directly by the voters, could block any legislation that failed to garner the support of two-thirds of both houses. Most of the Framers assumed that federal laws, like state legislation, would also be subject to review by the Supreme Court justices, whom they had placed at two removes from the electorate.[85]

Even the House of Representatives would not simply be a national version of the state assemblies that had evoked so much disgust from elite Americans. But the barriers that the convention placed between congressmen and their constituents were remarkably inconspicuous, as the next chapter shows.

CHAPTER 12

"DIVIDE ET IMPERA"

STATECRAFT

SOME OF THE HEFTIEST RESTRAINTS the Framers placed on popular power were also the least visible. The convention frustrated the Constitution's critics by accomplishing several crucial reforms through simple acts of omission. Even as British colonists, freeholders in many North American jurisdictions had enjoyed the right of instructing their representatives on how to vote, but the Constitution made no provision for instructing congressmen.[1] The Articles of Confederation—and even the "Virginia Plan," the blueprint upon which the Constitution was based—also made members of the lower house of the federal legislature "subject to recall."[2] This was another provision the Framers chose to leave out of the Constitution.[3]

The Constitution's denial of the rights of instruction and recall culminated an acrimonious debate, dating back to the struggle against Parliament, over whether elected officials were the "servants of the people" or the "Governor[s] of the people."[4] What should a representative do when he and his constituents disagreed? While populist essayists argued that the assemblyman must yield to the wishes of the people who had elected him, their opponents wanted him to exercise his own judgment. Indeed, Noah Webster said the relationship between constituent and representative was like a marriage: once an election had joined them together, the citizen had to yield to the superior judgment of the statesman in the same way that a married woman had to respect the authority of her husband. When William Paterson of New Jersey told his colleagues at the federal convention, "I came here not to speak my own sentiments, but the sentiments of those who sent me," his was very much a minority viewpoint.[5]

The members of the convention also harbored other expectations that they did not write into the Constitution. There seems to have been an understanding that the Senate would meet in secret, as it initially did. But the expectation of closed-door Senate sessions was itself a secret; nothing was put on paper. Nor was another of the delegates' shared expectations: that while members of the House of Representatives would travel to the capital for only a few months each year, senators would be a permanent part of the national government.[6]

The convention's most effective restraint on popular power was invisible for the simple reason that it was implicit in the whole idea of transferring certain key responsibilities from the states, where the median population was 250,000 souls, to a new national government that encompassed all 3.5 million Americans.

Most of the new state constitutions written during the Revolution had massively increased the membership of the assembly, in some cases doubling or tripling it.[7] That resulted in a proportionate reduction in the number of each assemblyman's constituents. The Philadelphia convention proposed a shift in the opposite direction, decreeing that the lower house of the federal legislature would be smaller than most of the state assemblies. That decision guaranteed that federal election districts would be huge. Each congressman would represent about ten times as many voters as the typical state assemblyman—a simple truth with powerful implications.

Several of the same convention delegates who argued against allowing ordinary citizens to elect their U.S. senators also wished to deny them the power of filling the lower house. Confessing that his republicanism had been chastened by the "levilling spirit" in the thirteen American republics, Elbridge Gerry of Massachusetts proposed that the voters in each congressional district elect a slate of candidates from which their state legislature would then choose their congressman for them.[8] General Charles Cotesworth Pinckney of South Carolina proposed to exclude voters from the process altogether. He would leave the selection of the powerful new Congress right where it had been when the United

States was a mere confederation: in the hands of the state legislatures. Pinckney told the convention that a "majority of the people in S. Carolina" had been "notoriously for paper money as a legal tender" for debts. But the assembly had voted to give creditors the option of refusing the paper money that it approved in October 1785, which indicated that state legislators would also be able to resist popular demands that they send men who supported measures such as fiat money to Congress.[9] Delegates like Gerry and Pinckney feared that a directly elected House of Representatives would adopt the same sort of tax and debt relief legislation that they and the other members of the convention had come to Philadelphia to abolish.

Other delegates thought the House of Representatives should be popularly elected. If the convention proposed a powerful new government in which the voters were not allowed to fill even one branch, they said, the Constitution would stand little chance of being ratified. Delegates who supported the direct election of congressmen lacked none of their colleagues' determination to prevent the adoption of legislation they considered irresponsible. They were simply proposing a different route to the same destination. James Madison spoke for many of his contemporaries when he asserted that in any given society, "the most enlightened and impartial people" would be outnumbered by "the unreflecting multitude."[10] The young Virginian believed he had found a way to get the unreflecting majority to give their votes to the enlightened minority. "If the Election is made by the Peop. in large Districts," he told the federal convention, "there will be no Danger of Demagogues." Decades later Madison remained confident that "large districts" were "manifestly favorable to the election of persons" with a "probable attachment to the rights of property." James Wilson agreed. "Bad elections proceed from the smallness of the districts which give an opportunity to bad men to intrigue themselves into office," he said.[11]

As Madison noted many years later, one reason larger districts rarely elect demagogues is that they diminish the influence of "personal solicitations," favoring instead the candidate who has achieved prominence long before the start of election season.[12] And to a generation that considered the quest for fame one of the noblest of human pursuits, it seemed that "merit and notoriety of character" were, as Madison put it, "rarely separated." Most of the delegates also correlated fame with the possession of a large amount of property. Sure, Indian captives and itinerant preachers sometimes acquired fame without amassing wealth, but most well-known Americans were also well-to-do. Once "the sphere of election is enlarged," Charles Cotesworth Pinckney would explain to his colleagues in the South Carolina legislature in January 1788, the wealthier candidate, with his more extensive reputation and wider sphere of influence (especially his network of customers, debtors, partners, employees, tenants, and suppliers), would start with a tremendous advantage over his rival, the "little demagogue of a petty parish or county," who "probably would not be known."[13] Thus the authors of the Constitution agreed with Herman Husband that large election districts tend to elect wealthy men, the only difference being that they celebrated what he bemoaned.

It would be too cynical to ascribe the Framers' desire to tilt elections in favor of wealthy candidates to the simple fact that most of them were men of means. Like many other Americans, the members of the convention genuinely believed property purchased virtue. For one thing, it was generally only the affluent who had acquired the "extensive information" that men such as William Plumer considered "requisite to form the statesman."[14] They also had more leisure time. Perhaps most crucially, property placed a man beyond the reach of bribery or economic intimidation. In his spring 1787 election sermon, presented to the Connecticut legislature two weeks before the opening of the federal convention, Durham pastor Elizur Goodrich affirmed that America's "natural aristocracy" was based not on social position but on merit. But he emphasized that "Riches" were nonetheless "necessary" to "raise the judge and counsellor above the temptation of transgressing for a piece of bread."[15]

Constitutional Convention delegates who wished to allow the voters to choose members of Congress pointed out that allowing the state legislatures to appoint congressmen would put the choice in the hands of assemblymen who were themselves elected in relatively small districts: the very men whose unjust and unwise relief policies had made the convention necessary. George Mason "was persuaded there was a better chance for proper elections by the people, if divided into large districts, than by the State Legislatures." Contending that in some states where assemblymen had emitted currency most of the voting public actually opposed it, Mason asked his convention colleagues if they really wanted to allow legislators who favored "paper money or any other Bad measure" to fill Congress with the friends of "these favorite measures."[16]

Despite Mason's fundamental difference of opinion with delegates like Pinckney and Gerry over where to lodge the power to choose congressmen, the examples the three men offered in support of their positions indicated that they shared a common goal. All were sworn enemies of paper money, and each was trying in his own way to ensure the election of congressmen who would protect creditors—and the economy—from its ravages.

Many federal convention delegates were so confident that large districts were likelier than state legislatures to choose virtuous officeholders that they wanted to allow the voters to elect U.S. senators—a right they did not actually obtain until 1913. When Elbridge Gerry argued the ultimately successful position that "the commercial & monied interest wd. be more secure in the hands of the State Legislatures," James Wilson replied that the members of the thirteen assemblies were the very ones who had "sacrificed the commercial to the landed interest."[17] "The great evils complained of were that the State Legislatures run into schemes of paper money &c, whenever solicited by the people," Madison reminded the convention. Letting the assemblies choose senators, far from "checking a like propensity in the National Legislature, may be expected to promote it," he said.[18]

The two most vocal delegates at the Constitutional Convention, Madison and Gouverneur Morris, even supported, at least in theory, a reform that Americans have still not achieved: popular election of the president. Why? Because "those little combinations and those momentary lies" that sometimes determined local elections would carry little weight in a vote taking place in a country the size of the United States, Morris believed.[19]

Another advantage of the vast new congressional districts was that they would allow representatives to reject irresponsible legislation without fear of repercussions at the polls. Federal incumbents would be difficult to defeat for the simple reason that they represented so many voters. This effect would of course have been magnified if the convention had allowed for popular election of the president, and one reason Morris was willing to entrust the choice of the chief executive to ordinary voters was that "the extent of the Country would secure his re-election agst the factions & discontents of particular States," in effect giving him a life term.[20]

Precisely how large should congressional districts be? Madison wanted to peg the membership of the First Congress at 130, which would give the average representative 15,000 to 20,000 constituents. Since Congress would be assuming some of the most important duties of the state legislatures, which had a combined membership of about 2,000, Madison's proposal to limit the number of congressmen to 130 was radical indeed.[21] In 1776, when Thomas Paine proposed a national government in his pamphlet *Common Sense*, he thought there should be "at least 390" congressmen.[22] But Madison's suggestion seems moderate compared with the number of seats the convention eventually decided to create in the First Congress: 65. Given that one of Madison's claims to fame is his zeal for enlarging election districts, it is jarring to discover that he considered the districts the convention created twice as large as they should have been. Indeed, Madison's proposal to double the membership of the House of Representatives was identical to one that would be offered a year later by Melancton Smith, a leading Anti-Federalist. Madison reminded his colleagues that legislation would not need 65 votes to pass, just a majority of the congressmen present. "A *majority* of a *Quorum* of 65 members, was too small a number to represent the whole inhabitants of the U. States," Madison declared. "They would not possess enough of the confidence of the people, and wd. be too sparsely taken from the people, to bring with them all the local information which would be frequently wanted."[23]

Madison's amendment was rejected, but on September 17, the very last day of the convention, the delegates took a small but dramatic step in the same direction. By this time the members had declared that every congressional district must contain a minimum of 40,000 constituents. Nathaniel Gorham of Massachusetts feared that number was too large. One way of "lessening objections to the Constitution," Gorham said, would be to reduce the minimum population of each district to 30,000 souls. Other delegates agreed. Since the first day of the convention, when George Washington was chosen as president, he had not entered into a single debate. Now, on the last day, he astonished the members by breaking his silence to support Gorham's motion. Washington was candid about his motives. He said he feared the immense size of the congressional districts would jeopardize ratification, and "it was much to be desired that the objections to the plan recommended might be made as few as possible."[24]

Washington's intervention ensured the success of Gorham's amendment. The minimum population of congressional districts would not be 40,000 people but 30,000. (There would be no maximum.) What was true of so many other elements of the Constitution would also be true of election districts. Although the immense new congressional constituencies were expected to make the federal government much less responsive to the public will than any of the states, the delegates' fear of jeopardizing ratification prevented them from going quite as far as some of them had desired.

Farmers' influence on legislation would be reduced not only by enlarging election districts but also by shifting authority over matters such as debtor-creditor legislation and continental taxation—arguably the two most important topics legislators confronted in peacetime—from the thirteen individual states to a new national polity that embraced all of them. George Mason reminded the convention that republics suffer from the constant "danger of the majority oppressing the minority"—a malady that "The Gen[era]l Government of itself will cure."[25] In a country where the population was rapidly moving toward the four million mark, Mason and other delegates believed, it would be very difficult for an angry populace to pull off an electoral sweep of the House of Representatives. By throwing so many heterogeneous groups into a single polity, the Framers made it much harder for any effort at influencing the government to attract a majority of the populace.[26]

In order to prevent relief proposals, which seemed to circulate like an "epidemic malady," from infecting officeholders, the Framers surrounded them with a series of concentric barriers.[27] In a nation of continental proportions, unlike in a state, a majority of the electorate would seldom experience the same grievance—or concur in a single remedy.[28] Suppose, for instance, that the bulk of the populace opposed redeeming speculators' government securities in gold and silver at face value. Voters would still disagree about whether to redeem them at market value, with paper money, or in some other way. "As the States will not concur at the same time in their unjust & oppressive plans," George Mason told the federal convention, "the general Govt. will be able to check & defeat them."[29]

Even if most Americans were to support some particular piece of legislation, the transfer of vital government functions from the state to the national level would make it harder for citizens to communicate with each other. "In small societies," Charles Cotesworth Pinckney told the South Carolina ratifying convention, "the people are easily assembled and inflamed." Pinckney believed it was no coincidence that paper money supporters achieved their aims in Rhode Island, "the most contracted society in the union." In neighboring Massachusetts, "where the sphere was enlarged, similar attempts have been rendered abortive," he noted. This salutary effect would be multiplied once control over matters such as paper money had been turned over to a government that embraced the even more "extensive territory" of the United States, since, Pinckney predicted, the sheer "number of its citizens will not permit them all to be assembled at one time, and in one place." Deprived of the ability to hold meetings, the "multitude will be less imperious."[30]

Pinckney had a point. If Congress had controlled the money supply in 1786, the paper money advocates who assembled in East Greenwich, Rhode Island, that February would have had to target federal, not state, incumbents, and they almost certainly would not have managed to defeat a majority of them.

Citizens seeking to exert collective pressure on their legislators could, of course, do so without actually assembling, yet the shift of power from the state to the national level would inhibit other forms of communication as well. In *Federalist* Number 60, which appeared on February 23, 1788, Alexander Hamilton predicted that critics of national legislation would rarely be able to form "a concert of views, in any partial scheme of elections."[31] One reason Gouverneur Morris was willing to allow voters to choose the president directly was that, though even "little combinations" could dominate elections "within a narrow sphere," voters would not be able to coalesce in "so great an extent of country" as the United States.[32]

The best-known champion of the large polity was, of course, Madison. The "Father of the Constitution" told his convention colleagues that by uniting Americans under one political roof, the new national charter would "divide the community into so great a number of interests & parties, that . . . they may not be apt to unite in the pursuit" of any particular goal.[33] The manner in which Madison expressed his thesis in *Federalist* Number 63 was strange but telling; he declared that the Constitution would protect citizens from "the danger of combining."[34] His October 24, 1787, letter to Jefferson was even bolder. "Divide et impera, the reprobated axiom of tyranny," Madison wrote, "is under certain qualifications, the only policy, by which a republic can be administered on just principles."[35]

"Divide et impera"—an explosive phrase. Throughout the 1780s Americans who tried to organize campaigns in favor of relief legislation had discovered again and again just how hard it was to "act unaformly" over an extensive territory. Madison had made the same discovery, and it became one of his principal motives for shifting power from the state to the national level. Seldom would a majority of United States citizens share the same grievance. Even when they did, they would rarely be able "to discover their own strength," much less "act in unison with each other."[36] It was the same strategy that Thomas Jefferson had urged Congress to employ against the United States's Indian neighbors— with the significant difference that Madison wanted to divide white Americans for their own good.

Would the new national government be equally impervious to every sort of grassroots pressure? Several Constitutional Convention delegates were sure that it would not, since some clusters of like-minded Americans would outdo others at achieving the unity that ensured influence. "The schemes of the Rich will be favored by the extent of the Country," Gouverneur Morris told his fellow delegates. Ordinary "people in such distant parts can not communicate & act in concert," placing them at a disadvantage compared with "those who have more Knowledge & intercourse" with each other.[37] In case any of the convention delegates doubted Morris's claim that the well-to-do would still be able to act in concert even after some of the state governments' most important duties had been transferred to a government that spanned all thirteen states, Elbridge Gerry supplied an illustration. On May 10, 1783, Continental Army officers had formed the Society of the Cincinnati, partly with the intention of making sure Congress and the states came through with their promised bonuses. One reason Gerry did not want to leave the election of the president to the voters was that groups such as the Cincinnati would be able to sway elections using their superior capability at "acting in Concert."[38]

Gerry's fellow delegates did not have to look far for proof of his point. Indeed, as they had gathered at the Pennsylvania statehouse in May 1787, another national convention, the triennial meeting of the Cincinnati, was adjourning just down the street. It was no coincidence that the federal convention and the Cincinnati assembled in the same city during the same month. Alexander Hamilton, who wrote the resolutions proposing the federal convention (he was acting on behalf of the few delegates who showed up for an abortive convention in Annapolis, Maryland, the previous September), set it for the same month—May 1787—as the triennial meeting of the Cincinnati, and several officers attended both sessions. One of the great ironies of America's founding is that the convention that wrote the nation's republican constitution was timed to coincide with a reunion of veteran officers who had not disguised their aristocratic ambitions.[39]

The members of the Cincinnati were by no means the only bondholders who kept in touch with each other during the 1780s. William Eustis, a former Continental Army surgeon who did not belong to the veterans' group, believed that by "holding a correspondence" with each other, the ex-officers could achieve sufficient unity to "promote their *pecuniary* interests," especially their goal of "rendering their securities more valuable."[40] Nonveterans also organized. "There are paper speculators dispersed over every part of the United States," Boston merchant George Flint told the firm of Constable Rucker & Company on December 17, 1785. "They keep up a constant & accurate communication. The information flies from one to another in every direction like an electrical shock."[41]

Bondholders were not the only interest that coalesced. Organizations of former army officers proved especially adept at obtaining congressional title, on highly favorable terms, to Indian land.[42] Other wealthy Americans with shared interests—among them merchants, lawyers, and university alumni—also formed associations, often with a view to increasing their political influence.[43]

These organizations of elite Americans did not escape the attention of their less fortunate fellow citizens. William Manning observed that "the greatest and only means by which the Few carry their plans into execution is by their associations and correspondences or complete organization." Choosing nearly the same metaphor as George Flint, he marveled that elite Americans seemed to "know each other's minds so as to dart their plans like flashes of lightning from one end of the continent to the other."[44] Farmers like Manning tended to overstate the unity of bondholders, retired officers, merchants, and other clusters of wealthy Americans. In several states, public creditors in particular were sharply divided. And when Gouverneur Morris claimed the Constitution would make it impossible for common farmers to "communicate & act in concert," he exaggerated their rural isolation. Myriad interactions connected ordinary farm families with their neighbors and even the wider Atlantic world.[45]

Yet few common citizens spun social webs as extensive as those of their wealthier countrymen. It was no secret that relief advocates seeking to influence elections to the upper house had achieved little success at coordinating across town borders (the one grand exception occurring in the petite state of Rhode Island). The difficulty of uniting a diverse collection of debtors and taxpayers became even more clear in the mid-1780s, when far-flung supporters of relief legislation tried to form statewide organizations.

Activists were not naïve about the challenges they faced, and they tried in often remarkable ways to overcome them. Sometimes relief advocates in different parts of a state would make a point of adopting identical proposals. On several occasions they tried to harness the power of the printed word.[46] One of the most intriguing of these efforts was launched in New Hampshire, where it must have seemed to citizens seeking an emission of paper money that their opponents in the legislature had adopted a deliberate strategy of divide and rule. In asking the town meetings to vote on its very modest paper money proposal, the assembly did not challenge them to take it or leave it (as the authors of the Constitution would do less than a year later), instead inviting them to propose amendments or alternatives. A month later a newspaper writer lamented that supporters of paper money had divided themselves among "so many different plans for funding and giving it a circulation." In January 1787 the legislature counted the returns and announced, to no one's surprise, that although two-thirds of the towns had voted in favor of some sort of paper money, none of the specific plans had obtained anything close to a majority. It declined to print any currency.[47]

Few of the other efforts to unite relief advocates behind a single proposal fared any better than the one in New Hampshire. Like its counterpart to the north, the Massachusetts legislature, which held a special session in the fall of 1786 to respond to Shays's Rebellion, was able to reject the most radical relief proposals as "inconsistent with each other."[48] Relief advocates seeking the power of unity would face even greater obstacles if control over the money supply, continental taxation, and other vital matters passed to a national government. Their opponents would, too, but the gap between the two groups' ability to exert collective pressure on elected officials was expected to widen. John Francis Mercer, a late-arriving federal convention delegate from Maryland, observed that senate districts in Virginia, his native state, were so large that voters could "not know & judge of the characters of Candidates." "The people in Towns can unite their votes in favor of one favorite," Mercer said, "& by that means always prevail over the people of the Country, who being dispersed will scatter their votes among a variety of candidates."[49] Since congressional districts would be even larger than the constituencies where Virginia senators were chosen, the disparity between "Town" and "Country" that Mercer had identified would be even greater in federal elections. That prospect by no means troubled the authors of the Constitution, who eagerly anticipated the day when the groups they considered most virtuous—including well-to-do city-dwellers (especially merchants), veteran officers, and investors in government bonds—could overcome irresponsible groups such as debtors and taxpayers.

Herman Husband had also noticed that enlarging legislative districts tended to thwart some factions more effectively than others. In a 1782 pamphlet Husband contended that the framers of the state constitutions had favored large legislative districts because they knew that in this system "the Body of the Governors" would be able to "combine," whereas "the Body of the Governed" was "cut off from the Benefit of the Circulation of Life and Knowledge, and so become dead and ignorant."[50]

• • •

Modern descriptions of the Constitutional Convention generally focus upon the series of "great compromises" that towered, like a chain of mountain peaks, over the members' day-to-day toil on more mundane matters. And yet twenty-first-century Americans are rarely exposed to what was arguably the greatest compromise of all: numerous explicitly elitist proposals, each of which would have obtained majority support if the delegates had had free rein, had to be abandoned—or at least replaced with more subtle devices—because they jeopardized ratification. These were compromises between the Framers and the American people. The convention nonetheless managed to construct a new national government that was considerably less democratic than even the most conservative of the state constitutions.

Recognizing that most of the members of the Constitutional Convention shared the desire to create a national government that was substantially immune to popular influence—and yet sufficiently democratic to be ratified—may make it possible to solve one of the convention's great mysteries. Biographers have often tried to place individual delegates along a continuum between democracy and elitism. But these efforts inevitably run into an insurmountable barrier: most of the members seem to have exhibited a remarkable inconsistency. For instance, on June 6, when Charles Pinckney of South Carolina suggested giving the power to choose congressmen to the state assemblies, his cousin Charles Cotesworth Pinckney agreed with him, but the leading advocate for the opposing position—popular election—was James Madison.[51] Less than three weeks later, on June 26, it was Charles Cotesworth Pinckney who took the democratic position that senators should serve short terms, while Madison thought they should remain in office for as long as nine years.[52] Likewise, James Wilson of Philadelphia is often depicted as one of the most democratic members of the convention, since he supported popular election of both branches of the federal legislature. But Wilson was one of the few delegates who wanted to deny Congress the right to override presidential vetoes.[53] Was Wilson more or less elitist than Roger Sherman, the Connecticut shoemaker-turned-attorney, who did not think the president should have an absolute veto—and yet also opposed the popular election of either branch of Congress?[54]

One way to explain the delegates' apparent inconsistency is to bear in mind that they faced the bracing challenge of persuading ordinary citizens to ratify a document that would reduce their power over lawmakers. The Framers knew the Constitution would have to contain a mixture of democratic and elitist elements—and yet no two delegates chose precisely the same combination.

By proposing to transfer control of the money supply and debtor-creditor relations to a new national government that would be much less responsive to the popular will than any of its state-level counterparts, the Founding Fathers underscored their conviction that the United States would never escape the recession of the 1780s while the thirteen state assemblies retained the power to rescue desperate debtors. The states had also acted too leniently toward taxpayers, the members of the convention affirmed, and as the next chapter will show, that belief accounts for another of their momentous decisions.

CHAPTER 13

"MORE ADEQUATE TO THE PURPOSES"

REVENUE

THE ARTICLES OF CONFEDERATION had delegated the duty of collecting "Continental" taxes to the thirteen states. Now, for the first time ever, national legislators would have the authority to levy taxes of their own. Until the adoption of the federal income tax in 1913, the Constitution allowed the federal government to impose three kinds of taxes: direct levies (such as property assessments), excises (such as fees on the production and sale of alcoholic beverages), and tariffs on merchandise entering the country from overseas. Most of the delegates were confident that the last of these sources of income—customs duties—would be sufficient to sustain the federal government during peacetime. If they proved correct, the effect of the adoption of the Constitution on ordinary taxpayers would be enormous.

The thirteen state governments relied upon a combination of tariffs and direct taxes. Direct levies, which consisted of poll (head) and property taxes, often demanded that farmers fork over gold and silver coin that simply did not exist in their communities. Tariffs, on the other hand, caused farmers little pain. They were collected at the water's edge, where gold and silver were most plentiful, and they were paid by merchants, not farmers. Some state governments—New York's being the classic example—derived a substantial portion of their revenue from tariffs, which allowed them to hold down direct taxes. Others—especially Delaware, New Jersey, and Connecticut, which received most of their foreign goods through Philadelphia or New York City, rather than from oceangoing vessels that sailed directly into their own ports—earned little from their tariffs. Officials in states that lacked large ports faced a constant dilemma: Should they pile more direct taxes on farmers who had no gold and silver with which to pay them, or should they allow their budgetary needs to go unmet? Even the states that did receive direct importations from overseas derived much less revenue from their tariffs than they theoretically might have, since even a slight increase in a state's tariff could drive trading vessels to other states' ports.

A federal tariff was a way for the government to obtain a vast sum of money while placing very little pressure on ordinary taxpayers. Often as much as half the money that a state government extracted from taxpayers was destined for the federal government. If these funds were instead raised through tariff duties, the states would be able to dramatically reduce the direct taxes that had inflamed farmers' protests throughout the 1780s. "For a long time the people of America will not have money to pay direct taxes," Gouverneur Morris warned the federal convention. "Seize and sell their effects and you push them into Revolts."[1] The abolition of direct taxes destined for federal coffers was one of the brightest prospects the Constitution offered. Many convention delegates even hoped to prevent the state assemblies from having to impose taxes on behalf of their own creditors. They wanted the federal government to assume responsibility for paying off all thirteen states' war debts, allowing the state governments to return to the modest tax levels of the colonial era.

Recognizing that the Framers hoped to reduce the average American's taxes may make it possible to solve one of the Constitution's paradoxes: If debt and tax relief legislation had proved to be an essential tool in preventing or quelling agrarian insurrections, what would the state assemblies do about insurgency after the Constitution disabled them from screening debtors and taxpayers? The answer lies in the expected economic impact of the proposed change in government. The very Constitution that prohibited the state legislatures from showing any sympathy for private debtors would, at the same time, prevent state assemblymen from ever having to impose high taxes during periods of monetary scarcity. Thus it would remove one of the largest causes of the agrarian insurrections of the 1780s.

At the same time that a federal tariff would provide relief to taxpayers, it would also, for the first time, enable Congress to pay its bills. For the foreseeable future the largest single line item would be interest payments to federal creditors. American historians spent much of the twentieth century debating the theory that one of the most powerful motivating forces behind the Constitution was the simple fact that many of its authors were bondholders who had not been paid. It is certainly true that bond speculators were among the Constitution's most enthusiastic supporters, but it is also clear that thousands of Americans, including several key federal convention delegates, supported federal taxation not because they owned bonds—many did not—but for other, more public-spirited reasons. Some viewed satisfying the public creditors as an imperative of justice.[2] Others considered it an essential tool in restoring the government's credit rating.

The delegates also believed that if the bondholders received their interest punctually, the market value of their securities would approach the face value, making them a valuable addition to the money supply. Since the scarcity of money had vastly increased the tax burden, allowing Congress to levy taxes on behalf of bondholders would, ironically enough, provide relief to taxpayers.

The Constitution did not explicitly require the federal government to redeem the war bonds. The first clause of Article VI simply stated that "All Debts contracted and Engagements entered into, before the Adoption of this Constitution, shall be as valid against the United States under this Constitution, as under the Confederation." Some delegates pushed for more explicit language, but they were defeated by realists such as Madison and Hamilton. Five years later, after he and Madison had parted company on the question of the public debt, Hamilton said he could "well remember" discussing the topic during "a long conversation which I had with Mr. Madison in an afternoon's walk." "We were perfectly agreed in the expediency and propriety of" requiring Congress to redeem the bonds, Hamilton said. But the two also concurred "that it would be more advisable to make it a measure of administration than an article of Constitution, from the impolicy of multiplying obstacles to its reception."[3] In this case as in so many others, the Framers chose subtlety over a more explicit approach that might have jeopardized ratification.

There were also other reasons to favor federal taxation. In the eighteenth century as in the twenty-first, the largest demand on government treasuries inevitably came from the military, and there was a nearly universal belief that the U. S. Army could not do its job without more money. Only with a well-financed military force could the federal government fulfill the preamble's commitment "to provide for the common defence." Alexander Hamilton reminded his colleagues of some of the duties the American army was expected to perform: "You have to protect your rights against Canada on the north, Spain on the south, and your western frontier against the savages."[4]

By the time of the federal convention, U.S. citizens recognized that the last of these goals—fighting Indians—was going to cost them even more than they had earlier believed. Native leaders had frequently compared the coalition they were trying to build to "the great white Meeting at Philadelphia"—a reference to Congress, which had met in Philadelphia until 1783.[5] In November and December 1786, the rebel Indians held a council at Brownstown across the Detroit River from the British fort and resolved to follow the white Americans' example.

Although during this very period many citizens of the United States lamented the lack of unity among the thirteen states and campaigned for a stronger national government, the theme of the Brownstown congress was that Native Americans needed to take a lesson in unity from white Americans. An Iroquois speaker said the reason "that large tract of Country, between our present habitations and the Salt water" was "not Still Inhabited by our own Colour" was that "Christians" had been "prudent enough to preserve . . . unanimity," and the Indians had not. "None of the divided Efforts of our Ancestors to oppose them had any Effect," he said. The only way for Native Americans to hang on to the territory they still occupied was to learn from their ancestors' failures and the British Americans' success. "Let us profit by these things and be unanimous," he declared.[6]

Today Americans debate whether the Framers of the Constitutic felt they had anything to learn from the Iroquois Confederacy. I clear that the builders of the anti–United States Indian coalition, of whom were Iroquois, were more interested in learning unity than teaching it.

One way for the Indians to foster unity was to embrace a concept that Europeans had invented within the previous century and a half: race. In an effort to persuade the disparate and divided native nations that they were really members of the same race, the Iroquois delegation at Brownstown told the western nations that the pan-Indian confederacy was of "high importance to all of us of the same Colour."[7]

Next to unity among themselves, the most important thing the Native Americans needed was British aid. Ever since the Revolutionary War, imperial officials had been encouraging anti–United States sentiment and supplying Indians with limited amounts of ammunition but dodging questions about whether they would provide firm military support. The Brownstown congress demanded that the British government give rebel Indians a "determined answer."[8]

The Brownstown meeting sent the U.S. Congress a message demanding that it renounce its claim to the land between the Ohio and Mississippi Rivers. The United States must also disavow the "partial" treaties its agents had negotiated with small numbers of Indians within the walls of Forts Stanwix (1784), McIntosh (1785), and Finney (1786). Insisting that "the chiefs had no power" to cede the vast tracts named in the fort treaties, the Brownstown congress demanded that future meetings be held "some place more central."[9] Although native diplomats had formed their confederacy and invented the idea of joint ownership of hunting ground only three years earlier (at a September 1783 meeting at Sandusky), they now referred to both the league and to joint ownership as though they were long-standing traditions: "the Lands they inherited by their Forefathers, and bequeathed to them was held in common, for the use & Benefit of the whole Confederacy, so no one Branch of that Confederacy could alienate any part of that without the Consent of the Whole." Thus the land cessions made at the three fort treaties of the mid-1780s, having been made by "particular Tribes," were "null & void." The council warned that if the United States "do not meet them upon fair and equal Terms, they are all Unanimously determin'd to defend their rights & privileges to the last Extremity."[10]

The growth of the native coalition alarmed citizens of the United States. In March 1787 Indian agent Richard Butler reported that Native American diplomats had "laboured exceedingly to form a general confederacy among themselves from North to South in order to become formidable." Butler warned that the United States might soon be drawn into "a general Indian war, *with European supplies and friends,*" a war that would "give a severe shock to our frontier."[11] It was becoming increasingly clear that fighting Indians was going to be the most costly task assigned to the new American army. Ultimately, however, it would also be the most lucrative. Once Congress managed to field a military force powerful enough to drive the Indians farther west, it could more than recoup that investment by auctioning off their land. If federal officials accepted war bonds from land office customers, as they had under the Articles of Confederation, they might finally be able to fulfill the old dream of using territory conquered from the Indians to liquidate the government's domestic debt.

Federal soldiers would also occasionally be used, as the preamble promised, to "ensure domestic tranquility." Although debtors and taxpayers would no longer be able to extract relief legislation from state assemblymen, the possibility remained that they would relieve their own distress—by freeing jailed debtors, forcing courts to close, or halting the sale of confiscated property. One of the Framers' principal criticisms of the Articles of Confederation was that, as Edmund Randolph told the convention, they made "No Provision agt. internal Insurrections."[12] Under Article I of the Constitution, the national government's authority to suppress rebellions would be unambiguous.[13] Congress would be permitted to raise sufficient tax revenue to field a powerful army, and it could also, in emergencies, take over the militias of the thirteen states.[14] None of these provisions would have been necessary—indeed, in many Americans' eyes, the Constitution itself could have been dispensed with—if farmers had not launched major rebellions during the 1780s. The most dramatic revolt was, of course, Shays's Rebellion in Massachusetts. Congress voted to raise an army to help suppress the uprising. (The official justification for raising the troops, to fight Indians, was widely recognized as false.) Yet only one state, Virginia, complied with the congressional requisition raising funds to recruit and equip the army.[15] The soldiers never took the field—an abject failure that became, for prominent citizens throughout the country, the final argument for strengthening the federal government.[16]

It is likely that many at the federal convention who swapped dire warnings about Shays's Rebellion would have traveled to Philadelphia and created a powerful national government even if the danger of revolt had remained hypothetical. But the Massachusetts insurrection did exert tremendous influence on one Framer, indeed the most important one. In December 1786, when the Virginia assembly informed George Washington that it had named him a delegate to the federal convention, he immediately wrote back declining the honor. Why should Washington risk his good name by taking part in a scheme that might well come to nothing (as the Annapolis Convention of 1786 had) or, worse, arouse suspicions of a conspiracy against liberty?

Washington also had another reason to avoid the convention. In 1784 he had been elected the first president of the Society of the Cincinnati. The group immediately stirred controversy, primarily because the original members decided to bequeath membership to their first sons and so on in perpetuity. Washington persuaded the society's national meeting to renounce the primogeniture rule, but most of the state chapters voted to retain it, and he thenceforth kept the Cincinnati at as great a distance as he decently could.[17] When Washington received his invitation to the federal convention, he had already told the Cincinnati he was unable to attend theirs. Too polite to supply his real reason for declining, Washington had explained that the "present imbecility of my health" did not permit him to leave the state. The fifty-four-year-old Washington really was ill much of that winter, suffering from "fever & ague" and even more from "rheumatick pains" that often forced him to wear one arm in a sling.[18] Having used his health as excuse, he wrote James Madison, "I could not appear at the same time & place . . . with out giving offence" to "the late officers of the American Army."[19]

Friends—including several members of the Cincinnati—implored Washington to change his mind, and the influence of these personal solicitations should not be discounted. But the single most important factor in persuading Washington to attend the convention—a decision that proved momentous, because it is hard to imagine the Constitution being ratified without his imprimatur—was Shays's Rebellion.[20] Most of the dispatches Washington received on the revolt bristled with wild exaggerations. To one particularly alarming report from his fellow Virginian Henry Lee, Jr., he replied darkly that "mankind left to themselves are unfit for their own government."[21]

Washington's greatest fear was that the revolt would spread to other states. A decade earlier, when the last royal governor of Virginia, Lord

Dunmore, offered freedom to Patriots' slaves who would rally to the king's standard, Washington, who had just taken command of the Continental Army, warned that if Dunmore was not crushed at once, his army would "increase as a snow ball by rolling."[22] The former commander now used the same metaphor to describe the possible effects of Shays's Rebellion. "Commotions of this sort, like snow-balls, gather strength as they roll, if there is no opposition in the way to divide & crumble them," he told David Humphreys, a former aide.[23] Washington also resorted to the same image that a host of other prominent Americans had used to describe how quickly agrarian insurgency might spread. "Fire, where there is inflamable matter, very rarely stops," he told David Stuart in December 1786, and three weeks later he was warning Henry Knox, his former chief of artillery, that "there are combustibles in every State, which a spark may set fire to."[24]

"Without some alteration in our political creed," Washington wrote James Madison (who needed no convincing), "the superstructure we have been seven years raising at the expence of much blood and treasure, must fall."[25] In describing the reforms he envisioned, the old general, still an accomplished horseman, employed the same image so many other elite Americans had used. "Let the reins of government then be braced in time & held with a steady hand," he wrote.[26]

Washington's letter declining appointment to the federal convention arrived in Richmond just after New Year's Day 1787. Governor Edmund Randolph wrote back saying he would postpone any announcement of the general's decision while awaiting the outcome of the Massachusetts convulsions, since Shays's Rebellion might well change Washington's mind.[27] Randolph was right. It was with a bittersweet mixture of reluctance and determination that on March 28, 1787, Washington wrote the governor accepting the appointment.[28]

Free farmers' insurrections were not the only ones the national government would help suppress. As several members of the convention pointed out, the powerful new army and the federalized militia could also be used against unruly slaves. White southerners' potential need for outside help was great; throughout the 1780s, "gangs of runaway negroes" were spotted in several sections of South Carolina. Some of the African Americans who had escaped their owners and joined forces with the British during the Revolutionary War had stayed behind when the redcoats left, but they clung to their freedom, remaining (as newspapers reported) "in a state of Rebellion." Whites were especially worried about the maroons who took refuge in the swampland around the Savannah River, which separates Georgia from South Carolina. In October 1786 the residents of a maroon village less than twenty miles from Savannah fought off two assaults by a Georgia military expedition before slipping away and pushing even deeper into the "almost impenetrable swamp." Early in May 1787, as the federal convention delegates were making preparations for their sojourn in Philadelphia, a joint force from South Carolina and Georgia, backed by Catawba Indians, captured the new maroon settlement—but few of its inhabitants.[29]

The expectation that the Constitution would help protect slaveholders from the people they claimed to own led delegates from all but the southernmost states to demand that Congress be allowed to ban the African slave trade. As Marylander Luther Martin put it, Congress deserved the power to block new shipments of Africans, since "slaves weakened one part of the Union which the other parts were bound to protect."[30] The Revolutionary War had shown that when African Americans formed alliances with foreign invaders—liberators, in their eyes—they became even more formidable. Decades earlier Spanish governors in Florida had offered freedom to all enslaved British colonists who could make it to St. Augustine—a policy that was widely blamed for the bloodiest North American slave revolt of the eighteenth century, the Stono Rebellion of April 1739.[31]

Near the end of the convention the issue of slave uprisings became intertwined with other conflicts between the regions. Southern delegates proposed to prohibit Congress from taxing exports. Their region's exports—primarily tobacco, rice, and indigo—were more valuable than those produced in the rest of the country, so the South would pay a disproportionate share of any export tax. On August 8 Rufus King of Massachusetts defended Congress's right to levy export tariffs. "If slaves are to be imported," he argued, "shall not the exports produced by their labor, supply a revenue the better to enable the Genl. Govt. to defend their Masters?"[32]

Other delegates linked slavery to trade protection. On August 29 a group of southern delegates tried to reduce the likelihood of Congress's imposing restrictions on their imports and exports. Under their proposal, no legislation favoring American merchants over their foreign competitors would be adopted without the support of two-thirds of both houses of Congress. Northern delegates rallied against this proposal. In their view, commercial concessions were the price white southerners owed their fellow citizens to the north for helping them put down slave revolts. The New England "States had no motive to Union but a commercial one," Nathaniel Gorham of Massachusetts declared with no little exaggeration. Northerners "were not led to strengthen the Union by fear for their own safety," he said, with the obvious implication being that slaveholders were.[33]

Some southern delegates, loath to make commercial concessions or to in any way impede the slave trade, claimed white southerners were actually fully capable of defending themselves.[34] Others, however, were willing to acknowledge what James Madison described as their "vulnerable situation." Such a concession came especially easy to Madison. A half century earlier, a jury had ruled his grandfather's death a murder, convicting two of the people he claimed to own, a man named Turk and a woman named Dido, as well as another slave from a neighboring plantation, of the crime.[35] General Charles Pinckney of South Carolina was also willing to admit "the interest the weak Southn. States had in being united with the strong Eastern [northern] States."[36]

Madison and Pinckney's admission that southern slaveholders might someday require federal protection proved prophetic. States' rights ideology did not prevent southern governors from requesting federal troops during all of the major slave insurrection scares of the nineteenth century: Gabriel's Rebellion in central Virginia in 1800; the Denmark Vesey conspiracy in Charleston, South Carolina, in 1822; Nat Turner's rebellion in Virginia in 1831; and John Brown's raid on Harpers Ferry, Virginia, in 1859. State militiamen were able to suppress most of the uprisings before U.S. troops arrived to assist them, but Brown's band held out until its position was stormed by U.S. Marines. Their commander, still two years away from his own rebellion against the federal government, was Robert E. Lee.

By the end of 1787 the legislature of every state but Rhode Island had complied with the federal convention's call for state-level conventions to consider the Constitution. The willingness of the majority of the state assemblymen to hold these ratifying conventions—not to mention many legislators' enthusiastic support for the Constitution—has led some scholars to deny that one of the Framers' primary motives was to rein in the thirteen legislatures. They ask how the legislatures and the Framers could possibly be described as enemies when a large percentage of the convention delegates had themselves served in the state assemblies. And besides, they say, if the legislatures had really perceived the federal convention as a threat, they could easily have thwarted its work by refusing to call ratifying conventions.[37]

Recall that many of the legislatures that granted relief to debtors and taxpayers during the 1780s did so unwillingly. When the assemblies imposed heavy taxes in the midst of dire shortages of circulating coin, farmers demanded relief, especially tax cuts and paper money. Representatives often felt they had no choice but to comply with these demands, but that did not make them friends of relief. John Jay sympathized with legislators whose constituents placed them in this predicament. In many states, he wrote, the governing party "may not always be able if willing to prevent the injustice meditated."[38]

By prohibiting state-level relief, the Constitution would eliminate the pressure on state representatives to adopt relief legislation, and that was a compelling reason for them to support ratification. What remained doubtful in the fall of 1787 was whether ordinary voters and the state ratifying conventions could be persuaded to see the Constitution in the same favorable light.

PART V
ESAU'S BARGAIN

CHAPTER 14

"TAKE UP THE REINS"

RATIFICATION

THE CONSTITUTIONAL CONVENTION was largely a response to the farmers' rebellions of the 1780s and the state assemblies' subsequent adoption of legislation that allegedly violated public and private contracts. Opponents of the new charter were quick to claim that it was itself an insurrection against the Articles of Confederation and a violation of that solemn agreement. Early in the convention New Jersey delegate William Paterson had implored his colleagues to limit themselves to their assigned mission of suggesting amendments to the Articles. Urging the delegates to reflect upon "The Nature of a Contract" that had been "Solemnly entered into," Paterson had asked, "Why break it[?]"[1] After the Constitution was presented to the public, one Massachusetts Anti-Federalist, John Quincy Adams, complained that the ratification procedure established by the Framers violated his state's constitution, which "was the only crime of our Berkshire & Hampshire insurgents."[2]

Adams's complaint raises a larger question. Why was it that, a decade after breaking away from the British Empire and creating thirteen sovereign states, free Americans decided to divest those states of some of their most important powers, transferring them to a new national government that would, as Robert Morris put it, "restrain the democratic spirit"?[3] Why did free Americans agree to give up so much of their power?

They did so for many reasons. Numerous citizens affirmed that they voted for the Constitution in order to make internal changes in the thirteen states. Less than a month after leaving Philadelphia, James

Madison was pleased to learn that his own most pressing concern was resonating throughout the country. Recall that on June 6, 1787, Madison had told his colleagues in Philadelphia that state-level "Interferences" with "the security of private rights, and the steady dispensation of Justice" were "evils which had more perhaps than any thing else, produced this convention."[4]

What, precisely, were the *"angry, oppressive, and destructive"* state laws from which the Constitution would rescue the country?[5] On that question, the Federalists were virtually unanimous. One clause of the Constitution was described as "Sufficient to outweigh all Objections to the System."[6] This was Article I, Section 10, which banned paper money and other state-level relief legislation. Given the solid backing that the Constitution would offer Americans seeking to collect from their debtors, their support for it was expected to be nearly unanimous. "Creditors, you know without being told, that the new constitution secures you against tender acts, &c. and will enable"—in fact require—"your debtors to pay you honorably," declared one Virginia essayist.[7] Alexander Hamilton expected the Constitution to earn "the good will of most men of property," since it would "protect them against domestic violence and the depredations which the democratic spirit is apt to make on property."[8]

As the Federalists anticipated, creditors greeted the Constitution like an army of liberation. "Our Courts have lately been very remiss," James Hunter of Portsmouth, Virginia, told an associate, but "we look forward to the new Constitution for general Reform."[9] In the fall of 1787 Thomas Smith warned Boston merchant John Dolbeare that if he were to sue a certain "Mr. B." during the existence of the state's "Tender Law" (which forced creditors to accept property from their debtors), "you will be likely to suffer." There was a glimmer of hope, however. "If the New Constitution takes place," Smith wrote, "the Tender Law will be at an end."[10]

Unpaid creditors were by no means the only Americans who rejoiced at the prospect of tearing down the protective barriers that state assemblymen and local officials had set up around debtors. "While legislative assemblies interfered between debtors and creditors," David Ramsay, the Charleston, South Carolina, physician asked, "what security could there be for property? . . . he that parted with his money could not tell when it would be replaced—hence a total want of confidence and of credit." Under the Constitution, however, "these evils will be done away." As soon as creditors feel certain of their ability to "recover payment. . . . That useful order of men, formerly called money lenders will be revived."[11]

The friends of the Constitution tailored their praise of Section 10 to the particular circumstances of their home states. Whereas the most common claim they made to Virginians was that abolishing debtor relief would persuade foreign—especially British—merchants to ship them merchandise on long credit, in Massachusetts they were more likely to assert that their own state abounded in private reserves of gold and silver that would be lent out as soon as relief was abolished.[12] Everywhere the Federalists' claim that the Constitution would revive credit reverberated in merchants' private correspondence. Falmouth, Virginia, trader William Allason's account books teemed with dormant debts that would spring to life if the Constitution was adopted. But Allason was convinced that creditors like himself were not the only ones who stood to benefit. He told John Likely of Greenock, Scotland, he had grown cautious about expanding his network of suppliers and customers. But "I very probably may extend it after . . . the New Fed[e]ral Constitution will take place," he said.[13]

Individual Americans were not the only ones who would find loans easier to obtain after the new federal charter was ratified. David Ramsay noted that little progress had been made on a proposed canal between the Santee and Cooper Rivers in South Carolina. "Much may be done to improve our inland navigation and facilitate our intercourse with each other," Ramsay observed shortly after his home state ratified. "But who would expend his capital on any project of this kind, while legislative assemblies claimed and exercised the right of making ex post facto laws?" he asked. Section 10 would set the shovels in motion. "Under the stability and energy which our new constitution promises, methinks I see the rivers of these states wedded to each other" and the "western country attached to the sea-coast," Ramsay declared.[14]

The crudest economic interpretations of the federal convention depict it as a cabal of public and private creditors who envisioned the new national government as a giant collection agency. It is true that large-scale creditors were fast friends of the Constitution. But some of the most avid supporters of the Constitution were not creditors but debtors.

Gouverneur Morris, the man who put the Constitution in its final form, had arrived at the federal convention carrying a tremendous, albeit invisible, burden: debts in excess of £20,000. Just weeks earlier, he had augmented his debt by nearly £8,000 in purchasing "Morrisania," the New York mansion where he was born, from the older brother who inherited it. Morris absented himself from the convention for most of June in order to confer with the overseer he had just hired. Soon after returning to Philadelphia, Morris plunged another £3,500 into debt purchasing more than 60,000 acres of land that the state of New York had acquired from the Six Nations of the Iroquois.[15] At first glance Morris might have been expected to fear the crackdown on debtors that the friends of the Constitution promised. Actually he celebrated it, because he saw his debt not as an albatross around his neck but as an investment. He believed his best chance of satisfying his creditors lay in borrowing even more money. That would permit him to make still more investments, the returns from which would pay all his debts. The Constitution would help Morris obtain those additional loans.

During the mid-1780s Morris and two partners (including his kinsman Robert Morris) had come up with the same idea that occurred to James Monroe and James Madison: borrowing money in Europe. Although records are incomplete, it appears that no one would lend them the money. Like Madison, Morris hoped the Constitution would increase the availability of loans by assuring would-be investors on both sides of the Atlantic that they would have no trouble collecting from their American debtors.[16]

Joshua B. Osgood was another debtor who believed the Constitution would allow him to borrow more. By the time the federal convention gathered, Osgood, having sunk into a morass of debt, was grasping helplessly for the additional loans he needed to extricate himself. Three weeks after the convention adjourned, the Fryeburg, Massachusetts, merchant assured a friend the Constitution would "give Energy to Government" and thereby "ristore Confidince between Men." Then, inevitably, "money will be obtainable by the Possession of real Estate," and Osgood, a landowner, would "find it in my Power [to?] command

Cash sufficient for my purposes."[17] Ratification would, in short, enable Osgood to borrow the money he needed to pay his debts. Osgood and Gouverneur Morris were by no means the only debtors who joined creditors in the coalition that supported the Constitution.[18]

If, as its promoters anticipated, the Constitution were to attract a massive infusion of capital to the American economy, the most obvious benefits would of course flow to the entrepreneurs who received the money—merchants, canal companies, land speculators, and agricultural improvers. But ratification was expected to bolster the entire economy. One Federalist traced an undeviating, albeit indirect, line connecting Section 10 to a future surge in the price of American farmers' crops. Once the new national government was ratified, he wrote, "public and private credit will be established; which circumstances must bring money amongst us," allowing farmers to "sell upon good terms."[19] The real estate market would also revive. George Washington attributed "the great fall in the price of property" throughout the United States to the fact that "money is not to be had." Ratification would end the monetary famine and raise the price of land. Men like Washington expected the Constitution to attract people as well as capital to American shores. If "property was well secured—faith and justice well preserved—a stable government well administered,—and confidence restored," he wrote, "the tide of population and wealth would flow to us, from every part of the Globe."[20]

Federalists said Section 10 would also foster economic growth by teaching Americans better habits. Recall that many leading citizens believed relief legislation had exacerbated two flaws in the national character: "torpor" (farmers' tendency to work too little) and extravagance (their penchant for excessive consumption).[21] The new national government would combat these failings. Farmers would no longer be able to escape their just debts, and many would be compelled to deliver up their property at a fraction of its value. But the ensuing hardship would ultimately pay dividends, Federalists argued. Forced to produce more, farmers would stimulate the growth of the American economy.

Although the supporters of the Constitution sincerely believed it would benefit nearly every free American, they knew better than to expect all their neighbors to see it in that light. At the same time that Section 10 made the Constitution attractive to creditors (and even to some debtors), it was bound to repel many Americans who could not pay their debts. Indeed, Oliver Ellsworth of Connecticut claimed, many Anti-Federalists were simply "debtors in desperate circumstances."[22] In assessing the chances for ratification in Massachusetts, Andover lawyer William Symmes, Jr., predicted that the "principal weight of opposition will hang" on Section 10.[23]

Federalists expected one group of debtors—those whose creditors were British merchants—to oppose the Constitution with special vehemence. The old Congress had been powerless to enforce the clause in the 1783 peace treaty requiring Americans to pay their prewar British debts. In sharp contrast, the Constitution would not only prohibit the state assemblies from violating treaties but allow British and other foreign creditors to seek redress in federal court. "The danger of every defendant" in a British debt case "being hurried sooner or later" to the new Supreme Court "is the most vulnerable and odious part of the constitution," Edmund Randolph—himself a British debtor—declared.[24] Although the opponents of the Constitution lodged numerous libertarian, states-rights, and democratic objections against it, Federalists like James Madison believed these were not "the true grounds of opposition." Actually, he said, "the articles relating to Treaties, to paper money, and to contracts, created more enemies than all the errors in the system, positive and negative, put together."[25]

In reply to the widely circulated claim that the Constitution would crack down on debtors, thereby persuading moneyed men and women to reopen the credit valve, most of the leading Anti-Federalists said almost nothing. Very few of the writers who attacked the Constitution in 1787 and 1788 criticized it for prohibiting the state legislatures from granting relief to debtors. Almost none defended paper money or property-tender laws. Even fewer Anti-Federalists denounced Section 10 in the state ratifying conventions.[26] Modern students of the Constitution sometimes interpret the Anti-Federalists' failure to attack Section 10 as evidence that the topic was not considered very important.[27] Actually, for many Americans who opposed the Constitution, the decision to ignore its procreditor provisions was strategic, for they feared that defending paper money would play into the hands of the numerous Federalists who claimed their adversaries were simply desperate debtors seeking to shirk their financial obligations.[28] Other Anti-Federalists avoided talking about relief for the simple reason that they themselves opposed it. All three of the federal convention delegates who refused to sign the Constitution—Elbridge Gerry of Massachusetts and George Mason and Edmund Randolph of Virginia—had expressed (in Mason's words) "a mortal hatred to paper money."[29]

By renouncing economic arguments, the Anti-Federalists paved the way for another misunderstanding as well. Since debtor relief was almost always described by its enemies rather than its friends, modern accounts of the controversy over the Constitution generally adopt, by default, the Framers' assumption that relief was unjustified.

Although the Framers were careful to eliminate every possibility of the thirteen state legislatures interfering in debt collection, they imposed no such restriction on the new national government. And yet the friends of the Constitution felt confident that Congress would rescue debtors only in the direst of circumstances—if then. Why? Because they expected the new national regime to be considerably less responsive to public pressure than any of the thirteen republics. The Federalists were not shy about affirming that one of the central problems the Philadelphia convention had tackled was what one Virginian called the state governments' "popular turn."[30] Noah Webster arrived at the antidemocratic ideology he articulated while campaigning for the Constitution by a circuitous route, passing from a belief that the "people in general are too ignorant" to a faith in "the common sense of mankind" and then, during the ratification fight, back to a conviction "that the mass of the people are corrupted"—all in the space of one year. The adoption of the Constitution put a period to Webster's vacillation. The elitist philosophy he articulated during the ratification campaign remained with him the rest of his life.[31]

The Federalists were considerably more candid about the deficiencies they had identified in the state governments than they were about the mechanisms by which the Constitution would eliminate them.[32] Once in a while, however, one of them would pay open homage to its imperviousness to popular pressure. In any free government, a Massachusetts Federalist pointed out, elected officials will invariably be tempted "to secure future elections" by "slacken[ing] the reins, and abat[ing] of that vigour and severity of administration which their sacred engagements and the common welfare require." But this "evil" would be "in some degree wisely guarded against, in the federal government, by the unfrequent elections."[33]

Of all the safeguards against popular influence devised in Philadelphia, Federalist speakers and essayists reserved some of their heartiest praise for the one that was least visible in the Constitution itself. This was the convention's decision to "extend the sphere"—to transfer several of the states' most critical duties to a new national government in which the only directly elected branch would be chosen in enormous districts. Noah Webster's October 1787 essay supporting ratification echoed a theme from the pamphlet that his fellow Connecticut native Benjamin Gale had published five years earlier. Gale had rejoiced in the statewide election of Connecticut's council of assistants, and Webster pointed out that Maryland senators enjoyed even more independence, since they were picked by electors who were themselves elected at large. In both states, Webster affirmed, the sheer number of voters involved in a statewide canvass helped ensure that few members of the upper house would ever be turned out of office. With "no particular number of men to fear or to oblige," the entrenched incumbents in the Maryland Senate and on the Connecticut Council had "prevented the most rash and iniquitous measures" from being adopted.[34] Webster felt confident that the large new election districts created by the Constitution would give congressmen the same sort of protection against voter revolts.[35]

Shifting control of certain key policies from the states to a new national government was also expected to help stop the wave of agrarian uprisings that had swept over the United States in the 1780s. "When the citizens are confined within a narrow compass, as was the case of Sparta, Rome, &c. it is within the power of a factious demagogue to scatter sedition and discontent, instantaneously, thro' every part of the State," John Stevens, Jr., declared in a November 1787 essay. "Republics, limited to *a small territory*, ever have been, and, from the nature of man, ever will be, liable to be torn to pieces by faction."[36] As eager as the friends of the Constitution were to hinder rebels, some of them recognized that they might someday regret doing so. In his October 24, 1787, letter to Thomas Jefferson touting large republics, Madison warned against constructing "too extensive a one," where "a defensive concert may be rendered too difficult against the oppression of those entrusted with the administration."[37]

The widespread allegation that the thirteen state governments suffered from an excess of democracy elicited the same response from the most famous Anti-Federalists as the related claim that state assemblymen had done too much for debtors and taxpayers. Here, too, the Federalists were without adversaries, because the leading opponents of the Constitution shared their belief that the state legislatures were too responsive to the public will. A week into the federal convention, Elbridge Gerry, George Mason, and Edmund Randolph affirmed that the thirteen state governments were, as Mason put it, "too democratic."[38]

Still, the elite Anti-Federalists' acknowledgment that the authors of the state constitutions had erred in one direction did not prevent them from accusing the Framers of trying to push the country too far the other way. They were especially concerned about the federal convention's decision to "extend the sphere" of government, enlarging legislative districts and shifting certain major government responsibilities from the state to the federal level. Most modern accounts of the ratification struggle focus on a single aspect of the Anti-Federalists' case against an American republic of continental proportions: their fear that it would degenerate into tyranny. Since that did not happen, the critics of the Constitution have acquired reputations as poor prophets.[39] But the other, overlooked, aspects of the Anti-Federalists' complaints about large polities and outsize legislative districts stand up much better under modern scrutiny. Many critics denounced the very features of the Constitution that its supporters most enthusiastically celebrated. Anticipating by four months Alexander Hamilton's contention that the Constitution would prevent "a concert of views, in any partial scheme of elections," an Anti-Federalist observed in October 1787 that if the Constitution were adopted, "the people in Georgia and New-Hampshire would not know one another's mind, and therefore could not act in concert to enable them to effect a general change of representatives."[40]

One of the most common complaints about the national government proposed in Philadelphia was that federal legislative districts would contain too many voters, blocking the flow of information both from citizens to the representative and in the other direction. Once members of Congress were "chosen within large circles," a Massachusetts essayist feared, "they will be unknown to a very considerable part of their constituents, and their constituents will be not less unknown to them."[41] In making the case that large election districts would prevent representatives from gathering sufficient information about their constituents, Anti-Federalist writers and speakers drew on the notion, popularized by Adam Smith in his 1759 *Theory of Moral Sentiments*, that all humans are "naturally sympathetic" with other people's sorrows, joys, and needs—but that they "feel . . . little for another, with whom they have no particular connexion." Since a representative with tens of thousands of constituents "can never be well informed as to the circumstances of the people," the "Federal Farmer" warned, he cannot "sympathize with them" either. Ironically, the ratifying convention delegate who drew most heavily on the notion of sympathy was George Mason. Back in Philadelphia he had enthusiastically endorsed the idea of shifting some of the states' power to a national polity with outsize legislative districts. But the convention's omission of a Bill of Rights and other crucial safeguards led Mason to reject its final product, and in speech after speech at the Virginia convention he claimed that the Constitution would sever the vital bond of "fellow-feeling" between the representative and his constituents.[42]

As alarming as the sheer number of constituents in every congressional district was to Anti-Federalist writers, it was not their paramount concern. An even greater threat lurked in the widespread expectation that the men elected in these large, new federal legislative districts would far surpass their constituents in wealth. If only *"eight men should represent the people of this Commonwealth,"* John Quincy Adams warned a cousin in December 1787, "they will infallibly be chosen from the aristocratic part of the community." In Connecticut the argument that the Constitution would ensure the election of wealthy men, oblivious to the problems of ordinary Americans, was made, surprisingly enough, by Benjamin Gale, the man who had praised the electoral invulnerability that Connecticut councilors received by being elected statewide. There were to be so few congressmen that they would assuredly all be "of the higher class of people who know but little of the poverty, straits, and difficulties of the middling and lower class of men," Gale said. The concern that Gale and other Anti-Federalists expressed hinged upon the notion of fellow feeling. "In order for one man properly to represent another," one critic of the Constitution declared, "he must feel like him, which he cannot do if he is not situated like him."⁴³

At the Constitutional Convention, Madison had also worried that officeholders would not be able to sympathize with members of social classes other than their own. "The man who is possessed of wealth, who lolls on his sofa or rolls in his carriage," he had said there, "cannot judge of the wants or feelings of the day laborer." Madison was apparently even more concerned about the corollary inability of the laborer to empathize with the needs of the man in the carriage; the point of his speech was that unless U.S. senators were given extremely long terms, they might someday cave in to popular demands that they redistribute rich people's property.⁴⁴ During the ratification debate, however, Madison abandoned his earlier claim that accurate representation required fellow feeling. The representative's "interest" and "ambition," he declared in *Federalist* Number 57, would ensure his "fidelity and sympathy with the great mass of the people."⁴⁵

Like several federal convention delegates, numerous opponents of the Constitution predicted that well-to-do Americans would outdo farmers and artisans at augmenting their influence by coordinating their efforts. "The great easily form associations," Melancton Smith told the New York ratifying convention on June 21, 1788, but "the poor and middling class form them with difficulty." He and other Anti-Federalists worried that once the government began holding plurality elections (in which the victory simply went to the candidate with the most votes, even if he fell short of a majority) in large districts, "the common people will divide, and their divisions will be promoted by the others." By contrast, "the *natural aristocracy*" would "easily unite their interests" behind slates of like-minded candidates.⁴⁶

The Framers had chosen not to require the state legislatures to carve the states into single-member congressional districts, and another Anti-Federalist, "Cornelius," explained the implications of this decision to Massachusetts voters. "The citizens in the seaport towns are numerous; they live compact; their interests are one; there is a constant connection and intercourse between them," he observed. Thus merchants and their followers would be able to "centre their votes" on a slate of like-minded candidates. Farmers, by contrast, were "scattered far and wide" and would thus find it much harder "to concert uniform plans for carrying elections." Even James Madison conceded that once the Constitution placed American voters in a more "extended situation," ordinary citizens would have trouble "combining," leaving them vulnerable to "the combined industry of interested men."[47]

Several opponents of the Constitution compared the United States to ancient Israel in the days of the prophet Samuel. "The Israelites were unsuccessful in war," Robert Lansing reminded the New York ratifying convention; "they were sometimes defeated by their enemies." So what did they do? "Instead of reflecting that these calamities were occasioned by their sins, they sought relief in the appointment of a king, in imitation of their neighbors."[48] Leaders of the twelve tribes came to Samuel saying, "Make us a king." When Samuel transmitted the appeal to Jehovah, He was furious, but He ultimately told Samuel, "Make them a king." Henceforth Israel was ruled by a long succession of monarchs—most of whom were tyrants. Now the United States stood upon the same precipice, the Anti-Federalists said. They pleaded with their countrymen not to hearken to those who, like the ancient Israelites, "in a frenzy . . . demanded a king."[49]

Federalists were not naïve about the challenge of reconciling ordinary citizens to a Constitution designed to drain away their political power. Benjamin Lincoln, who had commanded the army that suppressed Shays's Rebellion, warned that no one should expect "those men who were so lately intoxicated with large draughts of liberty and who were thirsting for more would in so short a time submit to a constitution, which would further take up the reins of government, which in their opinion were too strait before."[50]

CHAPTER 15

"MORE PRODUCTIVE AND LESS OPPRESSIVE"

TAXES

THE FEDERALISTS knew their best chance of conquering farmers' resistance to the new national government lay in persuading them that the Constitution would redress their two most pressing grievances, the monetary famine and their enormous tax burden.

Ratification would give the U.S. government something it had never before possessed: the right to levy an array of taxes, the most lucrative being a tariff on foreign goods entering American ports. The prospect of federal taxation endeared the Constitution to every American who had suffered at the hands of delinquent taxpayers. Foremost among the fiscal martyrs were citizens who owned federal securities, and their expectation that the Constitution would dramatically enhance the value of their bonds goes a long way toward explaining why they became Federalists at perhaps a greater rate than any other segment of society.[1] When George Washington asked Charles Lee what he should do with the certificates he had received as reimbursement for his wartime expenses, Lee said the answer would depend on whether the Constitution was adopted. If it failed, the certificates would be "extinguished." On the other hand, "if the proposed constitution be agreed to, . . . the public securities will appreciate and in a few years perhaps, be of considerable value."[2]

The bondholders' fondness for the Constitution invited a widely circulated Anti-Federalist allegation that it was their creation. Benjamin Gale told the Killingworth, Connecticut, town meeting that speculators feared that without the Constitution they would "finally lose their prize."[3] But public creditors were actually not the only Americans who exulted at the prospect of a reinvigorated Congress finally acquiring sufficient revenue to service its debt. Numerous citizens who owned no securities viewed satisfying the bondholders as a simple act of justice. It was also widely seen as the only way for the government to salvage its credit rating—a prerequisite for obtaining future loans.

Anti-Federalists worried that the federal government's desire to service the war debt would lead it to abuse its newly acquired power to levy taxes. John Quincy Adams warned that the Constitution would place Americans in the very predicament that Parliament had tried to force upon them: they would be "doubly taxed"—once by the federal government and once by the state.[4] "The people will bleed with taxes at every pore," Elbridge Gerry complained.[5] Encountering a man who did not share his opposition to the Constitution, Herman Husband invoked an image that had frequently been employed by the opponents of heavy state taxes. "I suppose, then, that we may properly call you an Issachar?" he asked. Husband reminded the man that the biblical Issachar had "bowed his shoulder, to bear every usurpation of tyrants, 'till he became a despicable slave," and he warned that ratification would subject Americans to the same fate.[6]

Some Federalists feared they would never persuade taxpayers to locate the power to levy and collect Continental taxes in a remote national government capable of resisting their demands for relief. At a time when nearly everyone agreed that the Confederation-era legislatures had levied "oppressive and unequal taxes," even Alexander Hamilton questioned whether pro-Constitution forces would be able to overcome "the disinclination of the people to pay taxes, and of course [consequently] to a strong government."[7] But most friends of the Constitution were only too happy to talk about taxation, because they considered it an issue they could win on. They believed they could persuade their fellow Americans that the Constitution would drastically reduce their taxes.[8]

For years taxpayers had been hearing that if the thirteen states had ratified the federal tariff, "you would . . . have paid all your public taxes without feeling it."[9] Starting in September 1787, Federalists made the same case. Since the new national government would be able to derive most of its income from fairly painless customs duties, a Virginian claimed, adoption of the Constitution would result in "an equality and lessening of internal taxes."[10] The largest windfall would go to taxpayers in the so-called non-importing states—those that received most of their foreign merchandise through ports in neighboring states. Unable to levy customs duties on goods arriving from overseas, Delaware, New Jersey, and Connecticut had been forced to obtain whatever money they sent Congress from painful direct taxes.[11] It was no coincidence that these were three of the first four states to approve the Constitution. Indeed, the Delaware and New Jersey conventions ratified unanimously. One Connecticut Federalist, Jeremiah Wadsworth, illustrated his case for federal taxation with the story of Issachar—the same archetypical beast of burden invoked by the Anti-Federalist Herman Husband. Until the federal government drew its sustenance from a national tariff, Wadsworth warned, Connecticut "may well be compared to the strong ass, couching down not only under two but twenty burthens, and they will finally crush us out of existence."[12]

North Carolina was the second-to-last state to ratify, but even there frustration at the government's inability to tax imported merchandise fueled Federalism. Hugh Williamson reminded his countrymen that two-thirds of the state's trade passed through Virginia or South Carolina, with the result that the legislature was able to "raise little by imports and exports." If the Constitution was rejected, he warned, the assembly would have to "encrease our taxes exceedingly, and those taxes must be of the most grievous kind; they must be taxes on lands and heads; taxes that cannot fail to grind the face of the poor."[13]

Anti-Federalists viewed the widely circulated claim that the Constitution would relieve the tax burden as the deadliest weapon in their opponents' arsenal.[14] Rather than wasting their strength in an unavailing effort to counter the compelling case for a national tariff, the critics of the Constitution sought to shift the fiscal battle to different terrain. They pointed out that the Framers had granted the national government a monopoly of tariff revenue. Since, under pressure from delegates representing staple-exporting regions, the convention had also prohibited state as well as federal taxes on exports, the Constitution would prevent the states from deriving any revenue from trade. So what, then, if the Constitution fulfilled its supporters' fondest expectations and diminished taxpayers' sacrifices on behalf of the federal government? It would at the same time magnify the tax burden imposed by the states.[15]

Nowhere did the prospect of increased state taxes create more misgivings than in Massachusetts. Even with a state tariff, Anti-Federalists there pointed out, the legislature had managed to pay interest on the $4 million state debt only by imposing the astronomical taxes that provoked Shays's Rebellion. One opponent of the Constitution, "Vox Populi," reminded his countrymen they had found "by woful experience, that an expectation of discharging [the state debt] with the proceeds of a dry tax on *polls* and *estates*, is a *baseless fabrick.*"[16] Several supporters of the Constitution responded to these apprehensions with a bold prediction: the federal government would assume the state governments' debts, satisfying the holders of state bonds while allowing the thirteen assemblies to revert to prewar tax levels.[17] Maryland senator Charles Carroll summed up the fiscal brief for ratification. A vote for the Constitution, he said, was a vote for "a better system of taxation" that would prove at once "more productive & less oppressive than the present."[18]

So persuasive were these arguments that numerous Americans who had championed the state-level relief measures proscribed in the Constitution nonetheless supported it in the hope that it would reduce their taxes. Thomas Rodney had used his influence as the speaker of the Delaware House of Representatives to shepherd a £10,000 currency emission through his chamber, only to see it defeated in the council. Rodney knew the Constitution would abolish paper money, but he could not bring himself to oppose it. "As I saw the people greatly oppressed," he explained, "I was in hopes it would afford relief."[19] Nearly half the New Hampshire towns that had asked the legislature to print paper money during the 1780s went on to elect ratifying convention delegates who supported the Constitution, which would ban currency emissions.[20] As the prospect of respite from crushing taxation drew more and more of the friends of expedients such as paper money to the Federalist banner, their abandoned allies accused them of selling their birthright, as Esau had, for a mess of pottage.[21]

The ranks of the Federalists were also swelled by Americans who were populists in the political realm but enemies of debt and tax relief. Chief among these was Thomas Paine. Although he called the Constitution "a copy, though not quite as base as the original, of the form of the British government," Paine was willing to sacrifice almost anything to eliminate the threat of paper money. During the war massive currency depreciation, with advances in artisans' wages and profits lagging far behind price increases, had ruined many of the men whose cause he championed. Paine once proposed that any legislator who tried to force creditors to accept paper money should be put to death. Artisans were also desperate to give Congress the power to protect American commerce. For all these reasons, most of them joined Paine in supporting the Constitution.[22]

Also bolstering support for the Constitution was the widespread expectation that federal taxation would finance an army capable of suppressing farmers' rebellions. "The flames of internal insurrection were ready to burst out in every quarter," James Wilson warned the Pennsylvania ratifying convention, which assembled in Philadelphia in November 1787. "From one end to the other of the continent, we walked on ashes, concealing fire beneath our feet."[23] Five days before the Constitution was adopted, the *Pennsylvania Gazette* warned that if Americans rejected the convention's plan, the news of June 1789 would read something like this: "We hear from Richmond, that the new statehouse lately erected there was burnt by a mob from Berkeley county, on account of the Assembly refusing to emit paper money. From the number and daring spirit of the mob, government have judged it most prudent not to meddle with them." On the other hand, if Americans ratified the Constitution, they would soon be reading that the rebellion of Connecticut squatters in the Wyoming Valley of Pennsylvania had been suppressed—and that the insurgent leaders were "to be tried for their lives."[24]

Actually, the federal army would rarely be called upon to subdue uprisings, pro-Constitution writers confidently predicted, because its very existence would give would-be rebels pause—a point that one New Hampshire wag made in verse. Invoking the names of Massachusetts insurgents Luke Day and Daniel Shays, he declared that after the Constitution was ratified, "Here Plenty and Order and Freedom shall dwell, / And your Shayses and Dayses won't dare to rebel."[25] Even many Americans who shared the Confederation-era insurgents' grievances nonetheless abhorred their tactics and welcomed the prospect of a government that would possess the power to "ensure domestic tranquility."[26]

It was not just citizens' rebellions that federal troops would suppress. The Constitution was also viewed as a powerful weapon against slave revolts. "Are we not weakened by the population of those whom we hold in slavery?" Virginia governor Edmund Randolph asked the state ratifying convention on June 6, 1788.[27] One indication of the trepidation with which Federalists viewed the threat of slave insurrection was their frequent recourse to the time-honored custom of referring to it euphemistically. In May 1788 Tench Coxe reminded white southerners their region was "crouded with *a dangerous species of population*."[28] Madison warned his fellow white southerners that they had to contend with certain "circumstances . . . which do not apply to the Northern States. They are therefore more interested in giving the Government a power to command the whole strength of the Union in cases of emergency."[29] Federalists also trumpeted the provision in the Constitution giving Congress the power to adopt a national fugitive slave act (which it did adopt in 1793). "We have obtained a right to recover our slaves in whatever part of America they may take refuge," federal convention delegate Charles Cotesworth Pinckney reported upon his return to South Carolina. This was "a right we had not before."[30]

The persistent threat of Indian attack was one more reason the United States needed a powerful national military establishment. Many western settlers—and indeed many coastal residents who had a financial stake in the West—supported the Constitution because they believed it would strengthen the United States in its battle against its Native American neighbors.[31] During the 1780s the farther south you traveled in the United States, the more talk you heard about the Indian threat. In Georgia, the southernmost state, citizens' anxiety about the Indians decisively influenced their assessment of the Constitution—with important implications for the ratification campaign as a whole.

A year or two earlier no state would have been less interested in establishing a national government than Georgia, where the legislature had not paid a dollar of the money Congress requisitioned from it. Assemblymen chose not to send a delegation to the Annapolis Convention in 1786, and the following year they initially voted not to be represented in Philadelphia, either—a decision they reversed only at the last minute. And yet on the last day of 1787 Georgians became not only the first southerners but the first Americans outside the Delaware Valley to ratify the Constitution. At the state ratifying convention, the yes vote was unanimous. Why did white Georgians' attitude change so dramatically in such a short time?[32]

The paramount reason was the state's conflict against the Creek Indian nation. Although most white Georgians still lived close to the Atlantic coast, they claimed the entire region bordered by South Carolina, Spanish Florida, and the Mississippi River—an area that was occupied by several powerful Indian nations. The most populous of these, with about fifteen thousand inhabitants, were the Creeks.[33] In the mid-1780s, Georgia officials persuaded a small number of Creeks to affix their names to deeds ceding much of their homeland. Thereupon the vast majority of the Creeks resolved, as headman Alexander McGillivray declared, "to take arms in our defence & repel those Invaders of our Lands, to drive them from their encroachments & fix them within their own proper limits."[34] Esteemed by his countrymen, McGillivray was actually only one-fourth Creek. His father was British, and he himself had been a Loyalist during the Revolutionary War, frequently leading Creek war parties in attacks against settlements in Georgia and other rebellious British colonies.[35]

McGillivray's mixed parentage gave him valuable contacts. Although the British government had ceded the Floridas to Spain in 1783, the British firm of Panton & Leslie was allowed to set up shop in Pensacola on the Gulf of Mexico. Spanish officials granted the firm a monopoly of the Indian trade in the region between the lower Mississippi and the southern Appalachians. McGillivray was an employee of the firm and thus had access to its weaponry and other vital supplies. An even more important contact for the Creeks was with the Spanish government itself. Spain desperately needed allies in this part of the world. While the United States claimed the 31st parallel as its southern border, Spain claimed that Spanish Florida reached all the way up to the Tennessee River. In 1784 and 1785 Spanish officials met with Creek and other native leaders and agreed to provide them with guns and ammunition.[36]

By 1786 the Georgia legislature was so sure that the Creeks were about to attack that it voted £50,000 to strengthen the militia. In the spring of 1787 a group of Creeks killed several Georgians. In June some friends and relatives of those killed went looking for Creeks and killed the first they found. These turned out to be neutralists who had favored accommodation with the United States. The attack outraged other Creek neutralists and drove many of them into the anti–United States camp. Now the Creeks were ready for all-out war against Georgia.

In May 1787 Nathaniel Pendleton would report from Savannah, Georgia, that the Creeks had "spread Terror thro every part of the State, and we have neither numbers, or resources sufficient to oppose their ravages." "We have made overtures," Pendleton wrote, but the Creeks were "sensible of our feeble condition, and the weakness of the whole Union," so Georgia's offer to negotiate would probably be "treated with Scorn."[37] One reason for the Creeks' confidence was the support they received from the Spanish. Congress and the Georgia legislature knew they could greatly weaken the Creeks if they could force Spain to evacuate its forts in the disputed region, especially Natchez on the east bank of the Mississippi River. But the United States was in no position to dictate to Spain.[38]

By October 1787, when the proposed Constitution arrived in Georgia, whites in the state were convinced that they were "involved in a general Indian war," and they attributed their vulnerability to the weakness of the federal union. "If we are to be much longer unblessed with an efficient national government, destitute of funds and without public credit, either at home or abroad," Nicholas Gilman declared, "I fear we shall become contemptible even in the eyes of savages themselves."[39]

The assembly, which had already been brought into special session to deal with the Creek threat, voted to call a ratifying convention. The convention quickly endorsed the Constitution, a decision that was widely attributed to fear of the Creeks. Massachusetts Anti-Federalist Mercy Otis Warren lamented that Georgia, "apprehensive of a war with the Savages, has acceded in order to insure protection."[40] Diplomats filed similar reports. "Georgia was the first of the five Southern States which adopted the new Constitution," a French envoy told his government. "Attacked by Indians, it was in its interest to appear federally inclined in order to obtain help from the present Union."[41]

Georgians were by no means the only Americans who hungered for Indian land. In *Federalist* Number 24 Alexander Hamilton asserted that U.S. settlers needed protection from the "savage tribes on our western frontier," who "ought to be regarded as our natural enemies."[42] One reason settlers in the western regions of Virginia and Maryland supported the Constitution in their state ratifying conventions was that Indians raided Clarksburg, Virginia, in the spring of 1788, reminding them of their vulnerability.[43] The United States had only "four or five hundred troops scattered along the Ohio to protect the frontier inhabitants, and give some value to your lands," Hugh Williamson reminded his fellow North Carolinians. "Those troops are ill paid, and in a fair way for being disbanded."[44] George Nicholas told white Kentuckians that the "present weak Government cannot protect them." Western citizens could "expect support and succour alone from a strong efficient Government, which can command the resources of the Union when necessary," he said.[45]

Absentee owners of western acreage would also benefit from the adoption of the Constitution. "Having claims to a considerable Quantity of Land in the Western Country," Williamson asserted, "I am fully persuaded that the Value of those Lands must be increased by an efficient federal Government."[46] For their part, Anti-Federalists ridiculed the claim that (as Patrick Henry put it) "the savage Indians are to destroy us" if the Constitution was not ratified.[47] William Grayson offered this sarcastic summary of the Federalists' appeal to white westerners: "The Indians are to invade us with numerous armies on our rear, in order to convert our cleared lands into hunting grounds."[48] John Tyler acknowledged to the Virginia ratifying convention that the existing national government was too weak to drive the Indians from their land, but professed not to be troubled. "Shall we sacrifice the peace and happiness of this country, to enable us to make wanton war?" he asked. "If we can defend ourselves, it is sufficient."[49]

In the Anti-Federalists' view, the standing army envisioned in the Constitution was not just unnecessary but dangerous. Had the proratification forces forgotten that one of the charges against George III was that he "had kept among us, in times of peace, a standing army without the consent of our legislatures"? The Federalists' imperial ambitions, like their proposal to enrich bond speculators at taxpayer expense, posed a threat to republican government. "A powerful and mighty empire is incompatible with the genius of republicanism," Patrick Henry warned his fellow Virginians.[50]

For once, the fabled orator had wasted his breath. As most free Americans saw it, a great point in the Constitution's favor was that it would give the United States the military muscle it needed to confront not only the Indians but their British allies. In *Federalist* Number 15, Alexander Hamilton pointed out that the United States had "valuable territories and important posts in the possession of a foreign power." Americans were in no "condition to resent, or to repel the aggression," because "we have neither troops nor treasury nor government."[51] The solution was clear. "The new Govt. and that alone," Madison declared on the eve of the Virginia ratifying convention, "will be able to take the requisite measures for getting into our hands the Western posts which will not cease to instigate the Savages, as long as they remain in British hands."[52]

The British forts figured in the campaign for the Constitution in another way as well. Imperial officials had a persuasive justification for holding on to the posts despite having pledged in the 1783 Paris peace treaty to give them up. They pointed out that the new American states had also violated the 1783 agreement by denying British merchant-creditors access to their courts. And so even as some Americans opposed the Constitution because they were reluctant to see British merchants' suits go forward, thousands of westerners supported it in order to get the courts open and the British out.[53]

One economically distressed backcountry region—the northwestern corner of Virginia, the area that later became West Virginia—initially wanted to keep British creditors out of the state's courts. Then the British foreign secretary, Lord Carmarthen, affirmed that his government would evacuate its Great Lakes forts only when the United Sates allowed British merchants to sue their American debtors. At the Virginia ratifying convention George Nicholas called the Constitution "the only chance we have of getting the Western posts."[54] Twenty-seven of the twenty-eight delegates from the Valley of Virginia and the region that later became West Virginia supported the Constitution. Recall that Virginia adopted by only a ten-vote margin. If the western Virginians had joined other westerners in opposing the Constitution—or even if they had split evenly—Virginia would not have ratified. Likewise, if the Indians had been as insignificant to the ratification campaign as they are usually portrayed, citizens would have had one less reason to support the Constitution.[55]

Thus the Constitution offered something of value to nearly every free American. It would cut taxes, service the war bonds, expand the money supply, and field an army powerful enough to defeat both Indians and domestic rebels of all kinds. And yet historians estimate that something like half the citizenry opposed it.[56] In Virginia—the most populous state—and in other critical states such as Massachusetts and New York, the majority of the men sent to the ratifying convention were, at least initially, Anti-Federalists. This raises a question. If the Constitution fell so far short of generating a consensus among free Americans, how were the Federalists able to secure favorable verdicts from nine state ratifying conventions—the number needed for ratification—and eventually from the other four states as well?

Some of the tactics deployed in support of the Constitution betrayed a certain desperate determination. For instance, Federalists predicted all sorts of dire consequences if it was not ratified. Leave the union in its current weakened state, proratification writers and speakers claimed, and it will dissolve altogether.[57] Massachusetts Anti-Federalist Mercy Otis Warren ridiculed supporters of the Constitution who "magnified the hopeless alternative, between the dissolution of the bands of all government, and receiving the proferred system *in toto*."[58]

In their desperation to see the Constitution adopted, some Federalists resorted to political chicanery. Several ratifying conventions, especially Pennsylvania's and South Carolina's, might have defeated the Constitution if the delegates had been allocated among the sections of the state in proportion to population. Instead, representation was tilted toward the eastern regions that favored ratification.[59]

Another indication of the Federalists' grim assessment of their prospects was their frequent recourse to false statements. Some claimed the members of the Philadelphia convention had unanimously approved the Constitution.[60] That was not true, but it was plausible, since the convention's plan received the unanimous approval of the eleven state delegations represented on the final day. (Each delegation voted as a unit; the New York delegation lacked a quorum.) In Massachusetts an essay attacking Anti-Federalist Elbridge Gerry asserted that he was the only delegate remaining in Philadelphia on September 17 who had refused to sign the Constitution.[61] The reality was that he had been joined by Virginians George Mason and Edmund Randolph. Another letter acknowledged that three delegates had withheld their signatures but complained that none of the three had chosen to "concert a single motion" for a bill of rights, as Anti-Federalists were now demanding. Actually Gerry had proposed a bill of rights, and Mason had seconded the motion.[62]

Fearing the members of Congress would either oppose the Constitution or suggest amendments to it, Federalists asked them merely to "transmit" it to the state ratifying conventions. Congress obliged, giving the Federalists an opening to affirm that the members had unanimously approved the Constitution.[63] Actually, although no entire state delegation opposed the weak resolution to transmit the convention's proposal to the states, several individuals did.

Appropriately enough, given that the *Federalist Papers* were the most systematic defense of the Constitution, the eighty-five essays by "Publius" contained some of the proratification side's most daring deceptions. To support his assertion that he was in a position to examine the Constitution objectively, Publius claimed he did not attend the federal convention. Actually, both of the principal authors of the *Federalist Papers*, Madison and Hamilton, had been among the most active delegates.[64] Publius's most valuable and enduring deception was contained in a single word. Back at the Philadelphia convention Madison had pointed out that under the Articles of Confederation, "the Union was a federal one among sovereign States." The Constitution, on the other hand, would give the United States "a national Governt."[65] But Madison, Hamilton, and Jay nonetheless chose to entitle their essays "The Federalist." Other supporters of the Constitution followed suit, and they are still known as Federalists today.

Proratification writers and speakers showed their pessimism regarding free Americans' enthusiasm for the Constitution by deceiving them not only about the process that had brought it into being but about its specific provisions. Madison warned many years later that when "consulting the contemporary writings, which vindicated and recommended the Constitution, it is fair to keep in mind that the authors might be sometimes influenced by the zeal of advocates."[66] Since Madison himself had been an especially zealous Federalist, it was perhaps inevitable that in promoting it, he surpassed most of them in stretching the truth. Like other supporters of the Constitution, Madison inflated the gravity of the problems it was designed to redress. In making the case that the states had proved themselves unstable, Madison declared that "every new election in the states is found to change one half of the representatives"—a gross exaggeration.[67]

The subject that opened the widest gap between the Framers' motives and the Federalists' rhetoric was the Senate. Most of the federal convention delegates had agreed that the members of the upper house of the national legislature should, as Madison declared on June 7, "come from, & represent, the Wealth of the nation."[68] Madison also affirmed that keeping the Senate small would make it a "more weighty check to the Democ[rac]y"—that is, to the House of Representatives.[69] The same motive explained the indirect election of senators. "In the formation of the Senate," John Dickinson said, "we ought to carry it through such a refining process as will assimilate it as near as may be to the House of Lords in England."[70] This elitist imperative is nowhere to be found in the Federalists' vindications of the Senate. They explained that long Senate terms would ensure stability, permit senators to oversee protracted treaty negotiations, and so on.[71] The friends of the Constitution said the Senate would provide what Benjamin Rush, a leader in the as-yet-unsuccessful effort to graft an upper house onto the Pennsylvania Assembly, called "a double representation of the people."[72]

Too much may be made of the deceptions used to secure the ratification of the Constitution. After all, the Anti-Federalists lied, too. George Mason angrily denounced the Framers' decision to allow Congress to restrict American trade by a simple majority. Often when Mason's essay was published in the North, where citizens expected to benefit from congressional trade restrictions, that particular criticism was dropped.[73] But to say that the friends and enemies of the Constitution were both willing to deceive their audiences is not to imply that they were equally successful at it. Every opponent of the Constitution who stretched the truth faced a flood of Federalist rebuttals, but the supporters of the Constitution had much less fear of being called to account. Most of the country's newspaper editors were on their side, and few offered their opponents anything like equal access. Some editors published Anti-Federalist essays—a small number of them, that is—solely for the purpose of giving pro-Constitution authors a chance to refute them. Some ran none at all.[74] In Connecticut only one newspaper printed one original essay opposing the Constitution. Even town meetings' antiratification votes were not deemed newsworthy.[75] When Philadelphia printer Thomas Lloyd published transcripts of the debates in the Pennsylvania ratifying convention, he simply left out almost everything the Anti-Federalists said.[76]

There was other chicanery as well, all of it betraying the Federalists' suspicion that their position had failed to gain majority support. The New Hampshire ratifying convention, which convened on February 13, seemed likely to vote the Constitution down, so the Federalist delegates called for a recess, which gave other state conventions time to create sufficient momentum in favor of the Constitution to carry New Hampshire into the yes column. In Massachusetts Federalists circulated the rumor that unless the delegates attending the ratifying convention approved the Constitution, they would not be paid. The tale was targeted at Anti-Federalist delegates who had run up bills for food and lodging that they could not pay on their own.[77] In New York, where two-thirds of the ratifying convention delegates had declared themselves Anti-Federalists when they were elected, the convention voted to ratify only after New York City threatened to secede from the state and join the new nation on its own. Rhode Island's ratification was extorted by the threat of a commercial boycott. "Never was there a political system introduced by less worthy means," George Richards Minot, the secretary of the Massachusetts ratifying convention and an ardent friend of the Constitution, flatly declared.[78]

But there was nothing nefarious about what was probably the most effective tactic employed by the friends of the Constitution: they promised to amend it. Back during the federal convention, when Elbridge Gerry had brought forward a bill of rights, most of his colleagues had contended that none was needed. The Constitution did not hand blanket authority to the federal government. It delegated only certain specific powers, they said, and since none of these duties infringed on Americans' basic civil liberties, there was no need for language protecting those freedoms from federal intervention. In fact, an enumeration of rights might be dangerous, since it could imply that the federal government had the right to enter every legal arena from which it had not been explicitly barred. Besides, Gerry had waited until the eleventh hour to make his proposal, and the delegates were tired. They had done what they had come to Philadelphia to do, and they wanted to go home.[79]

The convention's decision not to adopt a bill of rights was its greatest strategic blunder. The omission made Anti-Federalists out of a host of leading Americans who might otherwise have ranked among the Constitution's most zealous defenders. And yet the omission of a bill of rights also provided Federalists with something every negotiator likes to have: a fallback position. When the opponents of the Constitution seemed likely to carry the day in Massachusetts, Virginia, and New York, Federalists managed to win enough votes for ratification by pledging their support for the later inclusion of a bill of rights.[80] It is a remarkable but rarely noted irony that Americans owe their most cherished rights—among them freedom of speech and religion, the right to trial by jury, and protection against self-incrimination and illegal search and seizure—not to the authors of the Constitution but to its inveterate enemies.[81]

CHAPTER 16

"AS IF IMPOUNDED"

CONSOLIDATION

BACK IN 1782 Herman Husband had argued against the countywide election of Pennsylvania assemblymen, since only a county's wealthiest men were "generally known throughout the whole of it." To illustrate his point, Husband had taken it to what he considered an absurd extreme, pointing out that "this Defect would be still more easily seen and felt by all if we were to vote for a few Men in a whole State to sit in Congress." In November 1788 the Pennsylvania Assembly decided that the state's first members of the newly created United States House of Representatives would be chosen using the very system Husband had conjured up as an extreme example of unrepresentative government.[1]

The statewide election of congressmen favored candidates from the area around Philadelphia, and westerners took the lead in contending that it was, as Husband put it in 1789, "far from being satisfactory, for the bounds are too large for the common people to act in." Pennsylvania was not alone. As Anti-Federalists had predicted, legislators in several states decreed that the state's congressmen would be elected at large. Advocates for statewide voting believed it would ensure the selection of the most able men; their opponents maintained that unless congressmen were chosen in districts, they and their constituents would know too little about each other. Public pressure forced the Pennsylvania legislature to adopt the district method in 1791, but Husband warned that even in states where congressmen were chosen "in separate districts," federal constituencies were so large that the state legislatures "might as well have empowered the officers and wealthy men to have held those elections without mocking the public and the body of freemen."[2]

Connecticut also initially opted to elect its congressional delegation statewide, a decision that William Beers praised in a 1791 pamphlet that calls to mind Madison's faith in the power of "divide et impera." "Enlarge the acting body," Beers wrote, and "you augment the force of the wise, the uninfluenced and steady, and you divide and waste the strength of the opposite party." The following year another anonymous Connecticut writer, probably Windham lawyer, assemblyman, and future Federalist congressman Zephaniah Swift, echoed Beers's analysis of the impact of large election districts—except that what Beers celebrated, Swift bemoaned. Connecticut was divided into two mutually antagonistic classes, Swift declared. "Creditors are naturally rich, and debtors poor: the former are usually few, the latter many," he wrote. In a society characterized by this sort of "inequality of condition," Swift claimed, it was not difficult to predict the results of at-large voting. "The wide dispersion of the freemen in this state, with their consequent incapacity of acting in concert in these elections, appears to have been considered as recommending this mode by being advantageous to the cause of government," Swift wrote. "'Divide and rule' is a favourite maxim of despotism."[3] Swift suggested that being elected statewide made it easier for Connecticut congressmen to cast their votes for the Excise Act of 1791, which benefited bondholders—including those who sat in Congress—at the expense of taxpayers.[4]

In other states, too, nearly everyone agreed that congressmen elected statewide would be less dependent on the voters. An anonymous Marylander warned that single-member congressional districts would tilt elections in favor of politicians who would "not be too proud to court what are generally called the *poor folks*, shake them by the hand, ask them for their vote and interest, and, when an opportunity serves, treat them to a can of grog, and whilst drinking of it, join heartily in abusing what are called the *great people*."[5]

Some opponents of statewide congressional districts revived a claim that had been made by several Constitutional Convention delegates and numerous Anti-Federalists: that large congressional constituencies would thwart some attempts at organized political action more effectively than others. Swift noted that as the number of citizens sharing a particular interest increased, it became harder and harder for them to "act in concert." He contended that those whose "skill, wealth and connections, can most easily overcome these difficulties can the most easily effect their own particular wishes; and thus those persons possess the most liberty and power." William Findley told his colleagues in the Pennsylvania legislature that "while three fourths of the state are divided among five or six sets of men . . . the other one fourth may carry the election by acting in concert, and holding a correspondence with each other."[6]

Notwithstanding complaints such as these, extending the sphere of government was a much subtler way to reduce popular influence on government than most of the other devices that had been proposed at the Constitutional Convention. The notion that the republican form of government works best in a large area has been called America's single greatest contribution to political theory.[7] It might never have been developed if the authors of the Constitution had not feared that a more blatant method of dissipating grassroots influence—say, electing the House of Representatives indirectly—would provoke a public outcry. Zephaniah Swift paid rueful homage to his opponents' ingenuity when he noted that Connecticut's statewide congressional elections were "calculated to induce the freemen to imagine themselves at liberty, while they are thus destined to be allured or driven round as if impounded, being at the same time told that nothing confines them, although they have not the powers of escape."[8]

Once the expansion of legislative districts had penned freemen behind this invisible fence, Swift warned, fewer and fewer of them would turn out to vote. Herman Husband believed the process of inducing apathy had already begun with the first federal election. He claimed that anyone who examined the voting lists for Pennsylvania's at-large congressional election of 1788 would "find few who voted." Indeed, in many voting precincts, he wrote, "the people never opened any election."[9]

One of the first official actions of the newly organized federal Congress was to adopt a national tariff. A short time later James Madison introduced the amendments that became the Bill of Rights. Madison wanted to insert short phrases at various places in the Constitution guaranteeing some of the rights that the state ratifying conventions had requested. Instead Congress decided to gather all the proposed changes into a twelve-article Bill of Rights that became, after the states ratified all but two of them, the first ten amendments to the Constitution.

Numerous senators and congressmen wanted to shelve the Bill of Rights, but Madison and a majority of his colleagues pressed on. They acted upon a variety of motives ranging from honor to fear. Madison had vowed both as a Virginia ratifying convention delegate and as a candidate for Congress that there would be a bill of rights, and he probably could not have been reelected had he reneged on this promise. And yet the energy Madison brought to the fight for the Bill of Rights indicated that he had developed a deep personal commitment to the cause.[10]

Madison's colleagues agreed to his proposal for a variety of reasons. When the new federal government was being organized, North Carolina and Rhode Island still had not ratified the Constitution, and a bill of rights was seen—correctly, as it turned out—as a way to reconcile those last two states to the revolution in government.[11] Another reason the representatives decided to amend the Constitution was to prevent their fellow citizens from doing so. The New York and Virginia ratifying conventions had both endorsed the call for a second constitutional convention to draft a bill of rights. By the spring of 1789 the movement for a second convention was gaining momentum. The Constitution mandated that amendments could be proposed either by Congress or by a constitutional convention, but members of Congress did not want to lose control of the process. A second convention might propose radical changes. In particular, it might seek to reverse the course the Constitution had set by taking certain key responsibilities away from the new national government and returning them to the states. Benjamin Lincoln, the commander of the army that had suppressed Shays's Rebellion, called a second convention "a measure of all others to be dreaded."[12]

Perhaps the most pressing motive behind the Bill of Rights was, as Madison put it in an August 14, 1789, speech on the floor of Congress, "to conciliate the minds of the people."[13] Thus the first ten amendments, arguably the most cherished section of the Constitution, had something in common with the first seven articles that had been drafted in Philadelphia. The Bill of Rights would never have been adopted if leaders like Madison had not been feeling pressure from below.

On January 9, 1790, Secretary of the Treasury Alexander Hamilton gave Congress his plan for servicing the war bonds. The controversy ignited that day revived many of the battles Americans had waged during the previous half-decade—with an important difference. One prominent member of the coalition that had opposed debt and tax relief and then championed the Constitution—and only one—now switched sides. Madison argued that speculators who had bought up war bonds should be given only half their face value, with the residue going to the original recipients of the bonds—the farmers, merchants, and soldiers from whom the speculators had purchased them.[14] The Virginian also objected to Hamilton's suggestion that the federal government assume responsibility for paying off the state governments' war debts.

During the 1780s Madison had argued that speculators who had obtained their securities on the open market should be treated no differently from Americans who had received their bonds directly from the government and held on to them.[15] As late as the fall of 1789 he had not objected to the idea of the federal government redeeming the state bonds.[16] Why did he switch positions on these two crucial issues? Madison offered no satisfactory explanation for his conversion at the time, and it has remained a mystery ever since.

Madison's defection has been attributed to his disgust at the rapid concentration of state and federal debts between September 11, 1789, when Hamilton became secretary of the treasury, and the publication of his *Report on Public Credit* four months later. During that period bond trading entered a new—and in many Americans' eyes, grotesque— phase. Northern speculators chartered ships to rush their agents southward, where they scoured the countryside for bondholders who had not heard that the federal government was probably going to dedicate most of its income to servicing the war bonds. The most intense speculation was in state securities. Entrepreneurs anticipating federal assumption of the state debts—some of them benefiting from insider information supplied by Hamilton's assistant, William Duer—talked many of their fellow citizens into unloading their state bonds right be-

fore the flurry of speculative purchases sent their market price spiral-
ing upward. Perhaps the winter 1789–90 feeding frenzy convinced
Madison of a point that the bond speculators' critics had been making
all along: it was unfair to tax farmers—many of them Revolutionary
War veterans who had sold their bonds to speculators for a pittance—
to enrich the men and women who had purchased their bonds.

Another explanation for Madison's conversion is more cynical. His
support for the Constitution was sufficiently unpopular in his home
state to keep him out of the U.S. Senate, and it nearly prevented his
election to the House of Representatives. By January 1790, with a new
congressional election less than a year away, Madison realized that if he
wanted to represent Virginia in Congress, he had better start voting
like a Virginian.[17]

Both of these explanations are plausible, but the patterns Madison
had established earlier in his political career suggest a third. Only by
switching sides in the war bonds controversy could Madison remain
loyal to a principle. Since legislatures constantly try to abuse power, he
believed, they must constantly be opposed. Like most free Americans,
Madison feared parliamentary tyranny in the 1760s and early 1770s.
Once independence had been declared, the state assemblymen and the
voters who chose them became the new targets of his suspicion. Then
when the Constitution transferred a large measure of the states' sovereignty to the new national government, it was natural for Madison to
fear Congress—despite being a congressman—and to insist on strict
regard for constitutional restraints on its authority. By the winter of
1789–90 Madison believed bondholders exerted inordinate power over
a federal government that, for the first time, possessed the strength to
execute its writ. Thus he became their enemy on the same principle
that he had befriended them in the 1780s, when they had seemed so
weak. Comfort the afflicted, afflict the comfortable.[18]

Fortified by the acquisition of an ally of James Madison's caliber, the
bond speculators' critics offered a variety of alternatives to Hamilton's
plan. Shortly after the *Report on Public Credit* appeared, Herman Husband, who in 1782 had urged the Pennsylvania legislature to replace the
state's war bonds with gradually depreciating currency, proposed the
emission of federal paper money. Husband published a pamphlet arguing that Americans had a moral obligation to liquidate the government

debt in a single generation. It would be no more just to saddle future generations with the Revolutionary War debt than it would be "to oblige insolvent debtors to black their children in their infancy and sell them slaves for life," he said.[19]

The proposal to force bond speculators to split their proceeds with the former owners of the securities was based on similar plans that had been offered to the state assemblies. One champion of "discriminating" against the speculators—treating them differently from original holders—was William Manning, the Billerica, Massachusetts, farmer and tavern-keeper. Although Manning's essay, "Some Proposals for Makeing Restitution to the Original Creditors of Government . . . ," was not published at the time, it offers a rare glimpse into an ordinary farmer's thinking about a conflict that consumed the attention of the nation's most prominent politicians for nearly a year. Manning conceded that if the original recipients of government bonds had freely chosen to sell them—even far below the par (face) value—they would have no right to any additional compensation. But "did these poor soldiers act voluntarily in selling their certificates under par?" he asked.[20]

"Surely, no," Manning declared. "The original creditors of the government acted more like persons beset with robbers and prudently delivered up their purses rather than their lives." No weapons had been brandished in the faces of the original bondholders, of course, but they had in fact been compelled to sell. Farmers could not feed, shelter, or clothe their "needy families" with pieces of paper. And the same state and federal governments that failed to redeem the war securities also refused to accept them in discharge of taxes, requiring instead payment in gold and silver. For the government now to direct its entire compensation package to the speculators, giving nothing to the former soldiers, would be "glaringly unjust," Manning believed.[21]

Another claim that Manning, Madison, and other opponents of Hamilton's "Funding" bill borrowed from the state-level tax struggles of the 1780s was that heavy taxation for the benefit of bondholders endangered the nation's economic health. Funding would "take a capital from productive labor, and vest it in unproductive labor," Georgia congressman James Jackson declared.[22] Manning denied that funding the securities would make them a useful addition to the nation's depleted supply of currency. The new bonds came only in large denominations, and they were "chiefly owned in the seaports." Indeed, Funding might actually exacerbate the monetary famine in the countryside, since the "hard money" extracted from taxpayers on behalf of the bondholders would be "mostly sent out of the country or shut up in the banks by the merchants," Manning claimed.[23]

For more than a decade essayists, legislators, and petitioners had warned that imposing high taxes for the benefit of bondholders threatened the rough equality of property holding that was the soul of republican government. Many Americans perceived a similar threat in the Funding bill. Once the federal government had impoverished taxpayers and diminished the value of their farms, the bond speculators— "sharpers," Manning called them—would "be able with their securities to purchase whole townships at a time and bring us into lordships."[24] In April 1792 Congressman William Branch Giles of Virginia worried that the American middle class had already started to disappear. He called Congress's decision to pay off the speculators a "most powerful machine to stimulate this growing inequality in the distribution of wealth."[25]

Tax relief advocates were not the only participants in the Funding debate who dusted off the arguments they had perfected in state-level struggles. Americans who had received bonds directly from the federal government were furious at Hamilton's proposal that Congress redeem the war bonds, which paid 6 percent interest, with new securities paying a shade more than 4 percent. (In the end Congress decided upon a complex redemption system that also had the effect of bringing the interest rate below 6 percent.) They believed securities that had been purchased on the open market should be scaled down from their nominal value to the actual price the investors had paid for them. That would enable the government to pay 6 percent to Americans who had obtained their bonds directly from the government and then held on to them. Many owners of U.S. bonds opposed federal assumption of the state debts for the same reason: it would disable Congress from paying them everything they felt they deserved.[26]

As they had during the 1780s, the champions of the "original creditors" borrowed liberally from the rhetoric of the tax relief advocates.[27] Two Pennsylvanians who warned that Congress would undermine its ability to redeem original holders' securities at face value if it tried to extend the same privilege to speculators' bonds, Benjamin Rush and John Peters, resorted to one of the less savory tactics that had been used against bond speculators during the 1780s. In describing for his ally James Madison the forces arrayed on the opposite side of the Funding fight, Peters claimed "the Jews" had a "Fondness for Brokerage." Rush worried that if Congress adopted Hamilton's plan, "the whole profits of the war will soon center in the hands of American tories, Amsterdam Jews, and London brokers."[28]

Hamilton's critics claimed his pro-speculator proposals would, like the crushing taxes of the 1780s, violate the dictates of sensibility. The impoverished veterans' "sufferings" would "never be forgotten, while sympathy [remained] an American virtue," Madison declared on the floor of Congress in February 1790. The defenders of Funding, like the earlier advocates for rigorous collection of taxes and debts, claimed their opponents' arguments were (in Representative John Laurance's words) "improperly addressed to their feelings." The opponents of the proposal to discriminate against bond traders were especially dismayed to see Madison, their old ally, apparently being "led away by the dictates of his heart," as Elias Boudinot, a bondholder and New Jersey congressman, put it.[29]

Like relief advocates in the 1780s, supporters of Discrimination responded to these criticisms with a defense of sentiment. The "heart, in this instance, ought to govern," James Jackson said. One of the most impassioned claims that emotion had a role to play in politics appeared in a letter Benjamin Rush sent Madison after the opponents of Discrimination accused Madison of thinking with his heart. "The enemies of your motion concur in its being agreeable to *just* feelings," Rush told Madison, "but they say that reason alone should decide upon all great Questions of National policy. This is a new doctrine in Morals & Metaphysicks. In matters of *right & wrong feeling* alone should be our Guide."[30]

Hamilton's opponents echoed the mid-1780s relief advocates not only in their rhetoric and proposals but in their tactics. Just as Confederation-era writers and speakers had frequently threatened that high taxes would provoke agrarian rebellions, the opponents of Funding warned

Congress that "the people . . . will very ill brook the payment of taxes"—indeed they "would revolt at the idea" of "filling the pockets of the speculator."[31]

Hamilton's supporters made their own desultory attempt to elicit fears of civil conflict. A Connecticut newspaper writer assured bond-holders that Congress would meet their demands, if only because "to drive to despair two hundred thousand creditors and influential citizens, is an event too great to be hazarded." In reply, Funding opponent Thomas Scott ridiculed the notion that "the speculators will cut our throats, if we do not pay them twenty shillings for their half crown."[32]

As it had in the 1780s, the discussion of economic policy led both sides to reexamine the relationship between the officeholder and his constituents. Madison set off this phase of the debate by asserting that one reason to favor his Discrimination proposal was that "public opinion" seemed to support it. Several of Madison's opponents met him on his own ground, presenting evidence that the public actually opposed his amendment. John Laurance pointed out that the old Congress had opposed Discrimination (in an address written by Madison!), and he argued that public opinion "was better ascertained by the acts of public bodies than by squibs in the newspapers, or by pamphlets written by individuals." Fisher Ames likewise denied that public opinion supported Discrimination, but he went on to articulate a viewpoint that Madison himself would have found congenial only a few years earlier. It was all the "more a duty on Government to protect right when it may happen to be unpopular," Ames said.[33]

For all the similarities between the Funding battle and the controversies that had roiled state politics during the 1780s, James Madison's defection was but one of the important differences. What had previously been a set of internal conflicts within each of the thirteen states had, by 1790, already started to become a fight between sections of the country. Most, though by no means all, of the supporters of Funding came from north of the line that Charles Mason and Jeremiah Dixon had surveyed during the mid-1760s. That, after all, was where most of the bonds were. Prominent among the congressional supporters of Funding was Theodore Sedgwick, a forty-three-year-old lawyer from western Massachusetts. Sedgwick had long been a passionate supporter of redeeming the bonds. He was no friend of paper money or other relief measures. During Shays's Rebellion he paid for his unpopular views when a band of rebels raided his home. The story that an African American servant, Elizabeth Freeman, saved the family silver from the marauders by concealing it among her own humble possessions must be treated with skepticism, as it bears too strong a resemblance to the myth of the loyal plantation mammy. But it is true that Freeman had been a slave when she first met Sedgwick—and that he had represented her when she sued for her freedom, citing the Massachusetts declaration of rights, and won.[34]

Ranged against New England Federalists like Sedgwick were southerners like Madison who were growing leery of using southern tax dollars to enrich northern bond speculators.

Another difference between the mid-1780s fiscal and monetary debates and the Funding fight was that the adoption of the Constitution ensured that this new battle would be waged on very different terrain. Numerous speakers and writers on both sides of the conflict over the Constitution had predicted that transferring matters such as federal taxation and debtor-creditor relations from the state to the federal level would fundamentally change how they were decided, and those predictions proved accurate. Congressmen were, for the most part, wealthier than their state-level counterparts. They had so many constituents that they came into daily contact with only a small percentage of them— generally the wealthiest. Although the enlargement of legislative districts and the transfer of certain key governmental duties to the federal sphere diluted every interest group's influence on public officials, some factions lost more power than others. The Funding fight threw all of these differences between state and federal politics into sharp relief.

Hamilton's *Report on Public Credit* was officially a response to a petition the House of Representatives received from a group of public creditors living in Philadelphia at the end of August 1789. The bondholders asked Congress to devise a way to raise the market value of their greatly depreciated securities. When Madison proposed to force securities speculators to share the benefits of the Funding Act with the original owners of their bonds, including Continental Army veterans, his opponents demanded why, if this matter was so important to ordinary citizens, they had sent Congress "no petitions or remonstrances" of their own. In replying that the veterans "were so dispersed, that their interests and efforts could not be brought together," Madison observed that "the case of the purchasing holders was very different."[35]

Indeed it was. In his essay promoting his own Discrimination proposal, William Manning wrote that he expected "a formidable body of powerful men"—especially "those who have gotten their public securities for a trifle"—to "combine in opposition" to his plan. He feared they would succeed, too, since "the Few" had created a federal government "at such a distance from the influence of the common people that they think their interests and influence will always have the greatest sway."[36]

Madison and Manning were right to worry. When George Washington made his triumphal tour of New England during the summer of 1789, every member of the committee that escorted him into Boston was in the top rank of Massachusetts bondholders. During the battle over Funding, bondholders regularly corresponded with their counterparts in other states. As Congress debated the topic at Federal Hall in New York City, the reporter charged with transcribing the exchange noted that "the galleries were unusually crowded."[37]

It has never been entirely clear what had made Madison and other Constitutional Convention delegates so confident that extending the sphere of government would stymie irresponsible factions without also neutralizing virtuous ones.[38] The answer may lie in the Framers' belief that the very qualities that made some Americans more virtuous than others—their wealth, education, and frequent dealings with like-minded individuals in other states—would also enable them to unite.

The Federalists' opponents—the Anti-Federalists, the advocates for single-member congressional constituencies, and the Americans who thought even the state legislative districts were too large—agreed that shifting certain core governmental duties to national legislators would thwart some grassroots organizing efforts more effectively than others. All they denied was that the pernicious influences were the ones that would be filtered out.

Some bondholders were not satisfied with the Funding Act. Congress had decreed that everyone who turned in an old federal bond would receive two new ones. One, equal to two-thirds of the value of the original bond, would begin paying interest immediately. Interest on the other new bond, replacing the other third of the old bond, would not start until 1800. To Abigail Adams the idea of denying bondholders a third of their interest for ten years seemed manifestly unfair. She acknowledged that if the government had paid full interest immediately, "Some individuals might have accumulated great fortunes," but on the other hand "the National Honour would have stood much fairer with all honest Men."[39]

In December 1790 New Jersey and Pennsylvania bondholders petitioned Congress for better terms, but both groups were soundly rebuffed. In the Senate the only supporter of the Pennsylvania remonstrance was the man who had introduced it, Robert Morris.[40] During this same period John Brown of Providence, Rhode Island, wrote Samuel Breck of Boston proposing that New England bond traders circulate a petition of their own. Breck replied at the end of December that bondholders in his town were "apprehensive if Congress make any change in consequence of Petitions from the Creditors that such alterations in the System will justify others which may be less favourable to them."[41] Abigail Adams agreed. "The funding & Assumption Bills . . . are not what was wisht by many members" of Congress, she told Cotton Tufts on the eve of final adoption, "but the danger of finally loosing the Bill was so great, that it was consented to by both houses as an anchor that it would not do to quit, least the whole Should go to shipwreck."[42] By 1792 four out of every five dollars collected by the federal government were disbursed to bondholders.[43] If Congress were to revisit the issue, prudent speculators such as Breck and Adams realized, they could not be assured that their share of the federal pie would be enlarged.

In the early 1760s, when wealthy Virginians and Bostonians initiated the first organized protests against Parliament's aggressive new colonial policy, they set in motion a series of events that none of them could have anticipated. The protests provoked punitive action from Britain that led to more aggressive colonial resistance and eventually to a movement for independence. Perhaps most surprising of all, a colonial protest movement led by the most privileged Americans eventually sparked internal conflicts in which those same leaders had to face aggressive challenges from their social inferiors.[44]

In sharp contrast, the authors of the U.S. Constitution came very close to achieving the precise results they had projected. This was especially true in the all-important economic arena. Convinced that the United States would be a doomed nation until it did right by government bondholders and private creditors, the Framers placed state-level tax and debt relief beyond the realm of possibility.

The Constitution produced a massive shift in the balance of power between Americans who paid taxes and those who had invested in government bonds. With the adoption of the Funding Act in August 1790, the new national government committed itself to redeeming state as well as federal bonds. The owners of the old notes would receive new securities upon which punctual interest would be paid in gold and silver. "No country in the world affords such a field for speculations both in paper and land" as the United States, Noah Webster declared in 1791.[45] One of the most successful of the speculators was Abigail Adams.[46]

At the same time that the Constitution satisfied bondholders, it also permitted federal officials to keep a promise that numerous Federalists had made during the ratification campaign. After the Constitution was adopted, most Americans paid significantly lower taxes than they had during the previous decade.[47] Indeed, the new national government obtained almost all of its revenue from tariffs levied in the port towns, so farmers almost never had to try to come up with scarce gold and silver to pay federal taxes.

One of the states where taxpayers received the most dramatic relief was Massachusetts. There a heavy state government debt had necessitated punishing direct taxes. Once Congress assumed about 86 percent of the state debts (Massachusetts and several other states had run up such large government debts that Congress balked at assuming the entire burden), the General Court was able to grant the state's taxpayers a massive tax break.[48] There would be no repetition of Shays's Rebellion.[49]

The federal tax burden was even lighter than it appeared on paper, because the Constitution had the salutary effect of expanding the money supply. Just as the Federalists had predicted, punctual interest payments on the war bonds raised their market price to equivalence with their face value, transforming them into a circulating currency.[50]

In some regions of the country, however, the Constitution actually increased the tax burden. This would not have been the case if Congress had listened to James Madison and refused to assume the state debts. To service that additional debt load, lawmakers were forced in 1791 to levy an excise on domestically produced spirits.[51] Whiskey was an essential element in the backcountry economy. Because of its high value per pound, it was one of the few commodities that could be profitably shipped back east. Farmers paid day laborers a portion of their wages in whiskey, which reduced the amount of scarce gold and silver they had to obtain. But the Excise Act required Americans to pay taxes, in hard money, on every gallon of liquor they distilled—even whiskey that was not sold for cash but bartered to laborers.

Farmers in several regions of the country quietly decided to withhold their excise taxes.[52] Most of them got away with it, but the Washington administration decided to make an example of one group of tax resisters: those who lived just three hundred miles west of the temporary federal capital, Philadelphia. In 1794 an army marched to Westmoreland County, the westernmost region of Pennsylvania, and arrested hundreds of participants in the so-called Whiskey Rebellion. Significantly, the army was led by Treasury Secretary Alexander Hamilton.

One of the western tax resisters had urged his fellow insurgents not to use violence. Herman Husband was nonetheless arrested and taken to Philadelphia, where he was jailed for half a year awaiting trial. He escaped further punishment—indeed, the grand jury apparently refused to indict him—but the ordeal had broken his health. On his way home to Bedford he stopped at a tavern and died there sometime in June 1795. He was seventy years old—the biblical three score and ten.[53]

The tariff and the excise tax were not the federal government's only sources of revenues. During the 1780s Congress had actually netted a loss on its western land operations. With Indians standing in the way of white surveyors and settlers, land sales fell far short of financing the string of U.S. Army forts along the Ohio River. In the first years of the new government, western expenses only multiplied. Indeed, between 1790 and 1796—the first seven years in which Congress possessed its own authority to tax—nearly five-sixths of federal operating expenditures were devoted to fighting Indians. (This figure excluded payments to bondholders, which were actually greater than all other government expenditures combined.)[54]

In 1790 and again in 1791 the U.S. Army suffered devastating defeats at the hands of the Indians—a testament to the disparate native communities' success at achieving unity. But in 1794 the federal government's enormous investment in the West began to pay off. An army led by Anthony Wayne defeated the Indian confederation at Fallen Timbers in present-day Ohio, and the following year native diplomats signed over most of the land in the state. That was good news not only for land-hungry American settlers and speculators but for the federal government, which was finally able to realize the old dream of using western land sales to pay down its debt. The powerful new American army often proved sufficiently intimidating to achieve its objectives without even taking the field. In 1790, Creek Indians, desperate to keep federal troops from attacking their villages, ceded much of their territory to the new nation. A secret provision of the treaty made Creek headman Alexander McGillivray a brigadier general in the U.S. Army, guaranteeing him a substantial annual salary of $1,200. It was the first treaty ever ratified by the U.S. Senate.[55]

At the same time that the Constitution enriched the federal government, raised the value of the war bonds, and cut most Americans' taxes, it also revolutionized the relationship between the country's debtors and creditors. The magnitude of the transformation was evident in two letters that Theodore Sedgwick, a Massachusetts congressman, received from his countrymen in 1789. Both writers reported on events in the state's house of representatives, and both declared that they could only "thank God" that the Constitution had been adopted. One spelled out the reason for his relief: "it is not in their power to make paper money or to take many other disgraceful measures which we should undoubtedly be obliged to submit to but for that sovereign balm the Federal Constitution."[56]

Under the Constitution even Americans' least popular creditors—the British merchants who had sold them goods on credit before the Revolutionary War—were eventually able to collect from many of their American debtors. Especially after the Senate ratified Jay's Treaty with Britain in 1795, the new federal court system proved much more receptive to the merchant princes' suits than state courts had been. The very first state law overturned by the U.S. Supreme Court was a Rhode Island measure aimed at protecting a debtor from his British creditors.[57] Since 1912 the American money supply—which, ironically enough, is legal-tender paper money (creditors have no right to refuse it)—has been regulated by the Federal Open Market Committee. The committee consists of the seven Federal Reserve governors (appointed by the president, and confirmed by the Senate, to fourteen-year terms) and five of the regional Federal Reserve bank presidents, serving in rotation. The presidents of the regional banks are chosen by their boards of directors, two-thirds of whose members are appointed by private banks.[58] The Federal Reserve system perfectly fulfills the Framers' objective of removing control over the money supply as far as possible from the hands of ordinary Americans.

The constitutional ban on debtor relief not only pleased the nation's creditors but went a long way toward accomplishing the Framers' goal of transforming the United States into a more attractive place in which to invest. The benefits were not immediate. Less than a year after the Constitution was ratified, James Madison revived his plan to become a large-scale land speculator. He joined his fellow Virginian Henry Lee in a scheme to purchase and resell hundreds of town lots near the proposed site of the country's new capital city. Lee did what Madison had done in 1786: he wrote Thomas Jefferson, who was still in Paris, seeking his help in recruiting European investors. Once again Jefferson had to report that he could find no takers.[59]

In the long run, however, the Constitution did increase the flow of capital into the new nation. It is true that Americans benefited from Europe's disasters—a series of crop failures starting in 1788 and more than three decades of intermittent warfare beginning in 1793.[60] But the Funding Act and the constitutional ban on debtor relief also seem to have played their part. "The establishment of funds to maintain public credit has had an amazing effect upon the face of business and the country," Noah Webster declared in 1791. "Money circulates freely," and "Commerce revives."[61] "One reason for the boom of the 1790s," writes a careful historian of the Philadelphia business community, "was that the adoption of the Constitution and the introduction of Hamilton's financial program markedly increased the confidence of businessmen—both foreign and domestic—in the American economy."[62]

Thus the Constitution yielded tremendous economic benefits. But many Americans believed these came at an enormous political cost. The new national government was, by design, considerably less responsive to the public will than its state-level counterparts. The adoption of the Constitution spelled the end of annual elections, of grassroots instructions to representatives, and of popular control of the money supply—all of which dated back to the colonial era. Federal senators and congressmen, unlike the state legislators who had reigned supreme during the colonial and Revolutionary periods, would come into daily contact with only a small percentage of their constituents—generally the wealthiest.

EPILOGUE:

THE UNDERDOGS' CONSTITUTION

A NYONE WHO has broken off a chunk of the past and thoroughly scrutinized it will tell you the same thing: it always turns out that the truth of the matter is hidden under a thick coat of common misperceptions. What is striking about the genesis of the Constitution is that the confusion is not limited to the ill-informed. Indeed, a different set of myths seems to conceal the Framers' motives at every level of expertise.

The Americans who spend the least time thinking about the Constitution often confuse it with either the Declaration of Independence or the Bill of Rights. They credit the Framers with a passionate urge to safeguard civil liberties such as gun rights and freedom of religion and speech. Authors who mention the Constitution in passing—for instance, in biographies of the Founders and in textbooks—avoid that error. They say the dragon the Framers were trying to slay was the weakness of the federal government under the Articles of Confederation. That view is not wrong. But we will never fully understand why the Constitutional Convention was held until we grasp the full implications of James Madison's October 1787 assertion that the "mutability" and "injustice" of "the laws of the States" had "contributed more to that uneasiness which produced the Convention, and prepared the public mind for a general reform, than those which accrued to our national character and interest from the inadequacy of the Confederation."[1]

A growing number of historians of the Constitution acknowledge that one of its architects' most pressing goals was to transfer certain key responsibilities from the state legislatures to a new national government capable of resisting pressure from below. Some scholars go still further, showing that the Framers' antidemocratic ideology was rooted in their disgust at the damage the state governments had allegedly done to the economy. But most of these historians who focus on the elitist character of the Constitution commit an important error of their own, mistaking the Federalists' biased assessment of the crisis that led to the Constitution for reality. In the damage they do to American civic life, these writers surpass the amateurs and the ill-informed. During the 1780s, they say, some of the most prominent men in the nation accused the American farmer of proving himself incapable of running the country—and the farmer was guilty as charged. The Framers carved this accusation of plebeian incompetence into the cornerstone of the edifice they constructed in Philadelphia, and although the document has been amended, the attitude that spawned it has not. Today Americans exude immense pride in their democratic republic. But beneath that surface sentiment lurk nagging feelings, not only that you can't fight city hall but that you shouldn't, since we all know what happens when ordinary folk get their hands on the levers of power. Those, at least, are the messages conveyed both by the structure of the federal government (which was also the model used in subsequent revisions to the state constitutions) and by the history lessons that buttress it.

Of course the safeguards against grassroots pressure that were built into the American political system are much less rigid than those found in countries that do not even claim to be republics. On the other hand, they are considerably more insidious. The Framers designed the federal government to be much less accessible than it seems. As Zephaniah Swift put it in 1792, ordinary Americans are "told that nothing confines them," and yet they remain "impounded."[2] The sinister beauty of the Constitution—in particular, the immensity of congressional districts—is that when citizens find they cannot influence national legislation, their tendency is not to curse the system but to blame themselves.

The decade leading to the adoption of the Constitution is by no means the only period of American history that has been cited by intellectuals as illustrating the dire consequences of empowering simple farmers. For a hundred years historical orthodoxy held that the "Reconstruction" era that followed the Civil War was an unmitigated disaster. Scholars contended that during the 1870s the eleven recently defeated Southern states suffered the same affliction that the thirteen newly independent states had undergone in the 1780s: rule by unlettered agricultural workers (many of them, in this latter case, African American). The academic detractors of both the "Critical Period" and the Reconstruction era provided crucial justification for the not-so-pretty measures that were taken to bring both of these political experiments to a close. Actually what is true of the period leading up to the adoption of the Constitution is also true of the era that followed the Civil War. In both cases, the extent to which the farmers actually wielded power has been greatly exaggerated, as has their abuse of it.[3] Elitist analyses of the common people of both eras—articulated not only by their most prominent contemporaries but also by historians—were not founded in fact.

If historians want to paint a more accurate picture of the years leading up to the adoption of the Constitution, they will need to investigate more than one of the numerous contemporary perspectives on that period. It is not sufficient to report the arguments of the leading Anti-Federalists. Most of them shared the Framers' analysis of the economic and political crises of the 1780s, objecting to the Constitution solely because it seemed to threaten states' rights and civil liberties. We must also listen to the thousands of Americans who rejected the Framers' view that the Constitution was the only way out of the economic crisis of the 1780s. This is not to say that the Framers' analysis of the recession was inaccurate—only that it was one-sided. The authors of the Constitution sincerely believed that during the postwar era the thirteen state legislatures had bungled their way into a vivid demonstration of the perils of popular rule. Left to govern themselves, debtors and taxpayers had employed the might and power of government to cheat both their private creditors and the owners of government bonds. The result: moneyed men and women would neither lend cash to Americans—or to their government—nor ship them merchandise on credit. The country could never attract capital until it became less democratic. One of the primary motives for the Constitution was thus to wrest control of fiscal and monetary matters away from "the interested part of the community" and place it in the hands of men who took an objective view of the common good.[4]

Other Americans saw things differently. They pointed out that during the 1780s most of the state governments adopted higher taxes and tighter monetary policies than their colonial predecessors. It was this legislation, they contended, that had wrecked the economy. It had also enriched some free Americans while impoverishing others, endangering the very existence of republican government. Their great fear was not that excess democracy would scare off capital but that the methods being used to foster capitalism posed a threat to democracy.

Both sides were partly correct. For instance, the paper money advocates' claim that colonial-era loan offices had generally succeeded during peacetime is beyond dispute. But the Framers were certainly correct that many of the relief policies of the 1780s—including, in this new republican context, paper money—threatened Americans' collective credit rating. Was it realistic, however, for state assemblymen to lay on unprecedented taxes and expect their constituents not to demand a medium with which to pay them? Indeed, it would appear that the single greatest harm anyone inflicted on the economy during the 1780s was the state legislatures' adoption of fiscal and monetary policies so harsh as to make popular demands for tax and debt relief inevitable. This relief legislation—and in many cases, the mere threat that it might be adopted—persuaded would-be investors to steer clear of the American economy. One thing seems certain: the multifaceted, intertwined crises that beset the United States in the wake of the Revolutionary War do not prove what both the Framers and their historians have so often taken them to prove—that the reins of government reside most safely in the hands of the few.

On February 22, 1790, the House of Representatives concluded its debate on James Madison's suggestion that in redeeming the war bonds, the government should discriminate against stockjobbers. As House clerk John Beckley called the roll and recorded the votes on Madison's amendment—thirteen for and thirty-six against—the guests watching from the gallery included Abigail Adams, the vice president's wife. As she noted in a letter to her sister, Adams had chosen this very day to visit the House of Representatives "for the first Time."[5]

Neither Madison nor any of his colleagues knew that Adams was among the speculators his amendment targeted.[6] Adams still cherished a belief that Madison had, until quite recently, shared with her: that what was good for the bondholders was good for the country. But as Adams and other speculators peered down from the House gallery, Madison was beginning to have second thoughts.

During the 1780s Madison had allowed his disgust with the fiscal policies emanating from the state legislatures to persuade him that the bondholders' personal desires were synonymous with the public interest, that a government amenable to their influence would be a more virtuous one. Indeed, Madison had gone one step further, convincing himself that the bondholders were more capable than their natural adversaries, the taxpayers, of taking an objective view of the common good. Public creditors were among "the most enlightened and impartial people" who had to be protected from the "unreflecting multitude."[7]

Amid the speculative frenzy sparked by Alexander Hamilton's appointment as secretary of the treasury on September 11, 1789, Madison began to doubt bondholders' access to impartiality. Unlike Noah Webster, who admitted his "mistake" on the issue of taxation and declared, "The people were right," Madison made no public confession of error. But as the 1790s wore on, he backed further and further away from his earlier belief in the inseparability of wealth and virtue. Indeed, he began to swing to the other extreme. There is no reason for modern students of the origins of the Constitution to follow Madison as he veered toward a sanctification of popular virtue, but we might take a lesson from his dawning recognition that wealthy Americans did not actually possess a unique ability to perceive and pursue the common good. It is almost impossible to exaggerate the success of the government that the Constitution created. And yet historians err in echoing the Framers' belief that they had transferred power from the greedy to the selfless.

At the same time that historians neglect the views expressed by the segment of the population that pushed for tax and debt relief during the 1780s, they have also had very little to say about how relief advocates influenced the grand political events of that era. It is true that almost none of the fifty-five delegates who gathered in Philadelphia in the summer of 1787 for the Constitutional Convention were small farmers. So it is understandable that ordinary Americans remain invisible in traditional accounts of the origins of the Constitution. In a real sense, though, Americans who tilled the soil were present in the Pennsylvania statehouse that summer. It was small farmers' rebellions and threats that produced the state-level relief legislation that the authors of the Constitution were determined to overturn. With no rebellions, there would have been less tax and debt relief legislation, and without relief, there would have been much less need for a powerful new national government.

Farmers not only helped to bring the Constitution about but powerfully influenced its specific provisions. If the federal convention delegates had not feared that the nation's agrarian majority would reject it, they would have created a considerably more elitist document. The dread that farmers would refuse to ratify the Constitution also powerfully shaped gentry Federalists' rhetoric. It was largely in order to avoid turning smallholders against the new national government that its advocates disguised their antidemocratic intentions. In short, the new regime would have been a very different thing if small farmers had actually been what we once imagined them to have been: passive spectators of the "Miracle at Philadelphia." Indeed, the Constitution might never have been written.

What Americans admire most about their national charter is that it is, at its best, an underdogs' Constitution, a document that protects even the most unpopular religions and political ideas, the most mistrusted racial and ethnic minorities—and even people accused of crimes. But this book has argued that an underdogs' Constitution is precisely what the Framers did not intend to write. While there is no reason to question their claim that they hoped to benefit all free Americans, what they meant to give the ordinary citizen was prosperity, not power. Indeed, many of the Amendments that we most cherish today—the enfranchisement of African Americans and women, the direct election of senators, and others—do not just add to the Constitution. They directly contradict the Framers' antidemocratic intent.

For all the lip service Americans pay the authors of the Constitution, in their actions they have often shown much less respect for them than for the men and women with whom the Framers locked horns in the mid-1780s. There are people today who wish to give up their paper money and return to the gold standard, but they are generally viewed as crackpots. Few believe the wealthy possess special qualities of leadership. Most citizens expect their elected officials to do much more than clear away obstructions to private investment. That the nation's fundamental charter is an underdogs' Constitution is, for most Americans, a source of tremendous pride. It is richly ironic that what has arguably become history's greatest experiment in shielding the powerless began as a slur on the capacities of ordinary citizens.

NOTES

PREFACE

1. Alfred F. Young, "The Framers of the Constitution and the 'Genius' of the People," *Radical History Review* 42 (Fall 1988), 17; Kenneth R. Bowling, "A Tub to the Whale': The Founding Fathers and Adoption of the Federal Bill of Rights," *Journal of the Early Republic* 8 (Fall 1988), 223–51.

"EVILS WHICH . . . PRODUCED THIS CONVENTION": INTRODUCTION

1. Carl Van Doren, *The Great Rehearsal: The Story of the Making and Ratifying of the Constitution of the United States* (New York, 1948); Clinton Rossiter, *1787: The Grand Convention* (New York, 1966); Catherine Drinker Bowen, *Miracle at Philadelphia: The Story of the Constitutional Convention, May to September, 1787* (Boston, 1966); David O. Stewart, *The Summer of 1787: The Men Who Invented the Constitution* (New York, 2007).
2. Madison, June 19, 1787, in Max Farrand, ed., *The Records of the Federal Convention of 1787* (3 vols.; New Haven, Conn., 1911), 1:318.
3. Madison to Jefferson, Oct. 24, 1787, in William T. Hutchinson et al., eds., *The Papers of James Madison* (17 vols. to date; Chicago, 1962–), 10:212; Gordon S. Wood, *The Creation of the American Republic, 1776–1787* (Chapel Hill, N.C., 1969), 467.
4. Madison, ["Preface to Debates in the Convention of 1787"], in Farrand, ed., *Records of the Federal Convention*, 3:548; Mercer, Aug. 14, 1787, ibid., 2:288–89; Donald S. Lutz, *Popular Consent and Popular Control: Whig Political Theory in the Early State Constitutions* (Baton Rouge, La., 1980), 119; Lance Banning, *The Sacred Fire of Liberty: James Madison and the Founding of the Federal Republic* (Ithaca, N.Y., 1995), 114.
5. Plumer to Daniel Tilton, Dec. 16, 1787, quoted in Lynn W. Turner, *William Plumer of New Hampshire, 1759–1850* (Chapel Hill, N.C., 1962), 25; "A Citizen of Philadelphia" [Pelatiah Webster], *The Weaknesses of Brutus Exposed: or, Some Remarks in Vindication of the Constitution Proposed by the Late Federal Convention, Against the Objections and Gloomy Fears of that Writer* (Philadelphia, 1787), 18.
6. Hamilton, *Federalist* 85:3. I use the definitive edition of *The Federalist* edited by Jacob E. Cooke (Middletown, Conn., 1961) and cite it by essay number (in this case, Number 85) and paragraph.
7. "Publicus," *Middlesex Gazette*, Sept. 18, 1786.
8. Rep. Davenport, speech in Connecticut House of Representatives, May 12, 1787, *Middlesex Gazette*, May 28, 1787.
9. Hamilton, June 18, 1787, in Farrand, ed., *Records of the Federal Convention*, 1:301.
10. Henry Knox to Rufus King, June 8, 1787, in Charles R. King, ed., *The Life and Correspondence of Rufus King, Comprising His Letters, Private and Official, His Public Documents, and His Speeches* (New York, 1894), 1:222; "Extract of a Letter from a Gentleman in Washington County . . . ," *Albany Gazette*, June 21, 1787, *DHRC*, 13:141; Theodore Sedgwick to Nathan Dane, July 5, 1787, Sedgwick Family

Papers, MHS; Hartford dateline, *United States Chronicle*, June 1, 1786; Edmund Randolph, June 12, 1787, in Farrand, ed., *Records of the Federal Convention*, 1:218; J. Allen Smith, *The Spirit of American Government: A Study of the Constitution, Its Origin, Influence and Relation to Democracy* (New York, 1907), ch. 3–6; Wood, *Creation of the Republic*, 275, 513; Joyce Appleby, "The American Heritage: The Heirs and the Disinherited," *JAH* 74 (Dec. 1987), 798–813; Richard K. Matthews, *If Men Were Angels: James Madison and the Heartless Empire of Reason* (Lawrence, Kans., 1995). Compare Martin Diamond, "Democracy and *The Federalist*: A Reconsideration of the Framers' Intent," *American Political Science Review* 53 (Mar. 1959), 52–68; Bernard Bailyn, "The Ideological Fulfillment of the American Revolution: A Commentary on the Constitution," in Bailyn, *Faces of Revolution: Personalities and Themes in the Struggle for American Independence* (New York, 1990), 225–67.

11. Gouverneur Morris to George Washington, Oct. 30, 1787, in W. W. Abbot and Dorothy Twohig, eds., *The Papers of George Washington*, Confederation Series (6 vols.; Charlottesville, Va., 1992–97), 5:400; Roger H. Brown, *Redeeming the Republic: Federalists, Taxation, and the Origins of the Constitution* (Baltimore, 1993), 233.

12. Deane to Samuel B. Webb, July 16, 1785, in Worthington Chauncey Ford, ed., *Correspondence and Journals of Samuel Blachley Webb* (3 vols.; New York, 1893–94), 3:49; Samuel Wales, "A Sermon Preached before the General Assembly of the State of Connecticut, at Hartford," May 12, 1785, in Ellis Sandoz, ed., *Political Sermons of the American Founding Era, 1730–1805* (2nd ed., 2 vols.; Indianapolis, Ind., 1998), 1:852.

13. Drew R. McCoy, *The Last of the Fathers: James Madison and the Republican Legacy* (Cambridge, U.K., 1989), 73; Douglass Adair, "The Tenth Federalist Revisited," in Adair, *Fame and the Founding Fathers: Essays*, ed. Trevor Colbourn (orig. pub. 1974; Indianapolis, Ind., 1998), 111.

14. Ralph Ketcham, *James Madison: A Biography* (Charlottesville, Va., 1990), 51–52.

15. Irving Brant, *James Madison, Father of the Constitution, 1787–1800* (Indianapolis, Ind., 1950), 13; Banning, *Sacred Fire of Liberty*, 204; Jack N. Rakove, *James Madison and the Creation of the American Republic* (New York, 1990), 50.

16. Ketcham, *James Madison*, 51.

17. Ibid., 183.

18. Madison to Jefferson, Oct. 17, 1788, quoted in Colleen A. Sheehan, "The Politics of Public Opinion: James Madison's 'Notes on Government,'" *WMQ*, 3rd ser., 49 (Oct. 1992), 625.

19. Morris, July 2, 1787, in Farrand, ed., *Records of the Federal Convention*, 1:517.

20. Madison, June 6, 1787, ibid., 1:134.

21. Cumberland County citizens, memorial and remonstrance, Jan. 16, 1786, *New Jersey Gazette*, Feb. 6, 1786.

22. A[bigail] Dwight to Mrs. Morton, Jan. 10, 1785, Sedgwick Family Papers, MHS.

23. Madison, *Federalist* 10:1.

24. William Davie, speech in the North Carolina ratifying convention, July 29, 1788, in Farrand, ed., *Records of the Federal Convention*, 3:350.

25. Charles Pinckney, speech in South Carolina ratifying convention, May 20, 1788, in Jonathan Elliot, ed., *The Debates in the Several State Conventions on the Adoption of the Federal Constitution*... (4 vols.; Washington, D.C., 1836), 4:333; Edmund Pendleton to James Madison, Oct. 8, 1787, *DHRC*, 10:1773.

26. Randolph, speech in Virginia ratifying convention, June 17, 1788, in Farrand, ed., *Records of the Federal Convention*, 3:328.

27. Extract of a Letter from Salem County, West Jersey, Oct. 22, 1787, *Pennsylvania Herald*, Oct. 27, 1787, *DHRC*, 3:140–41; John Fiske, *The Critical Period of American History, 1783–1789* (Boston, 1888), 272–75.

28. Benjamin Rush to Jeremy Belknap, Feb. 28, 1788, in Bernard Bailyn, ed., *The Debate on the Constitution: Federalist and Antifederalist Speeches, Articles, and Letters During the Struggle over Ratification* (2 vols; New York, 1993), 2:256; James Wilson, speech in Pennsylvania ratifying convention, Dec. 4, 1787, *DHRC*, 2:500.

29. United States Constitution, in Farrand, ed., *Records of the Federal Convention*, 2:660.

30. Madison, *Federalist* 10:20–22.

31. Madison to Thomas Jefferson, Oct. 24, 1787, in Hutchinson et al., eds., *Papers of James Madison*, 10:214.

32. Greenbrier County court, order book, Sept. 21, 1784, in Helen S. Stinson, ed., *Greenbrier Co., W. Va. Court Orders, 1780–1850* (Moorpark, Calif., 1988), 37. I am grateful to Richard Franklin Neel, Jr., for sharing his research on Adonijah Mathews with me.

33. Winchester, Virginia, dateline, *New Hampshire Mercury*, Aug. 30, 1787; Henry Banks to [Edmund Randolph], Feb. 23, 1787, *CVSP*, 4:247.

34. Greenbrier County citizens, petition, Dec. 9, 1785, VLP; Otis K. Rice, *A History of Greenbrier County* (Lewisburg, W.V., 1986), 81–90.

35. John Francis Mercer to James Madison, Nov. 12, 1784, in Hutchinson et al., eds., *Papers of James Madison*, 8:135.

36. George Clendenin to [Edmund Randolph], Aug. 11, 1787, and Robert Renick, deposition, Aug. 20, 1787, enclosed in Edmund Randolph to Speaker of the House of Delegates, Oct. 15, 1787, Executive Communications, box 4, LiVi; Richmond dateline, *Virginia Gazette and Weekly Advertiser*, Sept. 20, 1787.

37. Richmond dateline, *Virginia Gazette and Weekly Advertiser*, Sept. 20, 1787.

38. Clendenin to [Randolph], Aug. 11, 1787, in Randolph to Speaker of the House of Delegates, Oct. 15, 1787, Executive Communications, box 4, LiVi.

39. Ronald P. Formisano, "Teaching Shays/The Regulation: Historiographical Problems as Tools for Learning," *Uncommon Sense* 106 (Winter 1998), 24–35.

40. James McClurg to James Madison, Aug. 22, 1787, in Hutchinson et al., eds., *Papers of James Madison*, 10:155.

41. Clendenin to [Randolph], Aug. 11, 1787, and Renick, deposition, Aug. 20, 1787, enclosed in Randolph to Speaker of the House of Delegates, Oct. 15, 1787, Executive Communications, box 4, LiVi.

42. Richmond dateline, *Virginia Gazette and Weekly Advertiser*, Sept. 20, 1787; Clen-

denin to [Randolph], Aug. 11, 1787, enclosed in Randolph to Speaker of the House of Delegates, Oct. 15, 1787, Executive Communications, box 4, LiVi.

43. Carl Lotus Becker, *The History of Political Parties in the Province of New York, 1760–1776* (Madison, Wisc., 1909), 22.

44. John Quincy Adams to Abigail Adams, Dec. 30, 1786, in Lyman H. Butterfield et al., eds., *Adams Family Correspondence* (8 vols. to date; Cambridge, Mass., 1963–), 7:418.

45. Gerry, Mason, Randolph, May 31, 1787, in Farrand, ed., *Records of the Federal Convention*, 1:48–51.

46. Mason, Aug. 16, 1787, in Farrand, ed., *Records of the Federal Convention*, 2:309; Gerry, June 7, 8, 1787, ibid., 1:154–55, 165; Edmund Randolph to Thomas Jefferson, July 12, 1786, in Julian P. Boyd et al., eds., *The Papers of Thomas Jefferson* (33 vols. to date; Princeton, N.J., 1950–), 10:133; Richard B. Morris, *The Forging of the Union, 1781–1789* (New York, 1987), 158; Brown, *Redeeming the Republic*, 206–8.

47. Brown, *Redeeming the Republic*, 212–13.

48. Bernard Bailyn, *To Begin the World Anew: The Genius and Ambiguities of the American Founders* (New York, 2003), 121–22. Bailyn is not alone. Edmund S. Morgan of Yale denounces the "legislative tyranny" of the period, and Gordon S. Wood of Brown writes that "paper money acts, stay laws, and other forms of debtor relief legislation hurt various creditor groups in the society and violated individual property rights." Morgan, "Just Say No," *New York Review of Books*, Nov. 18, 1999, p. 40; Wood, "Democracy and the Constitution," in *How Democratic Is the Constitution?* ed. Robert A. Goldwin and William A. Schambra (Washington, D.C., 1980), 8; Joseph J. Ellis, *Founding Brothers: The Revolutionary Generation* (New York, 2000), 52; Stanley Elkins and Eric McKitrick, *The Age of Federalism* (New York, 1993), 44; Banning, *Sacred Fire of Liberty*, 250.

CHAPTER 1: "BRICKS WITHOUT STRAW" — GRIEVANCES

1. Quoted in Jill Lepore, *A Is for American: Letters and Other Characters in the Newly United States* (New York, 2002), 40; Joseph J. Ellis, *After the Revolution: Profiles of Early American Culture* (New York, 1979), 163–64.

2. N[oah] Webster, *Pennsylvania Gazette*, May 9, 1787.

3. Ellis, *After the Revolution*, 162.

4. [Webster], "Political Paragraphs, Connecticut," *Connecticut Courant*, Nov. 20, 1786.

5. N[oah] Webster, *Pennsylvania Gazette*, May 9, 1787.

6. Forrest McDonald, *Alexander Hamilton: A Biography* (New York, 1979), 137; E. James Ferguson, *The Power of the Purse: A History of American Public Finance, 1776–1790* (Chapel Hill, N.C., 1961), 340–41.

7. Gordon S. Wood, *The Creation of the American Republic, 1776–1787* (Chapel Hill, N.C., 1969).

8. [John Jay], *An Address to the People of the State of New-York on the Subject of the Con-*

stitution Agreed Upon at Philadelphia . . . (New York, [1788]), in Paul Leicester Ford, ed., *Pamphlets on the Constitution of the United States, Published During its Discussion by the People, 1787–1788* (Brooklyn, N.Y., 1888), 73; Hamilton, speech in New York legislature, Apr. 12, 1787, in Harold C. Syrett, ed., *The Papers of Alexander Hamilton* (27 vols.; New York, 1961–87), 4:145; Hamilton, *Federalist* 85:3.

9. Jack N. Rakove, *James Madison and the Creation of the American Republic* (New York, 1990), 32.

10. Washington, quoted in Woody Holton, *Forced Founders: Indians, Debtors, Slaves, and the Making of the American Revolution in Virginia* (Chapel Hill, N.C., 1999), 3. On Washington's career as a land speculator, see Charles A. Beard, *An Economic Interpretation of the Constitution of the United States* (New York, 1913), 144; Holton, *Forced Founders*, 3–11, 37, 210, 215; Charles Royster, *The Fabulous History of the Dismal Swamp Company: A Story of George Washington's Times* (New York, 1999).

11. Washington, quoted in Irving Brant, *James Madison, The Nationalist, 1780–1787* (Indianapolis, Ind., 1948), 339.

12. Madison to Jefferson, Aug. 12, 1786, in William T. Hutchinson et al., eds., *The Papers of James Madison* (17 vols. to date; Chicago, 1962–), 9:97–98.

13. Madison to Monroe, Feb. 24, 1786, Madison to Jefferson, Aug. 12, 1786, in Hutchinson et al., eds., *Papers of James Madison*, 8:494, 9:97–98; Brant, *Madison, The Nationalist*, 339–40.

14. Madison to Jefferson, Aug. 12, 1786, in Hutchinson et al., eds., *Papers of James Madison*, 9:97–98.

15. Thomas Jefferson to James Madison, Dec. 16, 1786, in Hutchinson et al., eds., *Papers of James Madison*, 9:212–13; Holton, *Forced Founders*, 3–13, 32–37.

16. Madison to Jefferson, Mar. 18, 1786, in Julian P. Boyd et al., eds., *The Papers of Thomas Jefferson* (33 vols. to date; Princeton, N.J., 1950–), 9:334; Madison, "Agst. Paper Money, Novr. 1786 Virg: Assy.," in Hutchinson et al., eds., *Papers of James Madison*, 9:159.

17. Charles Jared Ingersoll (1825), quoted in Drew R. McCoy, *The Last of the Fathers: James Madison and the Republican Legacy* (Cambridge, U.K., 1989), 73.

18. Madison, *Federalist* 62:17.

19. [John] Templeman, "Live Teeth," *Massachusetts Centinel*, Aug. 16, 1786.

20. Doctor Le Mayeur, advertisement, *Virginia Independent Chronicle*, Mar. 7, 1787.

21. Gary B. Nash, "Thomas Peters: Millwright and Deliverer," in David G. Sweet and Gary B. Nash, eds., *Struggle and Survival in Colonial America* (Berkeley, Calif., 1981), 69–85 (revolution.h-net.msu.edu/essays/nash.html).

22. Benjamin Quarles, *The Negro in the American Revolution* (Chapel Hill, N.C., 1961); Sylvia R. Frey, "Between Slavery and Freedom: Virginia Blacks in the American Revolution," *Journal of Southern History* 49 (Aug. 1983), 375–98; Peter H. Wood, "'The Dream Deferred': Black Freedom Struggles on the Eve of White Independence," in Gary Y. Okihiro, ed., *In Resistance: Studies in African, Caribbean, and Afro-American History* (Amherst, Mass., 1986), 166–87; Robert A. Olwell, "'Domestick Enemies': Slavery and Political Independence in South

Carolina, May 1775–March 1776," *Journal of Southern History* 55 (Feb. 1989), 21–48; Frey, *Water from the Rock: Black Resistance in a Revolutionary Age* (Princeton, N.J., 1991); Holton, *Forced Founders*, 133–63; Simon Schama, *Rough Crossings: Britain, the Slaves and the American Revolution* (London, 2005); Gary B. Nash, *The Forgotten Fifth: African Americans in the Age of Revolution* (Cambridge, Mass., 2006); Cassandra Pybus, *Epic Journeys of Freedom: Runaway Slaves of the American Revolution and Their Global Quest for Liberty* (Boston, 2006).

23. George Robertson (Chesterfield County), petition, Nov. 8, 1785, VLP.

24. Harrison County citizens, petition, Dec. 5, 1786, Ohio County citizens, petition, Oct. 26, 1787, VLP.

25. "A Freeman," *Worcester Magazine* 2:28 (2nd week of Oct. 1786), 337; David Daggett, *An Oration, Pronounced in the Brick Meeting-House, in the City of New-Haven, on the Fourth of July, A.D. 1787* (New Haven, Conn., [1787]), 5; Holton, *Forced Founders*, 45–60, 215–16.

26. Unspecified Charleston newspaper, paraphrased in "Postscript," *Pennsylvania Herald*, Oct. 1, 1785.

27. "Plain Reason," *Virginia Independent Chronicle*, Sept. 5, 1787.

28. "Jonathan of the Valley," "The Warner," I, *Independent Chronicle*, June 16, 1785.

29. Anonymous essay, *New Haven Gazette*, Feb. 2, 1786; Robert R. Livingston to Hamilton, Mar. 3, 1787, in Syrett, ed., *Papers of Alexander Hamilton*, 4:103; Alfred F. Young, *The Democratic Republicans of New York: The Origins, 1763–1797* (Chapel Hill, N.C., 1967), 57.

30. Robert A. Becker, "Currency, Taxation, and Finance, 1775–1787," in Jack P. Greene and J. R. Pole, eds., *The Blackwell Encyclopedia of the American Revolution* (Cambridge, Mass., 1991), 367; Roger H. Brown, *Redeeming the Republic: Federalists, Taxation, and the Origins of the Constitution* (Baltimore, 1993), 33–36; Max M. Edling, *A Revolution in Favor of Government: Origins of the U.S. Constitution and the Making of the American State* (Oxford, 2003), 155–58; Woody Holton, "'From the Labours of Others': The War Bonds Controversy and the Origins of the Constitution in New England," *WMQ,* 3rd ser., 61 (Apr. 2004), 275–76.

31. The face value of the 1785 tax, passed in compliance with that year's $3 million congressional requisition, was £20,000, but Rhode Islanders were permitted to pay two-thirds of it using "indents" (certificates paid out as interest to holders of federal bonds) that had depreciated to about 33 percent of their face value, so its real cost was about £11,000. Ferguson, *Power of the Purse*, 225; John P. Kaminski, *Paper Politics: The Northern State Loan-Offices During the Confederation, 1783–1790* (New York, 1989), 169.

32. Robert A. Becker, *Revolution, Reform, and the Politics of American Taxation, 1763–1783* (Baton Rouge, La., 1980), 121–22; H. James Henderson, "Taxation and Political Culture: Massachusetts and Virginia, 1760–1800," *WMQ,* 3rd ser., 47 (Jan. 1990), 105.

33. "Answer of the Town of Greenwich to the Circular Letter from Boston," *Worcester Magazine* 2:35 (last week of Nov. 1786), 422; Daggett, *Fourth of July Oration*, 4–5, 14.

34. Theodore Sedgwick to Pamela Sedgwick, June 24, 1786, Sedgwick Family Pa-

pers, MHS; "Cincinnatus" [Arthur Lee], V, *New York Journal*, Nov. 29, 1787, in Bernard Bailyn, ed., *The Debate on the Constitution: Federalist and Antifederalist Speeches, Articles, and Letters During the Struggle over Ratification* (2 vols.; New York, 1993), 1:121.

35. Rufus King to John Adams, Oct. 3, 1786, in Paul H. Smith et al., eds., *Letters of Delegates to Congress, 1774–1789* (26 vols.; Washington, D.C., 1976–2000), 23:580–81.

36. Massachusetts General Court, "Address to the People," *Worcester Magazine*, 2:37 (2nd week of Dec. 1786), 445.

37. "An Act to Amend the Laws of Revenue, To Provide for the Support of Civil Government, and the Gradual Redemption of All the Debts Due by this Commonwealth" (Oct. 1787 session, chapter 1, passed Jan. 1, 1788), in William Waller Hening, ed., *The Statutes at Large: Being a Collection of All the Laws of Virginia, From the First Session of the Legislature, in the Year 1619* (Richmond, 1823), 12:412.

38. Brown, *Redeeming the Republic*.

39. "An Address of the House of Delegates of Maryland, To their Constituents," *Maryland Journal and Baltimore Advertiser*, Feb. 2, 1787; "Z," *Independent Chronicle*, July 20, 1786; Atkinson town meeting, Aug. 21, 1786, Fremont/Poplin town meeting, petition, June 5, 1786, in Isaac W. Hammond, ed., *Town Papers: Documents Relating to Towns in New Hampshire* (3 vols.; Concord, N.H., 1882–84), 11:123, 705; "A Friend to the Public," *Newport Mercury*, Feb. 13, 1786; Exodus 5: 6–19.

40. "A Friend to the Public," *Newport Mercury*, Feb. 13, 1786.

41. Manning, "Some Proposals For Making Restitution to the Original Creditors of Government and to Help the Continent to a Medium of Trade . . . ," Feb. 6, 1790, in Michael Merrill and Sean Wilentz, eds., *The Key of Liberty: The Life and Democratic Writings of William Manning, "A Laborer," 1747–1814* (Cambridge, Mass., 1993), 112.

42. Ibid., 105, 112.

43. "Tom Thoughtful" [Noah Webster], "The Devil Is in You," *American Museum* 1 (Feb. 1787), 114.

44. Dracut town meeting, petition, Sept. 25, 1786, Shays' Rebellion Collection, AAS; "An Inhabitant of Worcester County," *Worcester Magazine* 2:29 (3rd week of Oct. 1786), 348.

45. Virginia House of Delegates, "A Statement of the Revenues and Ordinary Expenditures of the Commonwealth of Virginia Arising from the Revenue of 1786 . . . ," in *Abstract and Statement* ([Richmond], [1788]); Leonard L. Richards, *Shays's Rebellion: The American Revolution's Final Battle* (Philadelphia, 2002), 74–83; Edling, *Revolution in Favor of Government*, 158; Holton, "From the Labours of Others," 277–81.

46. "An Act for Raising Supplies for the Year 1786," *Charleston Evening Gazette*, Apr. 3, 1786.

47. "Probus," *Massachusetts Centinel*, May 5, 1787.

48. Tucker, speech in South Carolina House of Representatives, Feb. 13, 1786, *Charleston Morning Post*, Feb. 14, 1786.

49. Madison, quoted in Lance Banning, *The Sacred Fire of Liberty: James Madison and the Founding of the Federal Republic* (Ithaca, N.Y., 1995).

50. Thomas Mansfield, petition, Sept. 27, 1786, Petitions Referred (1786), no. 1987, House of Representatives, MSA; Nathan Ordway, petition, Jan. 8, 1785, legislative petitions, NHSA.

51. *A Narrative of a Revolutionary Soldier: Some of the Adventures, Dangers, and Sufferings of Joseph Plumb Martin* (orig. pub. 1830; New York, 2001), 241–42; "H.J——," "Copy of a Genuine Letter, Written Some Time Since, By a Continental Invalid to His Wife," *Middlesex Gazette*, Mar. 12, 1787 (reprinted from *New York Morning Post*).

52. Daniel Rogers to Nicholas Brown, Nov. 13, 1786, Brown Papers, box 27, folder 6, JCB; Ferguson, *Power of the Purse*, 281; Irwin H. Polishook, *Rhode Island and the Union, 1774–1795* (Evanston, Ill., 1969), 118.

53. Greene and Pettit, articles of agreement, June 7, 1784, Greene to Jeremiah Wadsworth, June 7, 1784, in Richard K. Showman et al., eds., *The Papers of General Nathanael Greene* (13 vols.; Chapel Hill, N.C., 1976–2005), 13:323–24n.

54. Mary Beth Norton, *Liberty's Daughters: The Revolutionary Experience of American Women, 1750–1800* (Ithaca, N.Y., 1980), ch. 7; Joan R. Gundersen, *To Be Useful to the World: Women in Revolutionary America, 1740–1790* (New York, 1996), ch. 9.

55. Woody Holton, "Abigail Adams, Bond Speculator," *WMQ*, 3rd ser., 64 (Oct. 2007).

56. Abigail Adams to John Adams, Jan. 3, 1784, "Adams Family Papers: An Electronic Archive" (www.masshist.org/digitaladams/aea/), hereinafter cited as Adams Electronic Archive.

57. John Adams to Cotton Tufts, Sept. 5, 1784, in Lyman H. Butterfield et al., eds., *Adams Family Correspondence* (8 vols. to date; Cambridge, Mass., 1963–), 5:455.

58. Abigail Adams to Cotton Tufts, Sept. 8, 1784, ibid., 5:458.

59. John Adams to Cotton Tufts, April 24, 1785, ibid., 6:88–90.

60. Abigail Adams to Mary Cranch, Oct. 10, 1790, in Stewart Mitchell, ed., *New Letters of Abigail Adams, 1788–1801* (Boston, 1947), 61; Phyllis Lee Levin, *Abigail Adams: A Biography* (New York, 1987), 269.

61. Abigail Adams to John Adams, Apr. 25, 1782, John Adams to Abigail Adams, Oct. 12, 1782, Adams Electronic Archive; Lynne Withey, *Dearest Friend: A Life of Abigail Adams* (New York, 1981), 134–35, 215; Edith B. Gelles, *Portia: The World of Abigail Adams* (Bloomington, Ind., 1992), 45.

62. Abigail Adams to Cotton Tufts, [Apr. 26]–May 10, 1785, in Butterfield et al., eds., *Adams Family Correspondence*, 6:104.

63. Abigail Adams to Cotton Tufts, July 22, 1786, ibid., 7:280.

64. Abigail Adams to Cotton Tufts, [Apr. 26]–May 10, 1785, ibid., 6:108.

65. Abigail Adams to John Adams, June 17, 1782, Adams Electronic Archive.

66. Marylynn Salmon, *Women and the Law of Property in Early America* (Chapel Hill, N.C., 1986), 49–53.

67. Abigail Adams to John Adams, Dec. 27, 1783, Adams Electronic Archive.

68. Abigail Adams to Cotton Tufts, Oct. 3, 1790, Miscellaneous Manuscripts, New-York Historical Society, New York; Tufts to Abigail Adams, Jan. 7, 1791, *Microfilms of the Adams Papers Owned by the Adams Manuscript Trust and Deposited in the Massachusetts Historical Society* (microfilm, 608 reels, Boston, 1954–59), reel 374.

69. "Plain Reason," *Virginia Independent Chronicle*, Aug. 29, 1787; "On the Payment of the Massachusetts State Notes," *Hampshire Herald*, Feb. 14, 1786; "Justice," *Middlesex Gazette*, Mar. 6, 27, 1786. Compare "Zeno," *Middlesex Gazette*, Oct. 2, 1786.

68. *Massachusetts Centinel*, Mar. 25, 1789, in Joseph Stancliffe Davis, *Essays in the Earlier History of American Corporations* (2 vols.; Cambridge, Mass., 1917), 1:181.

71. John Webb to Samuel B. Webb, Mar. 22, 1786, in Worthington Chauncey Ford, ed., *Correspondence and Journals of Samuel Blachley Webb* (3 vols.; New York, 1893–94), 3:55; "A Friend to the Public," *Newport Mercury*, Jan. 30, 1786; Benjamin Guerard, speech in South Carolina House of Representatives, *Charleston Evening Gazette*, Oct. 4, 1785; John R. Nelson, Jr., *Liberty and Property: Political Economy and Policymaking in the New Nation, 1789–1812* (Baltimore, 1987), 30–31; Jackson Turner Main, *Political Parties Before the Constitution* (Chapel Hill, N.C., 1973), 51; Ferguson, *Power of the Purse*, ch. 12; Richards, *Shays's Rebellion*, 80.

72. James City County citizens, petition, Nov. 8, 1787, VLP; "Objections Against Reducing the Publick Debt Examined," *Massachusetts Centinel*, Mar. 1, 1786 (reprinted from *Hampshire Herald*).

73. "Nestor" [Rush], *Independent Gazetteer*, July 1, 1786.

74. Newcastle County citizens, printed petition, [Aug. 1787], Oct.–Nov. 1787 legislative petitions, record group 1111, DPA, reel 9, frame 119.

75. Abigail Adams to John Adams, Jan. 3, 1784, Adams Electronic Archive.

76. Cotton Tufts to Abigail Adams, Dec. 1, 1784, in Butterfield et al., eds., *Adams Family Correspondence*, 6:2.

77. Webster to Greenleaf, Oct. 13, 1791, in Harry R. Warfel, ed., *Letters of Noah Webster* (New York, 1953), 104.

78. Forrest McDonald, *E Pluribus Unum: The Formation of the American Republic, 1776–1790* (Boston, 1965), 131–32, 145–54; Van Beck Hall, *Politics Without Parties: Massachusetts, 1780–1791* ([Pittsburgh], 1972), ch. 4, 6, 7; Robert Arnold Feer, *Shay's Rebellion* (New York, 1988), 55–59; Richard Buel, Jr., "The Public Creditor Interest in Massachusetts Politics, 1780–86," in Robert A. Gross, ed., *In Debt to Shays: The Bicentennial of an Agrarian Rebellion* (Charlottesville, Va., 1993), 47; Ferguson, *Power of the Purse*, 245–48.

79. "Justitia," *Independent Chronicle*, June 22, 1786.

80. Jeremy Belknap, *The History of New-Hampshire . . .* (Boston, 1791), 2:461–62; Smithfield town meeting, representative instructions, Feb. 24, Apr. 19, 1786, PRAC-RISA; "Justice," *Middlesex Gazette*, Mar. 6, 27, 1786.

81. "Observator," *New Hampshire Gazette*, June 10, 1785.

82. John Adams to Thomas Jefferson, June 6, 1786, in Boyd et al., eds., *Papers of Thomas Jefferson*, 9:612; Richard Peters to James Madison, Mar. 31, 1790, in Hutchinson et al., eds., *Papers of James Madison*, 13:133.

83. "On the Payment of the Massachusetts State Notes," *Hampshire Herald*, Feb. 14, 1786.

84. George Richards Minot, *The History of the Insurrections in Massachusetts, In the Year [1786] and the Rebellion Consequent Thereon* (Worcester, Mass., 1788), 8–9; "Petition from Albemarle for Emission of Paper Money," [Nov. 3, 1787], *WMQ*, 2nd ser., 2 (July 1922), 214.

85. Campbell County citizens, petition, Oct. 30, 1786, VLP; Minot, *History of the Insurrections*, 8; Barrington town meeting, Nov. 18, 1786, Barrington Town Records, 1:608–9, NHSL; "Zeno," *Providence Gazette*, Feb. 25, 1786; Thomas Tudor Tucker, speech in South Carolina House of Representatives, Feb. 13, 1786, *Charleston Evening Gazette*, Feb. 14, 1786; Bernard Bailyn, *The Ideological Origins of the American Revolution* (enlarged ed., Cambridge, Mass., 1992), 48–51. Compare Alexander Hamilton to Robert Morris, Apr. 30, 1781, cited in Stanley Elkins and Eric McKitrick, *The Age of Federalism* (New York, 1993), 776n; "Speech of a Member of the General Court of Massachusetts, on the Question Whether the Public Securities Should Be Redeemed at Their Current Value," *American Museum* 1 (May 1787), 417.

86. "An Old Soldier," "Taxes Paid Easy!" *Independent Chronicle*, May 18, 1786; "An Honest Chearful Citizen," "A Word of Consolation for America . . ." *American Museum* 1 (Mar. 1787), 189; "A O.U.," *New Haven Gazette*, Aug. 23, 1787; "Extract from the Proceedings of the Senate," Jan. 5, 1787, *Maryland Journal and Baltimore Advertiser*, Jan. 16, 1787.

87. "A Friend to the Rights of Mankind," *New Hampshire Gazette*, June 3, 1785; Joshua Ewing to Peter Colt, Sept. 17, 1785, Wadsworth Correspondence, CHS.

88. "Observator," *New Hampshire Gazette*, May 20, June 10, 1785; "A O.U.," *New Haven Gazette*, Aug. 23, 1787; Johann David Schoepf, *Travels in the Confederation*, trans. and ed. Alfred J. Morrison (2 vols.; Philadelphia, 1911), 2:130; "The Observer," VII, *Pennsylvania Gazette*, Dec. 9, 1789; Smithfield town meeting, representative instructions, Feb. 24, 1786, cited in Brown, *Redeeming the Republic*, 90; James City County citizens, petition, Nov. 8, 1787, VLP.

89. Harmar to Francis Johnston, June 21, 1785, Harmar Letterbook, CL.

90. John Webb to Samuel B. Webb, June 25, 1786, in Ford, ed., *Correspondence of Webb*, 3:59; "An Old Republican," "Strictures upon County Conventions in General, and the Late Meeting Holden at Hatfield in Particular . . . ," V, *Hampshire Gazette*, Oct. 18, 1786; "Cousin Barnaby," *Virginia Independent Chronicle*, Sept. 26, 1787.

91. John Webb to Samuel B. Webb, Mar. 22, 1786, in Ford, ed., *Correspondence of Webb*, 3:56; Exeter town meeting, Oct. 16, 23, 1786, *New Hampshire Mercury*, Nov. 1, 1786.

92. ["Report of Board of Treasury on the Requisition for 1787"], Sept. 28, 1787 (submitted Sept. 29, 1787), in Worthington Chauncey Ford, ed., *Journals of the Continental Congress, 1774–1789* (34 vols.; Washington, D.C., 1904–37), 33:574.

93. Delaware citizens, printed petition, [August 1787], Oct.–Nov. legislative petitions, record group 1111, DPA, reel 9, frame 119.

94. Brown to George Benson, Oct. 12, 1785, Brown Papers, box 44, folder 10, JCB.

95. "Probus," *Massachusetts Centinel,* May 5, 1787; Richards, *Shays's Rebellion,* 78.

96. "Plain Reason," *Virginia Independent Chronicle,* Sept. 5, 1787.

97. "Impartial Observer," *Massachusetts Centinel,* Apr. 4, 1787; "A Customer," *Massachusetts Centinel,* Apr. 7, 1787.

98. Henry Lee, Jr., to George Washington, Oct. 1, 17, 1786, in W. W. Abbot and Dorothy Twohig, eds., *The Papers of George Washington,* Confederation Series (6 vols.; Charlottesville, Va., 1992–97), 4:282, 295; Henry Knox to George Washington, Oct. 23 and Dec. 17, 1786, ibid., 4:300, 460.

99. James City County citizens, petition, Nov. 8, 1787, VLP; "A Letter from a Gentleman in New-York to His Friend in Connecticut, on the Subject of Paper Money," *Connecticut Courant,* Feb. 5, 1787; Brown, *Redeeming the Republic,* 152.

100. "Objections Against Reducing the Publick Debt Examined," *Massachusetts Centinel,* Mar. 1, 1786 (reprinted from *Hampshire Herald*); Chester County citizens, petition, Feb. 20, 1786, in Lark Emerson Adams and Rosa Stoney Lumpkin, eds., *The State Records of South Carolina: Journals of the House of Representatives, 1785–1786* (Columbia, S.C., 1979), 440.

101. [Whiting], "Some Remarks on the Conduct of the Inhabitants of the Commonwealth of Massachusetts in Interupting The Siting of the Judicial Courts . . ." (Dec. 1786), in Stephen T. Riley, ed., "Dr. William Whiting and Shays' Rebellion," AAS *Proceedings* 66 (1957), 158.

102. Nathaniel Jemison to Samuel Salisbury, Apr. 20, 1785, Salisbury Papers, AAS.

103. John Welton, speech in Connecticut House of Representatives, May 30, 1787, *Middlesex Gazette,* June 18, 1787; Bruce H. Mann, *Republic of Debtors: Bankruptcy in the Age of American Independence* (Cambridge, Mass., 2002), 25, 63.

104. Unnamed representative, speech in Connecticut House of Representatives (paraphrase), May 25, 1787, *Middlesex Gazette,* June 18, 1787.

105. George Chandler, *The Chandler Family: The Descendants of William and Annis Chandler, Who Settled in Roxbury, Mass., 1637* (Boston, 1872), 153–54 (my thanks to Thomas Doughton for this reference).

106. New York dateline, *Middlesex Gazette,* June 25, 1787.

107. Hartford dateline, *Columbian Herald,* Aug. 10, 1785.

108. Charleston, South Carolina, dateline, *New Hampshire Mercury,* Feb. 1, 1786; Elizabeth-Town dateline, *New Jersey Journal, and Political Intelligencer,* May 30, 1787; New York dateline, *Massachusetts Gazette,* Nov. 28, 1785; Abigail Adams to Mary Cranch, Mar. 21, 1790, in Mitchell, ed., *New Letters of Abigail Adams,* 42; New York dateline, *Pennsylvania Gazette,* Apr. 3, 1755, May 16, 1765, Nov. 23, 1785 (my thanks to Heather B. Repicky for these references); Laurel Thatcher Ulrich, *A Midwife's Tale: The Life of Martha Ballard, Based on Her Diary, 1785–1812* (New York, 1990), 289–303.

109. Baltimore dateline, *Providence Gazette*, June 25, 1785; Charleston dateline, *Columbian Herald*, Apr. 18, 1785; Northampton dateline, *Middlesex Gazette*, Nov. 12, 1787; E. Wilder Spaulding, *New York in the Critical Period, 1783–1789* (orig. pub. 1932; Port Washington, N.Y., 1963), 26 (citing *Daily Advertiser*, May and June 1787).

110. Nathanael Greene to Henry Knox, Mar. 12, 1786, in Richard K. Showman et al., eds., *The Papers of General Nathanael Greene* (13 vols.; Chapel Hill, N.C., 1976–2005), 13:668.

111. Boston dateline, *Massachusetts Centinel*, July 19, 1786; Jeremiah Wadsworth to George Washington, Oct. 1, 1786, in Abbot and Twohig, eds., *Papers of George Washington*, 4:282–83.

112. "A Fellow Citizen"/ "Willing to Learn," *The True Policy of New-Jersey, Defined; Or, Our Great Strength Led to Exertion, in the Improvement of Agriculture & Manufactures, By Altering the Mode of Taxation, and by the Emission of Money on Loan . . .* (Elizabeth-Town, N.J., 1786), 11.

113. Petition from the citizens who closed the Worcester County court, *New Haven Chronicle*, Dec. 26, 1786.

114. "Crisis," *New Hampshire Gazette*, July 20, 1786.

115. Connecticut House of Representatives, journal, Oct. 27, 1786, *Middlesex Gazette*, Nov. 20, 1786.

CHAPTER 2: "THE FAULT IS ALL YOUR OWN"—REBUTTALS

1. "Mentor," *Maryland Journal and Baltimore Advertiser*, Aug. 18, 1786; Charleston dateline, *Columbian Herald*, Aug. 19, 1785; "Amicus Reipublicae" [Benjamin Thurston], *An Address to the Public, Containing Some Remarks on the Present Political State of the American Republicks, &c.* (Exeter, N.H., [1786]), 16; Massachusetts General Court, "Address to the People," *Worcester Magazine* 2:37 (2nd week of Dec. 1786), 447.

2. Jonathan M. Chu, "Debt Litigation and Shays's Rebellion," in Robert A. Gross, ed., *In Debt to Shays: The Bicentennial of the Agrarian Rebellion* (Charlottesville, Va., 1993), 89–91.

3. Springfield dateline, *Hampshire Herald*, June 6, 1786.

4. "A Bit of Advice to Connecticut Folks," *Norwich Packet*, Jan. 11, 1787 (reprinted from *Connecticut Magazine*); "Amicus," *Virginia Independent Chronicle*, June 13, July 4, 1787.

5. Jacob M. Price, *Capital and Credit in British Overseas Trade: The View from the Chesapeake, 1700–1776* (Cambridge, Mass., 1980), 16–19, 126.

6. T. H. Breen, *The Marketplace of Revolution: How Consumer Politics Shaped American Independence* (New York, 2004), 224, 242–43.

7. George Washington to George Mason, Apr. 5, 1769, in Robert A. Rutland, ed., *The Papers of George Mason, 1725–1792* (3 vols.; Chapel Hill, N.C., 1970), 1:98; Bruce A. Ragsdale, *A Planters' Republic: The Search for Economic Independence in Revolutionary Virginia* (Madison, Wisc., 1996), ch. 2, 3, 6, 7; Woody Holton,

Forced Founders: Indians, Debtors, Slaves, and the Making of the American Revolution in Virginia (Chapel Hill, N.C., 1999), 77–92, 99–105; T. H. Breen, *Tobacco Culture: The Mentality of the Great Tidewater Planters on the Eve of Revolution* (Princeton, N.J., 1985), 190–203; Breen, *Marketplace of Revolution*, ch. 6, 7, 8.

8. "Tom Thoughtful" [Noah Webster], "The Devil Is in You," *American Museum* 1 (Feb. 1787), 113.

9. Newburyport, Massachusetts, dateline, *South Carolina Gazette and Public Advertiser*, Nov. 10, 1785.

10. Boston dateline, *State Gazette of South Carolina*, Dec. 21, 1786; "A James River Planter," *Virginia Gazette and Independent Chronicle*, Dec. 9, 1786 (my thanks to Ruth Doumlele for this reference).

11. Anonymous essay, *Virginia Independent Chronicle*, Nov. 29, 1786; Breen, *Marketplace of Revolution*, 165–66.

12. Holton, *Forced Founders*, 104; [Thomas Chandler], *What Think Ye of the Congress Now? or, An Enquiry, How Far the Americans are Bound to Abide by, and Execute the Decisions, of the Late Congress?* (New York, 1775), 27.

13. "A Bit of Advice to Connecticut Folks," *Norwich Packet*, Jan. 11, 1787 (reprinted from *Connecticut Magazine*).

14. Anonymous essay, *Middlesex Gazette*, Dec. 11, 1786 (reprinted from *New Haven Gazette*); "Flirtilla," "An Answer to Blunt's Exhortation," *South Carolina Gazette and Public Advertiser*, Aug. 11, 1785; "T.B.," *Virginia Independent Chronicle*, Oct. 18, 1786; "Tom Thoughtful" [Noah Webster], "The Devil Is in You," *American Museum* 1 (Feb. 1787), 114.

15. "Zeno," *Middlesex Gazette*, Oct. 30, 1786.

16. "A Farmer," "Cause of, And Cure For, Hard Times," *American Museum* 1 (Jan. 1787), 12.

17. "Consequences of Extravagance," *American Museum* 1 (June 1787), 550.

18. "A Bit of Advice to Connecticut Folks," *Norwich Packet*, Jan. 11, 1787 (reprinted from *Connecticut Magazine*); "Adonis," *New Jersey Journal, and Political Intelligencer*, Aug. 15, 1787; "Consequences of Extravagance," *American Museum* 1 (June 1787), 551.

19. "Rusticus," *Massachusetts Centinel*, Apr. 13, 1785; "Consequences of Extravagance," *American Museum* 1 (June 1787), 551.

20. "Characters Out of Character," *South Carolina Gazette and Public Advertiser*, Nov. 19, 1785; "On Luxury," *New Jersey Magazine*, Jan. 1787, 22; "On Modern Dress, 1786: To the Ladies," *Massachusetts Centinel*, Mar. 1, 1786; "A Citizen of the United States" [Royall Tyler], *The Contrast, A Comedy: In Five Acts* (Philadelphia, 1790), 24.

21. Charleston dateline, *State Gazette of South Carolina*, May 29, 1786; "A Plain But Real Friend to America," "On American Manufactures," 1, *American Museum* 1 (Jan. 1787), 18; "The Worcester Speculator," III, *Worcester Magazine* 3:26 (4th week of Sept. 1787), 338.

22. "A Farmer," "Cause of, And Cure For, Hard Times," *American Museum* 1 (Jan. 1787), 12; "Americanus," *Columbian Herald*, Sept. 28, 1785.

23. "Abraham Long," *South Carolina Gazette and Public Advertiser*, Sept. 15, 1785 (reprinted from *Pennsylvania Herald*).

24. Mary Beth Norton, *Liberty's Daughters: The Revolutionary Experience of American Women, 1750–1800* (Ithaca, N.Y., 1980), 155–70; Breen, *Marketplace of Revolution*, ch. 6, 7, 8; Joan R. Gundersen, *To Be Useful to the World: Women in Revolutionary America, 1740–1790* (New York, 1996), 149–51.

25. "A Country-man," *Columbian Herald*, Sept. 28, 1785; "A Bit of Advice to Connecticut Folks," *Norwich Packet*, Jan. 11, 1787 (reprinted from *Connecticut Magazine*).

26. Boston dateline, *South Carolina Gazette and Public Advertiser*, Dec. 7, 1785.

27. "The Oeconomical Association," *Connecticut Courant*, Nov. 6, 1786; Norton, *Liberty's Daughters*, 245.

28. Hartford association and anonymous accompanying essay, *Middlesex Gazette*, Nov. 20, 1786, also appearing in *New Hampshire Mercury*, Nov. 22, 1786; *New Jersey Journal, and Political Intelligencer*, Nov. 22, 1786; *Virginia Independent Chronicle*, Nov. 29, 1786. On women's associations in other towns, see Portsmouth dateline, *New Hampshire Mercury*, Aug. 16, 1787 (on Halifax, N.C.).

29. Mary Cranch to Abigail Adams, July 10–11, 1786, quoted in Edith B. Gelles, *Portia: The World of Abigail Adams* (Bloomington, Ind., 1992), 126; Breen, *Marketplace of Revolution*, 24.

30. "Adonis," *New Jersey Journal, and Political Intelligencer*, Aug. 15, 1787.

31. Andover town meeting, n.d., *Worcester Magazine* 2:45 (2nd week of Feb. 1787), 547–48; David Daggett, *An Oration, Pronounced in the Brick Meeting-House, in the City of New-Haven, on the Fourth of July, A.D. 1787* (New Haven, Conn., [1787]), 19–20.

32. "Americanus," *Hampshire Herald*, Aug. 29, 1786.

33. Daggett, *Fourth of July Oration*, 13; Gordon S. Wood, "Interests and Disinterestedness in the Making of the Constitution," in Richard Beeman, Stephen Botein, and Edward C. Carter II, eds., *Beyond Confederation: Origins of the Constitution and American National Identity* (Chapel Hill, N.C., 1987), 77–79.

34. Newcastle Town citizens, petition, May–June 1786 legislative petitions, record group IIII, DPA, reel 7, frame 510.

35. George Richards Minot, *The History of the Insurrections in Massachusetts, in the Year [1786], and the Rebellion Consequent Thereon* (Worcester, Mass., 1788).

36. "An Undelivered Defense of a Winning Cause: Charles Carroll of Carrollton's 'Remarks on the Proposed Federal Constitution,'" ed. Edward C. Papenfuse, *Maryland Historical Magazine* 71 (Summer 1976), 248.

37. "Minimaltasperus," *New Hampshire Mercury*, Oct. 4, 1786.

38. "Extract of a Letter from Boston, June 18," *Virginia Independent Chronicle*, July 18, 1787.

39. "A Late Member of the General Court" [James Swan], *National Arithmetick; or, Observations on the Finances of the Commonwealth of Massachusetts, With Some Hints Respecting Financiering and Future Taxation in this State, Tending to Render the Publick Contributions More Easy to the People* (Boston, [1786]), viii.

40. "Crisis," *New Hampshire Gazette*, July 20, 1786.

41. "Modestus," *Worcester Magazine* 2:29 (3rd week of Oct. 1786), 351; "A Member of Convention," *Worcester Magazine* 2:33 (3rd week of Nov. 1786), 396.

42. Abigail Adams to John Adams, May 1, 1780, Adams Electronic Archive.

43. Abigail Adams to Mary Cranch, July 12, 1789, in Stewart Mitchell, ed., *New Letters of Abigail Adams, 1788–1801* (Boston, 1947), 15.

44. "Eliza," *American Magazine* (Mar. 1788), 241 (my thanks to Laurie Gingrich for this citation).

CHAPTER 3: "TO RELIEVE THE DISTRESSED"—DEMANDS

1. "A.B.," *Virginia Independent Chronicle*, Oct. 25, 1786 (reprinted from a Boston newspaper); lower part of Camden District citizens, petition, read Oct. 5, 1785, in Lark Emerson Adams and Rosa Stoney Lumpkin, eds., *The State Records of South Carolina: Journals of the House of Representatives, 1785–1786* (Columbia, S.C., 1979), 331; "An Old Citizen," *Charleston Morning Post*, Oct. 26, 1786.

2. Elizabeth-Town, New Jersey, dateline, *Virginia Independent Chronicle*, Dec. 6, 1786.

3. Harrison County citizens, petition, Oct. 22, 1787, James City County citizens, petition, Nov. 8, 1787, VLP; Lancaster town meeting, instructions to representative, Jan. 22, 1787, *Worcester Magazine* 2:44 (1st week of Feb. 1787), 533.

4. "Plain Reason," *Virginia Independent Chronicle*, Aug. 29, 1787.

5. "An Act to Alter and Supply Certain Parts of an Act, Intitled, *An Act Raising Ten Thousand Five Hundred Pounds for the Service of the Year One Thousand Seven Hundred and Eighty-Seven . . .*" (ch. 165, passed Nov. 10, 1787), in John D. Cushing, comp., *The First Laws of the State of Delaware* (2 vols.; orig. pub. 1792; Wilmington, Del., 1981), 2:912.

6. "J——," "Soliloquy," *Middlesex Gazette*, Mar. 27, 1786; Delaware citizens, petition, read Jan. 12, 1787, Jan.–Feb. 1787 legislative petitions, record group 1111, DPA, reel 8, frame 324; "A Friendly Evening's Dialogue, Between A. and B.," *Hampshire Herald*, Feb. 7, 1786; "A Farmer," *New Hampshire Gazette*, Oct. 7, 1785; "The Plan," cited in Terry Bouton, "Tying Up the Revolution: Money, Power, and the Regulation in Pennsylvania, 1765–1800" (Ph.D. diss., Duke University, 1996), 208–9 (see also Bouton, *Taming Democracy: "The People," the Founders, and the Troubled Ending of the American Revolution* [New York, 2007]); Rufus Hopkins to Nicholas Brown, Oct. 2, 1786, Hope Furnace Papers, Brown Papers, box 179, folder 6, JCB; anonymous essay, *Charleston Evening Gazette*, Oct. 1, 1785.

7. David P. Szatmary, *Shays' Rebellion: The Making of an Agrarian Insurrection* (Amherst, Mass., 1980), ch. 1; Michael Merrill, "The Anticapitalist Origins of the United States," *Review: A Journal of the Fernand Braudel Center* 13 (Fall 1990), 465–97.

8. "Publick Faith," *Massachusetts Centinel*, Feb. 8, 1786 (reprinted from *Hampshire Herald*, Jan. 31, 1786); anonymous essay, *Middlesex Gazette*, Mar. 27, 1786; "Jonas, Junior," *Hampshire Herald*, May 17, 1785.

9. "Publick Faith," *Massachusetts Centinel*, Feb. 8, 1786; "Excise," *Hampshire Herald*, Feb. 7, 1786.

10. "A Friend to Order," *Independent Chronicle*, Feb. 16, 1786; [Isaiah Thomas], editor's footnote to "Paper Money," *Worcester Magazine* 2:25 (3rd week of Sept. 1786), 294n.

11. Leonard Woods Labaree, ed., *The Public Records of the State of Connecticut . . .* (Hartford, Conn., 1943, 1945), 5:15–19, 432–33, 6:102; Whitney K. Bates, "The State Finances of Massachusetts, 1780-1789" (master's thesis, University of Wisconsin, 1948), 92–93; Henry Harrison Metcalf, ed., *Laws of New Hampshire . . .* (Bristol, N.H., 1916), 4:562–63 (Apr. 17, 1784); Newport citizens, memorial, *United States Chronicle*, Mar. 9, 1786.

12. "Publick Faith," *Massachusetts Centinel*, Feb. 8, 1786.

13. Botetourt County citizens, petition, Oct. 17, 1787, VLP.

14. Thomas Paine, "Dissertations on Government, the Affairs of the Bank, and Paper Money," in Philip S. Foner, ed., *The Complete Writings of Thomas Paine* (2 vols.; New York, 1945), 2:406, 409; "Primitive Whig" II, *New Jersey Gazette*, Jan. 16, 1786; "Patkick O'Punch," "Letter to a Gentleman in Town from an Irish Debtor, Received Yesterday," *Massachusetts Centinel*, Feb. 18, 1786; "The Republican," *New Hampshire Mercury*, Mar. 21, 1787; Amherst County citizens, petition, Nov. 6, 1787, VLP.

15. "A Friend to the Rights of Mankind," *New Hampshire Gazette*, June 3, July 1, 1785; Leviticus 25:8–17, 23–55; "A Letter from a Gentleman at New-York, dated April 19," *Massachusetts Centinel*, May 6, 1786; Acts 4:32.

16. Grayson to Madison, Mar. 22, 1786, in William T. Hutchinson et al., eds., *The Papers of James Madison* (17 vols. to date; Chicago, 1962–), 8:509.

17. Knox to George Washington, Oct. 23, 1786, in W. W. Abbot and Dorothy Twohig, eds., *The Papers of George Washington*, Confederation Series (6 vols.; Charlottesville, Va., 1992–97), 4:300.

18. Botetourt County citizens, petition, Oct. 17, 1787, VLP.

19. Jefferson to Alexander McCaul, Apr. 19, 1786, in Julian P. Boyd et al., eds., *The Papers of Thomas Jefferson* (33 vols. to date; Princeton, N.J., 1950–), 9:389; John Adams to James Warren, May 3, 1777, in Paul H. Smith et al., eds., *Letters of Delegates to Congress, 1774–1789* (26 vols.; Washington, D.C., 1976–2000), 7:21; Dumas Malone, *Jefferson and His Time*, vol. 1, *Jefferson the Virginian* (Boston, 1948), 161–63, 441–45.

20. Washington to George William Fairfax, June 30, 1786, in Abbot and Twohig, eds., *Papers of George Washington*, 4:137; Charles A. Beard, *An Economic Interpretation of the Constitution of the United States* (New York, 1913), 144–45.

21. *A Narrative of a Revolutionary Soldier: Some of the Adventures, Dangers, and Sufferings of Joseph Plumb Martin* (orig. pub. 1830; New York, 2001), 207–8.

22. "Centinel," *Salem Gazette*, July 26, 1785 (reprinted from an unnamed Boston newspaper); "A Looker On," *Independent Gazetteer*, Jan. 8, 1785 (reprinted from *Chronicle of Freedom*); anonymous essay, *Independent Chronicle*, Nov. 3, 1785; Jean Toscan to Marechal de Castrier, July 27, 1786, Toscan Papers, box 1, folder 10, NHHS; Alexander Hamilton, speech in New York Assembly, Feb. 18, 1787, *American Museum* 1 (June 1787), 524.

23. "An Old Soldier," *American Museum* 2 (July 1787), 38.

24. "Willing to Learn," II, *New Jersey Gazette*, Dec. 21, 1785; "The Petition from a

Number of Inhabitants of Westmoreland County Praying for the Opening of a
Loan Office," "read 1st time Aug. 12, 1784," Records of the General Assembly,
reel 3 (microfilm), PSA; Brunswick County citizens, petition, Oct. 28, 1786,
VLP; Baltimore dateline, *Columbian Herald*, July 15, 1785; Delaware assembly,
message to council, June 15, 1786, May–June 1786 legislative acts and bills, record
group 1111, DPA, reel 7, frame 317; E. James Ferguson, "Currency Finance: An Interpretation of Colonial Monetary Practices," *WMQ*, 3rd ser., 10 (Apr. 1953),
153–80.

25. Stanley Elkins and Eric McKitrick, "The Founding Fathers: Young Men of the
Revolution," *Political Science Quarterly* 76 (June 1961), 181–216.

26. Roger H. Brown, *Redeeming the Republic: Federalists, Taxation, and the Origins of the
Constitution* (Baltimore, 1993), 94.

27. John Fiske, *The Critical Period of American History, 1783–1789* (Boston, 1888),
168–79; Isaac Kramnick, "Introduction," in James Madison, Alexander Hamilton, and John Jay, *The Federalist Papers*, ed. Kramnick (orig. pub. 1788; London,
1987), 25; Francis D. Cogliano, *Revolutionary America, 1763–1815: A Political History* (London, 2000), 107. For the view that the "calls for paper money in the
1780s were the calls of American business," see Gordon S. Wood, "Interests and
Disinterestedness in the Making of the Constitution," in Richard Beeman,
Stephen Botein, and Edward C. Carter, II, eds., *Beyond Confederation: Origins of
the Constitution and American National Identity* (Chapel Hill, N.C., 1987), 78–81.

28. "A Friend to the Public," *Newport Mercury*, Jan. 30, Feb. 13, 1786.

29. New Hampshire House of Representatives, journal, June 23, 1786, in Albert
Stillman Batchellor, ed., *Early State Papers of New Hampshire* (Manchester and
Concord, N.H., 1891–93), 20:658.

30. Swanzey town meeting, instructions to representative, Aug. 28, 1786, in Isaac
W. Hammond, ed., *Town Papers: Documents Relating to Towns in New Hampshire*
(3 vols., Concord, N.H., 1882–84), 13:536.

31. Campbell County citizens, petition, Oct. 30, 1786, VLP; Woody Holton, "'From
the Labours of Others': The War Bonds Controversy and the Origins of the
Constitution in New England," *WMQ*, 3rd ser., 61 (Apr. 2004), 286–88.

32. "Q.Z.," *United States Chronicle*, Feb. 9, 23 (quotation), 1786.

33. "Proceedings of the General Court," *Boston Magazine* 3 (March 1786), 141.

34. Herman Husband, "Some Remarks on Religion, With the Author's Experience
in Pursuit Thereof . . . ," in William K. Boyd, ed., *Some Eighteenth Century Tracts
Concerning North Carolina* (Raleigh, N.C., 1927), 214.

35. Abigail Adams to Mary Cranch, Oct. 4, 1789, July 4, 1790, in Stewart Mitchell,
ed., *New Letters of Abigail Adams, 1788–1801* (Boston, 1947), 27, 53 (quotation).

36. Mark H. Jones, "Herman Husband: Millenarian, Carolina Regulator, and
Whiskey Rebel" (Ph.D. diss., Northern Illinois University, 1982), 8, 21, 26,
82–89; Marjoleine Kars, *Breaking Loose Together: The Regulator Rebellion in Pre-
Revolutionary North Carolina* (Chapel Hill, N.C., 2002).

37. Ibid.

38. Jones, "Herman Husband," 193.
39. [Herman Husband], *Proposals to Amend and Perfect the Policy of the Government of the United States of America, or, The Fulfilling of the Prophecies in the Latter Days, Commenced by the Independence of America* (Philadelphia, 1782), 31. For attribution of this pamphlet to Husband, see Jones, "Herman Husband," 272.
40. "Lycurgus III" [Herman Husband], *XIV Sermons on the Characters of Jacob's Fourteen Sons* (Philadelphia, 1789), v. For attribution of this essay to Husband, see Jones, "Herman Husband," 310.
41. [Husband], "A PROPOSAL, or a General Plan and Mode of Taxation, Throughout the American States, By Calling in All the Bills of Credit Now in Circulation, and Exchanging the Same for New Bills . . . ," in [Husband], *Proposals to Amend and Perfect the Policy*, 22.
42. [Husband], *Proposals to Amend and Perfect the Policy*, 16, 25–26; "Lycurgus III" [Husband], *XIV Sermons*, 32.

CHAPTER 4: "SAVE THE PEOPLE" — REQUISITION

1. Congressional requisition, Apr. 28, 1784, in Worthington Chauncey Ford, ed., *Journals of the Continental Congress, 1774–1789* (34 vols.; Washington, D.C., 1904–37), 26:312–13; congressional requisition, Sept. 27, 1785, ibid., 29:765–71; ["Report of Board of Treasury on the Requisition for 1787"], Sept. 28, 1787 (submitted Sept. 29, 1787), ibid., 33:570–71.
2. Congress reduced the 1784 requisition after discovering that some of its earlier demands had been higher than necessary; delegates made the opposite discovery in 1785. Congressional requisitions, Apr. 27–28, 1784, Sept. 27, 1785, ibid., 26:297–309, 311–14, 29:765–71.
3. Philip H. Jordan, Jr., "Connecticut Anti-Federalism on the Eve of the Constitutional Convention: A Letter from Benjamin Gale to Erastus Wolcott, February 10, 1787," *Connecticut Historical Society Bulletin* 28 (Jan. 1963), 18; George Richards Minot, *History of the Insurrections in 1786 and the Rebellion Consequent Thereon* (orig. pub. 1810; New York, 1971), 18; E. James Ferguson, *The Power of the Purse: A History of American Public Finance, 1776–1790* (Chapel Hill, N.C., 1961), 188. The first congressional resolve that paid interest on the Commutation certificates was adopted in April 1784, but it brought interest payments to federal bondholders only up through the end of 1783. The Commutation certificates were not issued until several weeks after March 22, 1783, when Congress approved the officers' bonuses. Nor did the April 1784 requisition require new taxes. Indeed, it actually *reduced* an earlier requisition by half and permitted the states to pay one-fourth of their reduced quotas using the indents that would be paid as interest on all federal bonds, including Commutation certificates. Continental Congress, requisition, Apr. 27–28, 1784, in Ford, ed., *Journals of the Continental Congress* 26:300–309, 311–14.
4. Ferguson, *Power of the Purse*, 155–64, 188.
5. Richard H. Kohn, "The Inside History of the Newburgh Conspiracy: America

and the Coup d'Etat," *WMQ*, 3rd ser., 27 (Apr. 1970), 187–220; Ferguson, *Power of the Purse*, 155–64.

6. Minor Myers, Jr., *Liberty without Anarchy: A History of the Society of the Cincinnati* (Charlottesville, Va., 1983), 9.

7. Edmund Randolph to James Madison, Apr. 26, 1783, William T. Hutchinson et al., eds., *The Papers of James Madison* (17 vols. to date; Chicago, 1962–), 6:499; ["Draft of a Speech by Benjamin Gale, 12 November 1787"], *DHRC* 3 (microfilm supp.), item 33-B, p. 154; "Massachusetts Soldiery," *Worcester Magazine* 2:45 (2nd week of Feb. 1787), 546; Lance Banning, *The Sacred Fire of Liberty: James Madison and the Founding of the Federal Republic* (Ithaca, N.Y., 1995), 29–33.

8. Richard Brookhiser, *Gentleman Revolutionary: Gouverneur Morris, The Rake Who Wrote the Constitution* (New York, 2003), 73.

9. John Resch, *Suffering Soldiers: Revolutionary War Veterans, Moral Sentiment, and Political Culture in the Early Republic* (Amherst, Mass., 1999), ix.

10. Joseph Barrell to Samuel B. Webb, June 29, 1784, in Worthington Chauncey Ford, ed., *Correspondence and Journals of Samuel Blachley Webb* (3 vols.; New York, 1893–94), 3:39.

11. Joseph Webb to Samuel B. Webb, May 9, 1783, ibid., 3:14; Charles Pinckney, speech to New Jersey assembly, Mar. 13, 1786, in *Pennsylvania Gazette*, Mar. 22, 1786.

12. New Hampshire citizens, petition, [1783], address, Nov. 27, 1783, in Isaac W. Hammond, ed., *Town Papers: Documents Relating to Towns in New Hampshire* (3 vols., Concord, N.H., 1882–84), 12:762–66; Christopher Collier, *All Politics Is Local: Family, Friends, and Provincial Interests in the Creation of the Constitution* (Hanover, N.H., 2003), 23–24.

13. Noah Webster, *Freeman's Chronicle* essay, quoted in Harry R. Warfel, ed., *Letters of Noah Webster* (New York, 1953), 10; Essex County citizens, petitions, read Nov. 27, 1783, *Votes and Proceedings of the Eighth General Assembly of the State of New-Jersey, at a Session Begun at Trenton on the 28th day of October, 1783 and Continued by Adjournments, Being the First Session* (Trenton, N.J., 1784), 34.

14. King to Elbridge Gerry, July 9, 1786, in Paul H. Smith et al., eds., *Letters of Delegates to Congress, 1774–1789* (26 vols.; Washington, D.C., 1976–2000), 23:393; Christopher Babbitt, *To His Excellency John Hancock, Esquire, Governor of the State of Massachusetts* (n.p., [1787]); William Manning, "Some Proposals For Making Restitution to the Original Creditors of Government and To Help the Continent to a Medium of Trade . . . ," Feb. 6, 1790, in Michael Merrill and Sean Wilentz, eds., *The Key of Liberty: The Life and Democratic Writings of William Manning, "A Laborer," 1747–1814* (Cambridge, Mass., 1993), 102; "A.B.," *Connecticut Journal*, Mar. 14, 1787; "The Looking Glass of 1787" (cartoon), in Collier, *All Politics Is Local*, 105, 158.

15. "Lycurgus III" [Herman Husband], *XIV Sermons on the Characters of Jacob's Fourteen Sons* (Philadelphia, 1789), 25.

16. Benjamin Gale, speech to Killingworth town meeting, Nov. 12, 1787, *DHRC*, 3:422, 429 n5.

17. Anonymous essay, *Boston Gazette*, Jan. 24, 1785; Manning, "Some Proposals," 102.

18. Compare Gordon S. Wood, *The Creation of the American Republic, 1776–1787* (Chapel Hill, N.C., 1969), 400.

19. "Cassius" [Aedanus Burke], *Considerations on the Society or Order of Cincinnati . . .* (Charleston, S.C., 1783), 29.

20. Ferguson, *Power of the Purse*, 223–28.

21. N[oah] Webster, *Pennsylvania Gazette*, May 9, 1787; [Elbridge Gerry] to Rufus King, Mar. 14, 1785, in Charles R. King, ed., *The Life and Correspondence of Rufus King, Comprising His Letters, Private and Official, His Public Documents, and His Speeches* (New York, 1894), 1:74.

22. "An Act for Raising a Revenue of [£31,259.5.0] Per Annum, For the Term of Twenty-Five Years, For the Purpose of Paying the Interest and Principal of Debts Due from the United States, Agreeably to a Recommendation of Congress of [Apr. 18, 1783] and for Appreciating the Same" (ch. 21, passed Dec. 20, 1783), *Acts of the Eighth General Assembly of the State of New-Jersey: At a Session Begun at Trenton the 28th day of October, 1783, and Continued Until the 24th Day of December Following* (Trenton, N.J., 1784), 44–57; "A Supplementary Act to an Act, Intitled, An Act for Raising a Revenue of Thirty-one Thousand Two Hundred and Fifty-Nine Pounds . . . ," *New Jersey Gazette*, Jan. 10, 1785; "Current Prices of Public Securities this Week," *Pennsylvania Gazette*, Aug. 16, 1786.

23. Nathan Dane to Caleb Davis, Feb. 19, 1786, in Smith et al., eds., *Letters of Delegates to Congress*, 23:155; "An Act for Emitting the Sum of Two Hundred Thousand Pounds in Bills of Credit, for the Purposes Therein Mentioned" (ch. 40, passed Apr. 18, 1786), *Laws of the State of New-York, Passed by the Legislature of Said State, at their Ninth Session* (New York, 1786), 76.

24. "An Act for Furnishing the Quota of this State towards Paying the Annual Interest of the Debts of the United States; And for Funding and Paying the Interest of the Public Debts of this State," *Pennsylvania Gazette*, Mar. 23, 30, 1785; "An Act for the Further Relief of Public Creditors" (ch. 7), *Laws Enacted in the Second Sitting of the Tenth General Assembly of the Commonwealth of Pennsylvania . . .* (Philadelphia [1786]), 17–22.

25. Madison to James Monroe, May 29, 1785, in Hutchinson et al., eds., *Papers of James Madison*, 8:285.

26. Ferguson, *Power of the Purse*, 225, 230.

27. "A Fellow Citizen," *Political Intelligencer and New-Jersey Advertiser*, Jan. 11, 1786; Charles Pinckney, speech to New Jersey assembly, Mar. 13, 1786, in *Pennsylvania Gazette*, Mar. 22, 1786.

28. Richard P. McCormick, *Experiment in Independence: New Jersey in the Critical Period, 1781–1789* (New Brunswick, N.J., 1950), 208–11, 235–44.

29. "X," *New Haven Gazette*, June 23, 1785; [Noah Webster], *ATTENTION! or, New Thoughts on a* Serious *Subject, Being an Enquiry into the Excise Laws of Connecticut . . .* (Hartford, Conn., 1789), 16.

30. "Agricola" [William Williams], *Connecticut Courant*, Oct. 9, 1786 (reprinted from

Connecticut Journal); "H.L.S.," "A Modern Courtier in His Elbow-Chair," *Middlesex Gazette*, Sept. 18, 1786.

31. Charles Burrall, Benjamin Chaplain, speeches in Connecticut House of Representatives, May 15, 1787, *Connecticut Courant*, May 28, 1787; table listing direct taxes in force and committee report on congressional requisition, both in House of Representatives, journal, Oct. 1785 session, in Leonard Woods Labaree, ed., *The Public Records of the State of Connecticut . . .* (Hartford, Conn., 1943, 1945), 6:102. The committee estimated that complying with the 1785 requisition would require a tax of fifteen pence on every pound of taxable property value. My estimate that approving the requisition would have required the Connecticut legislature to triple direct taxes is based on the assumption that, if the assembly had allowed taxpayers to pay two-thirds of the Continental tax with indents, the indents would have traded at one-third of their face value (as they did in Massachusetts), reducing the real value of the Continental tax from its face value of fifteen pence per pound to just above eight pence per pound—slightly more than double the hard money value of existing taxes.

32. Connecticut assembly, resolution, Oct. 1786, in Labaree, ed., *Public Records of Connecticut*, 6:232; Christopher Collier, *Roger Sherman's Connecticut: Yankee Politics and the American Revolution* (Middletown, Conn., 1971), 224; Stephen Reed Grossbart, "The Revolutionary Transition: Politics, Religion, and Economy in Eastern Connecticut, 1765–1800" (Ph.D. diss., University of Michigan, 1989), 249.

33. Woody Holton, "'From the Labours of Others': The War Bonds Controversy and the Origins of the Constitution in New England," *WMQ*, 3rd ser., 61 (Apr. 2004), 298.

34. Richmond town meeting, instructions to representative, Aug. 31, 1786, in Hammond, ed., *Town Papers*, 13:317; Aug. 2, 16, 1786, Bedford Town Records, 3:584–86, NHSL.

35. New Hampshire House of Representatives journal, Sept. 22, 1786, in Albert Stillman Batchellor, ed., *Early State Papers of New Hampshire* (Manchester and Concord, N.H., 1891–93), 20:709.

36. George Benson to Nicholas Brown, Mar. 16, 1785, Brown Papers, box 44, folder 10, JCB; Whitney K. Bates, "The State Finances of Massachusetts, 1780–1789" (master's thesis, University of Wisconsin, 1948), 77.

37. Benson to Brown, Mar. 23, 1785, Brown Papers, box 44, folder 10, JCB.

38. Ibid.; [Benson?], note dated Oct. 21, 1785, on the back of Brown to Benson, Oct. 12, 1785, ibid.

39. Theodore Sedgwick to William Whiting, Sept. 14, 1786, in Stephen T. Riley, ed., "Dr. William Whiting and Shays' Rebellion," AAS *Proceedings* 66 (1957), 138.

40. Massachusetts assembly, tax act, Mar. 23, 1786, *Acts and Laws Passed by the General Court of Massachusetts . . .* (Boston, 1786), 368–91.

41. Van Beck Hall, *Politics without Parties: Massachusetts, 1780–1791* ([Pittsburgh], 1972), 120–21; Richard Buel, Jr., "The Public Creditor Interest in Massachusetts

Politics, 1780–86," in Robert A. Gross, ed., *In Debt to Shays: The Bicentennial of an Agrarian Rebellion* (Charlottesville, Va., 1993), 53.

42. M. M. Hall to Nicholas Brown, June 26, 1786, Brown Papers, box 27, folder 5, JCB; "Price of Stocks," *Massachusetts Centinel*, July 26, 1786.

43. An additional 4 percent of the tax would make up a deficiency in Massachusetts's payment on Congress's 1784 specie requisition. Since the indent portion of the 1784 deficiency was intended to benefit domestic holders of federal bonds, I have merged it with the portion of the March 1786 tax that was intended to comply with the indent portion of the 1785 requisition.

44. Thomas Welsh to Abigail Adams, Oct. 27, 1786, in Lyman H. Butterfield et al., eds., *Adams Family Correspondence* (8 vols. to date; Cambridge, Mass., 1963–), 7:383.

45. "A Complaint against a Number Guilty of a Riot at a Court-House the 13th of June 1786," enclosed in Seth Padelford to Robert Treat Paine, June 19, 1786, in Edward W. Hanson, ed., *The Papers of Robert Treat Paine*, vol. 4 (forthcoming).

46. Ronald P. Formisano, "Teaching Shays/The Regulation: Historiographical Problems as Tools for Learning," *Uncommon Sense*, 106 (Winter 1998), 24–35.

47. Roger H. Brown, *Redeeming the Republic: Federalists, Taxation, and the Origins of the Constitution* (Baltimore, 1993), 117.

48. "Proceedings of the General Court," *Boston Magazine* 3 (Nov.–Dec. 1786), 428; Minot, *History of the Insurrections*, 20, 70; Ferguson, *Power of the Purse*, 248; Brown, *Redeeming the Republic*, 117–21; Leonard L. Richards, *Shays's Rebellion: The American Revolution's Final Battle* (Philadelphia, 2002), 119, 157.

49. Benjamin Lincoln to George Washington, Dec. 4, 1786–Mar. 4, 1787, in W. W. Abbot and Dorothy Twohig, eds., *The Papers of George Washington*, Confederation Series (6 vols.; Charlottesville, Va., 1992–97), 4:422.

50. Richards, *Shays's Rebellion*, 77–79.

51. "Probus," *Massachusetts Centinel*, May 5, 1787.

52. Bates, "State Finances of Massachusetts," 128.

53. Ferguson, *Power of the Purse*, 247.

54. Brown, *Redeeming the Republic*, 121.

55. David Howell to William Greene, Oct. 29, 1785, in William R. Staples, *Rhode Island in the Continental Congress, with the Journal of the Convention That Adopted the Constitution, 1765–1790* (Providence, R.I., 1870), 537; Jeremiah Wadsworth, speech in Connecticut House of Representatives, May 15, 1787, *Connecticut Courant*, May 28, 1787.

56. Irwin H. Polishook, *Rhode Island and the Union, 1774–1795* (Evanston, Ill., 1969), 124–26; John P. Kaminski, *Paper Politics: The Northern State Loan-Offices During the Confederation, 1783–1790* (New York, 1989), 177–78.

57. "A Friend to the Public," *Newport Mercury*, Jan. 30, 1786.

58. Ferguson, *Power of the Purse*, 280–82.

59. "North American," I, *Pennsylvania Journal*, Sept. 17, 1783, in Irving Brant, ed., "Two Neglected Madison Letters," *WMQ*, 3rd ser., 3 (Oct. 1946), 574–75 (few historians still ascribe this essay to Madison); "Cursory Remarks and Important Hints," *Connecticut Courant*, June 25, 1787.

60. Nathaniel Peabody to John Hancock, Jan. 24, 1785, Nathaniel Peabody Papers, box 1, folder 4, NHHS.

61. Ferguson, *Power of the Purse*, 40.

62. Abigail Adams to John Adams, June 1, 1777, Adams Electronic Archive.

63. Sept. 10, 1777, in Ford, ed., *Journals of the Continental Congress*, 8:730–31.

64. Morris to president of Congress, Aug. 28, 1781, quoted in Terry Bouton, "Tying Up the Revolution: Money, Power, and the Regulation in Pennsylvania, 1765–1800" (Ph.D. diss., Duke University, 1996), 138.

65. June 28, 1780, in Ford, ed., *Journals of the Continental Congress*, 17:567–69; Ferguson, *Power of the Purse*, 68.

66. Ferguson, *Power of the Purse*, 68–69.

67. James B. Hedges, *The Browns of Providence Plantations: Colonial Years* (Cambridge, Mass., 1952), 316, 322.

68. Sept. 27, 1785, in Ford, ed., *Journals of the Continental Congress*, 29:766; Ferguson, *Power of the Purse*, 69.

69. Smithfield town meeting, instructions to representative, Apr. 19, 1786, PRAC-RISA.

70. "Zeno," *Providence Gazette*, Feb. 25, 1786; "Z.," "Paper Money," *United States Chronicle*, June 1, 1786; Tiverton town meeting, instructions to representative, Mar. 6 (but endorsed "Read March 1 1786"), 1786, PRAC-RISA.

CHAPTER 5: "WHO WILL CALL THIS JUSTICE?"—QUARRELS

1. Mary Smith Cranch to Abigail Adams, Sept. 24, 1786, in Lyman H. Butterfield et al., eds., *Adams Family Correspondence* (8 vols. to date; Cambridge, Mass., 1963–), 7:342.

2. Abigail Adams to Mary Cranch, Sept. 1, 1789, Feb. 20, 1790, in Stewart Mitchell, ed., *New Letters of Abigail Adams, 1788–1801* (Boston, 1947), 22, 38.

3. Abigail Adams to Cotton Tufts, Mar. 10, 1787, in Butterfield et al., eds., *Adams Family Correspondence* 8:7; Benjamin Rush to Trustees of Dickinson College, [Apr.] 1786, in L. H. Butterfield, ed., *Letters of Benjamin Rush* (Princeton, N.J., 1951), 1:380–81.

4. Cotton Tufts to Abigail Adams, Dec. 18, 1787, in Butterfield et al., eds., *Adams Family Correspondence* 8:210.

5. Ibid.; "A Farmer," *Pennsylvania Gazette*, Feb. 3, 1790.

6. Charles Mortimer to John Mortimer, Sept. 1, 1787, quoted in Roger H. Brown, *Redeeming the Republic: Federalists, Taxation, and the Origins of the Constitution* (Baltimore, 1993), 164.

7. James Duncanson to James Maury, Mar. 11, 1788, *DHRC*, 8:478.

8. Battaile Muse to George Washington, Nov. 7, 1787, in W. W. Abbot and Dorothy Twohig, eds., *The Papers of George Washington*, Confederation Series (6 vols.; Charlottesville, Va., 1992–1997), 5:416.

9. Isaac Huger, memorial, n.d., 1787 General Assembly petitions, no. 15, SCDAH.

10. Boston dateline, *Middlesex Gazette*, Sept. 18, 1786; Boston dateline, *New Hampshire Gazette*, Sept. 14, 1786.

11. Randolph to Madison, Mar. 29, 1783, in William T. Hutchinson et al., eds., *The Papers of James Madison* (17 vols. to date; Chicago, 1962–), 6:415.

12. Pettit to Jeremiah Wadsworth, May 27, 1786, Wadsworth Correspondence, CHS; Terry Bouton, "Tying Up the Revolution: Money, Power, and the Regulation in Pennsylvania, 1765–1800" (Ph.D. diss., Duke University, 1996), 169.

13. Abigail Adams to Isaac Smith, Sr., Mar. 12, 1787, in Butterfield et al., eds., *Adams Family Correspondence* 8:8.

14. Abigail Adams to Mary Cranch, Feb. 20, 1790, in Mitchell, ed., *New Letters of Abigail Adams*, 38.

15. Washington to John Jay, May 18, 1786, Washington to Henry Knox, Dec. 26, 1786, in Abbot and Twohig, eds., *Papers of George Washington*, 4:56, 481.

16. "A Friendly Evening's Dialogue, Between A. and B.," *Hampshire Herald*, Feb. 7, 1786.

17. "Proceedings of the General Court," *Boston Magazine* 3 (Mar. 1786), 139.

18. Alexander Gillon, speech in South Carolina House of Representatives, Oct. 5, 1785, *Charleston Evening Gazette*, Oct. 18, 1785.

19. William Manning, "Some Proposals For Making Restitution to the Original Creditors of Government and To Help the Continent to a Medium of Trade . . . ," Feb. 6, 1790, in Michael Merrill and Sean Wilentz, eds., *The Key of Liberty: The Life and Democratic Writings of William Manning, "A Laborer," 1747–1814* (Cambridge, Mass., 1993), 112.

20. "O," *American Herald*, Feb. 4, 1788, *DHRC*, 5:855.

21. "Amicus," *Virginia Independent Chronicle*, July 4, 1787.

22. Springfield dateline, *Hampshire Herald*, Feb. 14, 1786.

23. Manning, "Some Proposals," 101.

24. "Proceedings of the General Court," *Boston Magazine* 3 (July 1786), 315.

25. [Herman Husband], *A Dialogue between an Assembly-man and a Convention-Man On the Subject of the State Constitution of Pennsylvania . . .* (Philadelphia, n.d.), 11; "Justice," *Middlesex Gazette*, Mar. 6, 1786; Newcastle County citizens, printed petition, [Aug. 1787], Oct.–Nov. 1787 legislative petitions, record group 1111, DPA, reel 9, frame 119; "Justitia," *Independent Chronicle*, June 22, 1786; "Observator," *New Hampshire Gazette*, June 10, 1785; "A Farmer," *Pennsylvania Gazette*, Jan. 27, 1790; "A Friend to Plain Reason," *Virginia Independent Chronicle*, Sept. 26, 1787.

26. Massachusetts General Court, "Address to the People," *Worcester Magazine* 2:35 (last week of Nov. 1786), 420.

27. B[enjamin] Goodhue to Samuel Phillips, Jr., Feb. 17, 1785, Phillips Family Papers, MHS; "An Old Republican," "Strictures upon County Conventions in General, and the Late Meeting Holden at Hatfield in Particular . . ." 5, *Hampshire Gazette*, Oct. 18, 1786.

28. Anonymous essay, *Middlesex Gazette*, Mar. 27, 1786; "Massachusetts Soldiery," *Worcester Magazine* 2:45 (2nd week of Feb. 1787), 545; Hunterdon County citizens, petition, Dec. 17, 1782, Legislative Petitions, box 15, NJBAH; Rock Bryn-

ner, "'Fire Beneath Our Feet': Shays' Rebellion and Its Constitutional Impact" (Ph.D. diss., Columbia University, 1993), 8, 67.

29. *A Narrative of a Revolutionary Soldier: Some of the Adventures, Dangers, and Sufferings of Joseph Plumb Martin* (orig. pub. 1830; New York, 2001), 247 (my thanks to Shelley Brooks McCabe for this reference).

30. "Americanus," *Columbian Herald*, Sept. 28, 1785.

31. "Tullius," *Gazette of the State of Georgia*, June 5, 1788, *DHRC* 3:301, 303.

32. [Husband], *Dialogue between an Assembly-man and a Convention-Man*, 11; "A Citizen of Philadelphia" [Noah Webster], "Thoughts on the Domestic Debt of the United States," *Pennsylvania Gazette*, Mar. 21, 1787.

33. "Lycurgus III" [Herman Husband], *XIV Sermons on the Characters of Jacob's Fourteen Sons* (Philadelphia, 1789), 13; Delaware citizens, petition, May–June 1786 legislative petitions, record group 1111, DPA, reel 7, frame 449; "Plain Reason," *Virginia Independent Chronicle*, Sept. 12, 1787; Representative Welton, speech in Connecticut House of Representatives, May 30, 1787, *Middlesex Gazette*, June 18, 1787; "A Friendly Evening's Dialogue Between A. and B.," *Hampshire Herald*, Feb. 7, 1786.

34. Delaware citizens, petition, May–June 1786 legislative petitions, record group 1111, DPA, reel 7, frame 451–52.

35. David Daggett, *An Oration, Pronounced in the Brick Meeting-House, in the City of New-Haven, on the Fourth of July, A.D. 1787* (New Haven, Conn., [1787]), 11–12; "An American," *Independent Chronicle*, Apr. 13, 1786; Portsmouth dateline, *New Hampshire Spy*, Nov. 14, 1786; "Martha Hardlines," cited in "Primitive Whig," VI, *New Jersey Gazette*, Feb. 13, 1786; "The Observer" 7, *Pennsylvania Gazette*, Dec. 2, 1789; Cumberland County citizens, petition, Nov. 19, 1787, VLP.

36. "Tom Thoughtful" [Noah Webster], "The Devil Is in You," *American Museum* 1 (Feb. 1787), 112–15; "Lucifer," "The Devil's Soliloquy on Monday, the Second Day of October, 1780," *Middlesex Gazette*, Nov. 6, 1786.

37. Newport dateline, *New Haven Chronicle*, Sept. 11, 1787; Providence, R.I., Episcopal Church, meeting, Nov. 12, 1787, *Middlesex Gazette*, Dec. 3, 1787 (reprinted from *Providence Gazette*).

38. William Plumer to John Hale, Oct. 6, 14, 1786, "Letters of William Plumer, 1786–1787," Colonial Society of Massachusetts, *Publications*, XI, *Transactions, 1906–1907* (Boston, 1910), 397–98.

39. "Plain Truth," "A Stimulant for the Conscience," *Middlesex Gazette*, Oct. 2, 1786 (my thanks to Douglas Winiarski for this insight).

40. "An Old Rogue," quoted in editors' note, *Massachusetts Centinel*, Feb. 15, 1786.

41. "The Plan . . . ," *Charleston Evening Gazette*, Nov. 19, 1785.

42. Christopher Babbitt, *To His Excellency John Hancock, Esquire, Governor of the State of Massachusetts* (n.p., [1787]).

43. "Modern Whig," III, *Connecticut Gazette*, Apr. 21, 1786.

44. Hunterdon County citizens, petition, Dec. 17, 1782, Legislative Petitions, box 15, NJBAH.

45. Plympton town meeting, petition, Feb. 12, 1787, Shays' Rebellion Collection, AAS; "Modern Whig," *Connecticut Gazette*, Mar. 24, 1786; Nehemiah 5.

46. "Paper Money, Raised from the Dead, Speaketh for Itself!" *Worcester Magazine* 2:25 (3rd week of Sept. 1786), 294.

47. "A.B.," *Connecticut Journal*, Mar. 14, 1787.

48. Merrill and Wilentz, eds., *The Key of Liberty*, 41–45.

49. Jan. 5, 23, 1785, "Diary or Memorandum Book Kept by Joseph Lewis of Morristown . . . ," *Proceedings of the New Jersey Historical Society* 60 (1942), 61–62; George Benson to Nicholas Brown, June 16, 17, 19, 1786, Brown Papers, box 44, folder 11, JCB.

50. "A Freeholder," *Virginia Independent Chronicle*, Apr. 9, 1788, *DHRC*, 9:728; Noah Webster, "Plan of Policy for Improving the Advantages and Perpetuating the Union of the American States," in Webster, *Sketches of American Policy* (Hartford, Conn., 1785), 48; "A Native of New-Jersey," *New Jersey Gazette*, Nov. 14, 1785; "Brutus," *Independent Chronicle*, Feb. 23, 1786; John Adams to David Ramsay, Aug. 1, 1786, *Microfilms of the Adams Papers Owned by the Adams Manuscript Trust and Deposited in the Massachusetts Historical Society* (microfilm, 608 reels, Boston, 1954–59), reel 113; Alexander Hamilton, speech in the New York assembly, Jan. 19, 1787, in Harold C. Syrett, ed., *The Papers of Alexander Hamilton* (27 vols.; New York, 1961–87), 4:7; "Amicus Reipublicae" [Benjamin Thurston], *An Address to the Public, Containing Some Remarks on the Present Political State of the American Republicks, &c.* (Exeter, N.H., [1786]), 26.

51. "A Freeholder," *Virginia Independent Chronicle*, Apr. 9, 1788, *DHRC*, 9:728; Henry Knox to George Washington, Jan. 14, 1787, in Abbot and Twohig, eds., *Papers of George Washington*, 4:522; James H. Hutson, "The Partition Treaty and the Declaration of American Independence," *JAH* 58 (Mar. 1972), 877–96. Compare "Answer of the Town of Greenwich to the Circular Letter from Boston," *Worcester Magazine* 2:35 (last week of Nov. 1786), 422.

52. Philip H. Jordan, Jr., "Connecticut Anti-Federalism on the Eve of the Constitutional Convention: A Letter from Benjamin Gale to Erastus Wolcott, Feb. 10, 1787," *Connecticut Historical Society Bulletin* 28 (1963), 19.

53. "Phydelius," *Connecticut Courant*, May 1, 1786.

54. Continental Congress, circular letter to the states, Sept. 13, 1779, in Worthington Chauncey Ford, ed., *Journals of the Continental Congress, 1774–1789* (34 vols.; Washington, D.C., 1904–37), 15:1060.

55. "The Petition of the Committee of Public Creditors of the City and Liberties of Philadelphia," *Pennsylvania Gazette*, Dec. 15, 1784; "Solon," "Consideration," *Independent Chronicle*, Feb. 23, 1786; "Monitor" 2, *New-Jersey Journal, and Political Intelligencer*, May 10, 1786; [Thurston], *Address to the Public*, 27; "Communication of Minister of France to Secry. Foreign Affairs," [received? Mar. 22, 1783], Joseph Jones Papers, MHS.

56. "Plain Reason," *Virginia Independent Chronicle*, Sept. 5, 1787; Pelatiah Webster, "A Seventh Essay on Free Trade and Finance; In Which the Expediency of Funding

the Public Securities, Striking Further Sums of Paper Money, and Other Important Matters, Are Considered" (1785), in Webster, *Political Essays on the Nature
and Operation of Money, Public Finances, and Other Subjects . . .* (Philadelphia, 1791),
277; "Jonas, Junior," *Hampshire Herald*, May 17, 1785.

57. "Publick Faith," *Massachusetts Centinel*, Feb. 8, 1786 (reprinted from *Hampshire
Herald*, Jan. 31, 1786); [Pelatiah Webster], *Pennsylvania Gazette*, Apr. 18, 1787.

CHAPTER 6: "IDLE DRONES"—ECONOMICS

1. New York dateline, *State Gazette of South Carolina*, May 29, 1786; Hamilton, *Federalist* 15:3; Edward C. Papenfuse, ed., "An Undelivered Defense of a Winning
Cause: Charles Carroll of Carrollton's 'Remarks on the Proposed Federal Constitution,'" *Maryland Historical Magazine* 71 (Summer 1976), 246; "A Late Member of the General Court" [James Swan], *National Arithmetick; or, Observations on
the Finances of the Commonwealth of Massachusetts, With Some Hints Respecting Financiering and Future Taxation in this State, Tending to Render the Publick Contributions More Easy to the People* (Boston, [1786]), 82; "An Account of the Insurrection
in the State of New-Hampshire . . . ," *Virginia Independent Chronicle*, Oct. 18,
1786; "Extract of a Letter from Washington, North-Carolina, March 27," *State
Gazette of South Carolina*, May 29, 1786; Cumberland County citizens, petition,
Nov. 19, 1787, VLP.

2. "Nestor" [Benjamin Rush], *Independent Gazetteer*, July 1, 1786; "Extract of a letter
from New-York, June 26," *New Hampshire Gazette*, Aug. 12, 1785; "A True Friend,"
Virginia Independent Chronicle, Nov. 14, 1787, *DHRC*, 8:162.

3. Madison to Jefferson, Mar. 18, 1786, in William T. Hutchinson et al., eds., *The Papers of James Madison* (17 vols. to date; Chicago, 1962–), 8:503; "Monitor," II, *New
Jersey Journal and Political Intelligencer*, May 10, 1786.

4. Madison, "Agst. Paper Money, Novr. 1786 Virg: Assy.," in Hutchinson et al., eds.,
Papers of James Madison, 9:159; "The Way to Make Money Plenty," *United States
Chronicle*, Mar. 16, 1786 (reprinted from an unnamed Philadelphia publication);
"Speech of a Member of the General Court of Massachusetts on the Question
Whether the Public Securities Should be Redeemed at the Current Value,"
American Museum 1 (May 1787), 417; "Sober Thoughts on the Present Scarcity of
Money," *New Hampshire Mercury*, Sept. 13, 1786; Robert Morris to Congress, July
29, 1782, in Worthington Chauncey Ford, ed., *Journals of the Continental Congress,
1774–1789* (34 vols.; Washington, D.C., 1904–37), 22:436–37; Hamilton, *Report on
Public Credit*, Jan. 9, 1790, in Harold C. Syrett, ed., *The Papers of Alexander Hamil-
ton* (27 vols.; New York, 1961–87), 6:70.

5. "Aristides," *Virginia Independent Chronicle*, Mar. 21, 1787; "Nestor" [Benjamin
Rush], *Independent Gazetteer*, July 1, 1786.

6. George Mason, "A Private Citizen begs leave humbly to submit the following
Queries to the consideration of the General Assembly now sitting," in Robert

A. Rutland, ed., *The Papers of George Mason, 1725–1792* (3 vols.; Chapel Hill, N.C., 1970), 2:861.

7. "A True Friend," *Virginia Independent Chronicle*, Nov. 14, 1787, *DHRC*, 8:161.

8. Ibid., 8:161, 163; "An Account of the Insurrection in the State of New Hampshire," *Virginia Independent Chronicle*, Oct. 18, 1786.

9. "Justice," *State Gazette of South Carolina*, Sept. 7, 1786.

10. Editors' note, Greene to George Washington, Apr. 22, 1784, and Robert Morris to Greene, Jan. 28, 1786, in Richard K. Showman et al., eds., *The Papers of General Nathanael Greene* (13 vols.; Chapel Hill, N.C., 1976–2005), 13:x–xi, 299, 656.

11. Louis Guillaume Otto to Jefferson, May 10, 1786, in Julian P. Boyd et al., eds., *The Papers of Thomas Jefferson* (33 vols. to date; Princeton, N.J., 1950–), 9:504–5 (my translation).

12. Stephen Collins to Harrison, Ansley, & Company, Apr. 29, 1786, container 32 (bound with incoming correspondence), Stephen Collins and Son Papers, LC.

13. Peter Colt to Constable, Rucker, & Company, June 9, 1787, pp. 80–81, box 153, Jeremiah Wadsworth Letterbook, CHS; "Willing to Learn" [Abraham Clark?], *Political Intelligencer and New Jersey Advertiser*, Dec. 14, 1785.

14. "Extract from the Proceedings of the Senate," Jan. 5, 1787, *Maryland Journal and Baltimore Advertiser*, Jan. 16, 1787; ["Jefferson's Report on Conversations with Vergennes"], [Dec. 1785], in Jefferson to John Jay, Jan. 2, 1786, in Boyd et al., eds., *Papers of Thomas Jefferson*, 9:143.

15. Morris to Congress, July 29, 1782, in Ford, ed., *Journals of the Continental Congress*, 22:436; "Amicus," *Virginia Independent Chronicle*, July 4, 1787; E. James Ferguson, *The Power of the Purse: A History of American Public Finance, 1776–1790* (Chapel Hill, N.C., 1961), 124; Ferguson "Political Economy, Public Liberty, and the Formation of the Constitution," *WMQ*, 3rd ser., 40 (July 1983), 402; Terry Bouton, "Tying Up the Revolution: Money, Power, and the Regulation in Pennsylvania, 1765–1800" (Ph.D. diss., Duke University, 1996), 132; Stanley Elkins and Eric McKitrick, *The Age of Federalism* (New York, 1993), 111, 115–18, 776–77n.

16. "A Native of Virginia," *Observations on the Proposed Plan of Federal Government . . .* , *DHRC*, 9:692; Major C. Phelps, speech in Connecticut House of Representatives, May 30, 1787, *Middlesex Gazette*, June 18, 1787.

17. Pendleton to Madison, Dec. 9, 1786, in Hutchinson et al., eds., *Papers of James Madison*, 9:201; David Ramsay, speech, May 27, 1788, in Bernard Bailyn, ed., *The Debate on the Constitution: Federalist and Antifederalist Speeches, Articles, and Letters During the Struggle over Ratification* (2 vols.; New York, 1993), 2:509; Roger H. Brown, *Redeeming the Republic: Federalists, Taxation, and the Origins of the Constitution* (Baltimore, 1993), 156–62.

18. Morris to Congress, July 29, 1782, in Ford, ed., *Journals of the Continental Congress*, 22:431; "A Farmer," *Maryland Journal and Baltimore Advertiser*, Feb. 6, 1787; "A Dialogue Between a Countryman and a Bostonian, Concerning the Times," *Boston Gazette*, Feb. 13, 1786; Amherst County citizens, petition, Nov. 6, 1787, VLP;

Charles Phelps, speech in Connecticut House of Representatives, May 30, 1787; *Middlesex Gazette*, June 18, 1787; "Eugenio III," *New Jersey Gazette*, Feb. 13, 1786; Brown, *Redeeming the Republic*, 231–33.

19. Charles A. Beard, *An Economic Interpretation of the Constitution of the United States* (New York, 1913), 47–48; Merrill Jensen, *The New Nation: A History of the United States During the Confederation, 1781–1789* (New York, 1950), 423–24.

20. Manning, "Some Proposals for Making Restitution to the Original Creditors of Government and To Help the Continent to a Medium of Trade . . . ," Feb. 6, 1790, in Michael Merrill and Sean Wilentz, eds., *The Key of Liberty: The Life and Democratic Writings of William Manning, "A Laborer," 1747–1814* (Cambridge, Mass., 1993), 114.

21. [Swan], *National Arithmetick*, 23; J. R. Pole, *Political Representation in England and the Origins of the American Republic* (London, 1966), 228; Terry Bouton, "A Road Closed: Rural Insurgency in Post-Independence Pennsylvania," *JAH* 87 (Dec. 2000), 858.

22. "Plain Reason," *Virginia Independent Chronicle*, Sept. 26, 1787; "Excise," *Hampshire Herald*, Feb. 7, 1786.

23. Bernardston town meeting, quoted in Brown, *Redeeming the Republic*, 112.

24. [Herman Husband], *Proposals to Amend and Perfect the Policy of the Government of the United States of America, or, The Fulfilling of the Prophecies in the Latter Days, Commenced by the Independence of America* (Philadelphia, 1782), 21; "Willing to Learn" [Abraham Clark?], *Political Intelligencer and New Jersey Advertiser*, Dec. 14, 1785; Bernardston town meeting, June 14, 1786, 1786 House of Representatives Petition no. 2043, MSA; Brown, *Redeeming the Republic*, 112.

25. Webster to Timothy Pickering, Mar. 24, 1786, Pickering Papers, MHS.

26. "A Fellow Citizen"/"Willing to Learn," *The True Policy of New-Jersey, Defined; Or, Our Great Strength Led to Exertion, in the Improvement of Agriculture & Manufactures, By Altering the Mode of Taxation, and by the Emission of Money on Loan . . .* (Elizabeth-Town, N.J., 1786), 22; Manning, "Some Proposals," 105; "A Friend to the Public," *Newport Mercury*, Feb. 27, 1786; "Tradesmen and Labourers of the Town of Portsmouth," petition to the Senate and House of Representatives, 1786(5), "Legislative Petitions," NHSA.

27. "A Fellow Citizen:"/"Willing to Learn," *True Policy of New-Jersey*, 12; Orange County citizens, petition, Nov. 17, 1786, no. 56, SCDAH.

28. Sanbornton citizens, petition, Oct. 24, 1785, in Isaac W. Hammond, ed., *Town Papers: Documents Relating to Towns in New Hampshire* (3 vols.; Concord, N.H., 1882–84), 13:399; [William Whiting], "Some Remarks on the Conduct of the Inhabitants of the Commonwealth of Massachusetts in Interupting The Siting of the Judicial Courts . . ." (Dec. 1786), in Stephen T. Riley, ed., "Dr. William Whiting and Shays' Rebellion," AAS *Proceedings* 66 (1957), 158; "Willing to Learn," *Political Intelligencer and New Jersey Advertiser*, Dec. 14, 1785; [Husband], *Proposals to Amend and Perfect the Policy*, 21; Cumberland town meeting, representative instructions, Feb. 25, 1786, PRAC-RISA; Brown, *Redeeming the Republic*, 112.

29. "Senex," *South Carolina Gazette and Public Advertiser*, June 1–4, 1785 (reprinted from *Maryland Journal*).

30. "A Member of Convention," *Worcester Magazine* 2:33 (3rd week of Nov. 1786), 395.

31. "A Citizen of Connecticut," *Connecticut Courant*, Apr. 3, 1786; "A Citizen," *Maryland Journal and Baltimore Advertiser*, July 21, 1786; Philadelphia dateline, *Virginia Independent Chronicle*, Aug. 15, 1787; "An Easy, Honest and Expeditious Way to Discharge the Publick Debt of the State of Massachusetts," *Hampshire Herald*, Sept. 26, 1786; delegates from 23 New Hampshire towns, petition, Nov. 27, 1783, in Hammond, ed., *Town Papers*, 12:765. Compare "One of the People," *Pennsylvania Gazette*, Oct. 17, 1787; anonymous essay, *Independent Chronicle*, Mar. 16, 1786 (reprinted from *New Jersey Gazette*); Buckingham County citizens, petition, Nov. 5, 1788, VLP.

32. "Publick Faith," *Massachusetts Centinel*, Feb. 8, 1786 (reprinted from *Hampshire Herald*, Jan. 31, 1786).

33. "A Citizen of Connecticut," *Connecticut Courant*, Apr. 3, 1786; Lancaster town meeting, instructions to representative, Jan. 22, 1787, *Worcester Magazine* 2:45 (2nd week of Feb. 1787), 532; Delaware citizens, petition, May–June 1786 legislative petitions, record group IIII, DPA, reel 7, frame 451; "A Fellow Citizen"/ "Willing to Learn," *True Policy of New-Jersey*, 22; "A Letter from a Gentleman in New-York to His Friend in Connecticut, on the Subject of Paper Money," *Connecticut Courant*, Feb. 5, 1787. Compare "A Farmer," *Maryland Journal and Baltimore Advertiser*, Feb. 6, 1787; "Eugenio," III, *New Jersey Gazette*, Feb. 13, 1786.

34. "Publick Faith," *Massachusetts Centinel*, Feb. 8, 1786 (reprinted from *Hampshire Herald*, Jan. 31, 1786); "Plain Reason," *Virginia Independent Chronicle*, Aug. 29, 1787; "A Husbandman," *Maryland Journal and Baltimore Advertiser*, June 6, 1786.

35. Sussex County citizens, petition, Jan.–Feb. 1787 legislative petitions, record group IIII, DPA, reel 8, frames 341–43; Delaware citizens, petition, May–June 1786 legislative petitions, record group IIII, DPA, reel 7, frame 448.

36. Lancaster town meeting, representative instructions, Jan. 22, 1787, *Worcester Magazine* 2:44 (1st week of Feb. 1787), 532.

37. "Proceedings of the General Court," *Boston Magazine* 3 (Mar. 1786), 139; David Daggett, *An Oration, Pronounced in the Brick Meeting-House, in the City of New-Haven, on the Fourth of July, A.D. 1787* (New Haven, Conn., [1787]), 12.

38. Delaware citizens, petition, May–June 1786 legislative petitions, record group IIII, DPA, reel 7, frame 448; "Modestus," *Maryland Journal and Baltimore Advertiser*, Apr. 10, 1787; "Publick Faith," *Massachusetts Centinel*, Feb. 8, 1786 (reprinted from *Hampshire Herald*, Jan. 31, 1786).

39. Brendan McConville, *These Daring Disturbers of the Public Peace: The Struggle for Property and Power in Early New Jersey* (Ithaca, N.Y., 1999); Allan Kulikoff, "Death and Rebirth of Class Analysis" (unpublished paper, 2001); Steven Rosswurm, *Arms, Country, and Class: The Philadelphia Militia and "Lower Sort" During the American Revolution, 1775–1783* (New Brunswick, N.J., 1987), 37–38; Alfred F. Young, *Liberty Tree: Ordinary People and the American Revolution* (New York, 2006), 36, 46–47, 217.

40. "Lycurgus III" [Herman Husband], *XIV Sermons on the Characters of Jacob's Fourteen Sons* (Philadelphia, 1789), 23; "A Fellow Citizen"/ "Willing to Learn," *True Pol-*

icy of New-Jersey, 34–35; "Honestus" [Benjamin Austin], *Independent Chronicle*, May 25 and June 22, 1786; "Crisis," *New Hampshire Gazette*, July 20, 1786.

41. Newton town meeting, instructions to representatives, *Virginia Independent Chronicle*, July 25, 1787.

42. "The Free Republican" [Benjamin Lincoln, Jr.], V, *Boston Magazine* 1 (Aug. 1784), 421.

43. "Plain Reason," *Virginia Independent Chronicle*, Sept. 5, 1787.

44. Henry Lee, Jr., to Richard Bland Lee, Apr. 4, 1786, in Paul H. Smith et al., eds., *Letters of Delegates to Congress, 1774–1789* (26 vols.; Washington, D.C., 1976–2000), 23:218; Theodore Sedgwick, Jan. 28, 1790, *Annals of Congress*, 1st Cong., 2nd sess., 1135; "Remarks on the Domestic Debt of the United States" 3, *New Haven Gazette and Connecticut Magazine*, June 14, 1787.

45. "Plain Reason," *Virginia Independent Chronicle*, Sept. 5, 1787.

46. "A Member of Convention," *Worcester Magazine* 2:27 (1st week of Oct. 1786), 322.

47. John Adams to Jefferson, July 16, 1786, in Boyd et al., eds., *Papers of Thomas Jefferson*, 10:140.

48. John Adams to John Jay, May 16, 1786, in Charles Francis Adams, ed., *The Works of John Adams, Second President of the United States, with a Life of the Author, Notes, and Illustrations* (Boston, 1853), 8:391.

49. Thomas Hartley, Feb. 16, 1790, *Annals of Congress*, 1st Cong., 1st sess., 1279.

CHAPTER 7: "THE FATE OF REPUBLICAN GOVT"—REDEMPTION

1. Madison, June 26, 1787, in Max Farrand, ed., *The Records of the Federal Convention of 1787* (3 vols.; New Haven, Conn., 1911), 1:423; "The Republican," II, *Connecticut Courant*, Feb. 12, 1787; Botetourt County citizens, petition, Oct. 17, 1787, VLP; "Camillus" [Fisher Ames], *Independent Chronicle* V, Mar. 15, 1787, reprinted in W. B. Allen, ed., *Works of Fisher Ames, as Published by Seth Ames* (Indianapolis, Ind., 1983), 1:75; Gordon S. Wood, *The Creation of the American Republic, 1776–1787* (Chapel Hill, N.C., 1969), 414–25, 466; Roger H. Brown, *Redeeming the Republic: Federalists, Taxation, and the Origins of the Constitution* (Baltimore, 1993), xi, 222–24.

2. [William Whiting], "Some Brief Remarks on the Present State of Publick Affairs," in Stephen T. Riley, ed., "Dr. William Whiting and Shays' Rebellion," AAS *Proceedings* 66 (1957), 133.

3. Representative Welton, speech in Connecticut House of Representatives, May 30, 1787, *Connecticut Courant*, June 11, 1787; John Trenchard and Thomas Gordon, *Cato's Letters, or, Essays on Liberty, Civil and Religious, and Other Important Subjects*, ed. Ronald Hamowy (2 vols.; Indianapolis, Ind., 1995), 1:253–54, 2:614.

4. Findley, quoted in Terry Bouton, "Tying Up the Revolution: Money, Power, and the Regulation in Pennsylvania, 1765–1800" (Ph.D. diss., Duke University, 1996), 219.

5. [Herman Husband], "A Plan for Raising Taxes to Pay the Debts of the United States in Forty Years . . . ," in *A Dialogue Between an Assembly-Man and a Convention-*

Man On the Subject of the State Constitution of Pennsylvania . . . (Philadelphia, n.d.), 11.

6. Albemarle County citizens, petition, Nov. 3, 1787, VLP; Eric Foner, *Tom Paine and Revolutionary America* (updated ed.; New York, 2005), 123–24.

7. Quoted in Foner, *Tom Paine and Revolutionary America*, 133; "A Friend to the Public," *Newport Mercury*, Feb. 27, 1786.

8. [Whiting], "Some Remarks on the Conduct of the Inhabitants of the Commonwealth of Massachusetts in Interupting the Siting of the Judicial Courts . . ." (Dec. 1786), 150–51.

9. Farmington town meeting, quoted in Christopher Collier, *All Politics Is Local: Family, Friends, and Provincial Interests in the Creation of the Constitution* (Hanover, N.H., 2003), 24.

10. "Monitor," II, *Political Intelligencer and New Jersey Advertiser* (reprinted from *New Jersey Journal*), May 10, 1786.

11. "Nestor" [Benjamin Rush], *Independent Gazetteer*, July 1, 1786; "A True Friend," *Virginia Independent Chronicle*, Nov. 14, 1787, *DHRC*, 8:161–62.

12. "A.Z.," "A Dialogue Between Obadiah and Timothy," *United States Chronicle*, Feb. 23, 1786.

13. Madison, "Agst. Paper Money, Novr. 1786 Virg: Assy.," in William T. Hutchinson et al., eds., *The Papers of James Madison* (17 vols. to date; Chicago, 1962–), 9:158–59; Madison, *Federalist* 44:5.

14. Joseph Albert Ernst, *Money and Politics in America, 1755–1775: A Study in the Currency Act of 1764 and the Political Economy of Revolution* (Chapel Hill, N.C., 1973).

15. "Eugenio," II, *New Jersey Gazette*, Jan. 30, 1786.

16. "Extract from the Proceedings of the Senate," Jan. 5, 1787, *Maryland Journal and Baltimore Advertiser*, Jan. 16, 1787.

17. Amherst County citizens, petition, Nov. 6, 1787, VLP.

18. "Nestor" [Benjamin Rush], *Independent Gazetteer*, July 1, 1786.

19. "Extract from the Proceedings of the Senate," Jan. 5, 1787, *Maryland Journal and Baltimore Advertiser*, Jan. 16, 1787.

20. E. James Ferguson, *The Power of the Purse: A History of American Public Finance, 1776–1790* (Chapel Hill, N.C., 1961), 243.

21. "A Marylander," *Maryland Journal and Baltimore Advertiser*, June 27, 1786.

22. "Senex," *South Carolina Gazette and Public Advertiser*, June 1–4, 1785 (reprinted from *Maryland Journal*).

23. Thomas Paine to Thomas Fitzsimons, Apr. 19, 1785, in *Pennsylvania Gazette*, Dec. 21, 1785.

24. Thomas Paine, "Dissertations on Government, the Affairs of the Bank, and Paper Money," in Philip S. Foner, ed., *The Complete Writings of Thomas Paine* (2 vols.; New York, 1945), 2:409–10.

25. Mrs. S. Livingston to William Livingston, Nov. 18, 1786, Livingston Papers, MHS; Earnest Wilder Spaulding, *New York in the Critical Period, 1783–1789* (Port

Washington, N.Y., 1960), 149; David Freeman Hawke, *Benjamin Rush, Revolutionary Gadfly* (Indianapolis, Ind., 1971), 340.

26. Hamilton, speech in New York assembly, Feb. 18, 1787, *American Museum* 1 (June 1787), 524.

27. "An Act [to] Prevent the Paper Or Any Other Money Being a Tender to Any of the Incorporated Bodies," Brown Papers, box 277, folder 5, JCB.

28. E. Wilder Spaulding, *New York in the Critical Period, 1783–1789* (orig. pub. 1932; Port Washington, N.Y., 1963), 150.

29. P[eregrine] Foster to Dwight Foster, Apr. 24, 1786, Foster Family Papers, AAS.

30. "List of State Notes Issued from the State of Rhode Is[lan]d, Belonging to Nicho. Brown Del[ivere]d to Mr. John Francis to Be Negotiated in Phila., March 14, 1788," Brown Papers, box 27, folder 6, JCB; James B. Hedges, *The Browns of Providence Plantations: Colonial Years* (Cambridge, Mass., 1952), 320.

31. "Plain Reason," *Virginia Independent Chronicle*, Aug. 29, 1787.

32. "A Native of New-Jersey," *New Jersey Gazette*, Nov. 14, 1785; "Z.," "Paper Money," *United States Chronicle*, June 1, 1786; "Rusticus," *Columbian Herald*, Sept. 26, 1785.

33. Jeremy Belknap, *The History of New-Hampshire . . .* (Boston, 1791), 2:463; Paine, "Dissertations on Government," 405–407; Madison, "Agst. Paper Money, Novr. 1786 Virg: Assy.," in Hutchinson et al., eds., *Papers of James Madison*, 9:158–59.

34. "Probus," cited in "Primitive Whig," IV, *New Jersey Gazette*, Jan. 30, 1786; New York dateline, *Worcester Magazine* 2:30 (4th week of Oct. 1786), 366; Patrick T. Conley, *Democracy in Decline: Rhode Island's Constitutional Development, 1776–1841* (Providence, R.I., 1977), 92–98.

35. Grayson to Madison, May 28, 1786, in Paul H. Smith et al., eds., *Letters of Delegates to Congress, 1774–1789* (26 vols.; Washington, D.C., 1976–2000), 23:320; "An Enquiry into the Principles on which a Commercial System for the United States of America Should be Founded . . . ," *American Museum* 1 (June 1787), 513.

36. "Nestor" [Benjamin Rush], *Independent Gazetteer*, June 3, 1786.

37. Richard Henry Lee to George Mason, May 15, 1787, in Rutland, ed., *Papers of George Mason*, 3:878; Benjamin Rush, *American Museum* 1 (Jan. 1787), 8–9; Philadelphia dateline, *Virginia Independent Chronicle*, June 20, 1787.

38. David Daggett, *An Oration, Pronounced in the Brick Meeting-House, in the City of New-Haven, on the Fourth of July, A.D. 1787* (New Haven, Conn., [1787]), 12.

39. "Extracts from Letters dated Berkshire County, Massachusetts," Sept. 16, 1786, *Connecticut Courant*, Oct. 2, 1786.

40. Adam Smith, *The Theory of Moral Sentiments*, ed. D. D. Raphael and A. L. Macfie (orig. pub. 1759; Indianapolis, Ind., 1984), 9.

41. Ibid., 86 (quotation), 90; Garry Wills, *Inventing America: Jefferson's Declaration of Independence* (Garden City, N.Y., 1978), 287.

42. Sheridan, quoted in Jay Fliegelman, *Declaring Independence: Jefferson, Natural Language, and the Culture of Performance* (Stanford, Calif., 1993), 26, 2.

43. Henry Home, Lord Kames, *Elements of Criticism* (1762), quoted ibid., 16.

44. James Rodgers, "Sensibility, Sympathy, Benevolence: Physiology and Moral Philosophy in *Tristram Shandy*," in L. J. Jordanova, ed., *Languages of Nature: Critical Essays on Science and Literature* (New Brunswick, N.J., 1986), 126–33.

45. Smith, *Theory of Moral Sentiments*, 36; Wills, *Inventing America*, 269; Norman S. Fiering, "Irresistible Compassion: An Aspect of Eighteenth-Century Sympathy and Humanitarianism," *Journal of the History of Ideas* 37 (Apr.–June, 1976), 195.

46. New Braintree town meeting, petition to governor and Council, Jan. 1, 1787, 205:6:50–56, Force Transcripts, LC.

47. "On Female Manners and Customs: Adapted to a Certain Place," *Massachusetts Centinel*, July 26, 1786; Murray, quoted in Andrew Burstein, *Sentimental Democracy: The Evolution of America's Romantic Self-Image* (New York, 1999), 21; Smith, *Theory of Moral Sentiments*, 190; Kenneth MacLean, "Imagination and Sympathy: Sterne and Adam Smith," *Journal of the History of Ideas* 10 (June 1949), 403; G. J. Barker-Benfield, *The Culture of Sensibility: Sex and Society in Eighteenth-Century Britain* (Chicago, 1992), xvii, 1, 23, 28, 117, 144.

48. Fiering, "Irresistible Compassion," 196, 204.

49. [Whiting], "Some Remarks on the Conduct of the Inhabitants," 157; "A Friend to the Public," *Newport Mercury*, Feb. 13, 1786; "A Fellow Citizen"/"Willing to Learn," *True Policy of New-Jersey*, 12; Kent County citizens, petition, May–June 1785 legislative petitions, record group 1111, DPA, reel 6, frame 282; "Americanus," *Columbian Herald*, Aug. 22, 1785; "A Tradesman," *New Hampshire Spy*, Nov. 14, 1786.

50. "Observator," *New Hampshire Gazette*, May 20, 1785; "A Planter," *Newport Mercury*, Feb. 20, 1786; "A Member of Convention," *Worcester Magazine* 2:33 (3rd week of Nov. 1786), 396; "A Farmer," *New Jersey Gazette*, Feb. 6, 1786.

51. "Probus," *Massachusetts Centinel*, May 5, 1787; Smith, *Theory of Moral Sentiments*, 55.

52. "North American," I, *Pennsylvania Journal*, Sept. 17, 1783, in Irving Brant, ed., "Two Neglected Madison Letters," *WMQ*, 3rd ser., 3 (Oct. 1946), 577; Smith, *Theory of Moral Sentiments*, 25.

53. Kent County citizens, petition, May–June 1785 legislative petitions, record group 1111, DPA, reel 6, frame 282.

54. "A Freeman," *Worcester Magazine* 2:28 (2nd week of Oct. 1786), 338.

55. "Another Correspondent," Philadelphia dateline, *New Jersey Journal, and Political Intelligencer*, Sept. 5, 1787.

56. Woody Holton, "'Divide et Impera': *Federalist* 10 in a Wider Sphere," *WMQ*, 3rd ser., 62 (Apr. 2005), 175–212.

57. Stephen Reed Grossbart, "The Revolutionary Transition: Politics, Religion, and Economy in Eastern Connecticut, 1765–1800" (Ph.D. diss., University of Michigan, 1989), 249.

58. Bouton, "Tying Up the Revolution," 156–71.

59. Newcastle County citizens, printed petition, [Aug. 1787], Oct.–Nov. 1787 legislative petitions, record group 1111, DPA, reel 9, frame 119.

60. Adams to Rufus King, June 14, 1786, in Charles R. King, ed., *The Life and Corre-*

spondence of Rufus King, Comprising His Letters, Private and Official, His Public Documents, and His Speeches (New York, 1894), 1:182.

61. Thomas Jefferson, "Explanations on Some of the Subjects of the Conversation . . . with . . . The Count de Vergennes . . . ," in Julian P. Boyd et al., eds., *The Papers of Thomas Jefferson* (33 vols. to date; Princeton, N.J., 1950–), 9:111–12; Jefferson to Archibald Stuart, Jan. 25, 1786, ibid., 9:217–18; Jefferson to Thomas Pleasants, May 8, 1786, ibid., 9:473; Jefferson to Lucy Ludwell Paradise, Aug. 27, 1786, ibid., 10:304–5.

62. John Adams to Cotton Tufts, Aug. 27, 1787, in Lyman H. Butterfield et al., eds., *Adams Family Correspondence* (8 vols. to date; Cambridge, Mass., 1963–), 8:149; Jefferson, *Notes on the State of Virginia*, ed. William Peden (New York, 1972), 164–65; Lynne Withey, *Dearest Friend: A Life of Abigail Adams* (New York, 1981), 259; Ruth H. Bloch, "The Gendered Meanings of Virtue in Revolutionary America," *Signs: Journal of Women in Culture and Society* 13 (Autumn 1987), 37–58.

63. Although records documenting Webster's ownership of at least £486 worth of federal securities do not specify whether he was an original or a secondary holder, the bitterness with which he attacked plans to pay interest to the secondary holders excludes all possibility that he was numbered among them. Certificate no. 4413, "Account of Certificates Delivered for Continental Certificates recd on Loan Per Act March 1786," book A, 137, record group 4 (microfilm), reel 5749, PSA.

64. Pelatiah Webster, "A Seventh Essay on Free Trade and Finance," in Webster, *Political Essays on the Nature and Operation of Money, Public Finances, and Other Subjects . . .* (Philadelphia, 1791), 282, 286.

65. Ibid., 302–3.

66. [Pelatiah Webster], *Pennsylvania Gazette*, Apr. 18, 1787.

67. Webster, "Seventh Essay," 283, 287; Webster, "A Sixth Essay on Free Trade and Finance," in Webster, *Political Essays*, 239; [Webster], anonymous essay, *Pennsylvania Gazette*, Apr. 18, 1787.

CHAPTER 8: "A REVOLUTION WHICH OUGHT TO BE GLORIOUS"—DISENCHANTMENT

1. "Aristides," *Virginia Independent Chronicle*, Mar. 21, 1787; Madison, July 26, 1787, in Max Farrand, ed., *The Records of the Federal Convention of 1787* (3 vols.; New Haven, Conn., 1911), 2:123.

2. Maclaine to Iredell, July 11, 1787, in Don Higginbotham, ed., *The Papers of James Iredell* (3 vols. to date; Raleigh, N.C., 1976–), 3:288.

3. C. Edward Skeen, "*Vox Populi, Vox Dei*: The Compensation Act of 1816 and the Rise of Popular Politics," *Journal of the Early Republic* 6 (Fall 1986), 268.

4. Patrick S. Brady, "The Slave Trade and Sectionalism in South Carolina, 1787–1808," *Journal of Southern History* 38 (Nov. 1972), 601–20.

5. Two years later the assembly reversed itself and temporarily banned the purchase of Africans. Ibid.; Camden District citizens, petition, read Sept. 27, 1785, and "Lower District of Camden" citizens, petition, read Feb. 4, 1786, in Lark

Emerson Adams and Rosa Stoney Lumpkin, eds., *The State Records of South Carolina: Journals of the House of Representatives, 1785–1786* (Columbia, S.C., 1979), 316, 372; Ralph Izard, speech in South Carolina House of Representatives, Oct. 1, 1785, *Charleston Evening Gazette*, Oct. 1, 1785.

6. "A Fellow Citizen"/ "Willing to Learn," *The True Policy of New-Jersey, Defined; Or, Our Great Strength Led to Exertion, in the Improvement of Agriculture & Manufactures, By Altering the Mode of Taxation, and by the Emission of Money on Loan . . .* (Elizabeth-Town, N.J., 1786), 40.

7. "Timoleon" [James Tilton], *The Biographical History of Dionysius, Tyrant of Delaware, Addressed to the People of the United States of America* (Philadelphia, 1788), 65; Nov. 2, 1787, in Claudia L. Bushman, Harold B. Hancock, and Elizabeth Moyne Homsey, eds., *Proceedings of the House of Assembly of the Delaware State, 1781–1792, and of the Constitutional Convention of 1792* (Newark, Del., 1988), 480–81; "An Act to Alter and Supply Certain Parts of an Act, Intitled, *An Act Raising Ten Thousand Five Pounds for the Service of the Year One Thousand Seven Hundred and Eighty-Seven . . .*" (ch. 165, passed Nov. 10, 1787), in John D. Cushing, comp., *The First Laws of the State of Delaware* (2 vols., orig. pub. 1792; Wilmington, Del., 1981), 2:910–12.

8. Jackson Turner Main, *Political Parties Before the Constitution* (Chapel Hill, N.C., 1973), 117; Roger H. Brown, *Redeeming the Republic: Federalists, Taxation, and the Origins of the Constitution* (Baltimore, 1993), 119.

9. "A Freeman," *Worcester Magazine* 2:28 (2nd week of Oct. 1786), 337.

10. "A.B.," *Connecticut Journal*, Oct. 23, 1776.

11. ["Honorius"], "An Address to the Discontented People of America," *Connecticut Courant*, Aug. 26, 1783; Oliver Wolcott, Sr., to Oliver Wolcott, Jr., Sept. 24, 1787 (typescript), *DHRC*, 3 (microfilm supp.), item 19, pp. 110–11; Richard J. Purcell, *Connecticut in Transition, 1775–1818* (orig. pub. 1918; Middletown, Conn., 1963), 124–29; Jackson Turner Main, *The Upper House in Revolutionary America, 1763–1788* (Madison, Wisc., 1967), 180–82; Richard Buel, Jr., *Dear Liberty: Connecticut's Mobilization for the Revolutionary War* (Middletown, Conn., 1980), 307–9; Stephen Reed Grossbart, "The Revolutionary Transition: Politics, Religion, and Economy in Eastern Connecticut, 1765–1800" (Ph.D. diss., University of Michigan, 1989), 210–11, 225–35.

12. "A Number of Freemen," *United States Chronicle*, Feb. 16, 1786.

13. James Manning to Brown, June 9, 1786, Brown Papers, box 367, folder 9, JCB.

14. "List of Persons Present 3d Apl. E Greenwich," box 277, folder 5, Brown Papers, JCB.

15. James Madison, "Influence of the Size of a Nation on Government," [1791–92?], in William T. Hutchinson et al., eds., *The Papers of James Madison* (17 vols. to date; Chicago, 1962–), 14:159; Brown, *Redeeming the Republic*, 86–93; Colleen A. Sheehan, "The Politics of Public Opinion: James Madison's 'Notes on Government,'" *WMQ*, 3rd ser., 49 (Oct. 1992), 614.

16. Bouton, "Tying Up the Revolution," 175–76.

17. "Tom Taciturn," *Worcester Magazine* 2:24 (2nd week of Sept. 1786), 287.

18. [William Whiting], "Some Remarks on the Conduct of the Inhabitants of the Commonwealth of Massachusetts in Interupting The Siting of the Judicial Courts . . ." (Dec. 1786), in Stephen T. Riley, ed., "Dr. William Whiting and Shays' Rebellion," AAS *Proceedings* 66 (1957), 157; "Impartiality," *New Hampshire Mercury*, Sept. 6, 1786.

19. "Sretaw Liph," *State Gazette of South Carolina*, June 29, 1786.

20. Chester County citizens, petition, Feb. 20, 1786, no. 31, SCDAH.

21. Philadelphia dateline, *Middlesex Gazette*, July 17, 1786; Lancaster County citizens, petition, Feb. 23, 1785, quoted in Bouton, "Tying Up the Revolution," 182.

22. Brunswick County citizens, petition, Oct. 28, 1786, VLP; Robert Arnold Feer, *Shay's Rebellion* (New York, 1988), 69; Jere R. Daniell, *Experiment in Republicanism: New Hampshire Politics and the American Revolution, 1741–1794* (Cambridge, Mass., 1970), 183; Terry Bouton, "A Road Closed: Rural Insurgency in Post-Independence Pennsylvania," *JAH* 87 (Dec. 2000), 887; Bouton, "Tying Up the Revolution," 213.

23. Reed, quoted in Feer, *Shay's Rebellion*, 73–74; Kent County citizens, petition, Nov. 10, 1783, May–June 1784 legislative petitions, record group III, DPA, reel 5, frame 374; "The History of the Mill . . . ," *Carlisle Gazette*, Mar. 21, 1787.

24. David Daggett, *An Oration, Pronounced in the Brick Meeting-House, in the City of New-Haven, on the Fourth of July, A.D. 1787* (New Haven, Conn., [1787]), 14; "A Citizen," *Maryland Journal and Baltimore Advertiser*, July 21, 1786.

25. "Plain Reason," *Virginia Independent Chronicle*, Aug. 29, 1787; Worcester County Convention, Sept. 26–28, 1786, *Worcester Magazine* 2:27 (1st week of Oct. 1786), 318.

26. William Lincoln, *History of Worcester, Massachusetts, From its Earliest Settlement to September, 1836, With Various Notices Relating to the History of Worcester County* (Worcester, 1837), 132; J. R. Pole, *Political Representation in England and the Origins of the American Republic* (London, 1966), 235.

27. Massachusetts General Court, "Address to the People," *Worcester Magazine* 2:37 (2nd week of Dec. 1786), 444; "Lucius Junius Brutus" [Fisher Ames], II, *Independent Chronicle*, Oct. 19, 1786, in W. B. Allen, ed., *Works of Fisher Ames, as Published by Seth Ames* (Indianapolis, Ind., 1983), 1:46.

28. Portsmouth dateline, *New Hampshire Spy*, Apr. 13, 1787; Massachusetts General Court, "Address to the People," *Worcester Magazine* 2:37 (2nd week of Dec. 1786), 444; Henry Lee, Jr., to Washington, Oct. 1, 1786, in W. W. Abbot and Dorothy Twohig, eds., *The Papers of George Washington*, Confederation Series (6 vols.; Charlottesville, Va., 1992–97), 4:281.

29. Leonard L. Richards, *Shays's Rebellion: The American Revolution's Final Battle* (Philadelphia, 2002), 144; Loudon selectmen, warrants for town meetings, May 19, 1786, Feb. 16, 1787, Mar. 10, 1787, and Loudon town meeting, [June 1, 1786, Mar. 5, 1787, Mar. 24, 1787], Loudon Town Records, 1:281–89, NHSL.

30. Cambridge town meeting, resolves, July 24, 1786, in *Worcester Magazine* 2:18 (1st week of Aug. 1786), 211.

31. Marlborough town meeting, Mar. 17, 1786, Oct. 19, 1786, Apr. 2, 1787, Marlbor-

ough Town Records, 2:252, 263, 272, NHSL; Deerfield town meeting, Sept. 26, 1785, June 6, 1786, Oct. 31, 1786, Mar. 20, 1787, Mar. 28, 1787, Deerfield Town Records, [1:] 181–82, 187–94, NHSL; Deerfield town meeting, June 6, 1786, in Isaac W. Hammond, ed., *Town Papers: Documents Relating to Towns in New Hampshire* (3 vols., Concord, N.H., 1882–84), 11: 488.

32. Paxton town meeting, instructions to representative, Oct. 30, 1786, *Worcester Magazine* 2:32 (2nd week of Nov. 1786), 387; Mary Smith Cranch to Abigail Adams, Feb. 9, 1787, in Lyman H. Butterfield et al., eds., *Adams Family Correspondence* (8 vols. to date; Cambridge, Mass., 1963–), 7:463; Braintree town meeting, Jan. 29, 1787, in Samuel A. Bates, ed., *Records of the Town of Braintree, 1640 to 1793* (Randolph, Mass., 1886), 569–70.

33. George Richards Minot to Nathan Dane, June 10, 1786, Nathan Dane Papers, Accession Number 7522, Beverley Historical Society (www.primaryresearch .org/PRTHB/Dane/Documents/Letters/7522.htm); Samuel Henshaw to Nathan Dane, May 21, 1786, Nathan Dane Papers, LC, quoted in Whitney K. Bates, "The State Finances of Massachusetts, 1780–1789" (master's thesis, University of Wisconsin, 1948), 123; "Rusticus," *New Hampshire Gazette*, May 25, 1786; William Plumer to Samuel Plumer, Jr., June 6, 9, 17, 1786, "Letters of William Plumer, 1786–1787," Colonial Society of Massachusetts, *Publications*, XI, *Transactions, 1906–1907* (Boston, 1910), 385.

34. Lunenburg town meeting, petition, Feb. 19, 1787, Force Transcripts, 205:6:46, LC; Albert Stillman Batchellor and Henry Harrison Metcalf, eds., *Laws of New Hampshire* . . . (Bristol, N.H., 1916), 5:134–35, 145, 194 (ch. 29, Feb. 28, 1786, ch. 39, Mar. 4, 1786, ch. 2, Sept. 14, 1786); Richard Donald Hershcopf, "The New England Farmer and Politics, 1785–1787" (master's thesis, University of Wisconsin, 1947), 74–75; Pole, *Political Representation*, 234; Van Beck Hall, *Politics Without Parties: Massachusetts, 1780–1791* ([Pittsburgh], 1972), 198.

35. "A Friend to Industry," *Pennsylvania Mercury*, June 23, 1786.

36. Frederick W. Marks III, *Independence on Trial: Foreign Affairs and the Making of the Constitution* (Baton Rouge, La., 1973), 52–95; Drew R. McCoy, *The Elusive Republic: Political Economy in Jeffersonian America* (Chapel Hill, N.C., 1980), 124–26; Brown, *Redeeming the Republic*, 144; Jack N. Rakove, *Original Meanings: Politics and Ideas in the Making of the Constitution* (New York, 1996), 26–27.

37. E. James Ferguson, *The Power of the Purse: A History of American Public Finance, 1776–1790* (Chapel Hill, N.C., 1961), 221, 231–32.

38. Monroe to Madison, Feb. 11, 1786, in Hutchinson et al., eds., *Papers of James Madison*, 8:492; [Pelatiah Webster], *Pennsylvania Gazette*, Apr. 18, 1787.

39. Jonathan Blanchard to Josiah Bartlett, Mar. 5, 1784, in Frank C. Mevers, ed., *The Papers of Josiah Bartlett* (Hanover, N.H., 1979), 311.

40. Congress, resolve, Sept. 27, 1785, in Worthington Chauncey Ford, ed., *Journals of the Continental Congress, 1774–1789* (34 vols.; Washington, D.C., 1904–37), 29:771.

41. Isabel Thompson Kelsay, *Joseph Brant, 1743–1807: Man of Two Worlds* (Syracuse, N.Y., 1984), ch. 9.

42. Joseph Brant, speech at conference at Sandusky (on the southern shore of Lake Erie in present-day Ohio), Sept. 7, 1783, *Collections and Researches Made by the Michigan Pioneer and Historical Society* (orig. pub. 1892; reprint, Detroit, Mich., 1912), 20:179.

43. Randolph C. Downes, *Council Fires on the Upper Ohio: A Narrative of Indian Affairs in the Upper Ohio Valley until 1795* (Pittsburgh, 1940), 282–301; Richard White, *The Middle Ground: Indians, Empires, and Republics in the Great Lakes Region, 1650–1815* (Cambridge, Mass., 1991), 413, 433–50.

44. Daniel K. Richter, "Onas the Long Knife: Pennsylvanians and Indians, 1783–1794," in Frederick E. Hoxie, Ronald Hoffman, and Peter J. Albert, eds., *Native Americans and the Early Republic* (Charlottesville, Va., 1999), 131–61.

45. Michael Huffnagle to Harmar, July [10?], 1785 [filed at the end of July 1785], David Luckett to Harmar, July 10, 1785, Harmar Papers, CL; Harmar to Henry Knox, July 16, 1785, Harmar Letterbook, CL; David Howell to William Greene, Aug. 23, 1785, in William R. Staples, *Rhode Island in the Continental Congress, with the Journal of the Convention That Adopted the Constitution, 1765–1790* (Providence, R.I., 1870), 535.

46. New York dateline, *South Carolina Gazette and Public Advertiser*, Sept. 1, 1785, *United States Chronicle*, Aug. 25, 1785, *Vermont Gazette*, Aug. 29, 1785, *New Hampshire Mercury*, Aug. 30, 1785.

47. Brant had intended to make the trip in the fall of 1784, but he had to delay it and did not actually leave for England until after Guyasuta and Cornplanter had reported his return. Kelsay, *Joseph Brant*, 361–64; Henry Hope to Evan Nepean, Nov. 5, 1785, CO 42/17, f. 212.

48. Gregory Evans Dowd, "The French King Wakes up in Detroit: 'Pontiac's War' in Rumor and History," *Ethnohistory* 37 (Summer 1990), 254–78.

49. Shawnee towns, message, Mar. 20, 1785, CO 42/48, f. 74; Fish Carrier [Cayuga], "At a Meeting Held at Fort Schlosser on the 27th March 1786 by the Principal Sachems and a Large Body of Warriors of the Six United Nations of Indians," CO 42/49; Alexander McKee to Arndt DePeyster, Sept. 8, 1783, *Collections and Researches Made by the Michigan Pioneer and Historical Society* (1888), 11:385.

50. Henry Knox, report, July 21, 1787, in Ford, ed., *Journals of the Continental Congress*, 33:388.

51. Philip Schuyler to Iroquois delegation, Jan. 1784, in Francis Jennings, ed., *Iroquois Indians: A Documentary History of the Diplomacy of the Six Nations and Their League* (microfilm, 50 reels, Woodbridge, Conn., 1984), reel 37.

52. John Johnson to Frederick Haldimand, Apr. 19, 1784, ibid.

53. Congress, resolve, Mar. 19, 1784, in Ford, ed., *Journals of the Continental Congress*, 26:153–54.

54. Council at Wakatomika Council House, Nov. 8, 1785, CO 42/49, f. 21; Captain Johnny (Shawnee sachem), speech, "At Council held at Wakitomiker, May 18, 1785 By the Chiefs the Shawenese, Mingoes, Dellawares, & Cherokee's," Native American History Collection, CL.

55. Todd to Randolph, Feb. 14, 1787, *CVSP*, 237; Henry Knox, report, July 21, 1787, in Ford, ed., *Journals of the Continental Congress*, 33:388.

56. Congress, ordinance, May 20, 1785, in Ford, ed., *Journals of the Continental Congress*, 28:375–81; Peter S. Onuf, *Statehood and Union: A History of the Northwest Ordinance* (Bloomington, Ind., 1987), ch. 2.

57. Obediah Robins to Harmar, Aug. 28, 1785, Harmar Papers, CL.

58. Joseph Ashton to Harmar, Oct. 23, 1785, Harmar Papers, CL.

59. "Examination of John Leith," Oct. 17, 1785, in William Henry Smith, ed., *The St. Clair Papers: The Life and Public Services of Arthur St. Clair . . .* (2 vols.; Cincinnati, 1882), 2:633.

60. John Cleves Symmes to Joseph Ward, July 24, 1786, in Paul H. Smith et al., eds., *Letters of Delegates to Congress, 1774–1789* (26 vols.; Washington, D.C., 1976–2000), 23:411.

61. George Brickell, Thomas Girty depositions, Sept. 13, 1786, Harmar Papers, CL; Jacob Springer to Thomas Hutchins, Sept. 2, 1786, "A Man Who For Many Reasons Wishes His Name Not to be Known Makes the Following Report," Sept. 14, 1786, in Archer Butler Hulbert, *Ohio in the Time of the Confederation* (Marietta, Ohio, 1918), 154–59; White, *Middle Ground*; James H. Merrell, *Into the American Woods: Negotiators on the Pennsylvania Frontier* (New York, 1999).

62. Winchester dateline, *Virginia Gazette and Winchester Advertiser*, July 25, 1787; R. Douglas Hurt, *The Ohio Frontier: Crucible of the Old Northwest, 1720–1830* (Bloomington, Ind., 1996), 148–52.

63. Philadelphia dateline, *Virginia Independent Chronicle*, Oct. 11, 1786.

64. Board of Treasury, report, Apr. 5, 1787, in Ford, ed., *Journals of the Continental Congress*, 32:156; Congress, resolve, Apr. 21, 1787, ibid., 225–26.

65. Hurt, *Ohio Frontier*, 155.

66. Land could be purchased, for an average price of less than $1.25 per acre, using federal securities that had depreciated to one-eighth of their face value. Committee report, July 23, 1787, in Ford, ed., *Journals of the Continental Congress*, 33:399–401; Harry M. Ward, *The Department of War, 1781–1795* (Pittsburgh, 1962), 56; Dorothy V. Jones, *License for Empire: Colonialism by Treaty in Early America* (Chicago, 1982), 163.

67. Congress, ordinance, July 13, 1787, in Ford, ed., *Journals of the Continental Congress*, 32:340; Reginald Horsman, "The Indian Policy of an 'Empire for Liberty,'" in Frederick E. Hoxie, Ronald Hoffman, and Peter J. Albert, eds., *Native Americans and the Early Republic* (Charlottesville, Va., 1999), 40; Andrew R. L. Cayton, *Frontier Indiana* (Bloomington, Ind., 1996), 123–24; Jones, *License for Empire*, 147, 164–69; Ward, *Department of War*, 68.

68. Henry Knox, report, July 21, 1787, in Ford, ed., *Journals of the Continental Congress*, 33:388.

69. Nathan Dane, speech, Nov. [9], 1786, paraphrased under Boston dateline, *New Hampshire Gazette*, Nov. 18, 1786.

CHAPTER 9: "A MURMURING UNDERNEATH"—REBELLION

1. Jerome J. Nadelhaft, *The Disorders of War: The Revolution in South Carolina* (Orono, Me., 1981), 155.

2. Bruce H. Mann, *Republic of Debtors: Bankruptcy in the Age of American Independence* (Cambridge, Mass., 2002), 26–27.

3. Freeman H. Hart, *The Valley of Virginia in the American Revolution, 1763–1789* (Chapel Hill, N.C., 1942), 125.

4. Richmond dateline, *Boston Gazette*, Oct. 10, 1785.

5. "Extract of a Letter from a Gentleman in New–York . . . ," *Connecticut Courant*, Apr. 10, 1786; David P. Szatmary, *Shays' Rebellion: The Making of an Agrarian Insurrection* (Amherst, Mass., 1980), 125.

6. Szatmary, *Shays' Rebellion*, 125.

7. Anonymous to Edmund Randolph, Sept. 6, 1788, *CVSP*, 477.

8. Edmund Randolph to James Madison, Apr. 26, 1783, in William T. Hutchinson et al., eds., *The Papers of James Madison* (17 vols. to date; Chicago, 1962–), 6:500.

9. John Thornton Posey, *General Thomas Posey: Son of the American Revolution* (East Lansing, Mich., 1992), 288–91.

10. Terry Bouton, "Tying Up the Revolution: Money, Power, and the Regulation in Pennsylvania, 1765–1800" (Ph.D. diss., Duke University, 1996), 244.

11. James Delaplain (Newcastle County) and Joseph Taylor (Kent County), petition, Jan.–Feb. 1786 legislative petitions, record group 1111, DPA, reel 7, frame 147.

12. Dorsey Pentecost, quoted in Bouton, "Tying Up the Revolution," 249.

13. William Grayson to [Patrick Henry], Jan. 22, 1785, Virginia Executive Papers (microfilm), reel 4918, LiVi; Augusta, Berkeley, Dinwiddie, Gloucester, Henry, Northampton, Powhatan, Prince Edward, Rockingham County sheriffs, petitions (summaries) [1787], *CVSP*, 377–78; L[eighton] Wood, Jr., to Edmund Randolph, Apr. 17, 1787 (enclosing memorial from former Chesterfield County sheriff George Robertson), *CVSP*, 270.

14. Bouton, "Tying Up the Revolution," 251–52.

15. Jan. 5, 1785, "Diary or Memorandum Book Kept by Joseph Lewis of Morristown . . . ," *Proceedings of the New Jersey Historical Society* 60 (Jan. 1942), 61; Sussex County citizens, petition, n.d., Legislative Petitions, item 58, box 19, NJBAH.

16. Jan. 5, 1785, "Diary . . . Joseph Lewis," 61; Justice [John Cleves] Symmes to William Livingston, Mar. 5, 1785, cited in David A. Bernstein, ed., *Minutes of the Governor's Privy Council, 1777–1789*, Mar. 16, 1785, in *New Jersey Archives*, 3rd ser., 1:261–62.

17. Richard P. McCormick, *Experiment in Independence: New Jersey in the Critical Period, 1781–1789* (New Brunswick, N.J., 1950), 114–15.

18. Henry Lee, Jr., to George Washington, Sept. 8, 1786, in W. W. Abbot and Dorothy Twohig, eds., *The Papers of George Washington*, Confederation Series (6 vols.; Charlottesville, Va., 1992–97), 4:240.

19. "Amicus Reipublicae" [Benjamin Thurston], *An Address to the Public, Containing*

Some Remarks on the Present Political State of the American Republicks, &c. (Exeter, N.H., [1786]), 20.

20. David Daggett, *An Oration, Pronounced in the Brick Meeting-House, in the City of New-Haven, on the Fourth of July, A.D. 1787* (New Haven, Conn., [1787]), 14; George Washington to Henry Knox, Dec. 26, 1786, in Abbot and Twohig, eds., *Papers of George Washington*, 4:482.

21. Benjamin Hawkins to Richard Caswell, Sept. 26, 1785, in Walter Clark, ed., *The State Records of North Carolina* (Goldsboro, N.C., 1909), 17:525; Roger H. Brown, *Redeeming the Republic: Federalists, Taxation, and the Origins of the Constitution* (Baltimore, 1993), 77.

22. "Sylvius" [Hugh Williamson], I, *American Museum* 2 (Aug. 1787), 107.

23. McClurg to James Madison, Aug. 22, 1787, in Hutchinson et al., eds., *Papers of James Madison*, 10:55.

24. Edmund Randolph to [Beverley] Randolph, Sept. 2, 1787, *CVSP*, 338; Henrico County citizens, petition to governor and council, Nov. 19, 1787, *CVSP*, 359.

25. Quoted in Bouton, "Tying Up the Revolution," 252.

26. Jordan, ed., "Letter from Benjamin Gale," 17; "Camillus," *Worcester Magazine* 3:1 (1st week of Apr. 1787), 3 (reprinted from *Independent Chronicle*); "Philolaos," *Worcester Magazine* 3:1 (1st week of Apr. 1787), 7.

27. "Zeno," *Middlesex Gazette*, Nov. 6, 1786.

28. Edward Carrington to Edmund Randolph, Dec. 8, 1786, in Paul H. Smith et al., eds., *Letters of Delegates to Congress, 1774–1789* (26 vols.; Washington, D.C., 1976–2000), 24:42.

29. Hamilton, June 18, 1787, in Max Farrand, ed., *The Records of the Federal Convention of 1787* (3 vols.; New Haven, Conn., 1911), 1:289; Thomas M. Doerflinger, *A Vigorous Spirit of Enterprise: Merchants and Economic Development in Revolutionary Philadelphia* (Chapel Hill, N.C., 1986), 274.

30. Mary A. Y. Gallagher, "Reinterpreting the 'Very Trifling Mutiny' at Philadelphia in June 1783," *Pennsylvania Magazine of History and Biography* 119 (Jan.–Apr. 1995), 3–35.

31. Jeremy Belknap to Josiah Waters, Sept. 24, 1786, in Belknap Papers, MHS Collections, 6th ser., IV (Boston, 1891), 3:315.

32. George Richards Minot, *The History of the Insurrections in Massachusetts, In the Year [1786] and the Rebellion Consequent Thereon* (Worcester, Mass., 1788), 96, 40.

33. [William Whiting], "Some Remarks on the Conduct of the Inhabitants of the Commonwealth of Massachusetts in Interupting The Siting of the Judicial Courts . . ." (Dec. 1786), in Stephen T. Riley, ed., "Dr. William Whiting and Shays' Rebellion," AAS *Proceedings* 66 (1957), 152.

34. "Answer of the Town of Greenwich to the Circular Letter from Boston," *Worcester Magazine* 2:35 (last week of Nov. 1786), 422; Dracut town meeting, petition, Sept. 25, 1786, Shay's Rebellion Petitions, AAS.

35. Jeremy Belknap to Josiah Waters, Sept. 24, 1786, Belknap Papers, 3:315.

36. Szatmary, *Shays' Rebellion*, 105.

37. Anonymous letter to James Bowdoin, quoted in Brown, *Redeeming the Republic*, 114.

38. John Dawson to James Madison, Apr. 15, 1787, in Hutchinson et al., eds., *Papers of James Madison*, 9:381.

39. Pittsylvania County citizens, petition, Nov. 5, 1787, VLP.

40. Stephen Ruddell (Hampshire County), petition, Nov. 6, 1789, VLP.

41. Anonymous Camden District citizens, resolves, Apr. 23, 1785, Grimké Papers, South Carolina Historical Society, Charleston; Robert A. Becker, ed., "John F. Grimké's Eyewitness Account of the Camden Court Riot, April 27–28, 1785," *South Carolina Historical Magazine* 83 (July 1982), 211–12; Becker, "Salus Populi Suprema Lex: Public Peace and South Carolina Debtor Relief Laws, 1783–1788," *South Carolina Historical Magazine* 80 (Jan. 1979), 68–69.

42. "Grimké's Eyewitness Account," 211–12.

43. Ibid., 211–13.

44. "H.T.," *Virginia Independent Chronicle*, Oct. 3, 1787 (in which "ripe" is misspelled "rife"); Benjamin Gale to Erastus Wolcott, Feb. 10, 1787, quoted in Christopher Collier, *Roger Sherman's Connecticut: Yankee Politics and the American Revolution* (Middletown, Conn., 1971), 222.

45. Henry, paraphrased by Archibald Stuart in Norman K. Risjord, *Chesapeake Politics, 1781–1800* (New York, 1978), 178.

46. "Remarks on the Domestic Debt of the United States," III, *New Haven Gazette, and Connecticut Magazine*, June 14, 1787; New York dateline, *South Carolina Gazette and Public Advertiser*, Aug. 11, 1785; "Lucius," *Political Intelligencer and New Jersey Advertiser*, Feb. 8, 1786; "Q.Z.," *United States Chronicle*, Feb. 9, 1786.

47. Seymour, speech in the Connecticut legislature, May 15, 1787, *Middlesex Gazette*, June 4, 1787; "A Letter from a Gentleman in New York to His Friend in Connecticut, on the Subject of Paper Money," *Connecticut Courant*, Feb. 5, 1787.

48. Gillon, quoted in Becker, "Salus Populi Suprema Lex," 74.

49. "A Friend to Justice," *Political Intelligencer* and *New Jersey Advertiser*, Oct. 19, 1784; "Extract from the Proceedings of the Senate," Jan. 5, 1787, *Maryland Journal and Baltimore Advertiser*, Jan. 16, 1787.

50. Bouton, "Tying Up the Revolution," 252–53.

51. Ibid., 232.

52. "A Husbandman," *Maryland Journal and Baltimore Advertiser*, June 6, 1786.

53. Gordon S. Wood, "A Note on Mobs in the American Revolution," *WMQ*, 3rd ser., 23 (Oct. 1966), 641.

54. "An Act to Amend the Laws of Revenue, To Provide for the Support of Civil Government, and the Gradual Redemption of All the Debts Due by this Commonwealth" (Oct. 1787 session, chap. 1, passed Jan. 1, 1788), in William Waller Hening, ed., *The Statutes at Large: Being a Collection of All the Laws of Virginia, From the First Session of the Legislature, in the Year 1619* (13 vols.; Richmond, 1819–23), 12:412–15.

55. McCormick, *Experiment in Independence*, 115.

56. Madison to George Washington, Dec. 7, 1786, in Abbot and Twohig, eds., *Papers of George Washington*, 4:449.

57. Hamilton, June 26, 1787, in Farrand, ed., *Records of the Federal Convention*, 1:425.

58. Grayson to William Short, Apr. 16, 1787, in Smith et al., eds., *Letters of Delegates to Congress*, 24:226; Roger Sherman, June 20, 1787, in Farrand, ed., *Records of the Federal Convention*, 1:341.

59. David Ramsay, quoted in Becker, "Salus Populi Suprema Lex," 74.

60. "Americanus," *Columbian Herald*, Aug. 22, 1785.

61. "Grimké's Eyewitness Account," 211; "The following paragraphs are extracted out of London papers . . . ," *Columbian Herald*, Sept. 30, 1785.

62. [Aedanus Burke], *A Few Salutary Hints, Pointing Out the Policy and Consequences of Admitting British Subjects to Engross Our Trade and Become Our Citizens . . .* (New York, 1786), 7; Ralph Izard, speech, South Carolina House of Representatives, Oct. 1, 1785, *Charleston Evening Gazette*, Oct. 1, 1785.

63. Moultrie, quoted in Brown, *Redeeming the Republic*, 78.

64. Burke, quoted in Becker, "Salus Populi Suprema Lex," 71; Alexander Gillon, speech in South Carolina House of Representatives, Sept. 30, 1785, *Charleston Evening Gazette*, Sept. 30, 1785.

65. Madison to Jefferson, Oct. 3, 1785, in Hutchinson et al., eds., *Papers of James Madison*, 8:375.

66. Rutledge, speech in South Carolina House of Representatives, Feb. 8, 1786; *Charleston Evening Gazette*, Feb. 9, 1786.

67. Hampshire County convention, resolves, *Hampshire Gazette*, Sept. 13, 1786; "Proceedings of the General Court," *Boston Magazine* 3 (Nov.–Dec. 1786), 428; Brown, *Redeeming the Republic*, 117–21.

68. Szatmary, *Shays' Rebellion*, 85–87.

69. Ibid., 102, 111, 115; Richards, *Shays's Rebellion*, 29, 36, 41.

70. Feb. 1787, Lee diary, New England Historic Genealogical Society, Boston.

71. Ibid.

72. Gerry, July 19, 1787, in Farrand, ed., *Records of the Federal Convention*, 2:57.

73. Boston dateline, *Connecticut Courant*, Oct. 2, 1786; Boston dateline, *Virginia Independent Chronicle*, Oct. 3, 1786.

74. Hartford dateline, *Connecticut Courant*, Oct. 2, 1786.

75. Williams, quoted under Hartford dateline, *Connecticut Courant*, Dec. 18, 1786; Williams, letter dated Dec. 26, 1786, *Connecticut Courant*, Jan. 1, 1787 (reprinted from *New London Gazette*).

76. Minot, *History of the Insurrections*, 17.

77. Randolph, May 29, 1787, in Farrand, ed., *Records of the Federal Convention*, 1:27.

78. Gerry, July 19, 1787, ibid., 2:57; Lawrence Shaw Mayo, *John Langdon of New Hampshire* (orig. pub. 1937; Port Washington, N.Y., 1970), 196.

79. Oakham town meeting, Shrewsbury town meeting, petitions to governor and council, Jan. 15, 1787, 205:6:3–5, 15–17, Force Transcripts, LC; Boston dateline, *Virginia Independent Chronicle*, Dec. 27, 1786; Benjamin Lincoln to George Washington, Dec. 4, 1786, to Mar. 4, 1787, in Abbot and Twohig, eds., *Papers of George Washington*, 4:421; Lucius R. Paige, *History of Hardwick, Massachusetts, With a Genealogical Regis-*

ter (Boston, 1883), 141; Rock Brynner, "'Fire Beneath Our Feet': Shays' Rebellion and Its Constitutional Impact" (Ph.D. diss., Columbia University, 1993), 67.

80. "A Friend to Government," *Massachusetts Centinel*, Mar. 3, 1787; Boston dateline, *Independent Chronicle*, Apr. 26, 1787; Riley, ed., "Dr. William Whiting," 130–31.

81. James Russell Trumbull, *History of Northampton, Massachusetts, from Its Settlement in 1654* (2 vols.; Northampton, Mass., 1898–1902), 2:479–82.

82. Editors' note, *Hampshire Herald*, Sept. 26, 1786.

83. Boston dateline, *Worcester Magazine* 2:24 (2nd week of Sept. 1786), 290; Boston dateline, *Middlesex Gazette*, Sept. 18, 1786.

CHAPTER 10: "EXCESS OF DEMOCRACY"? — REFORM

1. "Primitive Whig" [Livingston], II, *New Jersey Gazette*, Jan. 16, 1786.

2. "Diary of Timothy Ford, 1785–1786," *South Carolina Historical Magazine* 13 (Oct. 1912), 200.

3. Phelps, speech in Connecticut House of Representatives, May 30, 1787, *Middlesex Gazette*, June 18, 1787; George Mason, Aug. 13, 1787, in Max Farrand, ed., *The Records of the Federal Convention of 1787* (3 vols.; New Haven, Conn., 1911), 2:273.

4. "Batavus," *State Gazette of South Carolina*, Sept. 29, 1785.

5. "A Fellow Citizen"/"Willing to Learn," *The True Policy of New Jersey Defined; Or, Our Great Strength Led to Exertion, in the Improvement of Agriculture & Manufactures, By Altering the Mode of Taxation, and by the Emission of Money on Loan . . .* (Elizabeth-Town, N.J., 1786), 33–34.

6. [Herman Husband], *Proposals to Amend and Perfect the Policy of the Government of the United States of America, or, The Fulfilling of the Prophecies in the Latter Days, Commenced by the Independence of America* (Philadelphia, 1782), 6; "Biscayanus," *Virginia Independent Chronicle*, July 11, 1787 (reprinted from *London Public Ledger*); "Philodemus" [Thomas Tudor Tucker], *Conciliatory Hints, Attempting, By a Fair State of Matters, To Remove Party-Prejudices . . . And Proposing a Convention . . .* (Charleston, S.C., 1784), 17.

7. F. Nwabueze Okoye, "Chattel Slavery as the Nightmare of the American Revolutionaries," *WMQ*, 3rd. ser., 37 (Jan. 1980), 3–28; Frederick County citizens, petition, Nov. 8, 1785, VLP.

8. Larry E. Tise, *The American Counterrevolution: A Retreat from Liberty, 1783–1800* (Mechanicsburg, Pa., 1998), 109–10.

9. "A New Favourite Song for the Ladies," *New Hampshire Gazette*, Dec. 7, 1770; Judith Sargent Murray, "On the Equality of the Sexes" (1790), in Sheila L. Skemp, *Judith Sargent Murray: A Brief Biography with Documents* (Boston, 1998), 177–82; Joan R. Gundersen, *To Be Useful to the World: Women in Revolutionary America, 1740–1790* (New York, 1996), 147; T. H. Breen, *The Marketplace of Revolution: How Consumer Politics Shaped American Independence* (New York, 2004), 288.

10. Abigail Adams to John Adams, Mar. 31, 1776, Adams Electronic Archive.

11. "Timothy Foresight," *Independent Chronicle*, June 15, 1786 (reprinted from *Bristol Journal*).

12. Charleston dateline, *Columbian Herald*, May 26, 1785; Louise Belote Dawe and Sandra Gioia Treadway, "Hannah Lee Corbin: The Forgotten Lee," *Virginia Cavalcade* 29 (1979), 70–77; Cathy N. Davidson, "The Novel as Subversive Activity: Women Reading, Women Writing," in Alfred F. Young, ed., *Beyond the American Revolution: Explorations in the History of American Radicalism* (DeKalb, Ill., 1993), 299–300; Gundersen, *To Be Useful to the World*, 153.

13. *New York Gazetteer*, quoted under Portsmouth dateline, *New Hampshire Gazette*, Aug. 17, 1786; "A Freeman," *Worcester Magazine* 2:28 (2nd week of Oct. 1786), 338.

14. "A Conventioner," *Worcester Magazine* 2:29 (3rd week of Oct. 1786), 350; "Observator," *New Hampshire Gazette*, May 20, 1785; Robert A. Gross, *The Minutemen and Their World* (New York, 1976), 11.

15. Election notice, quoted in Terry Bouton, "Tying Up the Revolution: Money, Power, and the Regulation in Pennsylvania, 1765–1800" (Ph.D. diss., Duke University, 1996), 175–76.

16. [Husband], *Proposals to Amend and Perfect the Policy*, 10, 15.

17. Mary Beth Norton, *Liberty's Daughters: The Revolutionary Experience of American Women, 1750–1800* (Ithaca, N.Y., 1980), 219 (quotations), 222–24; Natalie S. Bober, *Abigail Adams: Witness to a Revolution* (New York, 1995), 71.

18. Samuel Haven, *An Election Sermon, Preached before the General Court of New Hampshire at Concord, June 8, 1786* (Portsmouth, 1786), 11–12.

19. "Political Paragraphs, Connecticut," *Connecticut Courant*, Nov. 20, 1786; "Political Paragraphs: Massachusetts," *Connecticut Courant*, Nov. 27, 1786.

20. "Minimaltasperus," *New Hampshire Mercury*, Oct. 4, 1786.

21. "Brutus," *Middlesex Gazette*, Apr. 2, 1787.

22. Henry Lee, Jr., speech in Virginia ratifying convention, June 9, 1788, *DHRC*, 9:1080; Jon Kukla, *A Wilderness So Immense: The Louisiana Purchase and the Destiny of America* (New York, 2003), 100.

23. "Political Paragraphs: Massachusetts," *Connecticut Courant*, Nov. 27, 1786; "Camillus," *Independent Chronicle*, March 1, 1787; Gordon S. Wood, *The Creation of the American Republic, 1776–1787* (Chapel Hill, N.C., 1969), 325.

24. Paraphrased under Portsmouth dateline, *New Hampshire Mercury*, Jan. 24, 1787.

25. Rutledge, quoted in Robert A. Becker, *Revolution, Reform, and the Politics of American Taxation, 1763–1783* (Baton Rouge, La., 1980), 209.

26. New York dateline, *Middlesex Gazette*, Oct. 2, 1786.

27. "Political Paragraphs: Massachusetts," *Connecticut Courant*, Nov. 27, 1786.

28. William Manning, "The Key of Libberty: Shewing the Causes Why a Free Government has Always Failed & a Reamedy Against It . . . ," in Michael Merrill and Sean Wilentz, eds., *The Key of Liberty: The Life and Democratic Writings of William Manning, "A Laborer," 1747–1814* (Cambridge, Mass., 1993), 125.

29. Ibid., 125–26.
30. [Husband], *Proposals to Amend and Perfect the Policy*, 10.
31. "The Censor," II, *Hampshire Herald*, Jan. 11, 1785.
32. "A Citizen of Connecticut" [William Beers], *An Address to the Legislature and People of the State of Connecticut, On the Subject of Dividing the State into Districts for the Election of Representatives in Congress* (New Haven, Conn., 1791), 31.
33. [Beers], *Address to the Legislature*, 17; "Atticus," IV, *Independent Chronicle*, Dec. 27, 1787, *DHRC*, 5:533.
34. "An Easy, Honest and Expeditious Way to Discharge the Publick Debt of the State of Massachusetts," *Hampshire Herald*, Sept. 26, 1786.
35. "Impartiality," *New Hampshire Mercury*, Sept. 6, 1786.
36. Worcester County convention, address, Nov. 23, 1786, quoted in George Richards Minot, *The History of the Insurrections in Massachusetts, In the Year [1786] and the Rebellion Consequent Thereon* (Worcester, Mass., 1788), 72; Wood, *Creation of the Republic*, ch. 5.
37. Mason, June 6, 1787, in Max Farrand, ed., *The Records of the Federal Convention of 1787* (3 vols.; New Haven, Conn., 1966), 1:133–34.
38. Cortlandt F. Bishop, *History of Elections in the American Colonies* (New York, 1893), 1–45.
39. Jeremiah Libbey to Jeremy Belknap, May 11, 1787, in Belknap Papers, MHS Collections, 6th ser., IV (Boston, 1891), 3:334.
40. Philadelphia dateline, *South Carolina Gazette and Public Advertiser*, Nov. 1, 1785.
41. Jack N. Rakove, *Original Meanings: Politics and Ideas in the Making of the Constitution* (New York, 1996), 41; J. R. Pole, *Political Representation in England and the Origins of the American Republic* (Berkeley, Calif., 1966), 300.
42. Willi Paul Adams, *The First American Constitutions: Republican Ideology and the Making of the State Constitutions in the Revolutionary Era*, trans. Rita and Robert Kimber (Chapel Hill, N.C., 1980), 245.
43. Wood, *Creation of the Republic*, 213; [Noah Webster], "An Examination into the Leading Principles of the Federal Constitution," in Bernard Bailyn, ed., *The Debate on the Constitution: Federalist and Antifederalist Speeches, Articles, and Letters During the Struggle over Ratification* (2 vols.; New York, 1993), 1:132; Marc W. Kruman, *Between Authority & Liberty: State Constitution Making in Revolutionary America* (Chapel Hill, N.C., 1997), 140–41, 199 n45.
44. Madison to Thomas Jefferson, Aug. 12, 1786, in William T. Hutchinson et al., eds., *The Papers of James Madison* (17 vols. to date; Chicago, 1962–), 9:95.
45. Newcastle County citizens, petition, Oct.–Nov. 1787 legislative elections, record group 1111, DPA, reel 9, frame 46; Pendleton, speech in South Carolina House of Representatives, Feb. 3, 1786, *Charleston Evening Gazette*, Feb. 3, 1786.
46. Boothbay town meeting, quoted in James S. Leamon, *Revolution Downeast: The War for American Independence in Maine* (Amherst, Mass., 1993), 169; Robert Arnold Feer, *Shays' Rebellion* (New York, 1988), 23; Stephen E. Patterson, *Political Parties in Revolutionary Massachusetts* (Madison, Wisc., 1973), 234–42.

47. "An Easy, Honest and Expeditious Way to Discharge the Publick Debt of the State of Massachusetts," *Hampshire Herald*, Sept. 26, 1786.
48. "Answer of the Town of Greenwich to the Circular Letter from Boston," *Worcester Magazine* 2:35 (last week of Nov. 1786), 423.
49. Patterson, *Political Parties in Revolutionary Massachusetts*, 218, 228, 230; Pole, *Political Representation*, 204, 234–35, 239.
50. "Petition of the Worcester County Convention to the General Court," "A Freeman," *Worcester Magazine* 2:28 (2nd week of Oct. 1786), 335–36; Bristol County convention, resolves, *Independent Chronicle*, July 27, 1786.
51. "A Number of Freemen," *United States Chronicle*, Feb. 16, 1786.
52. Camden District and York County citizens, petitions, read Sept. 27, 1785, in Lark Emerson Adams and Rosa Stoney Lumpkin, eds., *The State Records of South Carolina: Journals of the House of Representatives, 1785–1786* (Columbia, S.C., 1979), 316; Charleston dateline, *State Gazette of South Carolina*, Aug. 21, 1786; Little River District citizens, petition, read March 7, 1785, in Adams and Lumpkin, eds., *State Records of South Carolina*, 196; Chester County citizens, petition, Feb. 20, 1786, 1786 petitions, no. 31, SCDAH; [Tucker], *Conciliatory Hints*, 21–33; Rachel N. Klein, *Unification of a Slave State: The Rise of the Planter Class in the South Carolina Backcountry, 1760–1808* (Chapel Hill, N.C., 1990), 114.
53. Wood, *Creation of the Republic*, 181; Donald S. Lutz, *Popular Consent and Popular Control: Whig Political Theory in the Early State Constitutions* (Baton Rouge, La., 1980), 90–91.
54. *Rudiments of Law and Government, Deduced from the Law of Nature; Particularly Addressed to the People of South-Carolina, But Composed on Principles Applicable to All Mankind* (Charleston, 1783), 24; Hanover, Canaan, and Cardigan, joint town meeting, Nov. 27, 1776, in Nathaniel Bouton, ed., *Documents and Papers Relating to the State of New Hampshire During the Period of the American Revolution, From 1776 to 1783* (Concord, N.H., 1874), 8:422; Acworth town meeting, Dec. 9, 1776, ibid., 423; Haverhill, Lyman, Bath, Gunthwait, Landaff, and Morristown, joint committee meeting, Dec. 13, 1776, ibid., 425.
55. [Husband], *Proposals to Amend and Perfect the Policy*, 3–4, 8.
56. Ibid., 3–4, 10; [Swift], [Zephaniah Swift?], *The Security of the Rights of Citizens in the State of Connecticut Considered* (Hartford, Conn., 1792), 47n; Edmund S. Morgan, *Inventing the People: The Rise of Popular Sovereignty in England and America* (New York, 1988), 247.
57. Sean Wilentz, *The Rise of American Democracy: Jefferson to Lincoln* (New York, 2005), 14.
58. [Husband], *Proposals to Amend and Perfect the Policy*, 15.
59. "A Friend to his Country" [Benjamin Gale], *Brief, Decent, but Free Remarks, and Observations, on Several Laws Passed by the Honorable Legislature of the State of Connecticut, Since the year 1775* (Hartford, Conn., 1782), 32–33.
60. Ibid., 33; Timothy Dwight, *Travels in New England and New York*, ed. Barbara Miller Solomon (4 vols., orig. pub. 1822; Cambridge, Mass., 1969), 1:188–90.

61. Plymouth dateline, *New Hampshire Gazette*, June 17, 1785.

62. Madison, "Remarks on Mr Jeffersons Draught of a Constitution . . . ," in John P. Boyd et al., eds., *The Papers of Thomas Jefferson* (33 vols. to date; Princeton, N.J., 1950–), 6:315.

63. "Free Republican," VIII, *Independent Chronicle*, Jan. 12, 1786; Leamon, *Revolution Downeast*, 172–73.

64. *The People the Best Governors: Or A Plan of Government Founded on the Just Principles of Natural Freedom* (n.p., 1776), 10; Kruman, *Between Authority and Liberty*, 99–101.

65. "Americanus," *Virginia Independent Chronicle*, Aug. 29, 1787 (reprinted from *New York Daily Advertiser*).

66. Quoted in Wood, *Creation of the Republic*, 168–69.

67. "Lycurgus," *Connecticut Courant*, Apr. 17, 1786.

68. "Aristides," *Virginia Independent Chronicle*, Mar. 21, 1787.

69. Gerry, June 6, 1787, in Farrand, ed., *Records of the Federal Convention*, 1:132; Robert J. Taylor, *Western Massachusetts in the Revolution* (Providence, R.I., 1954), 142–43.

70. [Webster], "Examination into the Leading Principles of the Federal Constitution," in Bailyn, ed., *Debate on the Constitution*, 1:133; "Proceedings of Government," *Independent Chronicle*, Oct. 19, 1786; Pole, *Political Representation*, 230–32. Compare "A.W.," *Virginia Independent Chronicle*, Mar. 28, 1787.

71. "Sentinel," *New Hampshire Gazette*, Oct. 14, 1785; "A Message to the Council from the House of Assembly," June 15, 1786, and note on "Bill for Printing and Emitting Twenty One Thousand Pounds in Bills of Credit . . . ," May–June 1786 acts and bills, record group IIII, DPA, reel 7, frames 317, 333; Norman K. Risjord, *Chesapeake Politics, 1781–1800* (New York, 1978), 169–73; David P. Szatmary, *Shays' Rebellion: The Making of an Agrarian Insurrection* (Amherst, Mass., 1980), 54.

72. "Bill for Printing and Emitting Twenty One Thousand Pounds in Bills of Credit . . . ," May–June 1786 acts and bills, record group IIII, DPA, reel 7, frame 333.

73. "Extract from the Proceedings of the Senate," Dec. 30, 1786, *Maryland Journal and Baltimore Advertiser*, Jan. 16, 1787.

74. New York dateline, *Independent Chronicle*, Apr. 13, 1786; Providence dateline, *Middlesex Gazette*, May 22, 1786; Richard P. McCormick, *Experiment in Independence: New Jersey in the Critical Period, 1781–1789* (New Brunswick, N.J., 1950), 201; Jackson Turner Main, *Political Parties Before the Constitution* (Chapel Hill, N.C., 1973), 133.

75. "Sentinel," *New Hampshire Gazette*, Oct. 14, 1785.

76. Aubrey C. Land, "Economic Base and Social Structure: The Northern Chesapeake in the Eighteenth Century," *Journal of Economic History* 25 (Dec. 1965), 650.

77. Boston dateline, *Massachusetts Centinel*, July 29, 1786; Hanover, Canaan, and Cardigan, joint town meeting, Nov. 27, 1776, in Bouton, ed., *Documents and Papers Relating to the State of New-Hampshire*, 422; Haverhill, Lyman, Bath, Gunthwait, Landaff, and Morristown, joint committee, Dec. 13, 1776, ibid., 425; [Tucker],

Conciliatory Hints, 23; Patterson, *Political Parties in Revolutionary Massachusetts*, 222, 237.

78. Adams, quoted in Richard N. Rosenfeld, *American Aurora: A Democratic-Republican Returns: The Suppressed History of Our Nation's Beginnings and the Heroic Newspaper That Tried to Report It* (New York, 1997), 467; "A Song," *Middlesex Gazette*, Mar. 5, 1787; Noah Webster to Timothy Pickering, Aug. 10, 1786, Pickering Papers, MHS.

79. Madison, quoted in Rakove, *Original Meanings*, 41.

80. Pole, *Political Representation*, 301.

81. "The Free Republican," III, *Independent Chronicle*, Dec. 8, 1785.

82. "Honestus" [Benjamin Austin], *Independent Chronicle*, May 25, 1786; Kruman, *Between Authority and Liberty*, 78–79; Ronald Hoffman, in collaboration with Sally D. Mason, *Princes of Ireland, Planters of Maryland: A Carroll Saga, 1500–1782* (Chapel Hill, N.C., 2000), 311–13.

83. [Tucker], *Conciliatory Hints*, 21–22; Adams, *First American Constitutions*, 248; Kruman, *Between Authority and Liberty*, 81.

84. For citizens who asserted the right to instruct members of the lower house, see Essex County, New Jersey, convention, resolves, summarized in *Virginia Independent Chronicle*, June 6, 1787. For criticism of representative instructions, see George Washington to Bushrod Washington, Sept. 30, 1786, in W. W. Abbot and Dorothy Twohig, eds., *The Papers of George Washington*, Confederation Series (Charlottesville, Va., 1992–97), 4:278–79; Wood, *Creation of the Republic*, 379–81. For citizens who asserted the right to instruct members of the senate, see "A Freeman," *Worcester Magazine* 2:28 (2nd week of Oct. 1786), 337; "An Address of the House of Delegates of Maryland, To their Constituents," *Maryland Journal and Baltimore Advertiser*, Feb. 2, 1787. For denials of this right, see "Thoughts on the Constitution of Maryland . . . ," *Maryland Journal and Baltimore Advertiser*, Mar. 2, 1787.

85. Robert L. Brunhouse, *The Counter-Revolution in Pennsylvania, 1776–1790* (orig. pub. 1942; New York, 1971).

86. [Husband], *Proposals to Amend and Perfect the Policy*, 28.

87. "Consideration," *Connecticut Courant*, Feb. 5, 1787.

CHAPTER 11: "THE HOUSE ON FIRE"—CREDIT

1. Newport dateline, *New Haven Chronicle*, Apr. 17, 1787.

2. "Political Paragraphs: Massachusetts," *Connecticut Courant*, Nov. 27, 1786; Peregrine Foster to Dwight Foster, July 11, 1786, Foster Family Papers, AAS; Norwich, Conn., dateline, *The Palladium of Freedom, or the Baltimore Advertiser*, Aug. 8, 1787; "Consideration," *Charleston Evening Gazette*, May 27, 1786.

3. Richard Krauel, "Prince Henry of Prussia and the Regency of the United States, 1786," *American Historical Review* 17 (Oct. 1911), 44–51; Louise Burnham Dunbar, *A Study of "Monarchical" Tendencies in the United States from 1776 to 1801* (orig. pub. 1922; reprint, New York, 1970), ch. 3, 4, 5; Douglass Adair, " 'Experience Must Be Our Only Guide': History, Democratic Theory, and the United States Constitu-

tion," in Adair, *Fame and the Founding Fathers: Essays*, ed. Trevor Colbourn (orig. pub. 1974; Indianapolis, Ind., 1998), 168–69; David P. Szatmary, *Shays' Rebellion: The Making of an Agrarian Insurrection* (Amherst, Mass., 1980), 81–82; Alfred F. Young, "Conservatives, the Constitution, and the 'Spirit of Accommodation,'" in Robert A. Goldwin and William A. Schambra, eds., *How Democratic Is the Constitution?* (Washington, D.C., 1980), 118.

4. Lee, quoted in Roger H. Brown, *Redeeming the Republic: Federalists, Taxation, and the Origins of the Constitution* (Baltimore, 1993), 259.

5. Knox to Rufus King, July 15, 1787, Knox Papers (microfilm), reel 20, MHS.

6. Congress, resolve, Feb. 21, 1787, in Worthington Chauncey Ford, ed., *Journals of the Continental Congress, 1774–1789* (34 vols.; Washington, D.C., 1904–37), 32:74; "The Republican Federalist," I, *Massachusetts Centinel*, Dec. 29, 1787, *DHRC*, 5:552.

7. "Examiner," *Massachusetts Gazette*, Nov. 20, 1787, *DHRC*, 4:279; Garry Wills, *James Madison* (New York, 2002), 25–26.

8. Wilson, Aug. 30, 1787, Edmund Randolph, June 16, 1787, George Mason, June 20, 1787, in Max Farrand, ed., *The Records of the Federal Convention of 1787* (3 vols.; New Haven, Conn., 1911), 3:469, 1:255, 338.

9. C[hristopher] Gore to Rufus King, June 28, 1787, in Charles R. King, ed., *The Life and Correspondence of Rufus King, Comprising His Letters, Private and Official, His Public Documents, and His Speeches* (New York, 1894), 1:227; North Callahan, *Henry Knox: General Washington's General* (New York, 1958), 252.

10. John Lansing, William Paterson, June 16, 1787, in Farrand, ed., *Records of the Federal Convention*, 1:249, 274.

11. Donald Lutz, *Popular Consent and Popular Control: Whig Political Theory in the Early State Constitutions* (Baton Rouge, La., 1980), 119.

12. Madison, June 29, 1787, in Farrand, ed., *Records of the Federal Convention*, 1:471.

13. Randolph, June 21, 1787, ibid., 1:360; Brown, *Redeeming the Republic*, 190.

14. Madison, June 8, 29, 1787, in Farrand, ed., *Records of the Federal Convention*, 1:168, 476.

15. Madison to Jefferson, Mar. 19, 1787, in William T. Hutchinson et al., eds., *The Papers of James Madison* (17 vols. to date; Chicago, 1962–), 9:318.

16. Charles F. Hobson, "The Negative on State Laws: James Madison, the Constitution, and the Crisis of Republican Government," *WMQ*, 3rd ser., 36 (Apr. 1979), 220–21; Wills, *Madison*, 20–22.

17. Madison, June 8, 28, July 25, 1787, in Farrand, ed., *Records of the Federal Convention*, 1:164–65, 447 (quotation), 2:110; Shlomo Slonim, "Motives at Philadelphia, 1787: Gordon Wood's Neo-Beardian Thesis Reexamined," *Law and History Review* 16 (Fall 1998), 540–43.

18. Madison to Edmund Randolph, Apr. 8, 1787, in Hutchinson et al., eds., *Papers of James Madison*, 9:370; Madison to Washington, Apr. 16, 1787, in W. W. Abbot and Dorothy Twohig, eds., *The Papers of George Washington*, Confederation Series (6 vols.; Charlottesville, Va., 1992–97), 5:146; Madison, June 19, 1787, in Farrand, ed., *Records of the Federal Convention*, 1:317–18.

19. Madison, June 8, 1787, in Farrand, ed., *Records of the Federal Convention*, 1:164.

20. George Mason to George Mason, Jr., May 20, 1787, in Robert A. Rutland, ed., *The Papers of George Mason, 1725–1792* (3 vols.; Chapel Hill, N.C., 1970), 3:880; Apparent Outline of Pinckney Plan, in papers of Committee of Detail, in Farrand, ed., *Records of the Federal Convention*, 2:135; Edward Carrington to Madison, June 13, 1787, in Hutchinson et al., eds., *Papers of James Madison*, 10:52; Richard Henry Lee to George Mason, May 15, 1787, in Rutland, ed., *Papers of George Mason*, 3:879; [Tench Coxe], *An Enquiry into the Principles on Which a Commercial System for the United States of America Should be Founded . . .* (Philadelphia, 1787), *DHRC*, 13:104.

21. Edmund Randolph, May 29, 1787, Elbridge Gerry, June 8, 1787, in Farrand, ed., *Records of the Federal Convention*, 1:26, 165 (quotation); George Athan Billias, *Elbridge Gerry: Founding Father and Republican Statesman* (New York, 1976), 166–67.

22. Charles Pinckney, "Observations on the Plan of Government Submitted to the Federal Convention in Philadelphia on the 28th of May, 1787 . . . ," in Farrand, ed., *Records of the Federal Convention*, 3:113; Gerry, June 8, 1787, Lansing, June 16, 1787, ibid., 1:165, 250; Hobson, "Negative on State Laws," 227; Brown, *Redeeming the Republic*, 199.

23. Mason, paraphrased in Madison to Jefferson, Oct. 24, 1787, in Farrand, ed., *Records of the Federal Convention*, 3:136. For the idea of allowing the federal government to appoint state officials, see Mason, paraphrased in Madison to Jefferson, Oct. 24, 1787, ibid., 3:136; John Jay to George Washington, Jan. 7, 1787, in Abbot and Twohig, eds., *Papers of George Washington*, 4:503.

24. Lance Banning, *The Sacred Fire of Liberty: James Madison and the Founding of the Federal Republic* (Ithaca, N.Y., 1995), 148; Jennifer Nedelsky, "The Protection of Property in the Origins and Development of the American Constitution," in Herman Belz, Ronald Hoffman, and Peter J. Albert, eds., *To Form a More Perfect Union: The Critical Ideas of the Constitution* (Charlottesville, Va., 1992), 64.

25. U.S. Constitution, Article I, Section 10, in Farrand, ed., *Records of the Federal Convention*, 2:657.

26. Mark Douglas McGarvie, *One Nation Under Law: America's Early National Struggles to Separate Church and State* (DeKalb, Ill., 2004), 173–82.

27. Rev. James Madison to Thomas Madison, Oct. 1, 1787, *DHRC*, 8:30.

28. Charles Pinckney, speech in South Carolina ratifying convention, May 14, 1788, in Bernard Bailyn, ed., *The Debate on the Constitution: Federalist and Antifederalist Speeches, Articles, and Letters During the Struggle over Ratification* (2 vols.; New York, 1993), 2:586; Gouverneur Morris, Aug. 16, 1787, in Farrand, ed., *Records of the Federal Convention*, 2:309; Oliver Ellsworth, Aug. 16, 1787, ibid., 2:310.

29. Luther Martin, *The Genuine Information, Delivered to the Legislature of the State of Maryland, Relative to the Proceedings of the General Convention, Held at Philadelphia, in 1787 . . .* , in Farrand, ed., *Records of the Federal Convention*, 3:214, 206.

30. Davie, speech in North Carolina ratifying convention, July 29, 1788, ibid., 3:350.

31. Read, Aug. 16, 1787, ibid., 2:310.

32. Compare Banning, *Sacred Fire of Liberty*; Robert A. McGuire, *To Form a More Per-*

fect Union: A New Economic Interpretation of the United States Constitution (Oxford, 2003).

33. United States Constitution, Article VI, in Farrand, ed., *Records of the Federal Convention*, 2:663; Hobson, "Negative on State Laws," 228.

34. Hamilton, *Federalist* 78:12, *Federalist* 80:3; Luther Martin, July 21, 1787, Gouverneur Morris, July 23, 1787, in Farrand, ed., *Records of the Federal Convention*, 2:76, 92; Cecelia M. Kenyon, "Men of Little Faith: The Anti-Federalists on the Nature of Representative Government," *WMQ*, 3rd ser., 12 (Jan. 1955), 29–30.

35. Hobson, "Negative on State Laws," 228–29.

36. Thomas Jefferson to Madison, June 20, 1787, in Hutchinson et al., eds., *Papers of James Madison*, 10:64.

37. Madison to Jefferson, Oct. 24, 1787, ibid., 10:211.

38. Gouverneur Morris, July 21, Aug. 15, 1787, in Farrand, ed., *Records of the Federal Convention*, 2:76, 299.

39. "Camillus," *Independent Chronicle*, March 1, 1787.

40. Elizabeth Smith Shaw to Abigail Adams, May 20, 1787, in Lyman H. Butterfield et al., eds., *Adams Family Correspondence* (8 vols. to date; Cambridge, Mass., 1963–), 8:53.

41. Elaine K. Swift, *The Making of an American Senate: Reconstitutive Change in Congress, 1787–1841* (Ann Arbor, Mich., 1996), 28; Bailyn, ed., *The Debate on the Constitution*, 253, 308–11.

42. Rakove, *Original Meanings*, 220.

43. Gerry, July 19, 1787, in Farrand, ed., *Records of the Federal Convention*, 2:57.

44. Compare Don E. Fehrenbacher, *The Slaveholding Republic: An Account of the United States Government's Relations to Slavery*, ed. Ward McAfee (Oxford, 2001), 40.

45. Morris, Aug. 8, 1787, in Farrand, ed., *Records of the Federal Convention*, 2:222.

46. Madison, July 19, 1787, ibid., 2:56–57; Leonard L. Richards, *The Slave Power: The Free North and Southern Domination, 1780–1860* (Baton Rouge, La., 2000), 56–57.

47. Richards, *Slave Power* 42, 68–69, 80; Garry Wills, *"Negro President": Jefferson and the Slave Power* (Boston, 2003).

48. Swift, *Making of an American Senate*, 9.

49. Randolph, May 31, 1787, in Farrand, ed., *Records of the Federal Convention*, 1:51, 58.

50. Morris, July 19, 1787, ibid., 2:52; "Extract of a Letter from a Gentleman in Virginia . . . ," *Independent Gazetteer*, June 26, 1787, *DHRC*, 13:146; Swift, *Making of an American Senate*, 11.

51. Morgan, *Inventing the People*, 250.

52. Rakove, *James Madison*, 57–63.

53. Gerry, Pinckney, Mason, June 7, 1787, in Farrand, ed., *Records of the Federal Convention*, 1:154–56.

54. Dickinson, June 7, 1787, ibid., 1:150.

55. Madison to Jefferson, Aug. 12, 1786, in Hutchinson et al., eds., *Papers of James*

Madison, 9:95; Madison to Washington, Apr. 16, 1787, in Abbot and Twohig, eds., *Papers of George Washington*, 5:147.

56. ["James Madison: Note to His Speech on the Right of Suffrage"], ca. 1821, in Farrand, ed., *Records of the Federal Convention*, 3:454; Swift, *Making of an American Senate*, 49.

57. Gerry, June 12, 1787, in Farrand, ed., *Records of the Federal Convention*, 1:215; Young, "Spirit of Accommodation."

58. Alfred F. Young, "The Framers of the Constitution and the 'Genius' of the People," *Radical History Review* 42 (Fall 1988), 11–13.

59. Hamilton, June 18, 1787, in Farrand, ed., *Records of the Federal Convention*, 1:288, 299.

60. Johnson, June 21, 1787, ibid., 1:366; Douglass G. Adair, *The Intellectual Origins of Jeffersonian Democracy: Republicanism, the Class Struggle, and the Virtuous Farmer*, ed. Mark E. Yellin (Lanham, Md., 2000), 116, 119.

61. Young, "Spirit of Accommodation"; Young, "Genius of the People."

62. Mason, June 26, 1787, Dickinson, June 7, 1787, in Farrand, ed., *Records of the Federal Convention*, 1:428, 150; Swift, *Making of an American Senate*, 48–49.

63. Pinckney, Franklin, June 26, 1787, in Farrand, ed., *Records of the Federal Convention*, 1:426–27; Morris, July 2, 1787, ibid., 1:513.

64. Randolph, Aug. 13, 1787, ibid., 2:278–79.

65. Gerry, Dickinson, Aug. 13, 1787, ibid., 2:275, 278; Wood, *Creation of the Republic*, 563.

66. Carl Lotus Becker, *The History of Political Parties in the Province of New York, 1760–1776* (Madison, Wisc., 1909), 22.

67. Morris, quoted in Richard Brookhiser, *Gentleman Revolutionary: Gouverneur Morris, The Rake Who Wrote the Constitution* (New York, 2003), 20.

68. Ibid., 18–19.

69. Morris, Aug. 15, 1787, in Farrand, ed., *Records of the Federal Convention*, 2:299.

70. Gouverneur Morris, Thomas Fitzsimons, John Dickinson, Aug. 7, 1787, in Farrand, ed., *Records of the Federal Convention*, 2:201–2.

71. Oliver Ellsworth, George Mason, John Rutledge, Pierce Butler, Benjamin Franklin, Aug. 7, 1787, Nathaniel Gorham, Aug. 8, 1787, ibid., 2:201–205, 216; Young, "Spirit of Accommodation," 136–37; Rakove, *Original Meanings*, 226.

72. Madison, Aug. 7, 1787, Rutledge, Aug. 10, 1787, in Farrand, ed., *Records of the Federal Convention*, 2:203, 249; Nedelsky, "Protection of Property," 62.

73. Swift, *Making of an American Senate*, 27.

74. John Adams, "Thoughts on Government," in Robert J. Taylor et al., eds., *Papers of John Adams* (13 vols. to date; Cambridge, Mass., 1977–), 4:90; "The Observator," I, *New Haven Gazette*, Aug. 25, 1785; Jack N. Rakove, *The Beginnings of National Politics: An Interpretive History of the Continental Congress* (Baltimore, 1979), 364.

75. Madison, June 26, 1787, in Farrand, ed., *Records of the Federal Convention*, 1:431.

76. Morris, July 2, 1787, Alexander Hamilton, June 18, 1787, Reed, June 25, 1787, Robert Morris, June 25, 1787, ibid., 1:513–14, 288–89, 409; John Jay to George

Washington, Jan. 7, 1787, in Abbot and Twohig, eds., *Papers of George Washington*, 4:503.

77. Gerry, June 12, 1787, in Farrand, ed., *Records of the Federal Convention*, 1:220.

78. Pierce, June 12, 1787, Edmund Randolph, June 21, 1787, Gerry, June 26, 1787, Morris, July 24, 1787, ibid., 1:218, 360, 432, 2:205.

79. Bailyn, ed., *Debate on the Constitution*, 2:1091.

80. Madison, June 4, 1787, July 25, 1787, in Farrand, ed., *Records of the Federal Convention*, 1:108, 2:110.

81. Morris, Mason, July 21, 1787, Morris, Aug. 15, 1787, ibid., 2:76, 78, 299; John Jay to George Washington, Jan. 7, 1787, in Abbot and Twohig, eds., *Papers of George Washington*, 4:503.

82. Wilson, June 4, 1787, Gerry, July 21, 1787, in Farrand, ed., *Records of the Federal Convention*, 1:107, 2:78.

83. Mason, June 4, 1787, ibid., 1:106, 110.

84. Gouverneur Morris, Aug. 15, 1787, ibid., 2:299.

85. Luther Martin, July 21, 1787, ibid., 2:76.

CHAPTER 12: "DIVIDE ET IMPERA" — STATECRAFT

1. Elaine K. Swift, *The Making of an American Senate: Reconstitutive Change in Congress, 1787–1841* (Ann Arbor, Mich., 1996), 12, 32, 44.

2. "Resolutions Proposed by Mr Randolph in Convention," May 29, 1787, in Max Farrand, ed., *The Records of the Federal Convention of 1787* (3 vols.; New Haven, Conn., 1911), 1:20.

3. William Cranch to John Quincy Adams, Nov. 26, 1787, *DHRC*, 4:318–19.

4. "Giles Hickory" [Noah Webster], "Government," quoted in Carroll Smith-Rosenberg, "Dis-Covering the Subject of the 'Great Constitutional Discussion,' 1786–1789," *JAH* 79 (Dec. 1992), 853.

5. Paterson, June 16, 1787, in Farrand, ed., *Records of the Federal Convention*, 1:250.

6. Wilson, June 21, 1787, Gouverneur Morris, Aug. 8, 1787, Nathaniel Gorham, Aug. 14, 1787, ibid., 1:361, 2:224, 293.

7. Gordon S. Wood, *The Creation of the American Republic, 1776–1787* (Chapel Hill, N.C., 1969), 167.

8. Elbridge Gerry, May 31, June 7, 1787, in Farrand, ed., *Records of the Federal Convention*, 1:48, 154–55.

9. Charles Cotesworth Pinckney, June 6, 1787, John Rutledge, June 21, 1787, ibid., 1:137, 365.

10. Madison, June 12, 1787, ibid., 1:215, 219.

11. Madison, May 31, 1787, ["James Madison: Note to His Speech on the Right of Suffrage"], ca. 1821, James Wilson, June 6, 1787, ibid., 1:56, 3:454, 1:133; "Aristides" [Alexander Contee Hanson], *Remarks on the Proposed Plan of a Federal Government . . .* (Annapolis, Md., 1788) (my thanks to John Leonard for this reference); "An American Citizen," III, *Independent Gazetteer*, Sept. 29, 1787, *DHRC*, 15:525,

13:272; Albert Furtwangler, *The Authority of Publius: A Reading of the Federalist Papers* (Ithaca, N.Y., 1984), 116; Alan Gibson, "Impartial Representation and the Extended Republic: Towards a Comprehensive and Balanced Reading of the Tenth *Federalist* Paper," *History of Political Thought* 12 (Summer 1991), 270, 282–304.

12. ["James Madison: Note to His Speech on the Right of Suffrage"], ca. 1821, in Farrand, ed., *Records of the Federal Convention*, 3:454; ". . . An Old State Soldier . . . ," *Virginia Independent Chronicle*, Feb. 6, 1788, *DHRC*, 8:348.

13. Madison, "Remarks on Mr Jeffersons Draught of a Constitution . . . ," in Julian P. Boyd et al., eds., *The Papers of Thomas Jefferson* (33 vols. to date; Princeton, N.J., 1950–), 6:309; Charles Cotesworth Pinckney, speech in the South Carolina House of Representatives, Jan. 18, 1788, in Jonathan Elliot, ed., *The Debates in the Several State Conventions on the Adoption of the Federal Constitution . . .* (4 vols.; Washington, D.C., 1836), 4:302; Douglass Adair, *Fame and the Founding Fathers: Essays*, ed. Trevor Colbourn (Indianapolis, Ind., 1998), 3–36.

14. William Plumer to Samuel Plumer, Jr., June 6, 9, 17, 1786, William Plumer to John Hale, Aug. 13, 1786, in "Letters of William Plumer, 1786–1787," Colonial Society of Massachusetts, *Publications*, XI, *Transactions, 1906–1907* (Boston, 1910), 385–87.

15. Elizur Goodrich, "A Sermon Preached Before His Excellency Samuel Huntington . . . and the Honorable the General Assembly of the State of Connecticut . . . ," May 10, 1787, in Ellis Sandoz, ed., *Political Sermons of the American Founding Era, 1730–1805* (2nd ed., Indianapolis, Ind., 1998), 920–21; Gordon S. Wood, "Interests and Disinterestedness in the Making of the Constitution," in Richard Beeman, Stephen Botein, and Edward C. Carter II, eds., *Beyond Confederation: Origins of the Constitution and American National Identity* (Chapel Hill, N.C., 1987), 84–89.

16. George Mason, June 6, 1787, in Farrand, ed., *Records of the Federal Convention*, 1:134, 142.

17. Elbridge Gerry, James Wilson, June 7, 1787, ibid., 1:154–55.

18. James Madison, June 7, 1787, ibid., 1:154.

19. Gouverneur Morris, Madison, July 19, 1787, ibid., 2:54, 56–57; Catherine Drinker Bowen, *Miracle at Philadelphia: The Story of the Constitutional Convention, May to September, 1787* (Boston, [1966]), 42.

20. Gouverneur Morris, July 19, 1787, in Farrand, ed., *Records of the Federal Convention*, 2:54; [Webster], "An Examination into the Leading Principles of the Federal Constitution," in Bernard Bailyn, ed., *The Debate on the Constitution: Federalist and Antifederalist Speeches, Articles, and Letters During the Struggle over Ratification* (2 vols.; New York, 1993), 1:133, 140n.

21. Hamilton, *Federalist* 84:22; "Federal Farmer," *An Additional Number of Letters from the Federal Farmer to the Republican; Leading to a Fair Examination of the System of Government, Proposed by the Late Convention . . .* ([New York], 1788), IX, *DHRC*, 17:291.

22. Thomas Paine, *Common Sense and Other Writings*, ed. Nelson F. Adkins (Indianapolis, Ind., 1953), 31.

23. Madison, July 10, 1787, in Farrand, ed., *Records of the Federal Convention*, 1:568; Melancton Smith, June 20, 1788, John Williams, June 21, 1788, in Elliot, ed., *Debates in the State Conventions*, 2:229–30, 242; Edmund S. Morgan, "Safety in Numbers: Madison, Hume, and the Tenth *Federalist*," *Huntington Library Quarterly* 49 (Spring 1986), 106.

24. Gorham, Washington, Sept. 17, 1787, in Farrand, ed., *Records of the Federal Convention*, 2:643–44; Alfred F. Young, "Conservatives, the Constitution, and the 'Spirit of Accommodation,'" in Robert A. Goldwin and William A. Schambra, eds., *How Democratic Is the Constitution?* (Washington, D.C., 1980), 135; Jack N. Rakove, *Original Meanings: Politics and Ideas in the Making of the Constitution* (New York, 1996), 228.

25. George Mason, Aug. 13, 1787, in Farrand, ed., *Records of the Federal Convention*, 2:273; Edmund S. Morgan, *Inventing the People: The Rise of Popular Sovereignty in England and America* (New York, 1988), 268–69.

26. Larry D. Kramer, "Madison's Audience," *Harvard Law Review* 112 (Jan. 1999), 611–79; Robert J. Morgan, "Madison's Theory of Representation in the Tenth *Federalist*," *Journal of Politics* 36 (Nov. 1974), 852–55.

27. Madison, *Federalist* 10:22, 63:8; "The Petition of the Committee of Public Creditors of the City and Liberties of Philadelphia," *Pennsylvania Gazette*, Dec. 15, 1784; Elizabeth-Town dateline, *New Jersey Journal, and Political Intelligencer*, Oct. 4, 1786; "Camillus," *Worcester Magazine* 3:1 (1st week of Apr. 1787), 3; "Extract of a Letter from South-Kingstown, July 4," *Providence Gazette*, July 14, 1787.

28. Charles Cotesworth Pinckney, speech in South Carolina ratifying convention, May 14, 1788, in Bailyn, ed., *Debate on the Constitution*, 2:586; Garry Wills, *Explaining America: The Federalist* (London, 1981), 205.

29. George Mason, Aug. 13, 1787, in Farrand, ed., *Records of the Federal Convention*, 2:273–74.

30. Charles Cotesworth Pinckney, speech in South Carolina ratifying convention, May 14, 1788, in Bailyn, ed., *Debate on the Constitution*, 2:586; Wills, *Explaining America*, 205.

31. Hamilton, *Federalist* 60:3.

32. Gouverneur Morris, July 19, 1787, in Farrand, ed., *Records of the Federal Convention*, 2:54.

33. Drew McCoy, *The Last of the Fathers: James Madison and the Republican Legacy* (Cambridge, U.K., 1989), 73; Madison, June 6, 1787, in Farrand, ed., *Records of the Federal Convention*, 1:136; Madison, *Federalist* 63:8.

34. Madison, *Federalist* 63:8.

35. Madison to Thomas Jefferson, Oct. 24, 1787, in William T. Hutchinson et al., eds., *The Papers of James Madison* (17 vols. to date; Chicago, 1962–), 10:214; Madison, June 6, 1787, in Farrand, ed., *Records of the Federal Convention*, 1:136; Madison, *Federalist* 10:20–22; Douglass Adair, *The Intellectual Origins of Jeffersonian Democ-*

racy: Republicanism, the Class Struggle, and the Virtuous Farmer (New York, 2000), 123. (My thanks to Loren Young for his insight on this point.)

36. [Whiting], "Some Remarks on the Conduct of the Inhabitants of the Commonwealth of Massachusetts in Interupting The Siting of the Jucicial Courts . . ." (Dec. 1786), in Stephen T. Riley, ed., "Dr. William Whiting and Shays' Rebellion," AAS *Proceedings* 66 (1957), 153; Madison, *Federalist* 10:20; Madison, "Vices of the Political System of the U. States," [Apr.–June 1787], in Hutchinson et al., eds., *Papers of James Madison*, 9:356–57. Cherishing at once a republican belief in the importance of electing virtuous statesmen and a liberal realization that most people were actually pretty selfish, the Framers sought institutions that would force selfish constituents to choose virtuous representatives. Wood, *Creation of the Republic*, 475; John M. Murrin, "Fundamental Values, the Founding Fathers, and the Constitution," in Herman Belz, Ronald Hoffman, and Peter J. Albert, eds., *To Form a More Perfect Union: The Critical Ideas of the Constitution* (Charlottesville, Va., 1992), 30–31; Joyce Appleby, "The American Heritage: The Heirs and the Dis- inherited," *JAH* 74 (Dec. 1987), 803; Alan Gibson, "Impartial Representation and the Extended Republic: Towards a Comprehensive and Balanced Reading of the Tenth *Federalist* Paper," *History of Political Thought* 12 (Summer 1991), 302–4.

37. Gouverneur Morris, July 2, 1787, in Farrand, ed., *Records of the Federal Convention*, 1:514.

38. Gerry, July 25, 1787, Mason, July 26, 1787, ibid., 2:114, 119.

39. George Washington to Thomas Jefferson, Aug. 1, 1786, in W. W. Abbot and Dorothy Twohig, eds., *The Papers of George Washington*, Confederation Series (6 vols.; Charlottesville, Va., 1992–97), 4:184; Minor Myers, Jr., *Liberty without Anarchy: A History of the Society of the Cincinnati* (Charlottesville, Va., 1983), x, 95–96.

40. W[illiam] Eustis to Henry Knox, Feb. 3, 1785, Knox Papers (microfilm), box 17, item 165, MHS; E[lbridge] Gerry to Rufus King, Mar. 28, 1785, in Charles R. King, ed., *The Life and Correspondence of Rufus King, Comprising His Letters, Private and Official, His Public Documents, and His Speeches* (New York, 1894), 1:83; Sidney Kaplan, "Veteran Officers and Politics in Massachusetts, 1783–1787," *WMQ*, 3rd ser., 9 (Jan. 1952), 29–57.

41. George Flint, quoted in E. James Ferguson, *The Power of the Purse: A History of American Public Finance, 1776–1790* (Chapel Hill, N.C., 1961), 254; "The Remonstrance and Petition of the Proprietors of Loan-Office Certificates, in the City and Neighbourhood of Philadelphia, by Their Committee Chosen and Instructed for that Purpose, at a General Meeting of the Said Proprietors," *Independent Gazetteer*, Sept. 14, 1782; David Austin and Isaac Beers, announcement, *Middlesex Gazette*, Feb. 26, 1787; Benjamin Lincoln to Theodore Sedgwick, June 24, 1789, Sedgwick Family Papers, MHS; Joseph Stancliffe Davis, *Essays in the Earlier History of American Corporations* (2 vols.; London, 1917), 1:179; Alfred F. Young, *The Democratic Republicans of New York: The Origins 1763–1797* (Chapel Hill, N.C., 1967), 76; Myers, *Liberty without Anarchy*, 10.

42. Gerry to Rufus King, Mar. 28, 1785, in King, ed., *Life and Correspondence of Rufus King*, 83.

43. New York Chamber of Commerce, petition against paper money, *Independent Journal*, Mar. 8, 1786; Lynn W. Turner, *William Plumer of New Hampshire, 1759–1850* (Chapel Hill, N.C., 1962), 28.

44. William Manning, "The Key of Libberty: Shewing the Causes Why a Free Government has Always Failed & a Reamedy Against It . . . ," in Michael Merrill and Sean Wilentz, eds., *The Key of Liberty: The Life and Democratic Writings of William Manning, "A Laborer," 1747–1814* (Cambridge, Mass., 1993), 157.

45. Gouverneur Morris, July 2, 1787, in Farrand, ed., *Records of the Federal Convention*, 1:514; Laurel Thatcher Ulrich, *A Midwife's Tale: The Life of Martha Ballard, Based on Her Diary, 1785–1812* (New York, 1990), 91.

46. "Philodemus" [Thomas Tudor Tucker], *Conciliatory Hints, Attempting, By a Fair State of Matters, To Remove Party-Prejudices . . . And Proposing a Convention . . .* (Charleston, S.C., 1784), 29; Worcester County convention, proceedings, Sept. 26–28, 1786, *Worcester Magazine* 2:27 (1st week of Oct. 1786), 318; [William Whiting], "Some Remarks on the Conduct of the Inhabitants," 153; "Plain Reason," *Virginia Independent Chronicle*, Aug. 29, 1787.

47. "Discipulus," *New Hampshire Mercury*, Oct. 18, 1786. The legislative committee counted the number of citizens who had voted for and against paper money in the various town meetings and determined that it had lost by one vote. Jere R. Daniell, *Experiment in Republicanism: New Hampshire Politics and the American Revolution, 1741–1794* (Cambridge, Mass., 1970), 198–99; John H. Flannagan, Jr., "Trying Times: Economic Depression in New Hampshire, 1781–1789" (Ph.D. diss., Georgetown University, 1972), 306.

48. George Richards Minot, *History of the Insurrections in 1786 and of the Rebellion Consequent Thereon* (orig. pub. 1810; New York, 1971), 68; Massachusetts General Court, "Address to the People," *Worcester Magazine* 2:37 (2nd week in Dec. 1786), 444.

49. Mercer, Aug. 7, 1787, in Farrand, ed., *Records of the Federal Convention*, 2:205; Madison, "Remarks on Mr Jeffersons Draught of a Constitution," in Boyd et al., eds., *Papers of Thomas Jefferson*, 6:309.

50. [Herman Husband], *Proposals to Amend and Perfect the Policy of the Government of the United States of America, or, The Fulfilling of the Prophecies in the Latter Days, Commenced by the Independence of America* (Philadelphia, 1782), 8.

51. Charles Pinckney, Madison, Charles Cotesworth Pinckney, June 6, 1787, in Farrand, ed., *Records of the Federal Convention*, 1:132, 134, 137.

52. Charles Cotesworth Pinckney, Madison, June 26, 1787, ibid., 1:421, 423.

53. Wilson, June 4, 1787, ibid., 1:107.

54. Sherman, May 31, June 4, 7, 1787, ibid., 1:48, 99, 150.

CHAPTER 13: "MORE ADEQUATE TO THE PURPOSES"—REVENUE

1. Morris, Aug. 16, 1787, in Max Farrand, ed., *The Records of the Federal Convention of 1787* (3 vols.; New Haven, Conn., 1911), 2:307.

2. David Humphreys to George Washington, April 9, 1787, in W. W. Abbot and Dorothy Twohig, eds., *The Papers of George Washington*, Confederation Series (6 vols.; Charlottesville, Va., 1992–1997), 5:132.

3. Hamilton to Edward Carrington, May 26, 1792, in Farrand, ed., *Records of the Federal Convention*, 3:366–67.

4. Hamilton, June 18, 1787, ibid., 1:297.

5. "A Talk sent from Oconestota, the Corn Tassel & other head men of the Overhill Cherokees by the Warrior Sculacotta of that place to their brother & friend Le Roy Hammond," enclosed in Hammond to Benjamin Guerard, Dec. 27, 1784, Governor's Message no. 320, General Assembly Records, SCDAH.

6. "A Speech of the Five Nations to the Western Indians Novr., 1786," in Francis Jennings, ed., *Iroquois Indians: A Documentary History of the Diplomacy of the Six Nations and Their League* (microfilm, 50 reels, Woodbridge, Conn., 1984), reel 38.

7. Ibid.

8. Quoted in Richard White, *The Middle Ground: Indians, Empires, and the Republics in the Great Lakes Region, 1650–1815* (Cambridge, U.K., 1991), 434.

9. Winchester dateline, *Virginia Gazette and Winchester Advertiser*, July 25, 1787; Daniel Claus to Evan Nepean, May 5, 1787, CO 42/19, f. 128.

10. Daniel Claus to Evan Nepean, May 5, 1787, CO 42/19, f. 128.

11. Gregory Evans Dowd, *A Spirited Resistance: The North American Indian Struggle for Unity, 1745–1815* (Baltimore, 1992), 99.

12. Randolph, June 16, 1787, in Farrand, ed., *Records of the Federal Convention*, 1:273; "Extract from a Thanksgiving Sermon, Delivered in the County of Middlesex," *Worcester Magazine* 2:41 (2nd week of Jan. 1787), 493.

13. James Wilson, July 18, 1787, in Farrand, ed., *Records of the Federal Convention*, 2:47.

14. Madison, speech in Virginia ratifying convention, June 14, 1788, *DHRC*, 10:1294.

15. Madison to George Washington, Feb. 21, 1787, in Abbot and Twohig, eds., *Papers of George Washington*, 5:46.

16. William Grayson to Madison, Nov. 22, 1786, in William T. Hutchinson et al., eds., *The Papers of James Madison* (17 vols. to date; Chicago, 1962–), 9:174; Edward Carrington to Edmund Randolph, Dec. 8, 1786, in Paul H. Smith et al., eds., *Letters of Delegates to Congress, 1774–1789* (26 vols.; Washington, D.C., 1976–2000), 24:45; Thomas C. Cochran, *New York in the Confederation: An Economic Study* (orig. pub. 1932; Port Washington, N.Y., 1970), 179; David P. Szatmary, *Shays' Rebellion: The Making of an Agrarian Insurrection* (Amherst, Mass., 1980), 82–84.

17. Washington to Madison, Dec. 16, 1786, in Abbot and Twohig, eds., *Papers of George Washington*, 4:457–58; North Callahan, *Henry Knox: General Washington's General* (New York, 1958), 216.

18. Washington, quoted in Rock Brynner, "'Fire Beneath Our Feet': Shays' Rebel-

lion and Its Constitutional Impact" (Ph.D. diss., Columbia University, 1993), 208, 208n.

19. Washington to Madison, Nov. 18, 1786, in Abbot and Twohig, eds., *Papers of George Washington*, 4:383; Brynner, "Fire Beneath Our Feet," 207–8.

20. Gordon S. Wood, *The Radicalism of the American Revolution* (New York, 1992), 209; Brynner, "Fire Beneath Our Feet," 214, 220–21, 238.

21. Washington to Henry Lee, Jr., Oct. 31, 1786, in Abbot and Twohig, eds., *Papers of George Washington*, 4:318.

22. Washington, quoted in Peter H. Wood, "'Liberty Is Sweet': African-American Freedom Struggles in the Years before White Independence," in Alfred F. Young, ed., *Beyond the American Revolution: Explorations in the History of American Radicalism* (DeKalb, Ill., 1993), 170.

23. Washington to Humphreys, Oct. 22, 1786, in Abbot and Twohig, eds., *Papers of George Washington*, 4:297.

24. Washington to David Stuart, Dec. 6, 1786, and to Henry Knox, Dec. 26, 1786, ibid., 4:446, 482.

25. Washington to Madison, Nov. 5, 1786, and to David Humphreys, Dec. 26, 1786, ibid., 4:331, 479; Szatmary, *Shays' Rebellion*, 127; Brynner, "Fire Beneath Our Feet," 180–217; Leonard L. Richards, *Shays's Rebellion: The American Revolution's Final Battle* (Philadelphia, 2002), 1–3.

26. Washington to Henry Lee, Jr., Oct. 31, 1786, in Abbot and Twohig, eds., *Papers of George Washington*, 4:319.

27. Randolph to George Washington, Jan. 4, 1787, ibid., 4:501.

28. Washington to Randolph, Mar. 28, 1787, ibid., 5:113; Brynner, "Fire Beneath Our Feet," 209–10.

29. Charleston dateline, *Independent Chronicle*, July 13, 1786; Savannah dateline, *New Jersey Journal and Political Intelligencer*, June 20, 1787; Charleston dateline, *Independent Chronicle*, June 29, 1786; Savannah dateline, *Charleston Morning Post*, Oct. 26, 1786; Savannah dateline, *New Hampshire Spy*, Feb. 16, 1787.

30. Martin, Aug. 21, 1787, King, Gouverneur Morris, Aug. 8, 1787, in Farrand, ed., *Records of the Federal Convention*, 2:364, 220, 222.

31. Mason, Aug. 22, 1787, ibid., 2:370; Nathan Dane to Edward Pulling, Jan. 8, 1786, in Smith et al., eds., *Letters of Delegates to Congress*, 23:85.

32. King, Aug. 8, 1787, in Farrand, ed., *Records of the Federal Convention*, 2:220.

33. Gorham, Aug. 22, 29, 1787, Gouverneur Morris, Aug. 29, 1787, ibid., 2:374, 453, 450.

34. Rutledge, Aug. 21, 1787, Charles Pinckney, Hugh Williamson, Aug. 29, 1787, ibid., 2:364, 449–50.

35. Madison, Aug. 16, 29, 1787, ibid., 2:306–7, 452; Douglas B. Chambers, *Murder at Montpelier: Igbo Africans in Virginia* (Jackson, Miss., 2005), 5–9.

36. Pinckney, Aug. 29, 1787, in Farrand, ed., *Records of the Federal Convention*, 2:449–50.

37. William K. Boyd, review of *The Framing of the Constitution of the United States*, by Max Farrand, and *An Economic Interpretation of the Constitution of the United States*,

by Charles Beard, *South Atlantic Quarterly* 12 (July 1913), 272; Robert E. Brown, *Charles Beard and the Constitution: A Critical Analysis of "An Economic Interpretation of the Constitution"* (New York, 1956), 61; Forrest McDonald, *We the People: The Economic Origins of the Constitution* (Chicago, 1958), 11.

38. John Jay, *Federalist* 3:11.

CHAPTER 14: "TAKE UP THE REINS"—RATIFICATION

1. Paterson, June 16, 1787, in Max Farrand, ed., *The Records of the Federal Convention of 1787* (3 vols.; New Haven, Conn., 1911), 1:274; "Agrippa," XIV, *Massachusetts Gazette*, Jan. 29, 1788, *DHRC*, 5:822.
2. John Quincy Adams to William Cranch, Oct. 14, 1787, *DHRC*, 4:74.
3. Morris, quoted in Eric Foner, *Tom Paine and Revolutionary America* (updated ed.; New York, 2005), 190.
4. Madison, June 6, 1787, in Farrand, ed., *Records of the Federal Convention*, 1:134; Rev. James Madison to James Madison, [ca. Oct. 1, 1787], in William T. Hutchinson et al., eds., *The Papers of James Madison* (17 vols. to date; Chicago, 1962–), 10:184.
5. "A Citizen of Philadelphia" [Pelatiah Webster], *The Weaknesses of Brutus Exposed: or, Some Remarks in Vindication of the Constitution Proposed by the Late Federal Convention, Against the Objections and Gloomy Fears of that Writer* (Philadelphia, 1787), 18.
6. Edmund Pendleton to James Madison, Oct. 8, 1787, *DHRC*, 10:1773; Charles Pinckney, May 20, 1788, in Jonathan Elliot, ed., *The Debates in the Several State Conventions on the Adoption of the Federal Constitution . . .* (4 vols.; Washington, D.C., 1836), 4:333; William Davie, speech in the North Carolina ratifying convention, July 29, 1788, in Farrand, ed., *Records of the Federal Convention*, 3:350; ["Extract of a Letter from Salem County, West Jersey, 22 October"], *Pennsylvania Herald*, Oct. 27, 1787, *DHRC*, 3:140–41; James Wilson, speech in Pennsylvania ratifying convention, Dec. 4, 1787, in Elliot, ed., *Debates in the State Conventions*, 2:486.
7. "A Freeholder," *Virginia Independent Chronicle*, Apr. 9, 23, 1788, *DHRC*, 9:727, 754.
8. Hamilton, "Conjectures About the New Constitution," Sept. 1787?, in Bernard Bailyn, ed., *The Debate on the Constitution: Federalist and Antifederalist Speeches, Articles, and Letters During the Struggle over Ratification* (2 vols.; New York, 1993), 1:9.
9. Hunter, quoted in Brown, *Redeeming the Republic*, 227; Logan & Story to Stephen Collins, Nov. 2, 1787, *DHRC*, 8:141.
10. Smith to John Dolbeare, Nov. 15, 1787, *DHRC*, 4:236.
11. Ramsay, speech, May 27, 1788, in Bailyn, ed., *Debate on the Constitution*, 2:508–9.
12. "A True Friend," *Virginia Independent Chronicle*, Nov. 14, 1787, *DHRC*, 8:161; "A Native of Virginia," *Observations Upon the Proposed Plan of Federal Government . . .*, *DHRC*, 9:692; "A Dialogue Between Mr. Schism and Mr. Cutbrush," *Boston Gazette*, Oct. 29, 1787, *DHRC*, 4:165; "Truth," *Massachusetts Centinel*, Nov. 24, 1787, *DHRC*, 4:235.
13. William Allason to John Likely, May 24, 1788, *DHRC*, 9:588.
14. Ramsay, speech, May 27, 1788, in Bailyn, ed., *Debate on the Constitution*, 2:508;

Thomas Jefferson to James Madison, Dec. 16, 1786, in Hutchinson et al., eds., *Papers of James Madison*, 9:212–13.

15. Max M. Mintz, *Gouverneur Morris and the American Revolution* (Norman, Okla., 1970), 164–65, 173–75.

16. Ibid., 163.

17. Joshua B. Osgood to George Thatcher, Oct. 8, 1787, *DHRC*, 4:58.

18. "Extract of a letter from a Gentleman at Williamsburgh, Virginia to his Friend in Edinburgh, dated January 6, 1788," *Independent Chronicle*, May 22, 1788, *DHRC*, 9:843.

19. "A Freeholder," *Virginia Independent Chronicle*, Apr. 23, 1788, *DHRC*, 9:754.

20. Washington to John Armstrong, Sr., Apr. 25, 1788, *DHRC*, 9:761; John H. Flannagan, Jr., "Trying Times: Economic Depression in New Hampshire, 1781–1789" (Ph.D. diss., Georgetown University, 1972), 340.

21. "A Native of Virginia," *Observations Upon the Proposed Plan of Federal Government . . .* , *DHRC*, 9:692.

22. "Landholder" [Ellsworth] II, *Connecticut Courant*, Nov. 12, 1787, *DHRC*, 3:402; Henry Knox to George Washington, Feb. 14, 1788, *DHRC*, 7:1698; Jean Toscan, "Memoire Sur Differents Objets Relatifs à L'Etat du New Hampshire Pour L'Année 1787," Dec. 31, 1787, Toscan Papers, box 1, folder 13, NHHS; Jean de Crèvecoeur to William Short, Apr. 1, 1788, *DHRC*, 9:636; "Civis" [David Ramsay], *Columbian Herald*, Feb. 4, 1788, in Bailyn, ed., *Debate on the Constitution*, 2:153; William Allason to John Likely, May 24, 1788, *DHRC*, 9:588.

23. William Symmes, Jr., to Peter Osgood, Jr., Nov. 15, 1787, *DHRC*, 4:240; Madison to Washington, Oct. 14, 1787, in Hutchinson et al., eds., *Papers of James Madison*, 10:194.

24. Randolph to Madison, Oct. [29], 1787, in Hutchinson et al., eds., *Papers of James Madison*, 10:230.

25. Madison, quoted in Charles A. Beard, *An Economic Interpretation of the Constitution of the United States* (New York, 1913), 293.

26. For criticism of Article I, Section 10, see Luther Martin, *The Genuine Information, Delivered to the Legislature of the State of Maryland, Relative to the Proceedings of the General Convention, Held at Philadelphia, in 1787 . . .* , in Farrand, ed., *Records of the Federal Convention*, 3:214–15; anonymous essay, *Massachusetts Gazette*, Oct. 9, 1787, *DHRC*, 4:61.

27. Calvin H. Johnson, *Righteous Anger at the Wicked States: The Meaning of the Founders' Constitution* (Cambridge, U.K., 2005), 7.

28. Cecelia M. Kenyon, "Men of Little Faith: The Anti-Federalists on the Nature of Representative Government," *WMQ* 3rd ser., 12 (Jan. 1955), 32 n.

29. Mason, Aug. 16, 1787, in Farrand, ed., *Records of the Federal Convention*, 2:309; Gerry, June 7, 8, 1787, ibid., 1:154–55, 165; Edmund Randolph to Thomas Jefferson, July 12, 1786, in Julian P. Boyd et al., eds., *The Papers of Thomas Jefferson* (33 vols. to date; Princeton, N.J., 1950–), 10:133; Samuel Bryan, *The Letters of Centinel: Attacks on the U.S. Constitution, 1787–1788*, ed. Warren Hope (Ardmore, Pa.,

1998), 119; James B. Schick, "The Antifederalist Ideology in Virginia, 1787–1788" (Ph.D. diss., Indiana University, 1971), 305, 314.

30. ". . . An Old State Soldier . . . ," II, *Virginia Independent Chronicle*, Feb. 6, 1788, *DHRC*, 8:347.

31. [Webster], "Political Paragraphs: Connecticut," *Connecticut Courant*, Nov. 20, 1786; Webster, *Pennsylvania Gazette*, May 9, 1787; [Webster], "Examination into the Leading Principles of the Federal Constitution," in Bailyn, ed., *Debate on the Constitution*, 1:132; Sean Wilentz, *The Rise of American Democracy: Jefferson to Lincoln* (New York, 2005), 3–4.

32. Gordon Wood, "Democracy and the Constitution," in Robert A. Goldwin and William A. Schambra, eds., *How Democratic Is the Constitution?* (Washington, D.C., 1980), 15, 16.

33. "A.B.," *Hampshire Gazette*, Jan. 9, 1788, *DHRC*, 5:671.

34. [Webster], "An Examination into the Leading Principles of the Federal Constitution," in Bailyn, ed., *Debate on the Constitution*, 1:133, 140n.

35. Ibid., 1:140.

36. "Americanus" [John Stevens, Jr.], I, *Daily Advertiser*, Nov. 2, 1787, ibid., 1:229–30.

37. James Madison to Thomas Jefferson, Oct. 24, 1787, [Madison], "Consolidation," *National Gazette*, Dec. 5, 1791, in Hutchinson et al., eds., *Papers of James Madison*, 10:214, 14:138; Colleen A. Sheehan, "The Politics of Public Opinion: James Madison's 'Notes on Government,'" *WMQ*, 3rd ser., 49 (Oct. 1992), 614.

38. Elbridge Gerry, George Mason, Edmund Randolph, May 31, 1787, in Farrand, ed., *Records of the Federal Convention*, 1:48, 49, 51; Gordon S. Wood, *The Creation of the American Republic, 1776–1787* (Chapel Hill, N.C., 1969), 484.

39. "Brutus," I, *New York Journal*, Oct. 18, 1787, *DHRC*, 13:417; Kenyon, "Men of Little Faith"; Bernard Bailyn, *The Ideological Origins of the American Revolution* (enlarged ed., Cambridge, Mass., 1992), 347–49; Rosemarie Zagarri, *The Politics of Size: Representation in the United States, 1776–1850* (Ithaca, N.Y., 1987), 86, 93–94.

40. Hamilton, *Federalist* 60:3; "Brutus," I, *New York Journal*, Oct. 18, 1787, *DHRC*, 13:420.

41. "Cornelius," *Hampshire Chronicle*, Dec. 18, 1787, *DHRC*, 4:412; Zagarri, *Politics of Size*, 91–93.

42. Adam Smith, *The Theory of Moral Sentiments*, ed. D. D. Raphael and A. L. Macfie (orig. pub. 1759; Indianapolis, Ind., 1984), 86, 90; "Federal Farmer," *An Additional Number of Letters . . . , DHRC*, 17:281; George Mason, June 4, June 11, June 16, 1788, Patrick Henry, June 12, 1788, Edmund Randolph, June 6, June 17, 1788, George Nicholas, June 14, 1788, in Elliot, ed., *Debates in the State Conventions*, 3:30–31, 34, 262, 264, 426, 327, 123, 470, 393.

43. John Quincy Adams to William Cranch, Dec. 8, 1787, Benjamin Gale, speech, Nov. 12, 1787, "O," *American Herald*, Feb. 4, 1788, "Federal Farmer," *Observations Leading to a Fair Examination of the System of Government Proposed by the Late Convention . . . and to Several Essential and Necessary Alterations in It . . .* (New York, 1787), "Brutus," III, *New York Journal*, Nov. 15, 1787, *DHRC*, 4:401, 3:423, 5:855, 14:31, 123.

44. James Madison, May 31, June 26, 1787, ["James Madison: Note to His Speech on the Right of Suffrage"], in Farrand, ed., *Records of the Federal Convention*, 1:50, 431, 3:451.

45. Madison, *Federalist* 57:14; Hamilton, *Federalist* 35:5–11.

46. Melancton Smith, June 21, 1788, in Elliot, *Debates in the State Conventions*, 2:246; "Federal Farmer," *Additional Number of Letters*, DHRC, 17:280, 313–14; "A Real Farmer," *Hampshire Chronicle*, Nov. 5, 1788, in Merrill Jensen et al., eds., *The Documentary History of the First Federal Elections, 1788–1790* (4 vols.; Madison, Wisc., 1976–89), 1:471–72.

47. "Cornelius," *Hampshire Chronicle*, Dec. 18, 1787, DHRC, 4:414; Madison, *Federalist* 63:8; "Federal Farmer," *Additional Number of Letters*, DHRC, 17:312; Kenyon, "Men of Little Faith," 12–13, 40–41; William B. Allen, "Federal Representation: The Design of the Thirty-fifth *Federalist Paper*," *Publius* 6 (Summer 1976), 67.

48. Lansing, June 20, 1788, in Elliot, ed., *Debates in the State Conventions*, 2:218.

49. "Agrippa," XV, *Massachusetts Gazette*, Jan. 29, 1788, DHRC, 5:824; "Poplicola," *Boston Gazette*, Dec. 24, 1787, DHRC, 5:509–10; "A.B.," *Massachusetts Gazette*, Nov. 20, 1787, DHRC, 4:278–79; Melancton Smith, June 20, 1788, in Elliot, ed., *Debates in the State Conventions*, 2:225–26; "Lycurgus III" [Herman Husband], *XIV Sermons on the Characters of Jacob's Fourteen Sons* (Philadelphia, 1789), 20.

50. Benjamin Lincoln to George Washington, Feb. 3, 1788, DHRC, 7:1573.

Chapter 15: "More Productive and Less Oppressive"—Taxes

1. Philadelphia dateline, *Independent Gazetteer*, Aug. 22, 1787; "Freeholder," *Virginia Independent Chronicle*, Apr. 23, 1788, DHRC, 9:754; Hamilton, "The Defence of the Funding System" (July 1795), in Harold C. Syrett, ed., *The Papers of Alexander Hamilton* (26 vols.; New York, 1961–87), 19:5; Forrest McDonald, *E Pluribus Unum: The Formation of the American Republic, 1776–1790* (Boston, 1965), 34; E. James Ferguson, *The Power of the Purse: A History of American Public Finance, 1776–1790* (Chapel Hill, N.C., 1961), 340–41; Robert A. McGuire and Robert L. Ohsfeldt, "Economic Interests and the American Constitution: A Quantitative Rehabilitation of Charles A. Beard," *Journal of Economic History* 44 (June 1984), 509–19; John K. Alexander, *The Selling of the Constitutional Convention: A History of News Coverage* (Madison, Wisc., 1990), 148–49; Robert A. McGuire, *To Form a More Perfect Union: A New Economic Interpretation of the United States Constitution* (Oxford, 2003).

2. Lee to Washington, Apr. 11, 1788, DHRC, 9:734–35.

3. Benjamin Gale, speech to Killingworth town meeting, Nov. 12, 1787, DHRC, 3:422; "A Federalist," *Boston Gazette*, Nov. 26, 1787, DHRC, 4:322.

4. John Quincy Adams to William Cranch, Oct. 14, 1787, DHRC, 4:73.

5. Elbridge Gerry to James Warren, Oct. 18, 1787, DHRC, 4:94.

6. "Lycurgus III" [Herman Husband], *XIV Sermons on the Characters of Jacob's Fourteen Sons* (Philadelphia, 1789), 19; [Husband], *A Dialogue between an Assembly-man*

and a Convention-Man On the Subject of the State Constitution of Pennsylvania . . . (Philadelphia, n.d.), 11; Genesis 49:14–15.

7. "A Freeholder," *Virginia Independent Chronicle*, Apr. 9, 1788, *DHRC*, 9:727; Hamilton, "Conjectures About the New Constitution," [Sept. 1787], in Syrett, ed., *Papers of Alexander Hamilton*, 4:275.

8. "One of the Middle-Interest," *Massachusetts Centinel*, Dec. 5, 1787, *DHRC*, 4:388; "West-Chester Farmer," *New York Daily Advertiser*, June 8, 1787; "A Correspondent," Philadelphia dateline, *New Jersey Journal, and Political Intelligencer*, Aug. 15, 1787; Francis Corbin, speech in Virginia ratifying convention, June 7, 1788, *DHRC*, 9:1008, 1011.

9. "Connecticut Farmer," *Middlesex Gazette*, Sept. 11, 1786.

10. "A Freeholder," *Virginia Independent Chronicle*, Apr. 9, 1788, *DHRC*, 9:729; Hamilton, *Federalist* 12:12; Roger H. Brown, *Redeeming the Republic: Federalists, Taxation, and the Origins of the Constitution* (Baltimore, 1993), 213.

11. The fourth state to ratify early on was Pennsylvania. "A Farmer," *New Haven Gazette and Connecticut Magazine*, Oct. 18, 1787; Brown, *Redeeming the Republic*, 213.

12. Wadsworth, speech in Connecticut House of Representatives, May 12, 1787, *Middlesex Gazette*, May 28, 1787; Genesis 49:14–15.

13. Williamson, speech, Nov. 8, 1787, in Bernard Bailyn, ed., *The Debate on the Constitution: Federalist and Antifederalist Speeches, Articles, and Letters During the Struggle over Ratification* (2 vols.; New York, 1993), 2:233–34.

14. George Mason, speech in Virginia ratifying convention, June 11, 1788, *DHRC*, 9:1156.

15. Preston, Connecticut, town meeting, Nov. 26, 1787, *DHRC*, 3:440; Patrick T. Conley, "First in War, Last in Peace: Rhode Island and the Constitution, 1786–1790," in Conley and John P. Kaminski, eds., *The Constitution and the States: The Role of the Original Thirteen in the Framing and Adoption of the Federal Constitution* (Madison, Wisc., 1988), 281.

16. "Vox Populi," *Massachusetts Gazette*, Nov. 13, 1787, *DHRC*, 4:224–25.

17. Anonymous essay, *Massachusetts Centinel*, Oct. 13, 1787, *DHRC*, 4:70; William Cranch to John Quincy Adams, Nov. 26, 1787, *DHRC*, 4:319.

18. "An Undelivered Defense of a Winning Cause: Charles Carroll of Carrollton's 'Remarks on the Proposed Federal Constitution,'" ed. Edward C. Papenfuse, *Maryland Historical Magazine* 71 (Summer 1976), 246; "A Plebeian" [Melancton Smith], "An Address to the People of the State of New York . . . ," in Paul Leicester Ford, ed., *Pamphlets on the Constitution of the United States, Published During its Discussion by the People, 1787–1788* (Brooklyn, N.Y., 1888), 107; "The Observer," III, X, *Pennsylvania Gazette*, Nov. 18, 1789, Jan. 6, 1790; Max M. Edling, *A Revolution in Favor of Government: Origins of the U.S. Constitution and the Making of the American State* (Oxford, 2003), 203.

19. Rodney, quoted in Brown, *Redeeming the Republic*, 212.

20. John H. Flannagan, Jr., "Trying Times: Economic Depression in New Hampshire, 1781–1789" (Ph.D. diss., Georgetown University, 1972), 349–50.

21. "The Republican Federalist," V, *Massachusetts Centinel*, Jan. 19, 1788, *DHRC*, 5:751; Genesis 25:29–34.
22. Alfred F. Young, "The Framers of the Constitution and the 'Genius' of the People," *Radical History Review* 42 (Fall 1998), 16; Alfred F. Young, "Conservatives, the Constitution, and the 'Spirit of Accommodation,'" in Robert A. Goldwin and William A. Schambra, eds., *How Democratic Is the Constitution?* (Washington, D.C., 1980), 143–47; Eric Foner, *Tom Paine and Revolutionary America* (updated ed.; New York, 2005), 190, 198, 206.
23. Wilson, Dec. 11, 1787, in Jonathan Elliot, ed., *The Debates in the Several State Conventions on the Adoption of the Federal Constitution . . .* (4 vols.; Washington, D.C., 1836), 2: 521.
24. Philadelphia dateline, *Pennsylvania Gazette*, Sept. 12, 1787; "A Citizen of Philadelphia" [Pelatiah Webster], *The Weaknesses of Brutus Exposed: or, Some Remarks in Vindication of the Constitution Proposed by the Late Federal Convention, Against the Objections and Gloomy Fears of that Writer* (Philadelphia, 1787), 18; George Nicholas, James Madison, speeches in Virginia ratifying convention, June 14, 1788, *DHRC*, 10:1279, 1296.
25. Anonymous poet, quoted in Flannagan, "Trying Times," 347; Leonard L. Richards, *Shays's Rebellion: The American Revolution's Final Battle* (Philadelphia, 2002), 135.
26. "Valerius," *Massachusetts Centinel*, Nov. 28, 1787, *DHRC*, 4:334; William Manning, "The Key of Libberty: Shewing the Causes Why a Free Government has Always Failed & a Reamedy Against It . . . ," in Michael Merrill and Sean Wilentz, eds., *The Key of Liberty: The Life and Democratic Writings of William Manning, "A Laborer," 1747–1814* (Cambridge, Mass., 1993), 164–66.
27. Randolph, speeches in Virginia ratifying convention, June 6, 9, 1788, *DHRC*, 9:977–78, 983, 1086.
28. "An American" [Tench Coxe], *Pennsylvania Gazette*, May 21, 1788, *DHRC*, 9:839.
29. Madison, speeches in Virginia ratifying convention, June 11, 17, 1788, *DHRC*, 9:1145, 10:1339; Madison, *Federalist* 43:18; Charles Cotesworth Pinckney, Jan. 17, 1788, in Elliot, ed., *Debates in the State Conventions*, 4:285; George Washington to Bushrod Washington, Nov. 9, 1787, in W. W. Abbot and Dorothy Twohig, eds., *The Papers of George Washington*, Confederation Series (6 vols.; Charlottesville, Va., 1992–97), 5:422; Antoine de la Forest to Comte de Montmorin, Dec. 15, 1787, *DHRC*, 8:240.
30. Pinckney, Jan. 17, 1788, Madison, June [17,] 1788, in Elliot, ed., *Debates in the State Conventions*, 4:286, 3:453.
31. Antoine de la Forest to Comte de Montmorin, Dec. 15, 1787, *DHRC*, 8:240.
32. *DHRC*, 3:209–11n; Forrest McDonald, *We the People: The Economic Origins of the Constitution* (Chicago, 1963), 129–30.
33. Peter H. Wood, "The Changing Population of the Colonial South: An Overview by Race and Region, 1685–1790," in Wood, Gregory A. Waselkov, and

M. Thomas Hatley, eds., *Powhatan's Mantle: Indians in the Colonial Southeast* (Lincoln, Neb., 1989), 38.

34. Alexander McGillivray to Arturo O'Neill, Mar. 28, 1786, in John Walton Caughey, ed., *McGillivray of the Creeks* (Norman, Okla., 1938), 104; Gregory Evans Dowd, *A Spirited Resistance: The North American Indian Stuggle for Unity, 1745–1815* (Baltimore, 1992), 90–91.

35. J. Leitch Wright, Jr., *Anglo-Spanish Rivalry in North America* (Athens, Ga., 1971), 138–39, 142.

36. Dowd, *Spirited Resistance*, 98–99.

37. Pendleton to Jeremiah Wadsworth, May 10, 1788, quoted in Jackson Turner Main, *The Antifederalists: Critics of the Constitution, 1781–1788* (Chicago, 1961), 197.

38. Brown, *Redeeming the Republic*, 213; Frederick W. Marks III, *Independence on Trial: Foreign Affairs and the Making of the Constitution* (Baton Rouge, La., 1973), 21–23.

39. Gilman to John Sullivan, Nov. 7, 1787, *DHRC*, 3:262; Joseph Clay to John Pierce, Oct. 17, 1787, *DHRC*, 3:232; William Grayson to William Short, Nov. 10, 1787, *DHRC*, 3:262; George Washington to Samuel Powel, Jan. 18, 1788, *DHRC*, 3:263.

40. "A Columbian Patriot" [Mercy Otis Warren], *Observations on the New Constitution . . .* , Feb. 1788, in Bailyn, ed., *Debate on the Constitution*, 2:301.

41. G.J.A. Ducher to Comte de la Luzerne, Feb. 2, 1788, *DHRC*, 3:283.

42. Hamilton, *Federalist* 24:10.

43. Norman K. Risjord, *Chesapeake Politics, 1781–1800* (New York, 1978), 288.

44. Williamson, speech, Nov. 8, 1787, in Bailyn, ed., *Debate on the Constitution*, 2:233.

45. Nicholas, speeches in Virginia ratifying convention, June 10, 13, 1788, *DHRC*, 9:1129, 10:1252; James Madison to George Nicholas, May 17, 1788, *DHRC*, 9:805–6.

46. Williamson, quoted in Charles A. Beard, *An Economic Interpretation of the Constitution of the United States* (New York, 1913), 50.

47. Henry, speech in Virginia ratifying convention, June 9, 1788, *DHRC*, 9:1054.

48. Grayson, speech in Virginia ratifying convention, June 11, 1788, *DHRC*, 9:1167–68.

49. Tyler, speech in Virginia ratifying convention, June 25, 1788, *DHRC*, 10:1526–27.

50. Henry, quoted in Lance Banning, *The Sacred Fire of Liberty: James Madison and the Founding of the Federal Republic* (Ithaca, N.Y., 1995), 244.

51. Hamilton, *Federalist* 15:3.

52. Madison to George Nicholas, May 17, 1788, in William T. Hutchinson et al., eds., *The Papers of James Madison* (17 vols. to date; Chicago, 1962–), 11:49–50.

53. Augusta County citizens, petition, Oct. 25, 1786, VLP.

54. Nicholas, speech in Virginia ratifying convention, June 10, 1788, *DHRC*, 9:1129; Hamilton, *Federalist* 15:3.

55. E. Lee Shepard, *Reluctant Ratifiers: Virginia Considers the Federal Constitution* (Richmond, Va., 1988), 47.

56. Brown, *Redeeming the Republic*, 200, 217–18; Donald Lutz, *Popular Consent and Popular Control: Whig Political Theory in the Early State Constitutions* (Baton Rouge, La., 1980), 171–72, 186; Jackson Turner Main, *The Anti-Federalists: Critics*

of the Constitution, 1781–1788 (Chicago, 1961), 249; Gordon S. Wood, "How Democratic Is the Constitution?" *New York Review of Books*, Feb. 23, 2006, 27.

57. Hamilton, *Federalist* 11:5.

58. [Warren], *Observations on the Constitution*, in Bailyn, ed., *Debate on the Constitution*, 2:300; Albert Furtwangler, *The Authority of Publius: A Reading of the Federalist Papers* (Ithaca, N.Y., 1984), 70; Jack N. Rakove, *Original Meanings: Politics and Ideas in the Making of the Constitution* (New York, 1996), 123.

59. Jerome J. Nadelhaft, *The Disorders of War: The Revolution in South Carolina* (Orono, Me., 1981), 180–82; Terry Bouton, "Tying Up the Revolution: Money, Power, and the Regulation in Pennsylvania, 1765–1800" (Ph.D. diss., Duke University, 1996), 329n.

60. Worcester dateline, *Worcester Magazine* 4:1 (1st week of Oct. 1787), 15; Madison, *Federalist* 38:4; Richmond dateline, *Virginia Independent Chronicle*, Sept. 26, 1787.

61. "A.B." to Elbridge Gerry, *Massachusetts Centinel*, Nov. 14, 1787, *DHRC*, 4:229.

62. "A Freeman," III, *Pennsylvania Gazette*, Feb. 6, 1788, *DHRC*, 16:50.

63. George Washington to Madison, Oct. 10, 1787, in Abbot and Twohig, eds., *Papers of George Washington*, 5:366.

64. Garry Wills, *James Madison* (New York, 2002), 30; "Landholder" [Oliver Ellsworth], VI, *Connecticut Courant*, Dec. 10, 1787, *DHRC*, 3:491.

65. Madison, quoted in Rakove, *Original Meanings*, 60, 77.

66. Madison to Edward Livingston, Apr. 17, 1824, in Farrand, ed., *Records of the Federal Convention*, 3:463; Elaine K. Swift, *The Making of an American Senate: Reconstitutive Change in Congress, 1787–1841* (Ann Arbor, Mich., 2002), 13.

67. Madison, *Federalist* 62:12.

68. Madison, June 4, 6, 7, 26, 1787, Butler, June 26, 1787, William Samuel Johnson, June 29, 1787, in Farrand, ed., *Records of the Federal Convention*, 1:108, 135, 158, 431, 434, 461.

69. Madison and Dickinson's paraphrase of Madison, June 7, 1787, in Farrand, ed., *Records of the Federal Convention*, 1:158–59.

70. Dickinson, June 6, 1787, Gerry, June 7, 1787, ibid., 1:136, 152; Garry Wills, *Explaining America: The Federalist* (Garden City, N.Y., 1981), 229.

71. Rufus King, speech in Massachusetts ratifying convention, Jan. 19, 1788, *DHRC*, 6:1263.

72. [Rush], *Observations Upon the Present Government of Pennsylvania, In Four Letters to the People of Pennsylvania* (Philadelphia, 1777), 12; Gordon S. Wood, *The Creation of the American Republic, 1776–1787* (Chapel Hill, N.C., 1969), 445.

73. *DHRC*, 3:487n.

74. Wood, *Creation of the Republic*, 486–87; Flannagan, "Trying Times," 326.

75. Christopher Collier, *All Politics Is Local: Family, Friends, and Provincial Interests in the Creation of the Constitution* (Hanover, N.H., 2003), 87.

76. Rakove, *Original Meanings*, 146.

77. Henry Jackson to Henry Knox, Feb. 3, 1788, *DHRC*, 7:1571.

78. Minot, quoted in Rock Brynner, "'Fire Beneath Our Feet': Shays' Rebellion and Its Constitutional Impact" (Ph.D. diss., Columbia University, 1993), 243–44.

79. Stanley Elkins and Eric McKitrick, *The Age of Federalism* (New York, 1993), 59.

80. Nathaniel Gorham to Henry Knox, Jan. 30, 1788, *DHRC*, 7:1561; William Widgery to George Thatcher, Feb. 9, 1788, *DHRC*, 7:1690.

81. Kenneth R. Bowling, "'A Tub to the Whale': The Founding Fathers and Adoption of the Federal Bill of Rights," *Journal of the Early Republic* 8 (Fall 1988), 223–51; Young, "Genius of the People," 17.

CHAPTER 16: "AS IF IMPOUNDED"—CONSOLIDATION

1. [Herman Husband], *Proposals to Amend and Perfect the Policy of the Government of the United States of America, or, The Fulfilling of the Prophecies in the Latter Days, Commenced by the Independence of America* (Philadelphia, 1782), 3–4.

2. "Lycurgus III" [Herman Husband], *XIV Sermons on the Characters of Jacob's Fourteen Sons* (Philadelphia, 1789), 29; Rosemary Zagarri, *The Politics of Size: Representation in the United States, 1776–1850* (Ithaca, N.Y., 1987), 113–14.

3. "A Citizen of Connecticut" [William Beers], *An Address to the Legislature and People of the State of Connecticut, On the Subject of Dividing the State into Districts for the Election of Representatives in Congress* (New Haven, Conn., 1791), 17, 18, 29 (quotation), 35–36; [Swift], [Zephaniah Swift?], *The Security of the Rights of Citizens in the State of Connecticut Considered* (Hartford, Conn., 1792), 22, 75, 87; "Publius Secundus Americanus," *Daily Advertiser*, Nov. 10, 1788, in Merrill Jensen et al., eds., *The Documentary History of the First Federal Elections, 1788–1790* (4 vols.; Madison, Wisc., 1976), 3:210–11.

4. [Swift], *Security of the Rights*, 92–94.

5. *Maryland Journal*, Nov. 14, 1788, anonymous essay, *Daily Advertiser*, Nov. 7, 1788, in Jensen et al., eds., *History of the First Federal Elections*, 2:125, 3:209–10. Americans' positions in the debate over how to elect congressmen reflected not only their political philosophies but also their beliefs about which method was likely to favor their own party. Zagarri, *Politics of Size*, 113–18.

6. [Swift], *Security of the Rights*, 75; William Findley, speech in Pennsylvania assembly, Sept. 24, 1788, "A Real Farmer," *Hampshire Chronicle*, Nov. 5, 1788, in Jensen et al., eds., *History of the First Federal Elections*, 1:287, 471.

7. Ralph L. Ketcham, "Notes on James Madison's Sources for the Tenth Federalist Paper," *Midwest Journal of Political Science* 1 (May 1957), 20.

8. [Swift], *Security of the Rights*, 83–85.

9. "Lycurgus III" [Husband], *XIV Sermons*, 29.

10. Richard Labunski, *James Madison and the Struggle for the Bill of Rights* (Oxford, 2006).

11. Stanley Elkins and Eric McKitrick, *The Age of Federalism* (New York, 1993), 59.

12. Benjamin Lincoln to Theodore Sedgwick, Sept. 7, 1788, Sedgwick Family Papers, MHS.

13. Madison, speech in House of Representatives, Aug. 14, 1789, in Helen E. Veit, Kenneth R. Bowling, and Charlene Bangs Bickford, eds., *Creating the Bill of*

Rights: The Documentary Record from the First Federal Congress (Baltimore, 1991), 131; Nathaniel Barrell to George Thatcher, Feb. 20, 1788, *DHRC*, 7:1590; Virginia House of Delegates, resolution, Oct. 30, 1788, *DHRC*, 10:1764; anonymous essay, *Maryland Journal*, Dec. 12, 1788, cited in *DHRC*, 10:1764n.

14. Elkins and McKitrick, *Age of Federalism*, 143–44; E. James Ferguson, *The Power of the Purse: A History of American Public Finance, 1776–1790* (Chapel Hill, N.C., 1961), 297–99.

15. [Madison], "Address to the States, By the United States in Congress Assembled," Apr. 26, 1783, in Worthington Chauncey Ford, ed., *Journals of the Continental Congress, 1774–1789* (34 vols.; Washington, D.C., 1904–37), 24:282–83; Ferguson, *Power of the Purse*, 298; Elkins and McKitrick, *Age of Federalism*, 104.

16. Hamilton to Edward Carrington, May 26, 1792, in Max Farrand, ed., *The Records of the Federal Convention of 1787* (3 vols.; New Haven, Conn., 1911), 3:366–67; Elkins and McKitrick, *Age of Federalism*, 104.

17. Ferguson, *Power of the Purse*, 298.

18. Ibid., 297–99; Elkins and McKitrick, *Age of Federalism*, 136–42; Gordon S. Wood, "Is There a 'James Madison Problem'?" in David Womersley, ed., *Liberty and American Experience in the Eighteenth Century* (Indianapolis, Ind., 2006), 425–47.

19. [Herman Husband], *A Dialogue Between an Assembly-Man and a Convention-Man On the Subject of the State Constitution of Pennsylvania* . . . (Philadelphia, n.d.), 11; Ferguson, *Power of the Purse*, 299–302.

20. William Manning, "Some Proposals For Making Restitution to the Original Creditors of Government and To Help the Continent to a Medium of Trade . . . ," Feb. 6, 1790, in Michael Merrill and Sean Wilentz, eds., *The Key of Liberty: The Life and Democratic Writings of William Manning, "A Laborer," 1747–1814* (Cambridge, Mass., 1993), 101.

21. Ibid., 99, 101.

22. Jackson, Feb. 10, 1790, *Annals of Congress*, 1st Cong., 2nd sess., 1215.

23. Manning, "Some Proposals," 114.

24. Ibid., 99, 114.

25. Giles, Apr. 9, 1792, *Annals of Congress*, 2nd Cong., 2nd sess., 546.

26. "A Farmer," *Pennsylvania Gazette*, Jan. 27, 1790; Ferguson, *Power of the Purse*, 304.

27. "A Farmer," *Pennsylvania Gazette*, Jan. 27, 1790; "Equity," *Independent Chronicle*, Jan. 14, 1790.

28. Richard Peters to James Madison, Mar. 31, 1790, in William T. Hutchinson et al., eds., *The Papers of James Madison* (17 vols. to date; Chicago, 1962–), 13:133; Benjamin Rush to Thomas Fitzsimons[?], Aug. 5, 1790, in L. H. Butterfield, ed., *Letters of Benjamin Rush* Vol. I (Princeton, N.J., 1951), 1:569; "A Farmer," *Pennsylvania Gazette*, Feb. 17, 1790.

29. Madison, speech in House of Representatives, Feb. 11, 1790, in Hutchinson et al., eds., *Papers of James Madison*, 13:36; Laurance, Feb. 15, 1790, *Annals of Congress*, 1st Cong., 2nd sess., 1252; Boudinot, Feb. 11, 1790, *Annals of Congress*, 1st Cong., 2nd sess., 1238.

30. Jackson, Feb. 16, 1790, *Annals of Congress*, 1st Cong., 2nd sess., 1271; Benjamin

Rush to Madison, Feb. 18, 1790, in Hutchinson et al., eds., *Papers of James Madison*, 13:46; Madison, speech in House of Representatives, Feb. 18, 1790, ibid., 13:49.

31. Jackson, Abraham Baldwin, Alexander White, Feb. 16, 1790, *Annals of Congress*, 1st Cong., 2nd sess., 1272, 1277; "A Private Citizen," *Pennsylvania Gazette*, Mar. 10, 1790 (reprinted from *Connecticut Courant*); Elkins and McKitrick, *Age of Federalism*, 121.

32. "The Observer," IX, *Pennsylvania Gazette*, Dec. 30, 1789; Samuel Livermore, Feb. 9, 1790, Sedgwick, Scott, Jackson, Feb. 10, 1790, Ames, Feb. 15, 1790, Andrew Moore, Feb. 16, 1790, *Annals of Congress*, 1st Cong., 2nd sess., 1196, 1210, 1213–14, 1264, 1281; Ferguson, *Power of the Purse*, 303.

33. Madison, speech in House of Representatives, Feb. 11, 1790, in Hutchinson et al., eds., *Papers of James Madison*, 13:35; Laurance, Ames, Feb. 15, 1790, Boudinot, Feb. 17, 1790, *Annals of Congress*, 1st Cong., 2nd sess., 1252, 1263–64, 1296–97.

34. Sidney Kaplan and Emma Nogrady Kaplan, *The Black Presence in the Era of the American Revolution* (rev. ed.; Amherst, Mass., 1989), 244–48.

35. "The Memorial and Petition of the Public Creditors . . . of Pennsylvania . . . ," Aug. 21, 1789 (presented Aug. 28, 1789), in *Annals of Congress*, 1st Cong., 1st sess., 822–25; Boudinot, Feb. 17, 1790, in *Annals of Congress*, 1st Cong., 2nd sess., 1297; James Madison, speech in House of Representatives, Feb. 18, 1790, in Hutchinson et al., eds., *Papers of James Madison*, 13:52.

36. Manning, "Some Proposals," 112–13.

37. Theodore Sedgwick, Jan. 28, 1790, editor's footnote, in *Annals of Congress*, 1st Cong., 2nd sess., 1135, 1135n.

38. Alan Gibson, "Impartial Representation and the Extended Republic: Towards a Comprehensive and Balanced Reading of the Tenth *Federalist* Paper," *History of Political Thought* 12 (Summer 1991), 289–91; John Zvesper, "The Madisonian Systems," *Western Political Quarterly* 37 (June 1984), 244–47.

39. Abigail Adams to Cotton Tufts, Feb. 6, 1791 (misdated 1790), *Microfilms of the Adams Papers Owned by the Adams Manuscript Trust and Deposited in the Massachusetts Historical Society* (microfilm, 608 reels, Boston, 1954–59), reel 373.

40. Charles Adams to John Quincy Adams, Dec. 26, 1790, *Microfilms of the Adams Papers*, reel 374; Pennsylvania public creditors, "memorial and remonstrance," Senate resolution, *Senate Journal*, 1st Cong., 3rd sess., Dec. 20, 23, 1790, 223, 225; New Jersey public creditors, "memorial and remonstrance," Dec. 28, 1790, House of Representatives, resolution, Feb. 24, 1791, *Annals of Congress*, 1st Cong., 3rd sess., 1880, 2023.

41. Samuel Breck to John Brown, Dec. 30, 1790, Brown Papers, box 27, folder 6, JCB; Joseph Barrell to Samuel B. Webb, Jan. 31, 1790, in Worthington Chauncey Ford, ed., *Correspondence and Journals of Samuel Blachley Webb* (3 vols.; New York, 1893–94), 3:150.

42. Abigail Adams to Cotton Tufts, Aug. 2, 1790, Miscellaneous Manuscripts, New-York Historical Society, New York.

43. Leonard L. Richards, *Shays's Rebellion: The American Revolution's Final Battle* (Philadelphia, 2002), 158.

44. Gary B. Nash, *The Unknown American Revolution: The Unruly Birth of Democracy and the Struggle to Create America* (New York, 2005).

45. Webster to James Greenleaf, Oct. 13, 1791, in Harry R. Warfel, ed., *Letters of Noah Webster* (New York, 1953), 104.

46. Woody Holton, "Abigail Adams, Bond Speculator," *WMQ*, 3rd ser., 64 (Oct. 2007).

47. Brown, *Redeeming the Republic*, 236; Max M. Edling, *A Revolution in Favor of Government: Origins of the U.S. Constitution and the Making of the American State* (Oxford, 2003), 211–18; Max M. Edling and Mark D. Kaplanoff, "Alexander Hamilton's Fiscal Reform: Transforming the Structure of Taxation in the Early Republic," *WMQ*, 3rd ser., 61 (Oct. 2004), 713–44.

48. Ferguson, *Power of the Purse*, 321.

49. Elizabeth Smith Shaw to Abigail Adams, Feb. 14, 1791 (misfiled at Feb. 14, 1790), *Microfilms of the Adams Papers*, reel 373; Cotton Tufts to John Adams, Jan. 6, 1791, *Microfilms of the Adams Papers*, reel 374.

50. Noah Webster to James Greenleaf, Oct. 13, 1791, in Warfel, ed., *Letters of Noah Webster*, 103.

51. Benjamin Goodhue to Samuel Phillips, Jr., July 27, 1790, Phillips Family Papers, MHS; Thomas P. Slaughter, *The Whiskey Rebellion: Frontier Epilogue to the American Revolution* (New York, 1986), 95–105.

52. Richard H. Kohn, "The Washington Administration's Decision to Crush the Whiskey Rebellion," *JAH* 59 (Dec. 1972), 570.

53. Mark Jones, "Herman Husband: Millenarian, Carolina Regulator, and Whiskey Rebel" (Ph.D. diss., Northern Illinois University, 1983), 359–63.

54. Slaughter, *Whiskey Rebellion*, 94.

55. Gregory Evans Dowd, *A Spirited Resistance: The North American Indian Struggle for Unity, 1745–1815* (Baltimore, 1992), 101; Claudio Saunt, *A New Order of Things: Property, Power, and the Transformation of the Creek Indians, 1733–1816* (Cambridge, U.K., 1999), 78–79.

56. Quoted in J. R. Pole, *Political Representation in England and the Origins of the American Republic* (London, 1966), 241.

57. Patrick T. Conley, Jr., "First in War, Last in Peace: Rhode Island and the Constitution, 1786–1790," in Conley and John P. Kaminski, eds., *The Constitution and the States: The Role of the Original Thirteen in the Framing and Adoption of the Federal Constitution* (Madison, Wisc., 1988), 292; Patrick T. Conley, Jr., "The First Judicial Review of State Legislation: An Analysis of the Rhode Island Case of Champion and Dickason v. Casey (1792)," *Rhode Island Bar Journal* 36 (Oct. 1987), 5–9.

58. William Greider, *Secrets of the Temple: How the Federal Reserve Runs the Country* (New York, 1987), 50.

59. Lance Banning, *The Sacred Fire of Liberty: James Madison and the Founding of the Federal Republic* (Ithaca, N.Y., 1995), 500, n. 47.

60. Forrest McDonald, *Alexander Hamilton: A Biography* (New York, 1979), 173; Thomas M. Doerflinger, *A Vigorous Spirit of Enterprise: Merchants and Economic Development in Revolutionary Philadelphia* (Chapel Hill, N.C., 1986), 265;

Richard S. Chew, "Certain Victims of an International Contagion: The Panic of 1797 and the Hard Times of the Late 1790s in Baltimore," *Journal of the Early Republic* 25 (Winter 2005), 574.

61. Noah Webster to James Greenleaf, Oct. 13, 1791, in Warfel, ed., *Letters of Noah Webster*, 103; McCormick, *Experiment in Independence*, 274; Douglass C. North, *The Economic Growth of the United States, 1790–1860* (Englewood Cliffs, N.J., 1961), 17, 20, 25–54; Stuart Bruchey, *The Roots of American Economic Growth, 1607–1861: An Essay in Social Causation* (New York, 1965), 110–12; Stanley L. Engerman and Robert E. Gallman, "U.S. Economic Growth, 1783–1860," *Research in Economic History* 8 (1982), 17–19; Doerflinger, *Vigorous Spirit of Enterprise*, 267; Brown, *Redeeming the Republic*, 235–36, 240, 242; John J. McCusker, "Estimating Early American Gross Domestic Product," *Historical Methods* 33 (Summer 2000), 155–62.

62. Doerflinger, *Vigorous Spirit of Enterprise*, 267; Abigail Adams to Mary Cranch, Mar. 12, 1791, in Stewart Mitchell, ed., *New Letters of Abigail Adams, 1788–1801* (Boston, 1947), 71.

EPILOGUE: THE UNDERDOGS' CONSTITUTION

1. Madison to Jefferson, Oct. 24, 1787, in William T. Hutchinson et al., eds., *The Papers of James Madison* (17 vols. to date; Chicago, 1962–), 10:212.

2. [Zephaniah Swift], *The Security of the Rights of Citizens in the State of Connecticut Considered* (Hartford, Conn., 1792), 85.

3. John Hope Franklin, *Reconstruction: After the Civil War* (Chicago, 1961); Eric Foner, *Reconstruction: America's Unfinished Revolution, 1863–1877* (New York, 1988).

4. "A Native of New-Jersey," *New Jersey Gazette*, Nov. 14, 1785.

5. Abigail Adams to Mary Cranch, Feb. 20, 1790, in Stewart Mitchell, ed., *New Letters of Abigail Adams, 1788–1801* (Boston, 1947), 37; Feb. 22, 1790, *Annals of Congress*, 1st Cong., 2nd sess., 1344.

6. Cotton Tufts (Trustee to Mrs. Abigl. Adams), receipt for U.S. Treasury bonds, Aug. 21, 1792, Jeremiah Colbourn Autograph Collection, 7:243, property of the Bostonian Society, on deposit with MHS.

7. Madison, June 12, 1787, in Max Farrand, ed., *The Records of the Federal Convention of 1787* (3 vols.; New Haven, Conn., 1911), 1:215, 219.

Acknowledgments

Individuals

Joyce Appleby ▪ Susan Armeny ▪ Terry Bouton ▪ Kenneth Bowling ▪ T. H. Breen ▪ Timothy J. Bronstetter ▪ John L. Brooke ▪ Roger H. Brown ▪ Alex Bushel ▪ Daniel S. Clapper ▪ Ruth Doumlele ▪ Max M. Edling ▪ Lawrence Goodwyn ▪ Deborah S. Govoruhk ▪ Christopher Grasso ▪ Ann Gross ▪ Robert A. Gross ▪ Terri D. Halperin ▪ Travis Hardy ▪ Adrienne Huckabee ▪ Mary Jeske ▪ Roland Kankey ▪ Marjoleine Kars ▪ June Kim ▪ Allan Kulikoff ▪ Thomas LeBien ▪ Andrew Lewis ▪ Stuart Lipkin ▪ Gwynn Litchfield ▪ Tricia Manning ▪ Roderick McDonald ▪ Michael A. McDonnell ▪ Mark Douglas McGarvie ▪ John McGhee ▪ Richard F. Neel, Jr. ▪ David Nord ▪ Edwin J. Perkins ▪ Gretchen Ferris Schoel ▪ Rebecca M. Shewman ▪ Brent Tarter ▪ William R. VanderKloot ▪ Amanda G. Walsh ▪ Harry M. Ward ▪ Hugh West ▪ Douglas L. Winiarski ▪ Peter H. Wood ▪ Conrad E. Wright ▪ Robert E. Wright ▪ Alfred F. Young ▪ Michael Zuckerman

ORGANIZATIONS

The American Antiquarian Society (especially Thomas G. Knoles, Marie Lamoureux, and Philip J. Lampi) ▪ the Boston Early American History Seminar (especially Christine Desan, Pauline Maier, Kent Newmyer, and Lisa Wilson) ▪ the Bostonian Society (especially Lauren Mandel) ▪ the William A. Clements Library (especially Janet Bloom, Barbara deWolfe, and John Vann ▪ the Connecticut Historical Society (especially Barbara Austen) ▪ the Fall Line Early American Society (FLEAS) ▪ the John Carter Brown Library (especially Richard J. Ring) ▪ the Manuscripts Division at the Library of Congress (especially Jeff Flannery) ▪ the Library of Virginia (especially Minor Weisiger) ▪ the Massachusetts Historical Society (especially Peter Drummey, Nicholas Graham, Margaret A. Hogan, Megan Rose Milford, Cherylinne Pina, Melissa Pino, and Conrad E. Wright) ▪ the Massachusetts State Archives (especially Michael Comeau, Stephanie Dyson, Jennifer Fauxsmith, and Richard C. Kaplan) ▪ the National Archives of the United Kingdom ▪ the National Endowment for the Humanities ▪ the New England Historic Genealogical Society (especially Christopher G. Hartman) ▪ the New England Regional Fellowship Consortium ▪ the New Hampshire Division of Archives & Records (especially state archivist Frank C. Mevers) ▪ the New Hampshire Historical Society (especially William N. Copeley, Donna-Belle Garvin, and David Smolen) ▪ the New Hampshire State Library (especially Donna Gilbreth) ▪ the New Jersey State Archives (especially Bette M. Epstein) ▪ the Newberry Library (especially Sara Austin and the Newberry Library Seminar) ▪ the Society of the Cincinnati in the State of Virginia ▪ the South Carolina Department of Archives and History (especially Steven D. Tuttle) ▪ the Virginia Foundation for the Humanities (especially Ann Spencer)

INDEX